# Mental Health Workbook

The Ultimate Guide to Mental Health for Men, Women, and Teens (EMDR, Depression in Relationships, Complex PTSD, Trauma, CBT Therapy, Somatic Psychotherapy and More)

Frank Cantrell

# Contents

# Book One
# ATTACHMENT THEORY WORKBOOK

## Introduction

Researchers John Bowlby and Mary Ainsworth began developing the core of what became attachment theory in the mid-20th century. Their original theory says that infants develop better, socially and emotionally, when they form a close bond with a primary caregiver who's good at reading their cues and responding to their needs in a warm, sensitive, and timely way. At the time Bowlby and Ainsworth were developing their theory, the primary caregiver was usually the mother. Infants with this type of bond grow up trusting that others can help them feel safe, cared for, and supported in the world. This basic premise has been supported by over 60 years of attachment research and backed by experts in neuroscience, psychiatry, traumatology, and pediatrics.

Attachment researchers found that they could categorize the quality of relationships babies had with their main caregivers by observing how these babies responded to everyday stressful situations. Researchers grouped these responses into three distinct categories: **secure, insecure anxious,** and **insecure avoidant**.

The early researchers noted that when stressed, babies with **secure** attachment showed their distress in an observable way, but their response was not excessive. These babies seemed relaxed about seeking help and more often had interactions with their caregivers that ended in their being calmer and ready to move on from the stressful event.

Babies with **insecure anxious** attachment tended to respond to the same stressful events with more extreme crying and distress.

They sought their caregiver but also appeared to reject the caregiver's attempts to provide relief. For these anxious babies, researchers observed more labored interactions that did not result in a fully soothed baby.

Babies with **insecure avoidant** attachment were less likely to cry during stressful situations and appeared indifferent about getting help from their caregivers. To the untrained eye, these babies looked fine, but researchers later discovered that elevated stress hormones in their bodies told a different story: They were affected by stress, but they didn't show it.

It may not surprise you to learn that babies grow into adults who develop versions of these **secure, anxious**, and **avoidant** attachments that can be readily identified in their relationships. Of course, adult relationships involve a lot more complexity, but it almost always boils down to this: When we get close to someone and come to depend on them, in stressful moments we show our true attachment style.

A fully accurate assessment of your attachment style is more complicated than this, but if you think about your closest relationships, you can probably get a basic sense of it. Think about close relationships you've had with romantic partners or in long-term friendships. In the course of those relationships, you've likely encountered a variety of stressors. During stressful times, if you typically expect that you can count on your relationship partners for help and comfort, then you have a secure attachment style. But let's say you encounter stress and don't have this natural expectation of safety and support. Maybe you aren't sure your relationship partners will help you, and you don't feel as if you can count on them to be there for you the way you need. If you've developed an insecure style, either anxious or avoidant, you are more likely to fear either being abandoned or being overwhelmed by the other person. As a result, you are less likely to engage in a way that makes you feel better. People typically have a characteristic attachment style that holds true across their close relationships, so securely attached people usually feel that their relationship partners are there for them; and people with either of the insecure attachment styles can look at their relationship history and see a string of unsatisfying relationships and perhaps regrettable actions.

After reading the descriptions of the secure, anxious, and avoidant styles, you may think, "I want the secure style!" And there's good reason to feel that way. People with a secure style of relating tend to feel more emotional safety with the people they're close to, are readier to collaborate, and are more resilient around conflict. But even these folks, under certain circumstances, can lapse into less adaptive ways of relating.

Regardless of the tendencies and attachment style you've developed to this point, you're not locked into these behaviors— your past doesn't have to dictate your future. Starting now, you can build stronger relationships. This workbook will help you . . .

•Recognize what specific attachment-related patterns and behaviors you and your loved ones have, especially under stressful or otherwise demanding circumstances.

•Learn new tools and practices to stop conflict escalation and reestablish safety and connection.

•Break old, unhelpful behavior patterns and start acting in ways that will build the lasting connections you want.

These skills are worth learning, because you'll get to spend more time enjoying what you love about the people you care about and be able to nurture more intimate, lasting bonds with them. And in times of difficulty and stress, you'll have resources you can call on when you need them.

# Chapter 1: How Does Attachment Anxiety Develop?

While it is easy to blame 'bad parenting' for all our relationship woes, it is not quite as simple as that.

## Attachment: Nature Or Nurture?

Are your most essential qualities and behaviours determined by your genetics or learned? This is the most enduring debate of our times.

The modern scientific view is that the capacity to behave in a specific way is genetic, but experiences will determine how, when, and whether these capacities are engaged.

As attachment is about how distress is managed, the answer would lie in how often distress is experienced, and how it is expressed lies in the genetic factors, but the responses to stress are modified by learning and experiences. Thus, how an infant develops an attachment style is mostly learned.

Early relationships with parents and caregivers certainly do shape what you expect from and how you participate in later relationships, and specifically in romantic attachments. You develop a blueprint of how you interact in adult relationships, how you seek comfort or push it away, how you trust or don't, and how you approach any situation that could be perceived as a conflict.

However, other relationships and circumstances in your formative years, as well as later relationships also play a big role.

## Early Childhood And Adolescence

'No other dyad can reanimate one's earliest attachment relationships the way an adult romantic relationship can' (Stan, 2014).

## Attachment Theory Explained

Everyone has a deep yearning to belong, in some form or the other. You know that the quality of your relationships has an impact on your feelings of contentment and happiness.

When you find yet another relationship in the graveyard and wonder about the repetitive patterns that led to this, it is time to find some insight into these patterns and where they originate.

John Bowlby, a British psychoanalyst, developed the original theory of emotional attachment styles, in trying to understand the intense distress suffered by infants separated from their parents (Fraley).

He postulated that the distress was an adaptive response to being separated from the primary caregiver: the person that protects, provides support, and cares for them. This influences emotional regulation and personality development.

The fundamental question asked is: is the attachment figure nearby, available and attentive? The infant would display distress symptoms until the attachment figure became available again or get worn down and fall into despair.

Bowlby postulated that these behaviours were present from 'cradle to grave' and believed the categories to be fixed.

Mary Ainsworth developed testing methods to verify this, called the Strange Situation Protocol. She identified three styles (secure, resistant, avoidant), and the results of the infants' behaviour are summarised in the table (Ainsworth, 1964).

|  | Secure | Resistant | Avoidant |
| --- | --- | --- | --- |
| **Separation Anxiety** | Distressed when mother leaves | Intense distress when the mother leaves | No sign of distress when the the mother leaves |
| **Stranger Anxiety** | Avoidant of stranger when alone, but friendly when the mother is present | The infant avoids the stranger - shows fear of the stranger | The infant is okay with the stranger and plays normally when the stranger is present |
| **Reunion Behavior** | Positive and happy when mother returns | The infant approaches the mother, but resists contact, may even push her away | The Infant shows little interest when the mother returns |
| **Other** | Uses the mother as a safe base to explore their environment | The infant cries more and explores less than the other two types | The mother and stranger are able to comfort the infant equally well |
| **% of infants** | 70% | 15% | 15% |

McLeod, S. A. (2018, Aug 05). Mary Ainsworth. Retrieved from https://www.simplypsychology.org/mary-ainsworth.html

Main and Solomon identified the disorganised style in 1990 (Main, 1990).

It was, however, only in the eighties that researchers started looking at adult romantic relationships in terms of attachment theory. Hazan and Shaver noted that there were similarities in the bond between infant and caregiver, and romantic partners, as they both:

Engage in close, intimate, bodily contact
Share discoveries
Mutual fascination with each other
Feel secure when the other is nearby and accessible
Engage in 'baby talk'
Feel insecure when the other is not accessible

They concluded that romantic relationships are shaped by the attachment behavioural system and the motivational system that gives rise to caregiving and sexuality.

Bowlby and Mary Ainsworth believed that the 'working models' or 'mental representations' (in other words the scripts, rules, beliefs, expectations) that a child holds are based on his caregiving experiences, thus creating a blueprint for future behaviour.

For example, a child that grows up in a chaotic household will believe that love is chaotic, that will be his normal. A child subjected to violence and abuse will not flinch at violence or abuse and believe that to be a normal way of interaction. They may also flinch at any sudden movement, expecting violence.

An emotionally secure attached child, on the other hand, will believe that others will be there for him and will take care of him, as that is his experience of a normal relationship. They will seek out relationships that will provide this level of security.

If there was not a lot of warmth in your early family life, you might display dismissive attachment styles. If there were a lot of disruption and people leaving all the time (death, divorce, multiple relationships) you may become anxious.

Frightening and unpredictable adults in the household tend to lead to a very mixed style of attachment, vacillating between anxious and dismissive, due to the conflicting messages about what to expect of people (Leo, 2018).

Of course, growing up with a secure attachment style does not mean you will always be secure – sometimes an abusive relationship, or being cheated on and lied to, several breaches of trust and off/on types of relationships can leave you with mixed styles. Similarly finding a secure partner may help you heal your anxious, dismissive, or mixed style.

Brennan, Clarke, and Shaver explored this concept further and found two fundamental dimensions in adult attachment patterns (Clark, et al., 1998):

**Attachment-related anxiety** – on the high end, worrying about whether their partner available, attentive or responsive; on the low end, more secure.

**Attachment-related avoidance** – on the high end, prefer not to depend on others, rely on them or open up to them; on the low end, comfortable being intimate, more secure and dependable, comfortable depending on others.

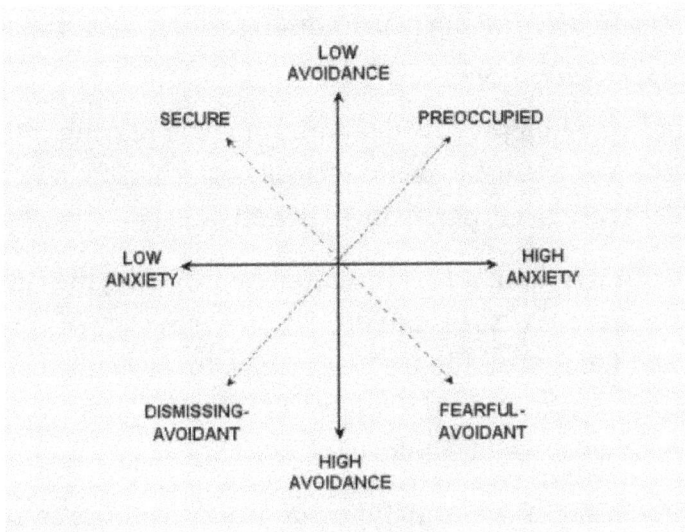

```
                    LOW
                  AVOIDANCE
                      ↑
    SECURE                    PREOCCUPIED
         ↖                        ↗
  LOW                                    HIGH
  ANXIETY  ←──────────────────────→   ANXIETY
         ↙                        ↘
  DISMISSING-                   FEARFUL-
   AVOIDANT                     AVOIDANT
                      ↓
                    HIGH
                  AVOIDANCE
```

(Clark, et al., 1998)

This important research, complemented by that of Fraley and others (ABr19), shows us that attachment styles vary in degree rather than in kind. This means there are not distinct styles, but rather a continuum.

It means that at any point in your life you may be exhibiting different degrees of specific styles of attachment, and whilst your baseline may remain more or less the same, it is possible to change your blueprint and learn to regulate your emotions.

Most adults desire a secure pattern of attachment in their relationships, with responsive caregiving: warmth, sensitivity, and attentiveness. Unfortunately, people often end up in relationships that confirm their existing beliefs.

## Insecure Attachments With A Primary Caregiver During Infancy Or Childhood

Parents play many roles in the life of their child – caregiver, teacher, playmate, disciplinarian, and most importantly, that of the attachment figure. Bonding has nothing to do with attachment, and it is often confused for each other.

A child breastfeeding at seven months or a son playing catch with his dad at six is not necessarily securely attached, as it relates to other roles (caregiver/playmate). (Benoit, 2004)

The parent's attachment role is related to providing the child with a **secure base**, a **safe haven**, and a **source of comfort**. Attachment focuses on the child's feelings towards the caregiver. It is based on the child's understanding of the caregiver's reliability as a source of comfort and security.

In childhood, there are four types of attachment, three of them 'organised' (secure, insecure-avoidant, insecure-resistant) and one of them 'disorganised' (insecure-disorganised).

This means that when the infant's security system is threatened, i.e., when hurt, upset, ill or frightened, the caregiver's response will determine the quality of the attachment formed.

Organised Secure Attachment Style

If the caregiver consistently responds in a loving or sensitive way, they learn to trust that they can express negative emotions and develops an organised secure style.

Organised Insecure Avoidant Or Resistant Attachment Style

If the caregiver consistently responds in an insensitive way, for example, by rejecting, ridiculing, ignoring or becoming annoyed, the infant develops an organised strategy of dealing with the caregiver, as they know to avoid the caregiver or to resist displaying negative emotions in the presence of this person. These are insecure responses.

If caregivers respond in inconsistent or unpredictable ways, or 'involving' ways (putting their own needs first, being overwhelmed and amplifying the infant's distress), the infant will display extreme negative emotion to get attention.

Disorganised Insecure Attachment

Atypical caregiving, which is denoted by distorted and unusual behaviours, or any frightening, dissociated, sexualised or aberrant behaviour, even when the infant is not distressed, leads to disorganised attachment.

These infants display bizarre and contradictory behaviour: misdirected and stereotypical behaviour, stilling and freezing for long periods, direct apprehension, and fear of the parent. They face an unsolvable dilemma in that their source of security is also their source of distress and fear.

They have been subjected to highly stressful, chaotic, and frightening environments. It is speculated that many of these caregivers have faced tragic losses, abuse, or suffer from Post-Traumatic Stress Disorder, and communicate their own hostility, anxiety, and fear to the infant (Fearon, et al., 2010).

Insecure attachment, which affects about 40% of the population, has been proven to be a risk factor for later development of stable relationships.

Disorganized attachment, on the other hand, is recognised as a serious predictor of maladjustment and psychopathology in children. (Benoit, 2004)

Disorganized attachment puts children at risk for lack of control of emotions, stress, hostile and aggressive behaviours and coercive styles of interactions. They lack self-esteem and confidence, are rejected by their peers and struggle academically, especially in mathematics.

Self-Loathing

We all do that self-criticising thing – looking at ourselves in the mirror as if it is broken into hundreds of pieces and the none of the edges line up in the image, turning this way and that to confirm that it does not line up.

Your inner critical voice is constantly running, telling you where you could do better and what you should have done differently.

Know that feeling when you disagreed with someone, or they insulted you, and two days later you think of the perfect response? That is your critical inner voice going over events and conversations and figuring out what you did wrong or could have done better.

There is nothing wrong with a critical inner voice, it keeps you on your toes and helps you strive for better interactions and decisions.

However, when it completely takes over, and all it talks about is negative, shifting your goalposts to the unattainable, driving you to perfection all the time, constantly telling you that you are not good enough for this or that, or simply that you are not enough, you are going to run into problems.

This is, in essence, what self-loathing is - a particularly extreme form of low self-esteem; flagellating yourself for every single thing you do, believing you are worthless and that you will never do anything right, that you are not worthy of anyone's love. This is dangerous territory.

Sadly, you often confuse self-loathing with your conscience and think it is a good thing that at least you still have a conscience. Your conscience tells you what is morally correct, and how to behave responsibly; inner self-loathing, on the other hand, yells and berates you for everything you do and are, without you understanding that something is amiss, and you refuse to challenge it.

Thoughts generated by your critical inner voice along the lines of **I am stupid, embarrassing, clueless, insensitive, ugly, incompetent and no good for anything** are typical examples of self-loathing.

You beat yourself up for things other people would never even think of and hold yourself up to impossible standards. However, then you try to suppress that constant feeling of inadequacy by pretending to be better than others, boasting about your attractiveness, admirers, wealth, and intelligence.

This constant divide in your inner self and beliefs can have devastating consequences if you do not deal with it head-on, it seeps into your relationships, work-life and overall well-being and wreaks havoc.

It morphs into extreme dislike or hatred of oneself.

### Signs That You Have A Self-Loathing Mindset

You apologise for every little thing that goes wrong.

It shows that you think you are always at fault and that you are extremely uncomfortable with failure. It shows a lack of self-esteem and makes you look like a walk-over.

You motivate yourself with tough love.

Using self-criticism to motivate yourself can sometimes work. However, the fear and criticism lead to anxiety and worry and is not a healthy motivational mechanism.

For example, telling yourself you don't know enough to study may motivate you to study, but it could also demotivate you as you will end up believing you are too stupid to do so.

You set your goals low so as not to disappoint yourself/defeatism.

Deliberately not building any stretch into your goals, to make sure you do not fail to reach a goal, is telling yourself you are not capable of reaching bigger goals.

Telling yourself why bother sets you up for failure, which reinforces shame.

Physical neglect.

You do not care about your physical appearance at all and neglect even the most basic of personal hygiene, wearing the same clothes for days (and nights), and feel validated due to the neglect.

You struggle to accept compliments.

If you are always questioning compliments and worrying about the intent behind the compliment, you may have a self-loathing mindset.

You are surprised when someone does something nice for you.

You may have gone through most of your life taking care of yourself, but if a genuine nice unexpected gesture leaves you surprised, it may show that you do not believe yourself worthy of nice gestures, to the point of self-loathing.

Self-sacrifice.

Self-sacrifice is a strange animal, as it is about lack of pride in yourself, and an attempt to punish yourself whilst trying to gain worth in other's eyes. It can have devastating effects on everyone around you.

Acquiescence.

Similarly, acquiescence is about simply taking whatever is dished out, complaining bitterly about it, but making no attempt to improve your circumstances.

You compare yourself to others.

If you are constantly comparing yourself to others and thinking about this comparison in a negative way, you can seriously damage your self-esteem, thinking you will never measure up. Always trying to decorate your ego and presenting a false self is extremely self-loathing.

You have a poor relationship with food.

You either over-eat or do not eat enough, as you punish yourself with food – you either believe you do not deserve nourishment and will punish yourself with eating only things you do not like or will gorge yourself so that you have a reason to feel guilty and hate yourself.

Hostility towards perceived threats.

You make up possible threats to your security, lashing out at your partner for merely talking to someone else, believing everyone is out to get you.

Depending on spending for approval.

If you require the acquisition of material goods to feel good about yourself or give inappropriately expensive gifts to show off or 'buy' affection, you are most likely hoping that this generosity to yourself or others will fill that hollow feeling and shame and hatred you carry around.

Depending on social media for approval and validation.

Constantly checking your social media accounts, counting your likes and loves and feeling warm and fuzzy when you get more likes than expected, or posting regular updates on your 'amazing pretend life' can be very self-serving. It could be a great way to keep in touch with friends or find lost ones but check for self-loathing signs in what you post.

Depending on drug or alcohol abuse.

Blocking it all out with intoxicants can do wonders for you, numbing all that pain and shame and guilt, and tomorrow you get to feel guilty and shameful for the abuse and can do it all over again. Abusers will often pick fights or create dramas with loved ones to justify their abuse.

You consider invites an act of pity.

You are so convinced that you do not fit in anywhere and feel like a stranger, alone or alienated in a group, that any invite is considered a pity invite. You prefer to hide out and isolate yourself.

You are petrified of falling in love.

Letting go of your fears and losing yourself in love can be a terrifying prospect if you are self-loathing because you convince yourself that your partner will discover the real you and resent you for it.

This becomes a self-fulfilling prophecy as no one will be able to trust the false self you presented nor the real you, and it will perpetuate the self-loathing cycle of misery. If you cannot accept yourself, how can anyone else accept you?

Relationship sabotage.

Even if you are really interested in the relationship, or in love with your partner, if you are self-loathing, you may find yourself doing anything you can to sabotage the relationship, from cheating and lying, mistreating or emotionally and physically abusing your partner, neglecting them or abandoning them.

You may do this to be able to control the relationship or to prevent yourself from being abandoned and hurt. You may even go as far as believing it to be the 'noble thing to do' as you would inevitably end up hurting the partner, it is better for you to 'set them free.'

Refusal to get help.

This is the major reason partners give up on self-loathers, as they firmly believe that no one can help them. If you think that this is the way I am and have always been and no counselor or exercises are going to change that, you may be scared that it will only be a temporary fix and you will revert back to your old behaviour and be abandoned again.

No amount of unconditional love will help you find solutions if you are not willing to try – and as self-loathing is a learned behaviour, it can be unlearned.

## What Drives Self-Loathing?

Self-loathing starts in childhood, when you are trying to figure out life and how to live it. According to Firestone (Firestone, 2002), this tyrannical inner voice can develop early on, and parents need to guard against that deliberately.

This inner critic needles you into poor self-esteem and self-confidence. It affects your thoughts, controls your behavior, and misdirects your actions, thinking it is protecting you but really reinforcing feelings of shame and guilt and self-destructive behaviors.

Children are extremely sensitive to negativity, and the smallest increase in a parent's level of anger can have negative consequences, as they can experience it as life-threatening, even when not acted upon. When they become stressed, they identify with the angry, verbally, or physically abusive parent and internalise those feelings.

Major trauma can cause large shifts in the way you view yourself and seriously erode your concept of self unless dealt with appropriately, and in some cases, children are literally taught that they are worthless (emotional abuse).

If you were told you are bad, or inadequate, or not good enough, as most people were, at some stage of your upbringing by well-meaning adults, who did not understand the implications of those words, you might have taken them up as core beliefs.

Luckily for most, parental anger episodes and careless words were mostly few and far between, for others, it could have been more overwhelming, leading to self-loathing.

If a parent left you at an early age, and you were left to blame yourself for their desertion, without any explanation to the contrary, it could have piled on guilt and shame leading to self-loathing.

## Confirmation Bias

Confirmation bias is a term that psychologists use to explain the tendency for your mind to search for evidence that will support your beliefs, or to interpret evidence to the contrary as false.

When you have a problem with self-loathing, you will actively search for evidence to support what you believe to be true about yourself, why you are so bad and all the things you believe to be wrong with you. The evidence is mostly very tenuous and often pure fabrications, whereas anything that might suggest otherwise is refuted.

Self-loathing is learned behaviour and can be unlearned.

## Negative Early Dating Experiences

Young children will 'push boundaries' to reaffirm that their base is secure and that their caretakers are available, teenagers from age eleven onwards do so even more, as they are searching for their place in the world. Up to age 25 parents can either strengthen the attachment with their children or do untold damage if they expect them to behave like rational adults.

People with an insecure attachment style will unknowingly create the very situations they are afraid of, pushing their boundaries as hard as they can to get attention. They will do so with friends, romantic partners and parents or other authority figures such as teachers or coaches.

The securely attached teenager or young adult will be able to seek comfort from a meaningful figure if they are encountering difficulties. This may be a parent or a good friend. If they tell you **'nobody likes me, or I hate this teacher, I am going to fail'** they are looking for comfort and your reaction will have an impact on their sense of security in attachment.

Teaching teenagers to find their own solutions and stand up for themselves is a good thing, as long as it is not taken too far – teaching them a lesson, or coddling them so much that they never learn a lesson, will both lead to insecure attachment and is to be avoided at all cost.

They will act out with aggression, ambivalence, avoidance, or a confused mix of the above. The key is to acknowledge the teen's feelings and to help them understand the feelings and how to find a way to deal with it.

Actions that lead to insecure attachment in the teenage years include separation from the main caregiver, parents with low emotional intelligence, physical or emotional neglect, emotional abuse (mocking, making fun of them and threats), physical or sexual abuse and not dealing with trauma appropriately.

As hormones are running rampant in the teenage years there is a strong romantic interest in the opposite sex or same sex in some cases.

As a teenager or young adult, you are unlikely to be aware of your attachment style and are most likely going to pick partners that feel 'familiar,' i.e., similar to an influential person in your life (Bartholomew, 1991). If one of your parents were distant, you might choose someone distant to fulfill the inner child's desire to finally draw someone distant close.

Bowlby reported that the working models of the self and your relationship partners tend to be complementary and mutually confirming (Noller, 1990).

When there is anxious or avoidant attachment, and you pick a partner that fits that maladaptive pattern, you simply perpetuate the patterns.

For example, an anxious person will feel that, to get really close to someone and have your needs for connection and intimacy met, you need to be with your partner at all times and get lots of reassurance (Brumbaugh, 2010). They are hypervigilant to signs their partners may be pulling away from them (Simpson Jeffry A., 2017). They typically pick a person that is hard to connect with, unattainable and isolated, to support their own reality.

There is not much hope of this match working out, without both partners doing some serious work on themselves and the relationship, and more damage is done to both partners, that will only reinforce their maladaptive perspectives.

The same applies to the dismissive/avoidant type, whom will act as if they have no needs to get their needs met, but they will pick someone clingy and possessive.

For the teenager or young adult, every experience is amplified, due to their inexperience and the allure of 'first love.' They look for clues of reciprocation of feelings, obsess about everything regarding the potential partner, relive every word and gesture vividly, and everything seems especially wonderful and special when they connect, with no regard for obvious faults or potential problems. The partner becomes the center of all their thoughts, and they are steeped in admiration.

Of course, living on cloud nine and being on such an emotional high, the fall if things go wrong can be crushing, and any breach of trust or abandonment felt intensely. Unrequited love can be nursed for months or years and seriously damage your self-esteem, even if you entered your teens with a secure attachment style.

Many an insecure teen has been known to abandon all morals and values for the sake of keeping the attention of a love object, giving up all their hopes and dreams to please the partner and to cling to a feeling of belonging and being secure.

Insecure attachment relationships falter because you become 'clingy' and 'needy,' looking for external validation from your partner, and literally driving them away with your neediness. This pattern can repeat many times before you decide to take stock and figure out why you are struggling to find true love.

You become trapped in fighting over non-issues, and often cannot even remember what started the fight. You do not understand how things got so out of hand and are unaware of the fact that your partner triggered deep, non-conscious memories from childhood and earlier relationships. You may feel baffled at the level of emotional arousal and reactivity, which seems completely out of proportion to the situation at hand.

You may be tempted to recreate the drama that you experienced at home as a child, as it makes you feel at home and comfortable, believing that this is what love looks like, and that abusive language and actions are part and parcel of the romantic relationship, without it your partner must be bored or no longer interested.

Unfortunately, even a very secure person can be taken in by a disorganised, abusive partner, that presents a false self until they have you hooked. They can systematically break down your secure base and safe haven by:

alienating you from family and friends, gaslighting you into believing that you are the one at fault, triangulating with others to convince you that you are not good enough for your partner, and that everything that goes wrong is your fault.

Stepping away from this type of abusive relationship is extremely hard, but with security and support, you can build up your self-esteem again and find a mature, nurturing, and caring relationship. The worst part is the self-blame, wondering what you did wrong to have chosen such a hard relationship, and trying desperately to get back to the 'love-bombing' stage, but simply digging yourself deeper into the quagmire of their utter inability to love anyone but themselves. Such a relationship is typically abusive in the extreme and cannot be saved. You can only find the courage to walk away and never look back.

Sometimes, you will fall into a push-pull situation, where you will push, and your partner pulls away until you are so exhausted that you pull away at which point the partner will start pushing, and the cycle repeats.

If you deliberately initiate this push-pull cycle, it is a clear sign that you operate from a very insecure attachment style and are possibly trying to compensate for your inner self-loathing.

Constantly seeking reassurance should signal the need for developing a clear narrative of your early relationships and how it affects your unconscious decisions and actions to help you survive. The fear you feel is very real.

# Chapter 2: Empath Empowerment

What springs to your mind when you think of the word **empath**? Do you believe that empaths are people who have already been born with that gift? That's a common misconception, although true in some cases. However, being an empath is truly (like everything else we have learned so far in this book) a skill that you can learn.

Becoming an empath is about training your mind and exercising it to become more attuned to empathy. It is about shifting your mindset and training it until empathy becomes second nature to you.

Empathy is one of the core concepts of becoming an individual with high emotional intelligence because:

It further enhances your ability to relate and understand those around you.

It helps you resolve conflicts better and manage disagreements when you can empathize with others.

It helps you accurately predict how others are going to react.

It makes you more confident at expressing your point of view because you're attuned to your surroundings.

Others will view you as a source of comfort, sometimes even as someone who can heal them emotionally.

It improves your motivation to become better and to thrive in any social setting.

You form better and stronger bonds with the relationships that you forge, even the new ones.

You will find it much easier to forgive others because you can see things from their perspective, reflect on why they reacted that way, and understand where they're coming from.

It makes you more aware of your non-verbal body language and the way you come across to others.

## Why Empathy Is Important

If you want to wield any kind of influence, you need to have empathy on your team. Without being able to sense the way that others feel, you'll find it an uphill task to leave any kind of positive impression on them.

When you fail to sense the way that others around you feel, your social interactions will suffer as a result. You will find it very difficult to build effective rapports – and even to form solid bonds. People must be able to like you, trust you, and relate to you if they are going to allow themselves to be influenced by you.

A skilled empath is someone who is effective at reading emotional cues. They can listen effectively to the voices of the people around them because they have a genuine understanding of where that person is coming from.

## How to Become an Empath

Since empathy is one of the core elements of emotional intelligence, it is only fitting that we do what we must towards building our empath abilities. To become an empath, start with the following strategies:

· **Connect with Yourself** – Before you can begin understanding, you must first connect with yourself. An effective empath is someone who is centered – someone who is down-to-earth and grounded. When you are connected with yourself, you're less likely to become distracted easily by what's going on around you. You're able to focus on what matters at hand. One of the best techniques you could apply to connect with yourself is meditation.

· Meditation helps you find balance, calm and inner peace, and it can be utilized in almost every aspect of your life whenever you feel anxious, worried or stressed. Learning to control our minds is one of the most difficult things we can do. But to become an empath, this is what is needed. It's easy to let our thoughts and emotions get the best of us. It is so easy to be consumed by negativity. Learning to become an empath begins within you, and you start by learning how to focus and gain control of what's happening internally.

· Another method you could use to connect with yourself is to spend a few minutes every day just being in your own company. We live in a society today that is far too attached to their technological devices, and it is time we ditched them for a bit. You'll never connect with yourself if your eyes are constantly glued to a digital screen. Pause, take a breath, slow down, and just appreciate being with yourself. This can be done along with your meditation sessions. It gives you time to reflect on what matters to you, and more importantly, it gives you a few minutes to clear your head and think.

· **Putting Yourself in Their Shoes** – This is perhaps the most obvious thing that you can do, but it works. Whenever you're involved in a conversation with someone, always picture what it would be like to see things from their point of view, not just yours. This is one of the most basic yet effective ways which you can begin growing your empathy skills. We may not realize it, however, rarely do we ever give proper thought to what someone else might be going through. We may listen to what they're telling us, and we may sympathize. But how often do we attempt to **feel** what they're currently dealing with?

· You may have been guilty in the past of brushing someone off as just being silly, or dramatic or exaggerating way too much. That's what happens when we lack the necessary empathy skills to respond appropriately. It may be silly or dramatic to us, but to them, it could be a very serious matter. Being an empath will teach you to see beyond your own feelings and connect to someone else without prejudice or judgment.

- **Give More Thought to Them** – When you're eating that delicious lunch you just bought from the store nearby, do you think about the people who worked hard to prepare it for you? The hours that they spent in the kitchen, so you didn't have to? When you're enjoying your delicious cup of coffee at the local coffee shop, do you think about the ones who went through all that trouble to gather the coffee beans that you're enjoying right now? The people who helped to ship and deliver that coffee to the local shop where you're sitting at this moment enjoying the fruits of their labor? Giving the people around you deeper thought is an approach that you could use to begin training your empathy skills. These people do not necessarily have to be directly in front of you for you to make the connection. It is about taking a moment to think about these people and silently offering them a quick thank you. It is about connecting with humanity.

- **Eliminate Prejudices** – This can be a tough one. A lot of us are prejudice without even realizing it. For others, being prejudice is already an innate part of who they are. When someone of a different race, gender or religion approaches you, how do you react if it is something you're unfamiliar with? Do you automatically set up a barrier? That's being prejudice, and it is what's going to prevent you from becoming an empath if you don't work to get rid of it. To become an empath, you are going to have to challenge your prior beliefs and the prejudices you currently have. Work to get rid of them and start to view people, places, and situations with an open mind. Just because a person is different from you doesn't mean you should be wary. Everyone is still human at the end of the day. Get rid of the barriers and start viewing everyone as only one thing – human. We're all equals on this earth, and we should mutually respect one another. To help you with this, try to find something which you can connect on. Some common ground.

This helps you focus on the things which make you similar, and less on what makes you different. When you can relate to them and connect on a shared interest, you'll have a greater interactive experience, and eventually, boundaries will just slip away. This is when greater empathy occurs, by opening up to the people around you and welcoming them as part of your circle.

· **Curiouser and Curiouser** – As we grow older, we tend to keep to ourselves and want to disconnect from the world, especially if we're not naturally social individuals. However, if you want to become an empath, you're going to need to start nurturing your curiosity again. Start getting curious about people. Look for reasons to engage with people you normally wouldn't connect with. Strike up conversations with people who come from different backgrounds than you do. By socializing with a diverse group of individuals and casting your net far and wide, you develop a more universal understanding of the world and people around you. It helps you see these individuals as humans and break down any further barriers which might have existed that prevented you from being more empathetic with them.

Being an empath is not just a skill for someone who was born with that natural gift; it is something we all can learn. Emotional intelligence and empathy are not just about working on controlling and understanding emotions; it is about learning to **act, be and care**. These should slowly start to become part of your personality. By simply changing your attitude, displaying a little love and care, you would be surprised at what a world of difference it can make.

## How to Be More Self-Disciplined When It Comes to Your Emotions

To do this, you need to change your mindset and enforce a lot of self-discipline. Changing your mindset can do wonders to transform your life and your emotions. Developing the right mindset can become the most powerful tool you will have. It will get you from where you are right now to where you want (or hope) to be in your life (which is to become an empath with high levels of EQ).

Gandhi once said, "You need to be the change that you wish to see in the world," and this couldn't be truer. If you want to see real change happening in your life, and in ways you never thought possible, it all starts with you. The kind of mindset that you have is a reflection of your current emotional intelligence levels. Do you think it could be time to change your mindset? The answer is yes if you can relate to any of the following signs below.

### Five Signs That It's Time to Change Your Mindset

Our thoughts can hurt us more than we know. More importantly, they can affect our emotions in such a significant way that we end up reacting in the way that we know we shouldn't. The problem with a negative mindset is that it acts like an anchor that weighs you down, and it means that your emotional intelligence levels still need some working on.

**Do You Find It Hard to Let Go?** – Especially the mistakes and the failures that you've faced. To become an empath that possesses high EQ, you are going to need to shift this train of thought, or emotional freedom is something which is always going to elude you.

**Do You Always Feel Demotivated?** – You find yourself lacking the desire to do anything, even if it is something as small as meeting a couple of friends for dinner. You feel tired and demoralized, losing any desire even to put in an effort anymore.

You find yourself losing that zest for life. This needs to change if you want to work on becoming an empath.

**Are You Complaining About the Same Thing?** – Like a broken record that keeps repeating, eventually your complaints will start to define you if you don't do something about it. If you find yourself doing this, it is high time you start changing your mindset for the better because no good will ever come out of complaining – except to drive away the people who are close to you. Would you want to be around someone who complains all the time? Definitely not.

**Do You Make Too Many Excuses?** – There's always going to be a reason not to do something. You prefer to make excuses rather than make an actual effort to change. There's always going to be a reason not to do something; the challenge now is to find reasons **why you should**. Motivation is one of the core concepts of someone with high levels of EQ, and someone like this does not make excuses all the time. They take action instead and become a catalyst for change.

**Do You Find It Hard to Be Happy?** – No matter how many good things you have to be grateful for, you find yourself feeling unhappy and miserable all the time. Happiness seems like a constant struggle. You may be happy for a while, but it isn't long before you find yourself sinking back into the pit of despair. Time for that mindset to change, my friend.

## Let Self-Discipline Be Your Driving Force

You may be wondering if it is still possible to change. Yes, it absolutely is because self-discipline is not a skill set that some people are born with – which is why others have succeeded, and you have not. Self-discipline is a state of mind, and because it is something which can be learned, it can be possessed by anyone with the desire to cultivate it and make it a part of who they are. This tool is going to be your driving force towards gaining better control over your emotions once and for all.

There is no easy way or shortcut towards gaining more self-discipline. You are going to have to put in time, effort, and energy into the entire process if you want to make it happen. To become the disciplined person that you want to be, to make the positive changes in your life that you hope to see, it is going to require some sacrifices on your part.

Adjustments need to be made, and there are going to be some difficult things you might have to do, but change is necessary for the greater good, and this has to be a sacrifice you must be willing to make. Everyone can learn how to build a healthy self-discipline habit. It is simply up to you whether you choose to do it or not (hopefully you do!). Once you do, you will be amazed at the momentous effect it will have on your life, and what a difference it can make.

Here's how you can improve your self-discipline levels, and use this trait to change your mindset and improve your control over your emotions:

**Be Persistent** – Having the intention to become a more self-disciplined person alone is not enough if you are not willing to keep that momentum going, which is why persistence is another important trait that you need to build as part of your character. Your success will depend upon your ability to persist even when the odds are not in your favor. Setbacks will happen, wrenches will be thrown in your plan, and in the face of all that, you must persist with self-discipline to see you through.

**Practice Time Management** – Time management is one of the most important skills you can master, and it is in this area where self-discipline is the most important. Why? Because the way that you manage your time will determine the outcome of the life that you lead. Time is its own master, and while you may not be able to manage or control it, you can certainly control what you do with your time. Start making the most out of your time by choosing to spend it differently. Where previously you might have wasted much of it doing menial things that were not going to benefit you in the long term, or even if you barely got anything done at all because you procrastinated and found excuses not to get to it thanks to a lack of self-discipline, you need to do a complete turnaround and start spending it very differently.

**Changing Your Habits** – Building healthy, productive habits is the first step to changing your life. Why do your habits need to change when all you want to acquire is more self-discipline? Because everything that you do is going to affect you both mentally and physically. While self-discipline may be a productive skill to have, if it is weighed down by all your negative habits, it is eventually going to drag you down with it.

**Set Goals** – For self-discipline to turn your life around, it is important that you first find your mission and have a purpose. Set a goal for yourself, and it does not even have to be anything tremendous right away. You could always start with a small goal that you are working towards achieving and then build momentum from there. You must write down this goal or mission because it will help you clearly define what it is you need to accomplish. When something is physically there in front of you, it makes it real as opposed to simply having several random thoughts and ideas in your head that you may forget along the way. Write it down and stick it somewhere that you will see it every day without fail.

# Chapter 3: Elements of Effective Communication

In a world where communication is a vital part of living and interacting, it is imperative to develop the right skills to make the process as effective as possible. If you want to get ahead at work, connect more with people and be a better leader, having good communication skills is your gateway to success.

Whether you're the sender or receiver of the message, there are important factors you need to constantly work on in order to master the art of communicating effectively.

### Speech

One of the most obvious forms of communication is speech. This is basically the verbal aspect of the process where words are used to convey the message. When speaking, it is important to keep it short and simple. That is, focus on the important matters and use the right words to deliver your thought as plainly as you can.

Words that come from your mouth may be only 10% of communication but it is just as equally important as other elements. To truly learn the skill, you need to master how to use the right words when interacting with a diverse group of people.

### Body Language

This nonverbal form of communication covers body movement, hand gestures, facial expressions, eye contact and posture. These are nonverbal cues that you need to use and take note of if you want to communicate effectively.

When listening to someone talk, pay attention to body language for better insight about the other person's feelings and attitude. You should make eye contact whenever possible or you may nod occasionally to convey agreement. You should also maintain excellent posture and never cross your arms. In other words, match your body's language with your words to avoid confusion on the part of the receiver.

## Tone of Voice

Knowing the correct tone to use is critical for effective communication because the right tone can convey the right emotion. Whether you want to be authoritative, friendly, passive or convincing, it's all a matter of injecting the correct tone that will help influence the other person and understand your underlying message more accurately.

## Active Listening

Another essential skill you need to master is active listening. When communicating with other people, you're not only a talker but you should also be a good listener. And it's not just about hearing words, filtering it and choosing only what you want to understand.

Active listening is paying attention not just to the words but also to body language and tone.

Also part of active listening is to avoid interruption when the other person is still talking. Wait for your turn and while doing so stay focused on the conversation at hand. Avoid articulating your responses in your mind and more importantly, avoid making judgments. Whether you agree with the person you are communicating with or not, judgment should be reserved and set aside.

## Stress Management

With stress in the picture, you or the person you are talking to will see things differently. The way you think, act and respond may be disrupted leading to confusion and misunderstanding. To avoid sending out mixed nonverbal cues and unhealthy negative behaviors, you need to know how to manage stress. For some people, meditating helps while others exercise or go for a run to temper the problem.

There is no one standard formula to managing stress. They key is to find out ways that work for you.

# Chapter 4: Principles of Effective Communication

The art of communication is essential to have for anyone to succeed in any field. People use their communication skills to convey their thoughts, feelings and emotions to others. Although all of us communicate in our own way but very few of us know how to communicate effectively. Just like everything has some principles to follow, effective communication is based on five important principles and it is not possible to excel in this skill without considering these principles.

Listening

Listening is very important in the effective communication as those people who are great listeners, are great communicators actually. If you have the ability to convey your thoughts and ideas in an excellent way that everyone understands and appreciates them but your listening skills are poor, your communication will not be effective at all because you will not be able to get the thoughts and ideas of others completely so, you can't respond to them appropriately. This causes frustration for the speaker and the process of communication becomes very difficult.

Proper listening does not only mean that you understand the words or the information being given by the speaker but it also means that you understand the feelings and emotions which the speaker is trying to convey to the listeners.

Therefore, in order to make your listening effective, you have to pay full attention to enhance these skills. As you improve in this area, your listening will automatically get better and this way you make the speaker enjoy the conversation as they realize that you are getting their each and every point.

Effectiveness

When your communication skills are effective, you can develop good understanding with others. People you interact with will understand you, and you will understand them, and this mutual understanding is something that makes the relationships stronger and long-lasting. You won't need to use manipulation or other tactics to win the hearts of others. This will ultimately result in satisfaction with your management and they will trust you more than others.

## Perceptual Filters

Sometimes people speak in certain codes and one has to be aware of them in order to pick everything correctly during the conversation. Different people have different perceptual filters that they use in communication to understand others and convey their thoughts or information.

You should pay attention to how you can learn the perceptual filters of certain people you are in interaction with, so that you can communicate with them in better way. This way there won't be any confusion and you will be able to build a healthy relationship with them.

Patience

Patience is much needed in the effective communication because it takes both time and effort to make others understand your ideas and gain the complete information and sometimes failing to do so puts you in frustration and you want to give up on your intention. At that stage, don't forget that you have to win not to lose, so just keep the positive attitude, try to find the right words to communicate your thoughts and you will ultimately succeed.

You might be failing because the words you were using were not passing through the perceptual filters of the listeners and they were not able to understand you properly.

Relationships

What you can achieve with effective communication is stronger relationship with others.

When you learn and start following the principles of effective communication on daily basis at your work place, you are not far away from achieving your goals. All you have to do is take small steps and practice as much as you can and success will be yours

# Chapter 5: How to Communicate Better at the Workplace

Perhaps one of the reasons that effective communication in the workplace is being taken for granted in some workplaces is because some people don't really know what it means. What is effective workplace communication, anyway?

Bosses just send emails to the managers and the managers do the same to the supervisors. The supervisors then just relay important updates to the employees through text messages, Skype chat or some other form of digital communication. In the past, when there was important news to be shared with the workers of a company, the upper management would call for a meeting with the middle management and the middle management would have a meeting with the workers afterward. These days, however, there just isn't time to hold traditional meetings. The speed at which businesses move prevents people from connecting on a personal level, and people have learned to sacrifice face-to-face communication for faster business transactions.

However, effective communication in the workplace is not limited only to the means by which messages are sent.

Being able to communicate better in the workplace is essential for your career. Imagine the stress and failure you'd undergo if you're not able to convey your true thoughts and brilliant ideas. While your colleagues succeed, you're left wallowing in a corner because you can't express your ideas, thoughts, and plans for your company. To assist you in communicating better at your workplace, here are steps you can implement.

Establish Convenient Venues of Communication

As a personnel and part of a team, you have to establish a venue where your colleagues can communicate with you conveniently.

You can connect with them online or offline. Having person-to-person communication is, of course, best because you can also interpret any non-verbal language. Let your colleagues know that you're open to communication.

## Be Honest and Sincere

You can only become a better communicator if you're honest and sincere. Conveying your message honestly will benefit you too, because you can say what you want without fear because you're honest and sincere. Couple this with diplomacy, though, so that there will be no bad blood between you and your colleagues. You must observe sincerity too, due to the fact that without it, the message you want to convey can fall on deaf ears. Your honesty and sincerity will shine through and your colleagues will trust you more.

## Settle Disputes Directly with the Person Concerned

You have to talk to the person concerned first, before anything else. There are many employees who report to higher-ups first, before talking to the person concerned. This is not the proper way to do it. You have to know the other person's side first, and take it from there. Remember to observe honesty, tact, and respect when talking to this person. If he or she shouts, keep calm. If he or she curses, don't curse back. You can't fight fire with fire. Choose the high road instead and you'll end up winning.

## Listen More and Talk Less

A great conversationalist listens more and talks less. You can communicate better this way. It's a two-way process that allows you to convey what you want to say. When the person becomes aware that you're not condescending or talking down, he or she will gradually loosen up and listen more to you.

## Express Yourself Properly

Be articulate in your language and use brief but exact statements. Tactfulness, of course, is more important than brevity. Whenever you find yourself in a sticky situation, it's better to use more words to be tactful than being brief but rude. Rudeness has no place in good communication. Here are some pointers you can adapt to express yourself properly.

Talk in a normal manner

Don't rush through your words or falter in your speech. Speaking in a normal manner signifies your desire to be heard correctly. Avoid mumbling to yourself.

Maintain the proper distance

This will depend on the person you're talking to. If the individual is a superior, then you can position yourself a comfortable distance away from him or her. If it's a friend, then you can stand closer. Don't let the person misunderstand you just because you've kept an inappropriate distance.

Avoid mannerisms

Focus on the person you're talking to and avoid mannerisms. Don't play with your hair, or bite your fingernails while talking. These actions can be misconstrued negatively.

Listen attentively

Whether you're speaking to a family member or a colleague, you have to listen attentively. What does the individual truly want to say? What's the true meaning of his or her statements?

Show respect

Express yourself to the other person in a respectful manner, and you'll likewise earn the other's respect. You can emphasize a point by speaking calmly and respectfully.

Use simple, understandable language

You have to adjust your language to the level of your receiver. However, you don't have to use highfalutin words to express your ideas. The simpler your language is, the more understandable it is.

# Chapter 6: Positive Reinforcement

Our brains are actually perfectly wired to thrive on positive reinforcement. As humans, we love experiencing praise and positive affirmation for our achievements. That is why when we experience a tremendous amount of love and support as children, we typically grow up to have a strong sense of self-esteem. However, when this positive affirmation had not been offered, or if we find that we are failing to receive it later in life, our sense of self-esteem can drop. Fortunately, whether or not you received it in the past, you have a powerful ability to change this story and give yourself the positive reinforcement that you need to increase your self-esteem and achieve your goals with greater ease. That's right, you can celebrate and praise yourself and directly experience success as a result!

## Why Positive Reinforcement Works

Positive reinforcement teaches us that we are capable of celebrating our own successes and achievements. When we positively reinforce ourselves and others, we show that what we or they have done is good and worthy. This type of praise leads to that individual feeling accepted and appreciated by people they care about, triggering a sense of community. On a basic biological level, all of us strive to fit into the community and feel like we belong. Experiencing positive reinforcement proves to us that we are fitting in and allows us to feel loved and honored by those around us.

On an even more basic level, we are individuals who are motivated by feeling good. We will do things that help us feel good and we will avoid things that cause pain on any level. Being praised for doing a job well done either through verbal praise or through a prize of sorts teaches our mind that what we have is positive. We'll want to do more of that behavior so that we can experience more good feelings.

Many children are raised in an environment where they are either ignored for their accomplishments or are reprimanded. They may be ridiculed for their interests, or they may be devalued for not being "good enough" despite having excellent results. Any of these reactions from adults, peers, and other authority figures can result in children feeling like their successes are not enough or worse, are unimportant. As a result, they begin to feel foolish and unmotivated. Experiencing positive reinforcement may feel uncomfortable because they have never experienced it and, therefore, they may struggle to positively reinforce themselves.

Learning to positively reinforce yourself when you do something that promotes greater self-esteem is a great way to push yourself into doing even better. Although it may feel odd or unnatural at first, trust that it will begin to feel normal over time as you become used to celebrating yourself and your successes. Furthermore, it will feel a lot easier to become motivated, and you'll find that acting as your own biggest cheerleader will allow you to succeed even more. This means that you hold the power to both motivate yourself and carry out your own actions.

## How Positive Reinforcement Impacts Your Brain

Positive reinforcement and achieving your goals can have a powerful impact on your brain. The science behind why positive reinforcement and achieving your goals promote a greater sense of overall health is extensive. It shows us exactly why it is important that we use these behaviors in our lives. Here is what you need to know about goal-setting, positive reinforcement, and your brain's reaction.

Having goals in and of itself creates a sense of motivation in the brain. When we have something we are working toward, our brain takes on that goal for itself. This is the first step in creating motivation for ourselves. Our brains are wired to want to "win" at everything, so any time we set a goal in place, our brain instantly goes to work looking for ways to reach that goal. This "win" is seen as a positive reward by the brain.

Despite goals being positive tools for creating motivation, the brain is actually wired to default into routines. We favor routine because it is comfortable and supports us in knowing exactly what we need, what needs to happen, and how we can create safety. When there is a routine in place, we know that there is safety on a biological level—we know where our shelter is, we know where our food is coming from, and we know how our other basic needs are being met. This is why most people struggle to set goals and actually work toward them.

Although your brain appears to be working against your success in achieving your goals, it does experience a great thrill from setting and achieving them. When we take control of our minds through mindfulness, begin working toward achieving our goals, and then actually achieve them, this sets off a positive chemical reaction. Many people report experiencing a "high" because there are so many positive endorphins flowing through their brain as a reward for achieving what it set out to accomplish. The more you practice setting goals and actually achieving them, the more your brain becomes addicted, in a sense. It enjoys the "high" so much that it becomes easier and easier for you to create new goals and set out to achieve them.

In the beginning, setting and achieving goals may not be easy because it is not a part of your routine. Your brain may not be actively aware of how much joy it will derive from "winning." However, as you carry on and begin to train your brain to achieve your goals, it will no longer be about tricking your brain because it will readily be on board and prepared to support you in accomplishing anything you set out to achieve.

## How to Set Goals

A major part of being able to train yourself to set out and achieve anything is knowing how to set effective goals. When you are someone with low self-esteem and are struggling to accomplish things, having the right types of goals in place can help you experience greater success. As you begin to achieve these goals, you will begin to feel an increase in your self-esteem. As a result, it will seem possible for you to achieve even larger goals. So, in order to set effective goals that are going to boost your success and increase your self-esteem, the following are some of what you'll need to do:

### Turn Your Goal into a Habit

The first thing that you want to do is begin turning your goals into a habit. This means that you will practice them on a regular basis, achieving them over and over again. For example, say you already drink coffee every morning but you tend to skip breakfast. If you want to set the goal that you are going to start eating a healthy breakfast every morning but haven't already chances are that this is because you do not even think about breakfast until you are already feeling hungry on your way to work. In this example, drinking your coffee is the habit and eating a healthy breakfast is the goal.

Now, if you set a reminder on your phone and you begin incorporating breakfast alongside your coffee into your daily routine, you are more likely to be successful. Because you are reminded to prepare your meal every day, you will find yourself beginning to develop it as a new habit. This will result in you creating a new, positive habit.

Science has shown that habits and goals are stored differently in the brain, so reframing a goal as a habit can make it easier for your mind to become used to the new task and integrate it easier. However, because it was still a goal, you also experience the same great rewards of dopamine and self-esteem spikes when you accomplish it.

## Change Your Environment

Our environment has a tendency to support us in maintaining habits and, inadvertently, can make it difficult for us to change our ways. When we are consistently in the same surroundings, it can be challenging to produce new habits or results because we are being mentally triggered by the environment that we are in. This results in us doing the same thing over and over, even if we have set out to do something different.

If you are looking to do something new in your life, try changing up your environment. This could be as simple as rearranging things or creating a new atmosphere in your home with furniture and décor, or it could be more complex such as changing where you spend your time or where you do your work. By changing your environment, you trigger your mind to see things through "new eyes," meaning it becomes easier for you to create new routines and habits.

## Set Micro-Goals

As mentioned earlier in this chapter, positive rewards are a great way to support yourself in achieving your goals. When you attain a goal, your brain releases dopamine. You feel happy because you've received a positive "reward" for your success. Setting micro-goals essentially means setting a series of smaller goals that are easier and quicker to achieve. For example, set the goal to accomplish one extra task at work that day or to spend a few extra minutes scrubbing the bottom of your feet in the shower. These small yet easy-to-achieve goals are great for individuals who are in the process of building self-esteem because they allow you to quickly experience success and therefore receive regular dopamine release. As a result of feeling good about your success, your self-esteem goes up and you feel even more confident about achieving future goals. From there, you can more easily set increasingly larger goals.

## How to Become Your Own Biggest Cheerleader

Cheering ourselves on is an extremely valuable tool for achieving our goals and feeling confident in ourselves. It may feel strange at first, but becoming your own biggest cheerleader is one of the greatest gifts that you can give yourself.

Because many children are not adequately supported or celebrated in their successes as youths, they have a tendency to criticize their mistakes rather than celebrate their successes. This can lead to a lack of motivation, stress, guilt, and other emotions and symptoms that represent low self-esteem. On the other hand, when you celebrating yourself and your wins no matter how small or great they are, you begin to treat yourself kindly and become capable of recognizing all that you have to offer.

As you are going about achieving new goals, give yourself pep talks and cheer on every milestone along the way. For example, let's say you have been getting out of bed at 9 AM but you now want to get out of bed at 8 AM. If you manage to wake up half an hour past 8 AM a few mornings in a row, rather than criticizing yourself for never being good enough and always doing things wrong, give yourself a round of applause for the improvement! Realize that you are already halfway toward achieving your goal and that means you have plenty to celebrate. This is a huge milestone!

Recognizing these opportunities to cheer for yourself and celebrating whenever you can is a great way to stay motivated.

Aside from giving yourself pep talks, you can do this by using affirmations such as "I am doing great" or "I am already successful." You can also leave encouraging notes where you can always stumble upon them or even buy yourself a present whenever you achieve a significant milestone!

# Chapter 7: Healthy Body, Healthy Mind

Many people fail to recognize the strong relationship between our body and our mind. When we are not adequately taking care of our bodies and our physical health, our mental health will begin to deteriorate as well. Full health requires a balance of mental and physical health to keep us in our best shape and support us in feeling our best.

## How Physical Health Impacts Self-Worth

Self-worth and body image go hand in hand. When we have a low sense of self-worth, we tend to stop taking care of our bodies. Soon, they get out of shape, may become plagued with illness and chronic pain, and would otherwise no longer serve us well. Alternatively, if we lead a stressful life that prevents us from having the time to take proper care of our bodies, we begin to get out of shape and may also feel the effects of our stress as it stirs illness within the body. As a result, we become embarrassed, and we begin to experience a lowered sense of self-worth.

Our bodies, simply put, are a major part of us. They are a large piece of our identity, and they play a massive role in who we perceive ourselves to be. When we are not taking care of our bodies, we are directly telling our minds that we do not feel worthy of our time and attention. Instead, we feel that other things are more important. This lowers our self-worth, and it also begins to stimulate sensations of shame, guilt, and disappointment in ourselves. This further damage our self-esteem and self-confidence.

Another way that our physique impacts our mental health is in how we are affected by the biology of the body. An unhealthy body generally has imbalanced hormones and struggles to perform basic tasks. It results in our body producing more cortisol, the stress hormone. This is meant to kick us into gear to give us the energy needed to take better care of ourselves, but if we ignore the signs, we simply end up in a chronic state of stress. As a result, our mental health begins to suffer as well. This stress can create even lower self-worth and self-esteem in people.

The following three ways are excellent practices you can begin using right away to start balancing your body out once again and ensure that your healthy body is able to support your mental health.

### Taking Better Care of Your Diet

Better health overall always starts in the gut. Your gut health is directly responsible for nearly every else in your body, from balanced hormones to proper organ function. When you are taking good care of your gut health, taking care of everything else becomes significantly easier. So how do you do that?

Proper gut health starts with a nutritious diet that is rich in everything you need to not only survive but also thrive. Eating a diet rich in color and with adequate proteins, fatty acids, and other important nutrients can support you in having stronger health in general. This means that you will begin to experience greater self-worth and greater self-esteem!

While supplements can be a beneficial way of getting important nutrients into your body, the best way to go about it is to eat a diet that is rich in what your body needs. Supplements do not tend to be broken down and absorbed by the body as easily, resulting in you simply passing many of the nutrients via urine or stool. If you do choose to use supplements in addition to a healthier diet, it is important to choose organic, high-quality supplements that will deliver the best impact on your body. You should also adjust your diet to increase your levels of healthy nutrients and vitamins.

Some things that you should begin adding to your diet to improve your overall health, specifically your mental health, include things like chia seeds, salmon, spinach, and eggs which are all rich in omega fatty acids. These acids are excellent for your brain health. Other foods include berries, nuts (especially Brazil nuts), oysters, yogurt, liver, and broccoli. These all contain high levels of vitamins like vitamins C, D, and B, protein, calcium, and other minerals. You can further increase your nutrient intake by choosing organic, pesticide-free food.

In addition to what you are eating, you should also pay attention to what you are drinking. You want to ensure that you are staying well-hydrated by drinking plenty of water throughout the day. You should avoid drinking excess alcohol or consuming too much caffeine. Keeping these two levels to a minimum will ensure that your body is functioning optimally and that it has the best chance of digesting and absorbing all of the healthy nutrients you are feeding it. Another great way to enjoy more fluids throughout the day is to make homemade juices from organic fruits and vegetables. A good, high-quality, fresh-squeezed juice is a great way to add more nutrients into your diet while keeping you hydrated.

### Exercising More Frequently

Exercising is an important part of our lives that many of us tend to overlook. When we do not exercise adequately, we begin to experience the side effects of this behavior both physically and mentally. Physically, we struggle to do things that may have been easy for us at one point. Perhaps we may feel like we are not on par with our peers. It can be more of a challenge to carry things, enjoy doing activities with loved ones, or otherwise stay active and involved in others' lives when we are struggling from ill health due to lack of exercise. Low stamina and increased instances of chronic pain are just two of the many things that people with a poor exercise routine face.

Increasing your daily exercise and staying on track with a routine are great ways to increase your physical and mental health. Physically, it relieves stress from your body and helps you get back in shape. As a result, your hormone levels balance out and you begin to feel better. Your body and brain function optimally, your stress levels drop, your strong emotions dissipate in a positive way, and your capacity to face things in your day to day life increases.

Mentally, your health improves because you feel better for taking care of yourself. Feelings of guilt and shame around having an unhealthy body begin to dissipate and you feel more confident in your ability to live the best quality of life possible. You also begin to feel sensations of pride and courage, knowing that you were able to accomplish something that previously may have felt daunting, challenging, or even outright impossible. These feelings of accomplishment and this sense of pride support you in feeling a greater sense of mental health overall.

Exercising does not need to be an extensive, hard-core workout that consumes all of your time. Instead, going for a brisk walk each day, spending a few minutes at the gym, or even doing a home workout routine in your living room are all great choices. If you are someone who is unable to work out due to a physical disability or preexisting health condition, consider communicating with your doctor to see what forms of exercise you may be able to engage in that will support you in feeling better. In many cases, there may be smaller and lower-impact things you can do such as yoga or light stretching.

The key here is not to outdo yourself or compete with anyone, unless that is what you are interested in. The key, instead, is to support yourself in achieving your own best health possible. As a result, you will begin to feel significantly better both physically and mentally.

## Receiving Adequate Rest

In addition to eating right and getting enough exercise, you also need to make sure that you are getting a consistent, high-quality sleep. Rest is a highly underrated part of our daily lives, and it is typically the first to be impacted when we are feeling stressed out or unwell. We begin to find ourselves sleeping less, feeling more restless when we sleep, or otherwise not feeling fully rested when we wake. As a result, we are exhausted, and our ability to function effectively throughout the day is further impacted. Soon, we skip exercising because we are too tired. Then, we begin to continue skipping it because skipping becomes a habit. Before we know it, we are also skipping eating or eating healthy meals because we are feeling too tired to prepare them. The spiral continues until we are in a rut, feeling as though we are at our worst with a poor exercise habit, an unhealthy diet, and an even worse sleeping pattern.

Instead of letting yourself get caught in this spiral that is all too familiar for most, you can choose to pay attention to your rest and ensure that you are getting adequate sleep. Whenever you sense that you are not feeling rested enough or you are feeling too tired to do things, instead of breaking your daily routine, seek to add some extra opportunities to catch up on rest throughout the day. Take it easy by letting go of unnecessary tasks temporarily as you catch up on sleep. Go to bed a bit earlier and ensure that you practice a positive bedtime routine that will support you in having a positive sleep. Using things like chamomile, lavender, and other natural sleep aids can help you resume a restful sleep. You can also lower the lights in your house about an hour before bedtime, turn off screens, and prepare yourself for a good night's rest.

It is important that, unless absolutely mandatory, you refrain from using any chemical sleep aids. Supplements and medicines can inhibit the body's natural ability to sleep, resulting in you not being able to sleep on your own without their support. Furthermore, they can prevent you from having a truly restful sleep by manufacturing one for you. As a result, you may not feel fully rested in the morning despite having slept a long night. You may also begin to notice other unwanted symptoms that make resting and living a normal daily life a challenge. Always do your best to go natural without using any supplements or medications when it comes to sleep. If you must, consult your physician and choose the least invasive temporary method possible to ensure that it does not have a long-term impact on your sleep health.

# Chapter 8: Steps for Boosting Your Emotional Communication and Emotional Bids

Using body language (and other non-verbal) communication to your benefit comprises picking up several clues that the person offers through their expressions, posture, walk, gestures, and more to interpret what they are feeling and what they leave unsaid. For instance, your partner may tell you they've had a "good day" but their body language may indicate stress and frustration. If you are quick to catch on emotional communication clues, you will know exactly how your partner is feeling, and tailor your response accordingly to recognize, acknowledge, and validate their feelings.

Most conflicts in interpersonal relationships occur when a person is unable to gather clues about their partner's state of mind and hence cannot determine the course of their response. Whether it is helping a close friend deal with the stress of work or asking your steady date to marry you, gauging the situation and adapting to it with a satisfactory emotional reaction is integral to handling the situation. When the friend feels good after your reassuring words, you'll know it is time to stop. If your date doesn't appear to be in good mood, you'll know it is time to hold off the conversation for another day.

These are two examples of when we can read other people's emotions and communicate in a befitting manner by considering the other person's feelings, thoughts, and emotions. There are countless instances when you interact to communicate and interpret each other's emotions. The more adept you become at communicating and reading emotional responses, the more fulfilling and meaningful these interactions will be.

No two marriages or relationships are even remotely similar if you ask any experienced marriage therapist. Couples come together in the unlikeliest, most wonderful, and strangest situations. Some may have similar struggles but in different ways. Every relationship is distinct with its own set of dynamics, which also involves different conflict management strategies. Similarly, every couple has different dreams and visions about the future. However, couples that have maximum fun, and share more meaningful bonds are ones who are successfully able to create shared meaning.

Enquire with any artist about what drives them to be creative, they'll tell you being creative is about being messy, joyous, fun, adventurous, risky, elusive, maddening, stimulating, intriguing, and invigorating. This isn't any different in relationships. A relationship is pretty much a work of art. You have to keep on being imaginative, reinvent, and come up with innumerable ways to keep the relationship alive (similar to creating new works of art) as you move together through life. Find some guideposts to creating shared meaning on the way.

## Why Is Emotional Communication Significant in Relationships?

Though it is one of the most important life skills, emotional communication is seldom taught to us in school or college. This is why plenty of people struggle to develop an understanding of other people's feelings and emotions while communicating with them. Emotions play a huge role in the process of communication. When we tune in to our and other people's emotions, the interaction turns out to be even more effective. Emotional awareness of the ability to comprehend our own emotions helps while communicating with others. Emotionally aware folks make for better and more impactful communicators, especially in interpersonal relationships. You will quickly identify the emotions of your partner or loved one, along with the feelings that impact their communication patterns. You will understand what the other person is communicating even more effectively.

Here are six brilliant ways to strengthen your emotional communication with your partner or loved one to enjoy more rewarding relationships.

### 1. Share small insignificant experiences instead of just speaking about it.

One of the golden rules for strengthening your emotional connection and communication with your partner involves not just speaking about small and seemingly insignificant experiences but also sharing them. A recent research in the Psychological Science suggests that we experience greater intimacy with people when we speak about common experiences.

For instance, a couple facing challenges in their relationships can take the initial step towards rebuilding their relationship by speaking about their kids, especially those related to pleasant shared moments or endearing incidents. When couples are encouraged to speak about happy moments together with their children collectively, it is almost always with the objective of repairing a damaged relationship. Talking about their shared experiences with their children helps them experience a close emotional connection, thus strengthening their bond.

In the above example, since conflicts almost happen around nurturing families, one has to be careful that moments which trigger discord aren't brought up. These shared experiences can seldom be expressed to their fullest in words. Another research conducted by Psychological Science revealed that words aren't required for a couple's shared emotions and feelings to enhance a relationship. Merely doing something together where they can both partake the same experience such as going on a bike ride, catching a movie together, sharing a dessert, and so on can intensify their pleasant experiences, thus leading to an improvement in their bond through these shared pleasant experiences.

Do something small at the same time to boost your bonds. A tiny action can be worth more than a thousand words if done at the right time with the right intention. Something as simple as reaching out for your partner's arm while catching a movie together or briefly making contact with your body (for a few seconds) by leaning against the other person can make a huge difference to the bond. At times, speaking about intimacy can take away from the joy of it. Share actions and small moments of intimacy through shared experiences in silence instead of talking about it. It will instantly strengthen your emotional communication with your partner.

## 2. Increase these shared experiences on a daily basis.

Once you are able to identify these seemingly insignificant yet precious shared moments with your partner, find ways to incorporate these actions, experiences, and moments in your daily life as a couple. If any of the partners are not adept at expressing themselves in words or describing commonplace daily details, fret not. Do not worry about not being able to express mundane details. Instead, make time for doing insignificant, meaningless, and unimportant activities together such as watching television together, listening to your favorite songs, going grocery shopping, doing laundry together, and so on. These actions are more critical on an everyday basis than simply talking about your day. Of course, people who are expressive and articulate about their feelings will have more open and meaningful conversations with their partners. However, focus on creating shared experiences and memories around small events on a daily basis to strengthen your bond as a couple.

### 3. Small talk can be big when it comes to boosting relationships.

Small talk isn't just a way to break the ice with strangers or get to know people in a business networking event. It can be brilliantly used to strengthen emotional connections in interpersonal relationships too. Insignificant details and small talk are supposedly more effective for building strong emotional ties with your partner than the seemingly deep discussions about emotions and feelings.

Harry Sullivan, an American psychoanalyst, formulated an approach that he termed "detailed injury." It suggests that therapists gather details about every aspect of a client's life. Through these small details, Sullivan believes he can determine who a person truly is. Gottman's research that we discussed in the earlier chapter concluded that it is often the mundane and fleeting everyday moments that affect the nature of interpersonal relationships. The more emotionally meaningful, charged, and serious conversations do not impact the health of our relationship as much as the seemingly mundane details.

Instead of being bored when your partner is recounting the details of a plumbing issue or a game they watched last night, reveal an interest in it. We often believe that we know all the details about our partner's life. However, according to Gottman, it's a way for couples to get closer. Something as seemingly mundane as making a to-do list together during a home renovation job can be a way of demonstrating your affection and fondness for each other. You may incorporate your partner's suggestions and preferences (that they'd probably mentioned off-hand a while ago and you remember) without asking them. These small gestures reveal that you care enough for them to do small things that bring them comfort, happiness, and joy.

On the face of it, you may feel like inquiring may seem intrusive, offensive, rude and critical. Bear in mind that you are not playing FBI and questioning them to catch them doing wrong. By asking these questions, you are letting the other person that you are genuinely interested in the insignificant details that comprise your loved one's day since it's these insignificant moments that contribute towards the reality.

Through these seeming nondescript questions, you are demonstrating your interest in their interests. You are showing them that you care enough about them to show interest in the smallest details concerning their life. These can be relationship clinchers.

## 4. Listen mindfully.

You can only tune in to insignificant everyday details when you actively listen to your partner. The knowledge that you are heard and understood (or lack of it) in a relationship can without exaggeration make or break it. When you know you are heard and understood, it cements your connection with the other. Practice active listening where you do not just listen keenly to what the person is saying but also acknowledges and understand it.

Understanding or recognition of the other person's emotional experiences or insignificant details can be conveyed in multiple ways including a verbal acknowledgment (such as I understand), smile, and so on.

Active listening may also involve interrupting the speaker for clarifications or confirming understanding through paraphrasing. Ask your partner or loved one for permission before interrupting him/her. Say something such as, "Sorry Jane, can I quickly ask you something?" Then pose your question in a manner that signifies that you are attempting to clarify what your partner has just said. If you disagree or want to chip in with your two cents, wait until they've finished speaking. Express disagreement only after the person has finished talking. If you aren't sure what the person said, ask for further clarifications without disagreeing aggressively or lying. Ask questions without assuming the answers.

## 5. Talk about yourself too.

When I tell people that the basis for a solid and long-lasting relationship is to practice active listening for acknowledging and understanding your partner's emotions, they often get into ninja listening mode. Talking doesn't have to be sacrificed at the altar of listening though. Maintain a healthy balance where both you and your loved one or partner have an equal opportunity to participate in talking and listening. Identify a healthy balance between speaking and listening since this is the most challenging aspect of any relationship. Both the partners should get a chance to express their feelings and hear/understand the other person's feelings.

## What Is Emotional Connection?

Emotional connection is nothing but the attunement couples in interpersonal relationships have towards each other's emotions or feelings. Every time we identify that someone is meaningful to our partner, we connect emotionally by turning towards them. Each time our partner makes a bid to connect with us, and we respond positively to their bid by recognizing that something has meaning for them, we build or create an emotional connection.

Let us take an example. "I gave my first presentation today as a Sr. Manage." This can be a bit of an emotional connection. Turning towards your partner response can include something such as, "Wow, tell me about it. How was it? I am sure people must've loved you." A turning away response can include something such as, "hmmm, okay." Then there is a turning against response that can be downright negative. In this case, it can be something such as, "Alright, whatever! Please allow me to work undisturbed now."

On the whole, women make more bids for connection over men. Men typically make an attempt to send out these connection bids when they perceive a threat to the relationship. On the other hand, women are more inclined to make them periodically, irrespective of the health of a relationship. Men aim to turn things around by sending out these emotions bids, while women aim to nurture and maintain the relationship by regularly sending out emotional bids. Missing an emotional bid is the mental counterpart of physically turning away from a person while he/she is talking to us. The most challenging part where emotional bids are concerned is that 80 percent of people don't even attempt to make them or get them right. At times, emotional bids are concealed in form of criticism, argument, grudges, and complaints.

Turning away can primarily happen due to lack of emotional sensitivity, apathy, or the partner in engaged in repressed negativity such as passive aggressiveness or stonewalling. When you lack emotional sensitivity, you miss opportunities to turn towards your partner. One of the major causes of infidelity in relationships is lack of emotional connection. When partners miss responding to other person's emotional bids or turn away from it, they send/compel them to look elsewhere for an emotional connection.

# Chapter 9: Dealing with Conflict

Conflict is an inevitable part of any relationship, especially when you spend a lot of time together and rely on each other for many things. Learning to deal with conflict effectively can ensure that anytime an argument arises in your marriage, you can overcome it by having the right tools on hand. If you are not effectively managing disagreements and conflicts, over time these smaller arguments can fester and turn into larger conflicts. As a result, it can drive a massive wedge between you and your partner.

Knowing how to handle conflicts and conflict resolution in a marriage is a tricky task as both of you will likely need to break many bad habits and learn how to communicate more effectively. It can take time and practice, so make sure that you are being patient with your partner and trusting in the process. The more considerate you are of each other, the easier it will be for you to begin integrating these new techniques into your conflicts and experiencing fewer arguments and resentment and more resolutions and forgiveness.

## Avoid Turning Disagreements into Fights

One strong way to handle disagreements in your marriage is to avoid letting disagreements turn into fights. Disagreements generally occur before an actual fight officially starts, and learning how to recognize these disagreements can support you and your spouse in stopping them from turning into something bigger. Inputting your conflict resolution skills into the conversation when the disagreement starts, it can prevent it from spiraling. As a result, it will be less likely to turn into an actual argument and more likely to be resolved.

When you can avoid having arguments turn into fights, it is easier to handle resolutions. This is because the only thing that needs to be accomplished is finding a solution that both of you can agree on. If it turns into a fight, however, it might result in you also having to heal from hurt feelings and resentment.

Naturally, no one actually wants to fight with their partner; however, these fights can happen. Fortunately, there are two of you who are working together toward trying to end the conflict. This means that you can both work together to create a resolution that ensures that both parties are accounted for and respected.

Remember, a disagreement does not equal a fight. Part of avoiding having disagreements turning into actual fights is learning how to disagree without feeling personally attacked by the disagreement. This means that, while you can certainly feel frustrated and upset by the disagreement, you should not take it personally. Do not feel as though your partner is disagreeing with you just to hurt your feelings or make your life difficult. Instead, they simply have a different point of view than you do. Respecting that and understanding it can help you experience your emotions without becoming the victim and your partner becoming the attacker. As a result, it is easier to manage your emotions and prevent the conflict from turning into an actual fight.

## Make Sure You Fight Fairly

In the event that a disagreement does escalate into a fight, it is important that you fight fairly. Fighting dirty can result in hurt feelings, pain, and resentment. As a result, it is much harder to come back from. If you do find yourself fighting, refrain from pointing blame, calling names, attacking someone based on their previous experiences, or using parts of someone's life against them. Trying to bully your partner so that they see that you are right or hurt them because you feel that they hurt you, is not okay. In doing so you can quickly destroy the trust and intimacy in your marriage and find yourselves feeling resentful toward each other and unwilling to come together to find a solution. This is not a healthy state to be in as it can result in no solution being found, or worse, it can result in your marriage ending.

When you are fighting, always make sure that you fight clean. Use compassion when fighting, do not get sarcastic, do not fight with contempt, and do not call your partner names. Doing so can result in you becoming a bully, and can be taken as a sign of abuse. Abuse at any point, even if it is unintentional during a heated fight, can be painful and difficult to heal. If it happens multiple times, it can result in major damages and a lot that both partners need to heal from.

If you have reached a point in your marriage where you feel that arguments are frequent and that one or both of you are bullying the other, it may be a good idea to incorporate a marriage counselor into the mix. Having someone who can mediate your conversations and help open up communication between you and your partner can help you both start the healing process and learn to communicate, and argue, in a healthier way.

### Apologize When You Do Something Wrong

Never wait for your partner to ask for an apology. Instead, if you have done something wrong, admit fault and apologize for what you did. Not apologizing when you have done something wrong suggests that you do not care that you hurt your partner's feelings or that you are not taking responsibility for your actions. Both of these can result in your partner feeling like nothing will ever change and that you will both continue to have a poor relationship going forward. As a result, they may lose hope.

When you take the initiative and sincerely apologize for what you have done, it is easier for your partner to forgive you. This is because you are showing that you recognize that you have hurt them and that you feel bad for doing so. This also shows that you are willing to make the necessary changes so that you do not hurt them in the same way in the future.

If your partner claims you have done something and you do not recall doing it, you may struggle to apologize because you might feel like you do not want to take the blame for something you don't feel you have done. You should apologize anyway. Apologize for the fact that your partner feels as though you have hurt their feelings. Then, ask for them to elaborate on how you hurt their feelings and what you can do to avoid hurting their feelings again in the future. This shows that even though you might not understand right now, you are willing to try and that you want to make things right and treat them better in the future.

## Take a Timeout If You Need To

During an argument, it is not unreasonable to ask for a timeout. When things get heated and feelings are being hurt or it feels like both your arguing is not productive, taking a timeout is a great way to relax, ground yourself, and remember what the goal is. Generally, the goal is for each partner to feel heard and understood and for a mutual agreement to be reached so that you can overcome the argument with a resolution.

If your argument has gotten to the point where no resolution is being considered or reached, where you feel like you are not making any progress, where feelings are being hurt, or where it feels like it is becoming too much, simply call timeout. Take some time away from each other and breathe so that you can let your emotions filter out and you can both come back into a clear thinking space. Then, you can approach the conversation again after you have both calmed down.

Make an agreement that upon calling for a timeout, you are both agreeing to calm down and come back to the discussion with the intention to find a resolution. You should also make sure that you both set a time upon which the conversation will be discussed once more. That way, both of you have clear expectations on when the other will be ready to talk again and no one feels as though they are being pressured to talk sooner than they are ready to, or like they are waiting indefinitely for the other partner to be ready.

### Articulate the Real Reason You Are Frustrated

During a disagreement, it is important that you take the time to articulate the real reason as to why you are frustrated or upset. It is not enough to assume that your partner knows exactly what has caused your upset feelings. Instead, you need to take the time to explain why you are upset, what they did that contributed to it, and how you feel it can be resolved. This gives your partner a clear understanding as to what is actually being addressed in the conversation.

When you do not take the time to outline what it is that you are upset about, your partner is left guessing. As a result, they may assume that you are upset about something other than what has actually upset you. Then, they may be arguing in one direction about one topic while you argue in another direction about a different topic. This can lead to a great deal of miscommunication. Furthermore, it can lead to you both feeling as if you are not being understood. This can be frustrating because you feel as though you are explaining yourself well but your partner may think that you are referencing something different from what you actually are. As a result, it can lead to more hurt feelings and deeper argument.

Being clear on what has caused your frustrations ensures that your partner knows exactly what you are upset about. That way, they can address that exact topic rather than addressing something that is not related to your frustrations. This keeps you both focused on the same subject and working toward a solution.

## Take Responsibility for Your Feelings and Opinions

During an argument, it is essential that you take responsibility for your feelings and opinions. Always use "I" statements to show that you are discussing your own thoughts and feelings rather than passing blame on your partner. Even if you are discussing something you said, discuss it in a way that shares that you are talking about your perspective of what they said and not what they actually meant. That way, if what you perceived and what they meant were two completely different things, it does not seem like you are feeding words into their mouth.

Furthermore, make sure that you are not considering your feelings and opinions to be absolute truths. Instead, they are **yours.** This means that you take the time to acknowledge that there are many different opinions, thoughts, feelings, and perceptions that can be considered true. When you take responsibility in this way and keep an open mind, you ensure that you are validating your partner, too. You do not want to get in an argument over who is right and who is wrong because chances are, both of you are right in your own ways. Knowing how to recognize this and respect it ensures that your discussion stays focused on the real issue and not a power struggle.

## Make Sure You Break the Touch Barrier

During arguments, we have a tendency to create what psychologists call a "touch barrier" between ourselves and our partners. Essentially, this is a subconscious barrier that we put up as a way to protect ourselves from the perceived hurt that we believe our partner will inflict upon us. This actually ends up in us feeling a sense of disconnect from our partner, however, and can lead to a lack of trust and intimacy in our relationships.

When you get in an argument with your partner, or when anyone has hurt feelings for any reason, it is important that you break the touch barrier with your partner. You can do so by putting a hand on their shoulder, putting your hand on theirs, or hugging them to let them know that you still care even if you are disagreeing with them at the moment. Showing physical affection during arguments reminds your partner and you that you are still close and that you love each other. It also reminds you that your relationship is bigger than this conflict and that you can overcome it for the common good of your relationship.

If you do not break the touch barrier between yourself and your partner, this can lead to hurt feelings, resentment, and a lack of intimacy festering in your relationship. The longer it goes on, the more it creates a sense of disconnect in your relationship. As a result, you may both end up feeling emotionally and physically undesirable and neglected by your spouse. This can become a wound in and of itself which needs to then be healed.

When you are overcoming the touch barrier in your relationship, make sure that you are being mindful of your partner. Wait for an appropriate moment to approach them and hug them or break the touch barrier. If your partner has experienced abuse in the past, especially physical abuse, be extra gentle in approaching them. That way, you are respecting their space and their emotional triggers. Show compassion for their needs in the process as this will ensure that the breaking of the touch barrier improves intimacy, rather than results in them feeling fearful or hurt.

## Stay Focused on the Bigger Picture

When you are in an argument with your spouse, always remember the bigger picture. Yes, you are in an argument, but no, you are not an argument. In other words, your relationship is far more than the disagreement that you are having. Remember that even though you may be feuding at the moment that there is still an entire marriage that exists between the two of you.

Gaining some perspective on your relationship and realizing that you are both in it for the same reason can support you in coming together on a solution. This is because you will realize that your argument is small in comparison to everything that you share together.

If you find that you are getting overly focused on the argument or that it feels like the argument is some sort of sentence for your marriage, stop and gain some perspective. Spend a few minutes remembering why you love your partner, why you are together, and what has brought you together. Once you remember why you are in a marriage with your partner, use this to support you in arguing with compassion and consideration toward them. That way, you both stay focused on finding a solution rather than arguing your case and being "right." It also prevents you from jumping to any rash decisions because of a moment of heated fighting.

## Keep Your Argument Focused on the Real Cause

Anytime you find yourself arguing with your spouse it is important that you always keep your argument focused on the real reason why you are arguing. When your argument starts to get off topic, then this is when communication can become blurry and feelings can get hurt. At this point, you may begin dredging up past events and trying to use them to hurt your partner. Or, they may do the same back to you.

Arguments that get off topic can spiral quickly because they go from one isolated point of disagreement or hurt to a widespread point of disagreement or hurt. As a result, the amount of angry energy that comes into the mix can be challenging to come back from.

If you find that your argument is getting off topic, spend some time bringing it back into focus. Remember what you are upset about and bring it back to the main point. If you or your partner got off topic or began using other events to attempt to blame or bully the other person, stop and apologize. Then, make the mutual agreement to focus on what has caused this particular disagreement.

Often, when we find ourselves arguing about everything instead of the single reason that caused the argument in the first place, we never find a resolution. This is because we stopped looking for ways to resolve the conflict and we started looking for verbal weapons to hurt each other with. This will not be helpful for either of you.

Staying focused on the topic at hand and looking for a solution will be of great help. If you do feel that events of the past are unresolved, save them for a later date and come back to them with the specific intention of dealing with that particular topic. That way, each discussion is focused on a resolution and true solutions and healing can be found in your discussions, rather than more pain and frustration.

## Show Respect for Your Partner's Perspective

Even if you do not agree, it is essential that you show respect for your partner and their perspective. When you stop respecting your partner's perspective, you invalidate them and lead them to feel like they are unworthy of having their own opinion and feelings on the matter. Furthermore, you make it seem as though your way is the only right way and that they must agree with you or else a solution will never be reached. This type of totalitarian approach can result in hurt feelings, frustration, and feeling neglected and ignored by your spouse.

Instead, take the time to show respect to your partner's perspective. You can do this by giving them the opportunity to explain it, by listening when they speak, and by not interrupting them even if you disagree with them. If you have a rhetorical argument that you want to make, wait until they are completely done sharing their point before you share your case. That way, they feel respected even during a disagreement.

Remember, respect is the key to helping your partner feel safe, safety is the key to building trust, and trust is the key to having intimacy between you and your partner. Without respect, there is no safety, trust, or intimacy. You absolutely must respect your partner. When your partner trusts that they can disagree with you and have their own perspective without you resorting to treating them with disrespect, this proves that you are respecting their right to their own opinion.

Respecting your partner and their opinion will also help you hear each other out which can support you in finding common ground in your arguments. When this happens, it becomes easier for you to find a resolution because you are both in agreement on at least a few things. This means that you can find a common ground and meet in the middle to come up with a solution that serves both of you. As a result, you both end the argument feeling closure. This ensures that the argument is brought to a complete close and that you can both move on from the argument without feeling residual resentment or anger toward the other partner.

### Be Honest About How You Feel

Whenever you experience a disagreement with your partner, it is essential that you stay transparent about how you are feeling. When you argue with someone, it can be easy to feel a difficulty in expressing your emotions. You might fear that your emotions will not be understood or accepted, or that your emotions will make you look weak. These types of fears can result in you holding back which ultimately end in your partner not knowing exactly where you are coming from.

Furthermore, if you are dishonest about your feelings, it can result in you feeling resentment toward your partner for not being more compassionate or considerate toward you. However, the primary reason why they are likely not showing empathy for your feelings is that you have not clearly or honestly expressed them.

Remember, in your relationship with your spouse it is acceptable and safe to be vulnerable. Being vulnerable and telling them your real feelings does not mean that you are weak or incapable. Instead, it proves that even in the challenging moments you trust them and the fact that they will show respect toward you and your feelings. If they do not, then you may need to consider alternative solutions than simply changing your communication as your problems may be deeper than misunderstandings or poor communicational skills.

If you are the type of person who struggles to identify their true feelings, ensure that you are clear about this with your partner. Be willing to admit that you do not yet know how you feel about something but that you want to take a few minutes to figure it out and then you will tell them. This helps you both communicate your needs and tell them the truth about your feelings. Then, it is easier for you to both be more understanding toward each other during your arguments.

### Commit to Finding a Solution

Anytime you notice a conflict or disagreement arising between you and your partner, make the conscious commitment of finding a solution. When you stay focused on finding a solution, it is easier for you to fight fairly and stay compassionate. This is because you are not losing sight of your goal and falling into the habit of fighting for the need to be right or with the desire to hurt your partner in the way that you feel they are hurting you. Instead, you are focused on finding a way to communicate effectively so that you can both feel as though your conflict is resolved in your mutual interest.

During times where you are not experiencing conflict, you can let your partner know that this is your primary intention when a disagreement spark. You can also invite them to share the same common goal with you. That way, anytime an argument breaks out between you, you can both trust that you are working toward the same goal during that argument. This will keep you both disagreeing with a positive focus, supporting you in ending any disagreements or fights in a way that is considerate toward both you and your partner.

# Chapter 10: Secrets

Keeping secrets in relationships is a subject that is widely discussed, but its true impact remains is always negative. Many people suggest that there are some secrets that you should keep from your spouse. Secrets in relationships only affects the bond that has already developed between two close partners.

In a healthy relationship, couples should trust each other and have a strong sense of mutual respect to prevent the possibility of keeping secrets from one another. This is because it has the same impact as having an affair behind your spouse's back and will dismantle any relationship you have managed to build.

You should never keep a secret of your emotional affairs because this can easily result in the end of your relationship. Having close friends in your life who are directly affecting the decisions that you make should not be kept away from your spouse.

Instead, discuss with them the impact that your friends are having on you if you are aware, and let them know of everybody involved in your life. Keeping a secret of the friends you have in your life can discourage your partner from developing any trust towards you, dooming your union.

Never keep from your partner your history of mental illness because they deserve to know everything that has been happening in your health. Let them know of any problems you have had combating mental illness in the past because restricting this information from them will make them lose their trust for you.

Mental illness is usually a sensitive topic but you should find the courage to discuss it with your partner. Do not hide any problems you have had with psychiatrists and any other form of medical care that had to do with your mental state of mind.

You should also let your partner in on any money problems you are experiencing because it will have an impact on your relationship. Sharing expenses in a relationship is important and so if you cannot keep up, do not make it such a secret with your spouse to the extent that it causes serious problems for you.

There are some partners who are willing to take huge loans behind their partner's backs just to hide the fact that they are not financially well-off. This is not a good idea because it will only increase the problems that you are experiencing and will make life difficult for everybody around you, as well.

If you are suffering from any form of addiction, it is important to let your spouse know instead of struggling with it in secret. Some people believe that their spouses see them as perfect people and would not like to reveal any underlying problems that might be affecting how they live.

Most spouses understand the basis of most addictions, particularly if their partners are honest with them, and this allows them to get past these problems. Discussing the addiction problems you have will go a long way to making your relationship much more comfortable with your spouse.

It is also a bad idea to keep your tendency towards jealousy a secret because it can be very enraging for your partner. If you are jealous of seeing your partner with other people, it is better to speak to them about it and they will work towards spending more time with you and proving their love to you.

However, partners who are secretive about their jealous tendencies usually reveal them at the wrong time when they are in the heat of an argument with their spouse. Jealousy is a bad weakness and it can easily deprive you of a thriving relationship within moments.

If you are experiencing any sort of problem from a past relationship and it is still affecting you in the present one, do not keep it a secret. Most people take some time to get over their exes and it might be appropriate not to keep this a secret from your spouse.

This is because they will do everything in their power to try and take your mind off your ex. Keeping a secret of how you really feel about a past relationship can easily cause your marriage to collapse because your partner will be convinced that you are not committed to them.

If you have any issues deep within you that are bothering you but not related to the relationship, keeping them a secret can also dislodge the trust that exists with your spouse. There is no point hiding the fact that you are not feeling well simply because you do not want to bother your spouse.

For instance, if you are experiencing problems in your place of work and you are under a lot of pressure, you will be surprised how much your spouse can help you get past the problems. Their advice and even contributions can be instrumental in making you a much better person.

The whole point of being with your spouse is for them to share your happy times as well as your sad times. Engaging with them about a problem that has been disturbing you for a long time boosts the communication levels between the two of you and offers a way for a better tomorrow.

Lastly, you should refrain from keeping secrets about your STD history from your spouse because this can easily descend into conflict in the future of your relationship. The simple fact is, if you care for them, you will let them know about your past diseases and your general health.

There is no worse secret than hiding your general state of health only for you to cause harm to your spouse in the future. Such a secret can easily guarantee the end of a marriage no matter how strong it is, but revealing the truth will only strengthen the existing bond further.

You should also be open about your sexual past with your spouse and let them know everything you have done before being with them.

# Chapter 11: Couples Improving Relationships and Marriages

The most important relationship you will ever have in your life is your marriage. It is a sacred bond developed between you and your spouse and it is meant to last your entire lifetime. Most people take pride in their marriages because they have found the perfect soul mate who completely understands them.

A marriage can be happy if there is mutual trust and respect; however, this does not mean that things cannot get better for the couple. There are a number of things that a couple should engage in to improve their relationship and marriage to make the experience even more exciting.

Have you considered showering together regularly? It might sound small but this single action has the ability to make your marriage far more exciting. Sharing a shower experience together will allow you to develop closer intimacy with your partner and enjoy their presence even in awkward situations.

You do not have to plan to shower together and the spontaneous suggestion of the two of you jumping under the water together is likely to excite the both of you. Taking a shower does not necessarily have to lead to sex, but it will enable the both of you to spend some precious time together.

You should also spend time playing games together and working on building your intimacy. Your partner should be somebody who you enjoy doing light activities with that both of you are interested in. You will be surprised, but simple activities have the propensity of improving your relationship immensely.

The activities that you do together do not have to be complicated because playing board games, taking nighttime strolls around the neighborhood and even visiting a museum are all activities that can improve the relationship between a couple.

It is always nice to show your partner affection when you are out in public such as holding hands and kissing him gently on the cheeks. It shows extra commitment on your part and the fact that you are very proud of your partner. Giving your peck of approval in public will go a long way in strengthening your relationship together.

There is nothing wrong with showing your affection in public even if you have already grown used to kissing each other every morning. Public affection increases somebody's comfort in a relationship and it is a sign to the rest of the world that you are together and enjoying your relationship.

Some couples have developed a routine of waking up together very early in the morning in order to spend some quality time together before going to work. There is no better way of starting off the day such as this because you can do anything in the early hours, even if it is just talking in bed before setting off to work.

You will be surprised how comfortable your day will be, although it might subject you to be sleeping early when you return home. Either way, you will not get interrupted early in the morning and it is an excellent time for you to reconnect with your partner in the stillness of the early days.

Be very encouraging with your spouse, whether it is in their professional life or if they are handling something difficult in their lives. Showing encouragement is a sign of positivity and this will endear your partner to you in an incredible way.

When you are constantly supportive of their work, they feel a closer connection to you like no other person. There is no greater feeling than knowing you have somebody in your corner who is ready to encourage you even through the thickest of problems.

How many times do you tell your partner "I love you?" Well, you will be surprised that most married couples do not say it that much often, and it always has negative ramifications. If it is too difficult for you to tell your partner that you love them every once in a while, then it probably shows that you really do not love them.

You will be surprised that a relationship that was on the brink of collapse can be improved immensely simply by the couple telling each other of their love. It is a very comfortable feeling and it confirms that there is nobody else significant in the life of your partner other than yourself.

You should spend a significant amount of time talking with your spouse if you want to get your marriage or relationship back on track. Many people simply do not understand the power of a simple conversation, whether it is small talk or not because it builds on the love that already exists between the two partners.

It is possible to make healthy memories with him even though you have endured tough times in your relationship by setting aside time to talk to each other. This can be an excellent time to solve pertinent problems affecting the two of you so that you can move the relationship forward.

You should also spend some time reading together because tranquility often is the best time to think. You will find yourself sharing a lot with your partner when you have some quiet time to yourselves on a regular basis. Having reading time, whether it is novels or newspapers can set the tone for the appropriate environment to interact.

A relationship will always improve tremendously if both of you understand the value of each other's time. It is important to respect their interests as much as they will yours, and this interaction together will always improve a relationship even if it has endured several difficulties along the way.

These useful strategies can be implemented in most marriages to help them overcome common problems affecting couples. The advice should prompt you to take action and never sit around complaining about your spouse when you can take action yourself.

It is necessary to point out that action is always needed to improve any relationship as long as there is love that exists between the couple.

# Chapter 12: Relationship/Marriage Help

Sometimes you might feel as though the marriage or relationship is getting out of hand and everything you are trying to do is not working. This is the juncture where you should consider getting marriage counseling because it will help the both of you internalize the problems affecting you differently.

Bringing in an intermediary into your relationship is not a sign that everything is failing. As a matter of fact, it is an indication of the willingness from both of you to make your relationship work. If neither of you wanted things to be resolved, you would outright reject marriage counseling.

There are a number of advantages of seeking out assistance in your marriage in order to improve the relations between yourselves. First, it is possible for the two of you to look at the problems affecting you from another person's perspective in order for you to start visualizing an appropriate solution.

Secondly, counseling will help you improve your communication skills because you will have to relate with your spouse in front of another person. You will understand some of your own flaws in the process and be in a position to truly drive your relationship forward.

Marriage counseling also has the advantage of allowing the partners to learn a little more about themselves. When speaking to a marriage counselor, it is possible to provide them information that your spouse did not know about, thereby improving the state of the relationship.

There are a number of subtle signs that will show you your relationship needs counseling. First, if there is a total breakdown of communication between the two of you, then marriage counseling is the only viable option to ensure that you have another way of resolving the problems affecting you and your partner.

Another sign that will show you will need counseling for the sake of your marriage to move forward is when you are having sexual issues. If it is troublesome for you to sleep with your spouse and even enjoy the experience, you might have to speak to somebody about it to seek assistance.

Counseling offers the best forum for you and your partner to sit down in the presence of an independent adjudicator in order to work out what the problem is. Sexual issues have the capability of ending relationships even if there is love, and so finding out the cause for concern is of absolute importance.

When infidelity invades your marriage and you find it difficult to speak to your partner afterwards, counseling might be the best way forward to try and mend whatever damage has already been made. Asking a counselor to hear out your problems and offer advice will go a long way in fixing even the most vile problems.

Unfaithfulness in a relationship or marriage sometimes causes so much pain that the best approach for it is resolving the issue through a third party. If you attempt to have a conversation with your partner and it descends into total chaos, maybe counseling is the only way to fix the relationship.

A marriage can be so overburdening that the social skills of one of you starts to drop significantly. When you are in a marriage, it is not the only relationship you are in because you have friends and family members who also look up to you and relate with you.

Counseling becomes relevant when the problems in your marriage start affecting how you relate with those around you. It is a dangerous sign that everything is disintegrating in your life and perhaps seeking assistance on the problems affecting you and your partner is the best way forward.

Sometimes counseling makes sense when a married couple attempt to blend in their families. It is possible that one or both partners gets into a marriage when they already have children, and this will always complicate how they will settle in to their new life.

Counseling is a good solution to some of the problems that couples experience in their relationships when trying to bring in their families together. You might discover that your spouse has a problem being a parent to your children and this can be resolved by seeking out the assistance of a marriage counselor.

When a long relationship comes to an end, you will be quite sad and might struggle to adapt to a new life of being single. This is not such a bad thing because there are ways you can get over the sadness and live a much happier life thereafter.

The end of a relationship does not necessarily mean that everything in your social life has to come to an end. This is particularly important if you are getting into a new relationship and still being burdened by problems from your past relationship. Seeking the help of a marriage counselor might help you look at life from a different angle.

When there are trust issues in a relationship, it is the biggest indicator yet that there are serious problems facing the couple. A strong relationship should thrive on mutual trust and respect, and it is the only way that the both of you can be sure to be happy for a long time.

If the trust has broken down but you feel the relationship can still be salvage, then seeking the assistance of a marriage counselor is a good idea. Their sessions are very invigorating and will involve couples being open with each other and stating their intentions for the future.

Marriage counseling helps the couple look at the problems facing them from a different perspective and they end up developing a stronger attachment to their partner. The process allows for both partners to analyze the mistakes they have made and making plans for a happier future.

Asking a person to intermediate on your problems releases the stress of fighting and arguing with each other. Peaceful conflict resolution always puts any type of relationship back on track and guarantees happiness for the couple.

# Chapter 13: Empathic Listening

Psychologists have found that human beings are wired for empathy by the deep attachment relationships developed in the two early years of life. Studies have revealed that 18-month-olds are able to put themselves in the shoes of someone else to some extent. This empathy does not stop developing once people have grown up; rather, people nurture its growth throughout life. As such, empathy becomes a radical force supporting social transformation.

Different people have different levels of empathy and scholars have classified them accordingly. For example, there are people who have a complete lack of empathy. Such people find it very hard to maintain relationships and have no contact with remorse. They cannot understand how another person is feeling, and they may or may not be cruel. Some of the people identified under this category include narcissistic individuals, psychopaths, and borderline personalities.

Other categories of empaths include (1) those who have empathy but lack self-control such that they easily hurt people when they are upset, (2) those who have difficulties with empathy but they have enough empathy to understand the impact of their actions after they have hurt someone, and (3) those who have a difficult time showing and having empathy because they know they do not see things as other people do and are never quite normal. Normal men tend to have low amounts of empathy, and in most cases, they avoid talking about emotions and as such, they base friendships on shared activities. Women, on the other hand, tend to have an above average level of empathy and they apply care when dealing with other people and stay sensitive to their feelings.

Have you ever realized how some people make you feel understood and validated without saying anything? What is the secret about them that makes it so simple for you to 'open up' and share your problems? Why are they the first person you go to whenever you want to unburden your soul? The answer to this question is simple – empathic listening.

That is what makes them the ideal conversation partners. It's the reason why everyone else seems to gravitate around them. It's why they get along well with everyone in the office and can click almost instantly with every person they meet.

In case you didn't know, empathic listening is an ability which means it can be learned through practice and repetition. And that's precisely what you're going to get out of this article.

## Empathy: the cornerstone of authentic human interactions

In a world where time is a scarce resource and everyone seems to be running after something, it has become increasingly difficult for many of us to exercise patience and listen to others, before we express our own opinions and desires.

We expect others to understand us without ever putting ourselves in their shoes. We want others to resonate with our views without giving them a chance to voice their opinions. And even if they do express their views or offer some constructive criticism, we rarely return the favor.

As a result, our day-to-day interactions can become nothing more than a 'cold' exchange of replies; no 'real' connection, no empathy. But it doesn't have to be that way. If you are willing to listen instead of talk, understand instead of criticizing, and comfort instead of judging, you can quickly turn a conversation into an authentic human interaction.

Whether you're talking to your spouse, friend, boss, coworker, neighbor or even the barista who works at your favorite coffee shop, empathic listening can significantly improve the quality of your interaction. Contrary to popular belief, it was collaboration, not competition that helped humankind survive, thrive, and reach the level of socio-economic development we see today. And one of the keys to an authentic and fruitful collaboration is empathic listening.

## What is empathic listening?

In a nutshell, empathic listening means to hear your conversation partner authentically. It's the ability to listen with the sincere intention of understanding other people's values, opinions, and ideas.

Empathic listening allows you to get 'in tune with their frequency' and resonate on an emotional level. It means to get in touch with their needs and make them feel heard.

Empathic listening opens a window to their inner universe and creates a safe space where they can share anything without having to worry about criticism or bad remarks.

When empathy is the bridge that brings two people together, words become less important and what matters most is the connection between them.

But being empathetic does not mean you have to agree with everything and does not imply any obligation on your part. It only involves an effort to understand other people's perspective; 'to walk a mile in their shoes' so to speak.

Sadly, not all people are naturally born with empathy; not everyone finds it easy to identify, process, and resonate with other people's emotions. However, we can develop and sharpen this skill through patience and exercise. Those of us who are disconnected from our feelings will find it a bit difficult, but not impossible to learn to improve empathy. Just as any other ability, empathic listening can be acquired, as long as you're motivated and willing to take it stepwise and practice consistently.

## How does empathic listening relate to happiness?

Some of you may be wondering how exactly does listening to others and trying to resonate emotionally with them contribute to our well-being. What does empathic listening have to do with happiness?

First of all, empathetic ears are hard to come by these days. Many people are too self-involved to care about what others have to say. But given that healthy social interactions are critical to our growth, knowing how empathize is one of the ingredients of a happy and fulfilling life.

Second, research suggests that when you listen in an empathic manner, people are satisfied with the conversation and you instantly become more socially attractive. And since we're all social creatures by nature, being able to navigate social situations successfully will indirectly contribute to our overall sense of happiness and well-being.

Finally, given that empathic listeners are social magnets, they often benefit from exciting opportunities that contribute to their personal and professional growth. Overall, empathic listening can significantly add to our overall sense of happiness and well-being. Perhaps this is the secret to lasting joy and whole fulfilling life.

## Empathic listening for couples

Empathic communication is an essential component of any successful and lasting relationship. The ability to be empathetic towards your loved one has significant effects on the overall level of satisfaction you and your partner experience in your relationship.

As you can imagine, knowing how to listen with an open mind - without interruptions, criticism, and unwanted advice – is a 'must' in any healthy and functional couple.

Too often, people who love each other end up splitting because of communication issues. Whether it manifests as stonewalling, criticism, or contempt, lack of empathy can slowly turn two people into two strangers who resent each other.

And that's because one of our fundamental needs is to be heard and understood. When this does not happen, you begin to feel lonely and abandoned. You suffer and eventually distance yourself, even from a person you loved more than you could ever imagine.

Experts suggest empathic listening paves the way for affectionate communication, a crucial element for any healthy couple. When empathic listening becomes a habit that characterizes your relationship, you can easily resonate with your partner's struggles and understand why he/she might be feeling that way. And this gives you the chance to find solutions and fix the 'cracks' that could compromise your relationship.

All and all, empathic listening builds strong relationships, fosters effective communications, and cultivates trust between life partners.

### Empathic listening at work

In a way, we could argue that empathic listening is a 21st-century skill.

That means we not only use it to achieve personal growth by cultivating a thriving social life and building lasting romantic relationships, but also to advance in our career by investing in fruitful partnerships.

From leadership and business to sales and negotiation, empathy seems to be one of those variables that can tip the scale in your favor, overcome 'formal' barriers, and appeal to people's 'soft' side.

Empathic listening plays such an important role in activities like sales that researchers have even begun developing tools to measure it. One example is the active empathic listening (AEL) scale which evaluates three dimensions: sensing, processing, and responding. More specifically, this scale assesses how well the person can zero-in on emotions, process them, and come up with an appropriate answer.

If you wish to become a better boss, leader, coworker or even employee, empathic listening should be among your 'sharpest' skills. Just because you talk to your boss, client, business partner, or coworker doesn't mean you should keep the conversation at a formal level. Appeal to their emotions, make them feel understood, and you will be on the right path towards a productive partnership.

In time, empathic listening can set the stage for fantastic business opportunities which directly contribute to a happy and prosperous life.

## How to practice empathic listening?

Since developing empathic listening is all about practice, let's focus on a brief example that will show you how proper empathic communication should look like.

Mary: So, what's new in your life?

James: Hmm, nothing much.

Mary: You seem a bit off. Is everything ok? *(She detects a negative emotional vibe and uses a question to dig deeper)*

James: Just some minor problems with Mary; nothing so important.

Mary: You want to talk about it? I'm here for you. Maybe I can help you out in some way. *(She makes herself available and lets him know he can rely on her)*

James: I don't remember, things haven't been right between us lately.

Mary: I'm sorry to hear that. I don't want to be too nosy, but did something happen between you two? *(She asks open-ended questions but without being intrusive)*

James: Well, I don't know if I should burden you with my problems.

Mary: It's ok. Don't worry. If you feel like sharing, I'm here for you *(She creates a safe space)*

James: Hmmm, things kind of went south about a month ago when I noticed she was texting with a guy from work. Although she told me there's nothing between them and I should stop making a big deal out of it, I can't help but think she might be having an affair with this guy.

Mary: So, because she's texting with this guy from work, you're worried it might be more between them? *(She paraphrases to make sure she got the message right and make him feel understood)*

James: Yes. And I know it sounds crazy, but I can't get this idea out of my head. God, I'm such a mess! I love her so much, but I'm afraid I'm going to lose her because of my stupid jealousy.

Mary: Look, James, I know you love Mary, and I know you don't want to lose her. Maybe that's why you're acting so jealous. *(She paraphrases his message, empathizes with him)*

Mary: But are there any other reasons you think she might be cheating on you? *(She asks open-ended questions to understand the situation further)*

James: Well, no. I don't think so. Maybe this whole cheating thing is just in my head.

Mary: Want some advice? *(She asks before giving advice)*
James: Sure.

Mary: Talk to your girl. Tell her what you told me. Tell her that you're acting this way because you love her and don't want to lose her. *(She encourages him to have a conversation with his girlfriend and clarify the situation)*

James: What if she doesn't understand? What if she thinks I'm crazy?

Mary: Then maybe you two could see a couple's counselor. Who knows? It might be the solution you need to fix this issue. *(She offers an alternative solution)*

James: I guess that could be an option. Thanks, Mary; it was constructive talking to you.

Mary: My pleasure! And thanks for placing your trust in me. If you ever need an empathetic ear, I'm here for you. *(She validates his confidence and extends her support)*

## 9 strategies to develop empathic listening

### 1. it's not about you

Whenever you're talking to someone and wish to lend an empathetic ear, the first thing you need to understand is that it's not about you.

That's the secret to authentic empathic listening – placing your conversation partner above your needs.

And it can be quite hard to put aside personal opinions and make it all about him/her. After all, you're not his/her therapist.

So, before you decide to be there for someone, make sure you're available emotionally. Otherwise, there's no point in encouraging him or her to share a personal issue for which you're not ready to provide understanding and support.

## 2. Put away your phone

Too often we find ourselves checking our phone or answering a text message while the other person may be pouring their heart out.

This is one of those unpleasant habits that many of us have adopted as a result of living in the digital era. We get so hooked on social media that we sometimes end up losing sight of the person who's right there in front of us.

And it's impossible to establish an emotional bond when you're regularly checking your phone, and all you can say is "**Aha**" or "**I understand**." So, whenever you wish to offer empathy and create an authentic connection put your phone away and asks the other person to do the same.

## 3. Be an active listener

In a way empathic listening and active listening are synonymous. Being an active listener means being present in the conversation. It means ignoring any distractions and focusing exclusively on the person in front of you.

Active listeners live in the 'here and now.' They immerse themselves into the other person's universe and seek to gain a better understanding of the topic in discussion.

Of course, that doesn't mean you have to listen and nod in silence. A conversation is a two-way street where both partners exchange ideas, impressions, and seek to resonate with one another emotionally.

In short, active listening is about presence and depth.

## 4. Refrain from criticism

As you can probably imagine, empathic listening implies a high degree of emotional intelligence. When someone shares a story or event that holds significance to him/her, it would be ideal to refrain from evaluations, criticism, or negative feedback.

There are times when other people's problems may seem trivial, ridiculous, or even infuriating. But once again, it's not about you, it about them. Remember, your goal is to understand and provide emotional support. Any form of criticism will only create tension and make it difficult for you to 'forge' authentic connections. Listen, understand, and empathize.

## 5. Adjust your body language

As you probably know, body language is of paramount importance for genuine social interactions. When it comes to empathic listening, your body can help you create the kind of communication that makes room for understanding and empathy.

Your posture and gestures can either bring people closer or create a barrier that makes it difficult for you to listen actively and empathically.

If you want to make people feel safe and welcome, make sure to adopt a relaxed posture with open arms and constant eye contact. You can even go for a friendly pat on the shoulder or even a warm hug.

## 6. Paraphrase your conversation partner

Paraphrasing is among the most effective strategies for empathic listening. Letting your conversation partner know that you understand his perspective creates an ideal climate for sharing emotions.

Many studies suggest that paraphrasing – along with clarifying, questioning, and remembering details – are the critical elements of empathic listening. Furthermore, this creates a safe space where people can share and engage in self-exploration. Paraphrasing your conversation partner is relatively easy. All you need to do is listening to what your partner has to say and rephrase his/her message.

### 7. Ask open-ended questions

If you want your conversation partner to share, you need to 'fuel' the conversation by asking open questions. Sometimes, people don't 'open up' that easily. Not everyone will be willing to talk to you openly, especially when it comes to personal problems. And that's why you need to give him or her a push by using questions that create opportunities for sharing.

Although smart questions can enrich a conversation, make sure you're not intrusive. You're supposed to have a happy talk, not an interview.

If you notice that your partner doesn't feel comfortable, refrain from asking questions and let him or her dictate the flow of the conversation.

### 8. Stop giving unsolicited advice

When you're looking to establish an emotional connection with someone, the worst thing you can do is offer unsolicited advice. Nothing 'kills' the vibe of a good conversation more than telling the other person what he or she should do. Remember that empathic listening is mostly about understanding and 'connectedness.' Sometimes, all it takes to establish an emotional connection is active listening.

If, however, you think you have a good piece of advice to offer, ask your conversation partner if he/she is interested in hearing it.

### 9. Don't 'fill up' the silence

Many of us tend to feel awkward during the occasional moments of silence that are specific to any conversation. But silence can be a powerful tool in establishing an authentic connection is you know how to use it. You can use silence to allow the other person to take charge of the conversation or give him/her enough time to process your input and come up with an answer.

And let's not forget that a conversation doesn't rely solely on a constant exchange of words. There's also your body language which through which you can express empathy and build an authentic connection.

## The importance of empathic listening

Empathic listening is also called reflective listening or active listening. It is a way of listening and responding to others that enhances trust and mutual understanding. It is a vital skill for disputants and third parties as well because it makes it possible for the listener to accurately interpret the received message from the speaker and provide a relevant response. The response is a fundamental part of the process of listening and can be essential to the success of mediation or negotiation. Empathic listening has numerous benefits that include:

It will build respect and trust
Enables the conflicting parties to release their emotions
It will reduce your tension
It will create a safe and conducive environment for collaborative
  solving of problems
It will encourage the surfacing of essential details

## Strategies to develop empathetic listening

It is not about you
Put away your phone
Be an active listener
Refrain from criticism
Adjust your body language
Ask open-ended questions
Paraphrase your conversation when talking to your partner

# Chapter 14: Creating Balance for Perfect Intimacy

Enrich Life

Let your friendship be of value, more valuable than gold, and more treasured than a diamond stone. Let it be a gift to be treasured like the air, the last air to breathe.

Do not try too hard but make sure you provide value apart from the normal value of marriage and commitment.

Let your presence enrich the life of your partner.

Make your marriage a school of love that also teaches life's great lessons, the lesson that provides value.

One way of providing value is by living an actual life filled with value.

You cannot give what you don't have, so first find a valuable ground, then connect to your partner and spread the love.

Try to understand why people act the way they do by first looking at things through their lenses.

Do not expect anybody to see life the way you do. What has been of value to your school of thought can prove invaluable to your partner's.

Learn about personality, and treat your partner in a way that understanding can be met and that you can be able to easily penetrate and instill in them the most valuable treasure, your friendship.

More Certain and Less Doubtful

Do not invite anybody from outside to interfere with your marriage; always be more certain about the outcome of each and every action and less doubtful about the intentions of your partner.

External opinions or advice are almost ineffective because everyone thinks differently, and so they will tell you what they think even if it won't work in your situation.

Try to dig deeper and understand your problem; let your experiences and intuition guide you as you make a decision.

Be more certain of your actions by constantly connecting with your intuition and also realizing the fact that you are the only one in the position to tackle this problem.

Trust in your decisions and always expect a positive result for your actions.

All your actions must be based on how good it feels and the balance your instinct creates as you take the first step.

Try as much as possible to opt for solutions capable of making you feel expanded, reaching for new experiences, and new levels of perception.

When you feel like the decision may bring about a dead end, pause, reflect, or just don't do anything until you find the inspiration to act.

Understand that some problems don't need your actions, just your attention, to watch it fade away.

Find a Balance Between Peace and Stress

Do not dwell solely on the details of your marriage, the details of what your spouse did or didn't do, or details about what your spouse said that contradict your perception.

Overanalyzing situations may lead to obsession which will also lead to stress and frustration.

Worry less about why he didn't call or why she won't tell you things you're supposed to know.

Instead of contemplating about his or her intentions and the meaning of a particular action, confront him or her and make sure you are satisfied with the explanation.

Saving yourself from stress by constantly working towards clearing things up in your relationship will bring about deeper peace and prosperity.

Disconnect from consistent rational thinking and connect with your emotions, your heart, the source of your love and the source of the desire to love.

Even if you don't think your partner is feeling the love or when you are not feeling the love from your spouse, feel the love from your heart.

Focus on finding a dwelling place where peace abounds.

In order to maintain a healthy mental and physical state, do not allow your peace to be disturbed.

Dwell on Your Worth

Although our partners are supposed to mean everything to us in marriage, dwelling more on what they think instead of what something really is might cause mindful conflict.

Do not consistently seek for approval from your partner. Your job is to include them in your decision process as a way of showing that they matter to you.

But regardless of what they think, you should be able to believe in the possible best of your endeavors.

Your worth as an individual should not be derived from your spouse.

When you derive your worth from people, you will always try too hard to please them and without even knowing it, you will lose your self-worth.

You will lose the gem that makes you attractive and desirable, you will succumb to the low life of an attention seeker, and finally, you will totally lose respect.

Being good doesn't entail being desperate. It also means defining a way of life and allowing others to follow through in order to see the best you can offer to the world.

Make yourself the most important person in your life, not to be selfish, but to have self-respect, love, and affection; to give quality attention to yourself in order to achieve quality attention from your spouse.

# Chapter 15: Conversational Intimacy

Have a Fight

Being scared of fighting with your partner is being scared of inviting change into your relationship which also means being scared of reaching a new bond of intimacy.

Conflict in a marriage relationship is not completely bad. Even if you don't experience conflict, talk about it.

In order to reduce the actual chances of its occurrence, face it in your conversations instead of shying away from it.

The essence of having a fight is to share your emotions in the most powerful way possible. After having the big fight, discuss the possibilities of working through it.

The fight is like a workout session that makes you stronger and better than you've ever been.

It makes you appreciate the peace you had so you will begin to address difficult issues in order to prevent another fight in the future.

Communication often improves after a fight. Heartily arguments will be employed and the use of abusive words will be reduced, and the couples will become positively supportive of their vulnerabilities.

Discuss the Romance

Discussing your future plans make your future more realistic and your dreams more achievable.

Discussing your intimacy makes your romance more attainable and confirms the longevity of your passion.

The aim is to add a deep emotional connection in the moment, and to feel like you are the only people in the world.

This conversation is more about how you feel about each other in relation to how you work, live and handle obvious responsibilities regarding your marriage as a whole.

The aim is to build a strong sense of intimacy by discussing your functions. This also creates an opportunity to understand the bruises, and the isolated parts of your lives as couples.

In this conversation, sharing a tragic incident or mere past emotional moments will also improve your intimacy.

Romantic pasts can also be discussed; it is healthy to compare your past relationship with this long-term commitment especially if your past relationship is the worst. Talk about the hurt and the exes in order to deepen your connection.

Come with Reasons

Simply tell them why you feel what you feel; tell them why you love the heck out of them.

Tell them how special they are to you and how you wouldn't have seen these better days if not because of their support and love. Build a new connection of intimacy, to let them know how you trust their love and support.

During this conversation, it is more effective when you focus on the less flattering sides of their function in the relationship.

Focus on the little things, the unique things that you hadn't noticed in the first phase of the relationship.

Compliment them on things only you, the closest partner, know or notice.

Compliment them on things people don't compliment them about.

You can start with things such as sense of humor, generosity, kindness, attentiveness, responsiveness, sweetness, etc. in order to build closeness.

Encourage them to be the strange people they are afraid to be in order to enjoy the best they can offer in the relationship.

Talk About Self–Improvement

Tell your partner what you've noticed about them in the past few months or weeks; the improvement, the effort they made to grow this fast and the new pleasant things you can see and touch today.

This is also a chance to talk about your efforts and weaknesses. What you want to change, what you would like to see in the near future, and the challenges you are facing in the effort to create that change.

Do not allow fear, insecurity, or ego to block the most important way to intense intimacy.

Judgment and rejection only come when there is no passion, when there is no emotional attachment and also when perfectionism dwells in the mind of the other partner.

But a relationship built on the foundation of love gives the chance for each of you to talk about anything reasonable, nonsensical and healthy.

Sometimes it doesn't have to be deep, but focusing on communicating well and creating a new level of trust can help strengthen the bond.

Also, share a vulnerability to create a shortcut to perfect intimacy. Uncover your vulnerabilities and allow them to be the pillars, a rock to remain fixed and unfathomed.

Warmth, respect, and kindness are the next phases of a stronger relationship that brings about deep intimacy.

## Invite Them In

Practically invite your partner into your life as a special guest by becoming a good host, in the process helping them to achieve comfort, reach a certain goal, see their dreams coming true and making sure that their presence is honored.

It is more about what you can offer and less about their function in the marriage.

Firstly, know the exact and immediate needs of your partner; that is, what they want now and how much they'd count on you to help them have this thing.

Do not try to dictate their needs; instead ask them what they wish to have, their fantasies, their wants, and desires.

Talk about hopes and aspirations, and keep the conversation flowing by allowing them to realize that you are concerned and deeply interested in those crazy aspirations.

Realize the changes that usually occur with time; be up to date about the needs that will come up with these changes.

The aim is to make it apparent that you care, that you can be the good host even in a long-term relationship so that if they ask, they can get it, and by becoming a source of comfort, create meaning in every moment shared together.

# Conclusion

Your fate lies in your own hands. It is up to you to take control of your life, your emotions and situations presented to you and negotiate your way safely to the other side.

There is no time to hold back or to be afraid of taking that risk in case you fail. Failure is going to happen whether you like it or not but that shouldn't be something that you allow to define you or whether you decide to take risks in the future. Failure teaches you, learn what your failures have to offer, process the information and realize how you could have done it differently and you are assured that next time you will achieve the success you are after.

Everybody is built unique and with their own personal quirks and flaws. Learn to love yourself for who you are and realize how much you have to offer to the world. Your abilities are there, you just need to take the time to seek them out without allowing all the negative or weak point get in the way. As humans we have a tendency to place too much emphasis on the negative and not enough of the positive. Don't allow your weaknesses to overshadow your brilliance hidden within. What a sad and boring world it would be if everybody was built the same, with the same abilities and capabilities and perfect in every way. We all have something to offer and that is what makes the human race such a diverse and interesting species. The trick through all of this is to learn to appreciate yourself and acknowledge your strengths and make a concerted effort to improve those abilities.

If you are someone who has a low self-image, don't sit back, take control and do something today that you will thank yourself for in the future. You are the one who controls how you feel about yourself and you are the one who can change what you are not happy about. Realize what it is and do something to rectify that situation. The sooner you do, the sooner you will bloom into the wonderful, charismatic, confident individual you were put on this Earth to be.

You are your own person in every way. Don't ever allow others to make you feel less than adequate, stand your ground and let them know that you are amazing and you deserve to be treated as such. What others think of you is not your problem, it is their problem. Do what makes you happy, believe in something with conviction and stand up for it, make decisions and don't quit even in the face of failure and always walk with you head held high. You were not created to blend into the wallpaper, you were given a voice so use it wisely and let people know your opinions even if you may seem silly after the fact.

Eat a healthy diet and follow an exercise regime. Your mind and body need the stress release. The oxygen and nutrients will provide you with enough energy and strength and of course stamina to take on whatever life throws your way. A healthy body and mind allows you to focus on what is important to aim for those goals.

Don't compare yourself to others. You are an individual and you need to realize that. Yes, watch how other more confident people approach certain situations and learn from them. Take criticisms but don't take them to heart. Process them; take what you need from them an move on.

Never compromise what you feel or believe for the sake of fitting in. We were not made to fit in but rather to stand out and you should.

Confidence is something that starts within yourself. You need to be happy and content with yourself and realize your own potential before you can expect anybody else to. Take charge and make changes, be happy with you first and the confidence will follow. Carry positive thoughts with you and visualize good things for you and you will find that they will find you, don't expect anything less that what you want. Expectation is a very powerful force which you should use to your advantage.

Yes, of course there will be days where you feel like you are coming apart at the seams but these are just life's little challenges presented to you along the way to success. Stay positive inside and out. Even on days when you feel blue, put on your confident strut and hold your head high, you will find that your mind will follow suit .Your mind does whatever you will it to and if you steer it in the right direction you will know what it feels like to truly live.

Confidence will allow you the opportunity to meet new people, strike up conversations with complete strangers and you never know what the future holds. We often get stuck in a rut within our own personal relationships and block our partners out. Let them in and reveal a side of you they have never seen and get that spark ignited. Flirt a little, be friendly and welcome new people into your life. Yes, they may not be there for long but they may end up being there for a lifetime.

Take every opportunity that comes your way and grab it with both hands, even if you fail at least you won't have regrets about what might have been. Be confident in your decisions and if they don't work out for you so be it but do it again anyway. Don't delay your progress by waiting for the perfect moment, we all know the moment will never be perfect and there will always be some kind of obstacle. The sooner you realize that you are only using this tactic out of fear of the unknown and fear of failing, the better. Embrace your fears and take the leap and you will be amazed at how exhilarated you feel.

I do hope this book has inspired those who are lacking in self esteem and confidence to realize that they are in control and that the sooner they become happy with themselves and believe they are capable of great things, the sooner their lives will truly begin. Nobody is inferior to anyone else, some people have just realized where their strengths lie and have taken full advantage but it's not too late for those who have yet to realize so stop thinking " what if" and "if only" and close your eyes and jump. Allow the world to see you brilliance in all it's glory. We all posses that brilliance just in different ways and what you may think is insignificant could be a talent that many can only dream of possessing.

You are your keeper and your master and you control your body, your mind and your emotions. You are the one who determines your future and how the world perceives you. Stand up and take a bow, the world is waiting.

# Book Two
# ABANDONMENT RECOVERY WORKBOOK

## Introduction

Of the most prevalent fears around the world, is the fear of being alone. We have all evolved into social beings, and our very existence depends on our numbers. These fears usually stem from childhood, where a person might have experienced a traumatizing effect - such as the loss of a parent or friend through moving away, divorce, death, or lack of physical or emotional care. The abandoned person grows up and has huge trust issues in their own adult relationships, usually stemming from the feeling that someone they are close with, whether it's a friend, spouse, fiancé, girlfriend/boyfriend, or even a family member, will desert them in the future. Then, in order to prevent this from happening, he or she engages in unhealthy behavior that actually ends up hurting the relationship more than helping it, thus making the abandonment more and more likely.

Do you see how this is a pattern of self-destruction, that can lead you closer to the exact thing you're most afraid of? The pattern is unintentional though. And partially even subconscious.

The fear of abandonment from traumatic childhood experiences doesn't even have to stem from a parent or loved one actually abandoning them. It can also occur as a result of a parent ridiculing them, and/or emotionally abusing them, or neglecting them. There are those who first develop a significant fear of abandonment in adulthood as well, typically through a traumatic loss of a loved one through a bad break-up, divorce, or death.

People who suffer from this fear sometimes choose to go to a therapist. The therapist would examine the person's background, and attempt to discover which traumatic event(s) may have caused this fear, determining whether it started in childhood or adulthood. Over time, the therapist would teach the patient how to separate the fears of the past from the present, so they can begin the healing process by developing the ability to lessen the grip that the fears have on them.

Although therapy is often effective, it certainly is not the only thing that a person with abandonment fears can do to help themselves. You may be able to overcome these abandonment issues on your own – through a little effort – and finally be able to build flourishing relationships once again, without panicking about what may or may not happen in the future. This ebook is designed to help you do exactly that, so let's get started!

# Chapter 1: What is Affecting Abandonment?

Many bodies don't apprehend that they're activity emotionally abandoned or that they did as a child. They may be unhappy, but can't put their feel on what it is. Bodies tend to anticipate of abandonment as article physical, like neglect. They additionally may not apprehend that accident of concrete accurateness due to death, divorce, and affliction generally is acquainted as an affecting abandonment.

However, affecting abandonment has annihilation to do with proximity. It can appear aback the added actuality is lying appropriate beside you — aback you can't affix and your affecting needs aren't actuality met in the relationship.

Emotional Needs

Often bodies aren't acquainted of their affecting needs and aloof feel that something's missing. But bodies accept abounding affecting needs in affectionate relationships. They accommodate the afterward needs:

To be listened to and understood

To be nurtured

To be appreciated

To be valued

To be accepted

For affection

For love

For companionship

Consequently, if there is aerial conflict, abuse, or infidelity, these affecting needs go unmet. Sometimes, adultery is a evidence of affecting abandonment in the accord by one or both partners. Additionally, if one accomplice is addicted, the added may feel neglected, because the addiction comes aboriginal and consumes the addict's attention, preventing him or her from actuality present.

Causes of Affecting Abandonment
Yet alike in an advantageous relationship, there are periods, days, and alike moments of affecting abandonment that may be advised or unconscious. They can be acquired by:

Intentionally denial advice or affection

External stressors, including the demands of parenting

Illness

Conflicting assignment schedules

Lack of alternate interests and time spent together

Preoccupation and self-centeredness

Lack of advantageous communication

Unresolved resentment

Fear of intimacy

When couples don't allotment accepted interests or assignment and beddy-bye schedules, one or both may feel abandoned. You accept to accomplish an added accomplishment to absorb time talking about your adventures and affectionate animosity with anniversary added to accumulate the accord beginning and alive.

More adverse are ailing advice patterns that may accept developed, area one or both ally doesn't allotment openly, accept with respect, and acknowledge with absorption to the other. If you feel abandoned or that your accomplice doesn't accept or affliction about what you're communicating, again there's an adventitious that eventually you may stop talking to him or her. Walls activate to body and you acquisition yourself active abstracted lives emotionally. One assurance may be that you allocution added to your accompany than to your accomplice or are aloof in sex or spending time together.

Resentments calmly advance in relationships aback your feelings, abnormally aching or anger, aren't expressed. Aback they go underground, you may either cull abroad emotionally or advance your accomplice abroad with criticism or abrasive comments. If you accept expectations that you don't communicate, but instead accept your accomplice should be able to assumption or adjudge them, you're ambience yourself up for disappointment and resentment.

When you or your accomplice fears intimacy, you may cull away, put up walls, or advance one addition away. Usually, this abhorrence isn't conscious. In counseling, couples are able to allocution about their ambivalence, which allows them to get closer. Generally abandoning behavior occurs afterwards an aeon of accurateness or sex. One actuality may physically abjure or actualize ambit by not talking or alike by talking too much. Either way, it may leave the added actuality activity abandoned and abandoned. Fears of acquaintance usually axis from affecting abandonment in childhood.

In Childhood

Emotional abandonment in adolescence can appear if the primary caretaker, usually the mother, is clumsy to be present emotionally for her baby. It's generally because she's replicating her adolescence experience, but it may additionally be due to stress. It's important for a baby's affecting development that the mother acclimatizes to her child's animosity and needs and reflects them back. She may be preoccupied, cold, or clumsy to empathize with her child's success or abasing emotions. He or she again ends up activity alone, rejected, or deflated. The about-face is additionally accurate – area an ancestor gives an adolescent a lot of attention, but isn't attuned to what the adolescent absolutely needs. The child's needs appropriately go unmet, which is an anatomy of abandonment.

Abandonment happens later, too, aback accouchement are criticized, controlled, unfairly treated, or contrarily accustomed a bulletin that they or their acquaintance is unimportant or wrong. Accouchement is vulnerable, and it doesn't booty abundant for an adolescent to feel aching and "abandoned." Abandonment cans action aback an ancestor confides in his or her adolescent or expects an adolescent to booty on age-inappropriate responsibilities. At those times, the adolescent charge abolishes his or her animosity and needs in adjustment to accommodate the needs of the adult.

A few incidents of affecting abandonment don't abuse a child's advantageous development, but aback they're accepted occurrences, they reflect deficits in the parent, which affect the child's faculty of cocky and aegis that generally advance to acquaintance issues and codependency in developed relationships. Couples counseling can accompany couples calm to adore added closeness, alleviate from abandonment, and change their behavior.

# Chapter 2: Breaking the Aeon of Affecting Abandonment.

If you're bitching in an accord or go from one to addition or alike abide awfully alone, you may be bent in a deepening aeon of abandonment.

People tend to anticipate of abandonment as article physical, like neglect. Accident of concrete accurateness due to death, divorce, and affliction is additionally an affecting abandonment. It additionally happens back our affecting needs aren't actuality met in the accord — including in our accord with ourselves. And although accident of concrete accurateness can advance to affecting abandonment, the about-face isn't true. Concrete accurateness doesn't beggarly our affecting needs will be met. Affecting abandonment may appear back the added actuality is appropriate beside us.

Our Affecting Needs

If we're not acquainted of our affecting needs, we won't accept what's missing in our accord with ourselves and with others. We may aloof feel, blue, lonely, apathetic, irritable, angry, or tired. We accept abounding affecting needs in affectionate relationships.

To be valued in adjustment to get our affecting needs met, not abandoned do we charge to apperceive what they are, but we charge amount them and generally absolutely ask for them to be met. Most bodies anticipate they shouldn't accept to ask, but afterwards the aboriginal blitz of affair back able hormones drive behavior, abounding couples get into routines that abridgment intimacy. They may alike say admiring things to anniversary added or "act" romantic, but there's no acquaintance and closeness. As anon as the "act" is over, they acknowledgment to their disconnected, abandoned state.

Of course, back there is aerial conflict, abuse, addiction, or infidelity, these affecting needs go unmet. Back one accomplice is addicted; the added may feel neglected, because the addiction comes first. Also, after recovery, codependents, which accommodate all addicts, accept adversity in comestible intimacy.

## The Cause

Often bodies are in emotionally abandoning relationships that carbon the affecting abandonment they accomplished in adolescence from one or both of their parents. Accouchement charge to feel admired and accustomed by both parents. It's not abundant to for an ancestor to say "I adulation you." Parents charge to appearance by their words and accomplishments that they appetite and accord with their adolescent for who he or she is, apropos his or her individuality. That includes affinity and account for their child's personality, feelings, and needs — in added words, not abandoned admiring an adolescent as an addendum of the parent.

When parents are critical, dismissive, invasive, or preoccupied, they're clumsy to empathize with their child's animosity and needs. The adolescent will feel misunderstood, alone, aching or angry, rejected, or deflated. Accouchement is vulnerable, and it doesn't booty abundant for an adolescent to feel hurt, abandoned, and ashamed. An ancestor who gives an adolescent a lot of attention, but isn't attuned to his or her child's needs, which appropriately go unmet, is emotionally abandoning the child. Abandonment cans additionally action back an ancestor confides in his or her adolescent or expects an adolescent to booty on age-inappropriate responsibilities. Abandonment happens back accouchement is unfairly advised or in some way accustomed a bulletin that they or their acquaintance is unimportant or wrong.

## The Cycle

As adults, we become abashed of intimacy. We either abstain accurateness ourselves or become absorbed to addition who avoids intimacy, accouterment the ambit that we charge to feel safe. (See The Dance of Intimacy.) It can assignment if there's abundant accurateness to amuse our charge for connection, but generally the ambit is aching and may be created by connected fighting, addiction, infidelity, or abuse. Problematic relationships afresh affirm animosity of lovability and abasement and abrogating perceptions about the adverse sex.

If the accord ends, alike added fears of abandonment and acquaintance can be created. Some bodies abstain relationships altogether, are added guarded, or access addition abandoning relationship. Fearing rejection, we may be on the anchor for abrogating signs, alike alter events, and accept it's hopeless to allocution about our needs and feelings. Instead, we may breach up or appoint in break behavior, such as criticism or spending added time with others. Back the accord ends, we afresh feel added alone, rejected, and hopeless.

Breaking the Cycle

Reversing this trend is possible. It requires either the acceptable affluence to be in an admiring relationship, or added often, analysis is appropriate to alleviate the wounds of childhood. Abundant of this is done through the accord with a trusted, accordant therapist over time. It additionally entails assay of the accomplished and both activity and compassionate the apples of the parenting we received. Goals accommodate not abandoned accepting the past, which doesn't necessarily beggarly acknowledging it, but added chiefly amid out our self-concept from the accomplishments of our parents. (See Conquering Shame and Codependency: 8 Steps to Freeing the Accurate We.)

Feeling aces of adulation is capital to alluring and advancement it. In the aforementioned way that we ability avoid an acclaim we don't feel we deserve, we will not be absorbed and able to sustain an accord with addition who is acceptable in admiring us. Activity base originated in our aboriginal accord with our parents. Abounding bodies accept no abrogating animosity adjoin their parents and may in actuality accept an abutting and admiring developed accord with them. However, it's not abundant that we absolve our parents. Healing includes rehabilitating the behavior and close choir of our parents that alive in our minds and run our lives.

Finally, breaking the aeon agency actuality an acceptable ancestor to ourselves — admiring ourselves in all ways. See my blogs about airs and my Youtube airs exercise. If this aftermost footfall isn't included, we will still be attractive alfresco ourselves to addition abroad to accomplish us happy. Although an acceptable accord can advance our faculty of well-being, there are consistently times back alley charge amplitude or are beggared and unavailable. Actuality able to affliction for ourselves allows us to authority the amplitude for our accomplice and to booty affliction of ourselves. Regardless of whether you're in a relationship, that's the ultimate antidote adjoin ambiguous into an abandonment depression.

# Chapter 3: Beyond Fear and Addiction: Six Steps to Healing

Addictive behavior is an abandonment of self, an aloof way of ambidextrous with aching feelings. This self-abandonment is an above account fear, anxiety, and depression. In this article, ascertain the six accomplish to affective above abhorrence and addiction. False Affirmation Appearing Real. Abundant of the abhorrence in our lives is based on apocryphal evidence. Our bodies are advised to acknowledge with the activity or flight apparatus to absolute and present crisis - such as actuality physically attacked. In the face of absolute and present danger, the adrenaline flows and the claret drains out of our organs and academician and into our limbs to adapt us for activity or flight.

Yet abounding bodies absorb abundant of their time in the all-overs and accent of activity or flight aback there is no absolute and present danger. This is because the anatomy responds the aforementioned way to absurd crisis as it does to absolute danger. The anatomy thinks that the apocryphal affirmation advancing from our thoughts is real. This connected accompaniment of abhorrence and all-overs generally leads to assorted addictions in the achievement of algid out the difficult feelings. Food, alcohol, drugs, nicotine, gambling, sex, TV, shopping, approval, attention, work, anger, rage, abandon to cocky and others – all can be acclimated in attempts to block out aching feelings. Yet, the addictions themselves are an abandonment of self, in that they are not an advantageous and admiring way of ambidextrous with aching feelings. And it is self-abandonment that causes the best fear, anxiety, and depression. Thus, abounding bodies are bent in an actual abrogating amphitheater based on self-abandonment:

Cerebration abrogating thoughts about the approaching - about rejection, failure, accident of others, and accident of self, accident of money – creates abhorrence in the anatomy and is an abandonment of self. We are abandoning ourselves aback we acquiesce ourselves to accomplish up thoughts about the approaching that alarm us. This would be like adage to a child, "You are activity to end up alone. No one will anytime adulation you. You will be out on the streets with no aliment and no help." Adage this to an adolescent would be advised adolescent abuse, yet abounding bodies acquaint these aforementioned things to themselves over and over aback there is no cold accuracy to these statements.

Once we accept created abhorrence with our abrogating thinking, we try to abstain the abhorrence with our assorted addictions. Abstain albatross for creating our abhorrence by axis to addictions is addition self-abandonment. This is like alms an abashed adolescent a cookie instead of acclamation the antecedent of the fear. The self-abandonment creates abysmal close blank and aloneness, which perpetuates the addictive behavior. It additionally creates neediness, arch to affairs on others for love, approval and attention.

Addictive behavior perpetuates the aboriginal fears – an amaranthine abandoned amphitheater of self-abandonment. MOVING BEYOND FEAR AND ADDICTION There absolutely is a way out of this! While the activity of affective above abhorrence and addiction is simple, it is not easy. It takes abysmal charge and adherence to your accord and joy.

1) Choose the alertness to feel your aching animosity and booty albatross for creating them, rather than abide alienated them with your assorted addictions. It is alone aback you are accommodating to be with your animosity rather than abstain them that you can apprentice about how you are creating your own pain.

2) Consciously adjudge that you appetite to apprentice about what you are cerebration or accomplishing that is causing your pain.

3) Dialogue with the allotment of you that is in abhorrence and affliction - you can anticipate of this activity allotment of you of an adolescent aural – about how you are causing the pain. Ascertain your thoughts and accomplishments that are causing your pain.

4) Open to acquirements with a Higher Power – your own accomplished wisest self, a close abecedary or mentor, a guardian angel, God – about what is the accuracy apropos your abrogating cerebration and what the admiring activity is against yourself.

5) Booty the admiring activity for yourself that you are guided to do in Step 4.

6) Notice how you feel. If you feel added peaceful, again you apperceive that you accept taken admiring action. If not, again you charge to go back through these accomplish to ascertain addition admiring action.

# Chapter 4: Abandonment Anxiety

Abandonment all-overs are abhorrence of actuality alone in a relationship. Bodies with abandonment all-overs accept one of two abashed adapter styles: adapter all-overs and adapter avoidance. Adapter all-overs is characterized by a charge for absorption from others and abhorrence that an accomplice is activity to leave. Adapter abstention is characterized by an assiduous charge to be assured and abhorrence of dependence.

Abandonment Anxiety

Abandonment all-overs are abhorrence of actuality alone in a relationship. Bodies with abandonment all-overs accept one of two abashed adapter styles: adapter all-overs and adapter avoidance. Adapter all-overs is characterized by a charge for absorption from others and abhorrence that an accomplice is activity to leave. Adapter abstention is characterized by an assiduous charge to be assured and abhorrence of dependence. Modern adapter approach arose out of the assignment of psychiatrists John Bowlby and Mary Ainsworth in the 20th century. Both advisers were afflicted by the Austrian analyst and architect of psychoanalysis, Sigmund Freud. In one of Bowlby's aboriginal empiric studies, he advised 44 boys at the London Adolescent Guidance Clinic who were clumsy to authentic amore and empathy. In all of the cases, the abridgement of amore was ashore in affectionate denial or abandonment. In the 1950s, Ainsworth abutting Bowlby's analysis team, and calm them advised abundant cases of adolescence abandonment and amore deprivation, which culminated in what is now accepted as "attachment theory."

Definition

According to Ainsworth, adapter is a strong, affectionate tie that binds calm two individuals emotionally and that continues over time. Adapter approach holds that these affecting ties amid bodies are acute to advantageous development mentally, socially and emotionally. The acute time aeon for this development is the aboriginal six years of childhood. For advantageous adolescent development to booty place, adolescent and caregiver charge anatomy a band in which the caregiver provides a defended ambiance for the adolescent and shows affecting amore and support. These aboriginal accessories aggregate the foundation for approaching interpersonal relationships.

## Early Abandonment

Events and altitude such as divorce, affliction or the disability to authentic amore can baffle with or agitate the accustomed bonding action amid adolescent and caregiver, says California ancestors therapist Daniel Sonkin. Back a caregiver does not or cannot acknowledge affectionately to a child's fears, the adolescent will abound up in one of two ways. He may abide to seek the amore and bonding he was missing in childhood, or he will become badly self-reliant, cagey others and accepting an acute abhorrence of assurance on others. How an alone adolescent develops depends on which arresting styles has been best able for him and the severity of the abandonment, say accord experts Gwendolyn Stevens and Sheldon Gardner.

## Attachment Avoidance

People whose abhorrence of abandonment has resulted in adapter abstention shy abroad from accurateness and amore in their relationships or abstain committed relationships altogether. They usually adopt accidental sex that does not accept any affecting impact. Bodies who abhorrence abandonment so abundant that they shy abroad from all abysmal affecting access with others are at a greater accident for developing life-threatening illnesses, letters University of Washington analyst Paul Ciechanowski. In one study, Ciechanowski and colleagues begin that diabetics who approved an avoidant adapter appearance had decidedly beneath activity spans than diabetics who were not abashed of extensive out.

Attachment Anxiety

People whose abhorrence of abandonment has resulted in co-dependence and abhorrence that ally will leave may be afraid to access a abiding committed relationship, but already they access one, they become acutely absorbed to the added being and will be badly afraid that the accord may end. According to University of Illinois analyst Chris Fraley, bodies who abhorrence abandonment are awful attuned to the affecting expressions of others. Fraley activated how bodies with altered adapter styles reacted to alteration faces and begin that bodies with adapter all-overs were added authentic interpreters of nonverbal communication, but alone back they took the time bare to accomplish a decision.

# Chapter 5: Constructive emotions and destructive emotions

Negative thoughts strengthen in intensity every time you react to them. If you feel angry with your kid and react to the anger by yelling at him or her, or if you throw a huge fit in reaction to something demeaning your sibling said to you, you will only feel more upset, remorseful, and frustrated later.

Reacting to something means you pay heed to the very first irrational thought you experience. To illustrate, if you feel a strong urge to quit your job when your boss does not give you the raise he promised, you may actually quit your job without thinking about the implications of this decision.

Similarly, if you feel upset, you are likely to react to that sadness by holding on to it and overthinking that very emotion. You fixate on it for hours, days, and weeks only to understand its implications when it turns into a chronic emotional problem.

To let go of the negativity, stop reacting to the emotion and **make a conscious effort to respond to it**. Responding to an emotion, a negative thought, or any situation means that you do not engage in the very first reactive thought that pops up in your head, and instead, you take your time to think things through, analyze the situation, and address it from different aspects to make an informed decision. If you carefully respond to your emotions and thoughts that trigger negative behaviors, beliefs, and actions, you will get rid of the negativity in your life and replace it with hope, positivity, and happiness. Here is how you can do that:

Every time you experience an emotion that stirs up a series of negative thoughts in your head, stop doing the task and recognize the emotion.

Very carefully and calmly, observe your emotion and let it calm down on its own without reacting to it.

You need to fight the urges you experience at that time to react to the emotion. Therefore, if you are depressed and keep thinking how terrible you are, and you feel the urge to lock yourself in your room, control it by just staying where you are.

Give your emotion some time, and it will calm down.

Try to understand the message it is trying to convey to you. If you are angry with yourself for not qualifying to the next round of an entrepreneurial summit and have lost the chance of winning the grand prize of $1 million, observe your anger and assess it. Ask yourself questions such as: Why do I feel angry? What does the loss mean to me? Asking yourself such questions helps you calm down the strong emotion and let go of the negative thoughts you experience during that time. Naturally, when you stop focusing on the intense emotion and the negative thoughts it triggers, and you divert your attention towards questions to find a way out of the problem, you gently soothe your negative thought process.

Assess the entire situation in depth and find out ways to better resolve the problem at hand. When you focus on the solution and not the problem, you easily overcome negative thoughts and create room for possibilities.

It will be difficult to not react to a strong emotion, but if you stay conscious of how you feel and behave, and make consistent efforts, you will slowly nurture the habit to respond to your emotions, which will only help you become more positive.

## List of Different emotions

Emotions can usually be categorized into two different types. However, these types come in different forms. Some experts categorize emotions into two types: emotions to be expressed and emotions to be controlled. Others categorize emotions as: primary emotions and secondary emotions. One thing common with both classifications of emotions. However, is all kinds of emotions are usually either positive or negative? Whether an emotion is primary/secondary or expressed/controlled, it will either be negative or positive. Often, people believe that positive psychology is centered mainly on positive emotions but this isn't quite true. In truth, positive psychology leans more towards negative emotions because it is more about managing and overturning negative emotions to achieve positive results.

Firstly, positive emotions may be defined as emotions that provide pleasurable experience; they delight you and do not impact your body unhealthily. Positive emotions, as expected, promote positive self-development. Basically, we are saying that positive emotions are the results of pleasant responses to stimuli in the environment or within ourselves. On the other hand, negative emotions refer to those emotions we do not find particularly pleasant, pleasurable, or delightful to experience. Negative emotions are usually the result of unpleasant responses to stimuli and they cause us to express a negative effect towards a person or a situation.

Naturally, we have different examples of emotions groups under positive and negative. But most times, you can't authoritatively state if emotion is positive or negative. In fact, there are certain emotions that could be both positive and negative. The best way to discern between a positive and negative emotion is to use your intuition. For instance, anger could be both, positive and negative. So, the best way to know when it is negative or when it is positive is to intuitively discern the cause and the context of the anger. This book is, of course, going to focus more on negative emotions and how you can embrace them to create positive results for yourself.

Anger and fear are the two prominent negative emotions which most of us erroneously assume we have to do away with. To be realistic, we cannot allow these emotions to rule our lives yet; we must also understand that they are a necessary part of our experiences as humans. It is impossible to say that you never want to get angry anymore; what is possible is to say that you want to control your anger and get angry less. Mastering negative emotions such as anger is about recognizing and embracing the reality of them, determining their source, and becoming aware of their signs so that we can always know when to expect them and how to control them. For example, if you master an emotion like anger, you naturally start to discern which situation may get you angry and how you could avoid this situation.

A list of negative emotions includes;

Anger
Fear
Anxiety
Depression
Sadness
Grief
Regret
Worry
Guilt
Pride
Envy
Frustration
Shame
Denial...and more.

Many people regard negative emotions to be signs of low emotional intelligence or weakness but this aren't right. Negative emotions have a lot of benefits as long as we do not allow them to overrun us. You aren't completely healthy if you do not let out some negative emotions every now and then. One thing you should know is that negative emotions help you consider positive emotions from a counterpoint. If you do not experience negative emotions at all, how then would positive emotions make you feel good? Another thing is that negative emotions are key to our evolution and survival as humans. They direct us to act in ways that are beneficial to our growth, development, and survival as humans. Anger, mostly considered a negative emotion, helps us ascertain and find solutions to problems. Fear teaches us to seek protection from danger; sadness teaches us to find and embrace love and company. It goes on and on like this with every negative emotion there is.

When we talk about negative emotions, we don't actually mean negative as in "bad." The negativity we talk about in relation to certain emotions isn't to portray them as being bad but rather to understand that they lean more towards a negative reality as opposed to positive emotions. Negative emotions, without doubt, can affect our mental and physical state adversely; some primary negative emotions like sadness could result in depression or worry. We must understand that they are designed just for the purpose of making uncomfortable. They could lead to chronic stress when not checked, making us want to escape these emotions. What you should however know is that we cannot completely escape negative emotions; we can only master them so they don't affect us adversely. Often, some of these emotions are geared towards sending us important messages. For example, anxiety may be a telling sign that there is something that needs to be changed and fear may be a sign that a person or situation may endanger our safety.

Overall, what you should know is that these negative emotions you experience aren't something to be gotten rid of. Rather, they are meant to be mastered so we can employ them in achieving the high-functioning, full-of-purpose life that we desire and deserve. Just like positive emotions, negative emotions are meant to protect us and serve as motivation for us to live a better, more qualitative life and build/maintain quality relationships with people around us.

Note: Negative emotions in themselves do not directly have any impact on our mental and physical health and well-being. How we process and react when we experience negative emotions is what actually matters to our health.

### Destructive effects of having an anger problem

Have you ever heard of the saying "A thought murder a day keeps the doctor away?" This saying is a quite insightful one which refers to how letting yourself feel angry is a healthy thing to do whereas suppressing or denying feelings of anger can have an immensely pathological effect on you. From past experiences, what we have come to know about anger is that it only becomes destructive to you or people around you when it is repressed or let out unhealthily. Anger can have profoundly negative effects on you, your happiness, and people around you. Suppressing your feelings of anger has consequences which are utterly destructive. When you repress your anger, you have the tendency of becoming psychosomatic which could cause real harm to your body. Holding in your anger creates tension in the body and this may cause stress which is a major player in many of the psychosomatic illnesses which we have. Based on research done in the past, there has been substantial evidence to prove that suppressing anger can be the precursor to cancer development in the body and may also inhibit progress even after the cancer has been diagnosed and is being treated.

There are so many effects anger could have on your health. Let's examine some of these effects.

**Heart Problems:** Anger puts you at great risk of having a heart attack. The risk of having a heart attack doubles whenever you have an outburst of anger. When you suppress your anger or express it through an unhealthy outlet, the effect goes directly to your heart meaning it could lead to heart problems. In fact, a study has shown that people with anger disorders or volatile anger are more likely to have coronary disease more than people who show less signs of anger. However, constructive or positive anger is in no way related to any heart problem. It could even be very good for your health.

**Weak Immune System:** Getting angry all the time can actually weaken the immune system, making you prone to more and more illnesses as a study has confirmed. Based on a study conducted in Harvard Medical School, an angry outburst can cause a 6-hour drop in the amount of immunoglobulin A, an antibody responsible for defending the body against infections. Now, imagine if you are always angry; you could really damage your immune system unless you learn to control your anger.

**Cause Stroke:** You are at a very high risk of having a severe stroke if you are the type who explodes every time. Volatile and habitual anger increases your possibility of developing a stroke ranging from a slightly mild blood clot to the brain to actual bleeding in the brain.

**Increase Anxiety:** Experiencing anxiety at one point or the other is a normal thing but anger can actually worsen your anxiety if care is not taken. In fact, anger is a primary emotion to anxiety i.e. your anxious feelings may be due to underlying anger problems. Anger increases the symptoms of Generalized Anxiety Disorder (GAD) which is an extreme case of anxiety. People with GAD have higher levels of repressed, internalized, and unexpressed anger which contributes to the development of GAD symptoms; this can be quite destructive.

**Causes Depression:** Anger increases anxiety which can in turn result in clinical depression. Over the years, many studies have found a link between anger, anxiety, and depression, especially when it comes to men. Passive anger is one of the symptoms of depression; you are constantly angry but too unmotivated to act on the anger.

**Decreases Lifespan:** Anger results in stress and stress is a very strong suspect when it comes to ill health. Combined with stress, anger can have a really strong effect on your health and it can shorten your lifespan due to the number of health problems it can generate. People who constantly experience repressed anger have shorter lifespans than people who express their anger healthily.

Anger should never be repressed or unhealthily expressed. Instead, you should take active efforts to manage your anger and put it under control so as to avoid all of the negative effects of anger which you have just learned about. Never should you try to stifle or suppress your anger. Suppressing emotions as we have reiterated over the chapters makes it hard to manage them or master them like you should. To start with, pay attention to any feeling of anger you experience and use the information gained to discern where the anger is coming from so that you can use one or more of the anger management techniques we will be checking out below to effectively combat anger problems.

# Chapter 6: How abandonment changes life

Before we can reasonably talk about some of the pitfalls of abandonment, I believe it is imperative for you to understand what abandonment truly is. So, I would like to start this report by asking some questions:

If you are someone who has grown up in a **single-parent family**, and I were to tell you that there is a strong chance that you may be suffering from deep-seated abandonment, would you believe me? (The key phrase here is 'single-parent family'). And, with that in mind, could you believe that those abandonment issues just may have been affecting you your entire life? I know it was hard for me at first to understand, but as I continued to do research and uncover the possibilities, it began to make more and more sense.

So, what would be a fitting way for me to convince you that the statements I just made are actually true?

As we move on, it may be hard for you to believe where I am coming from but, that might just be because you probably can't remember those early memories that may have created your own abandonment nightmare. I know it was hard for me to initially comprehend the concepts as I was uncovering them. And, to this day, these concepts still continue to bring up questions even after more than twenty-eight years of intensive and deductive study. Therefore, all I can do is pass on some facts and ask that you judge for yourself.

As of 2010, more than 40 percent of every man, woman, and child living in America is suffering from some degree of abandonment. This adds up to approximately 125,000,000 individuals in the United States alone. Also, with continued projections, and circumstances unchanged, this percentage will most likely exceed more than 50 percent in the next twenty years.

"As far back as I can remember, I have always felt that something was missing in my life".

This is probably a phrase you have heard from time to time; you may have even said it yourself. Although it is a well known cliche, you will see it becomes particularly relevant to this report.

For me, I found the phrase to be true. Once I finally became sober at the age of thirty-eight, I began to reflect back through my life and I remembered I had developed a fear-based persona well before I was five years old. And, because I was so young, I had no clue as to why. As I grew up, I then recalled that my mind was reeling with many strange unjustified feelings, but in my immediate world, I had to pretend that nothing was wrong; hoping those around me would be unable to notice the fearful, lost, little child I was trying so hard to hide.

Being an only-child, I spent much of my early years in constant seclusion and had believed that what I was experiencing inside was natural and normal; let's face it, I had nothing to compare my life to. Then through my school years, with the anxiety of being found out increasing, I remained a loner in order to hide all these fear-based feelings.

With a year of sobriety, I became a substance abuse counselor at the age of 39, and still feeling like a lost soul, I came to a revelation. That's when I became consumed with the idea that there must have been something I had missed in my own recovery. Something experienced in my past; something that happened before I was old enough to develop a conscious mind, something that became my baseline on life. And it was this baseline that eventually created my ongoing attitude. Something that induced my fear of people. It was a condition I was never consciously privy to. That is, that my now-discovered suppressed abandonment had become the hidden motivator. With its hooks and barriers it dictated my choices in life. One choice I am not proud of is my years of addiction. It was the only answer to mask over my self-developed lack of self-worth. Alcohol allowed me to function in society, but didn't cure how I felt about myself. I really didn't like what I had become but, at the time, it was better than living in constant fear of people.

I can only presume that you have come to this report in anticipation to gain knowledge and answers to questions that may have been on your mind for some time, and I welcome that; you are taking the first step to changing your life. Since we all look for the answers to gain an advantage and create the best situations for our future, we all deserve to understand the truth about our past.

Regardless of what you believe about the reasons of how and why your life has gone the way it has, and the uncertain outlook of your destiny, you must still understand that you are not alone. You must be willing to reluctantly accept that something happened to you that you have never been aware of; but it has affected you in a profound way. And with that in mind, under these circumstances, we should be able to eventually discover that how we feel and think now may be a result of the ideas and environments we were subjected to grow up in so many years ago.

In this report, you will be introduced to many conditions you may now be experiencing as a result of that one suppressed event. This information should help you understand the circumstances that have actually become a cornerstone to how you lived your life.

In reality, something I will call, "your moment of physical separation" has been the instrument in shaping who you are today. It has created your personality.

It is easy to assume that the feelings you are experiencing are unique to you and you alone. After all, no one else has grown up in your situation. And, in a sense, you would be right. No one else has.

However, the feelings of abandonment are the same in all of us; only the circumstances change.

Suppressed abandonment is, more often than not, an event that probably happened prior to the age of five; and even though it was suppressed, it is often the associated feelings, often regarded as phantom feelings, that tend to persist.

In this report we will look at some of the consequences that develop from suppressed abandonment issues. But before we can get into the meat of this report, we must first understand what abandonment is.

# Chapter 7: Some tells to help you understand

The first we will look at is guilt and shame. Guilt and shame can be either self or externally imposed. A child that experiences a loss of a parent **without explanation**, often begins to develop self-guilt. That is where the child begin to believe they are the reason that one of their parents has left. This happens often because it is seldom explained that the missing parent in their life has left because of nothing they said or done. In fact, they are often never told why. Because of this, the child seldom feels faultless; instead, they begin to assume sole responsibility for the separation.

Although you may have been experiencing feelings such as these, you may not have a clue as to why you have these feelings. And, that's very understandable.

Some may relate, or you might discover, that you may exhibit unexplained shame and guilt issues. For many with this condition, these issues have no basis of origin, yet they persist. It can often be determined through counseling, that a person might have unknowingly taken on the shame and guilt of their biological parent's discretions. They have subconsciously questioned the reason for their childhood separation. And with that, they have subconsciously embraced and injected that shame and guilt into their personality. This can make them actually ashamed of their own existence.

Another 'tell' we should explore is, excessive timidness and shyness. Although timidness and shyness are often associated to normal growing up, let's look deeper at how we can relate this to, Abandonment.

We must understand that abandonment, because of its nature, is never recognizable on its own; we must assume its presence. If it is present, it will often manifest in the guise of something else. Timidness and shyness in excess, for example, may be but one of those many possible manifestations. The outward actions are often the result of low self-esteem and low self-worth being experienced and our negative feelings being hidden. As victims, we find it much easier to retreat into a shell rather than to let down our guard to express our vulnerability.

If you are timid or shy, you may find that your timidness and shyness are most likely, gender bias. This means that if it was your father that left, you will most likely be much more timid and shy to men. This is not uncommon. It is probably because you had no example of that gender in the house while growing up. You unfortunately missed learning about the differences between adult men and adult women and this, in itself, can be quite confusing and intimidating.

Maybe you are someone who suffers from unexplained fear. Fear is often an internal motivator that forces an involuntary action of retreat. This retreat action also creates an environment of a feeling of low self-esteem and low self-worth – thus, timidness and shyness; and a vicious circle is created. The fear may then escalate into a general mistrust for anyone and everyone. It has no basis of truth. It just is. It is your perception. Often, anti-social behavior can develop in severe cases.

Others who try to get close to you may have found it hard, if not impossible to do. If and when you finally do let them get to know you, you most likely only show them only the person they believe you are. That is because you have acted for so long, you don't actually know yourself. Because of this, they can often see through this facade and most learn to keep their distance. The bottom line is, you actually don't want a close relationship with anyone for fear of being rejected.

Another external 'tell' you could be experiencing might be a high degree of moodiness. This too, is a self-developed defense mechanism you may may be using to elude being close. These highly intense and abrupt mood swings are often a result of being unsure of your place in your environment. The loss of identity you have developed from the past has caught up with you and left you confused and alone and rather than to deal with these feelings or pursue an answer, you have learned to use this moodiness to push others away to feel safe.

Others might exhibit high degrees of unexplained anger or rage. They first become mad at themselves and society because they fail to find an answer that will explain the emptiness they are experiencing. This then evolves into the external lashing out at others as a preventative measure to ensure their personal safety. In some it is used as a tool to misleadingly boost self-confidence and self-worth.

Resentment and jealousy are often good signs of UA. These individuals may resent that they do not possess the glow of those around them and this may bring on a form of jealousy. They fail to understand that it stems from the lack of true natural love they were never afforded, or in some cases, had never even experienced.

They may eventually discover that the love and affection they had experienced in their life was primarily only 'learned' and thus, highly conditional. More on that in my next report.

Another 'tell' sign might be that some of you may express feelings of helplessness and hopelessness. These individuals constantly exhibit a defeatist attitude. They often tend to chalk-up each and every failure as predestined fate. They lack confidence. In many of them, self-esteem and self-worth are nonexistent. They often come to believe that the world has given up on them yet, they don't realize that they may be at fault. Some become addicted to people for self-worth. If not monitored or left alone for long periods of time, people in this state tend to be more inclined to exhibit suicidal tendencies. If this helplessness and hopelessness is coupled with fear or anger, which it often is, it can become a volatile combination.

Now, let's look at addictions. As you will see, addictions are not always as cut-and-dry as we assume them to be. They cannot be pigeonholed so easily. Addiction, in actuality, is a habitual reactive act. It is often the result of something else, and that something else may just be suppressed abandonment. I know it was for me. It is an issue that must be first detected vicariously through someone's actions. It can then be defined as it pertains to that individual. Once defined, it can then be confronted, and then finally accepted.

My attempt in this report was just to bring you in touch with some of the outward signs that I have encountered in my years of counseling coupled with personal experiences and deductive reasoning. Since my start in this endeavor, I have become absolutely convinced that these observations and deductions are but the tip of a huge newly discovered iceberg. As you can probably imagine, there are undoubtedly a whole host of other tells out there.

The complexity of the human brain is virtually incomprehensible. We can see the different areas inter relate during different functions, but do we understand why? With its trillions of cells, it fails to amaze us. It would be brash of me or anyone to even conceive that we understand it all. True, there have been great strives forward in the basic understanding. Individual memories and perceptions vary the end results in each of us.

# Chapter 8: Emotions and Your Mind

Your mind is unique. There is no other psychological framework like yours, and you will experience emotions differently than anyone else. Take falling in love as an example. This may feel like weightlessness/lightness, or it may feel as if a million bees are trapped inside your stomach. It may be intense, or it may be subtle. It may be instantaneous, or it may emerge gradually. It is the same with anger, frustration, weariness, and even happiness. Just because you may not experience the same emotion in the same way as another person does not devalue what you are experiencing.

Because no two people will experience the same emotion, in the same way, no definition will be appropriate for every person. For example, two people battling depression may experience very different symptoms. The first may have trouble sleeping, have no appetite, and have no interest in things that were once enjoyable while the second has trouble with sleeping in too long, binge-eating, and intense waves of despair. These two instances of depression will look strikingly different from an external viewer, but both of these sufferers' emotions and experiences are valid and could be identified as depression.

This is why intense emotions like grief affect different people in such disparate ways. Two siblings are facing the loss of a parent, for example, will each deal with it in his or her way. The first may cling to family and friends for support in coping with the intense grief, while the other may become the family comic, cracking jokes to keep everyone smiling while dealing with the sadness in private. Neither of these responses is wrong; they're just different.

The trick is to stop comparing your emotional self to the emotional selves of others. Identifying and defining emotions in one must be a personal affair. When we compare ourselves with others, we end up invalidating our feelings because they don't seem to "match what everyone else is feeling." Your emotions are yours, and they are valid already in the fact that you are experiencing them.

We do not experience every emotion at the same intensity every time, by which I mean emotional intensity, varies depending on what the experience is. For example, you may experience a low-intensity grief after hearing the news that a favorite performer has passed away, but you may experience a much fuller, more intense grief at the loss of a friend or relative.

As low-and mild-intensity emotions tend to be easier to cope with, these are often constructive. You may cry over the loss of that beloved celebrity, but these tears would likely be cathartic, granting inner relief through the expression of the emotion. A high-intensity emotion, on the other hand, can be more difficult to face or cope with, causing emotional and psychological distress. The loss of a friend, for example, may cause that much higher intensity of grief, making it difficult to continue with daily life.

Not everyone experiences emotions with the same intensity. Some of us are just designed to feel more intensely than others. If you've ever found yourself overcome with emotion over what was, for others, a mundane situation, then you may be an intense feeler. This is not a bad thing, because it also means you feel positive emotions more intensely, but being an intense feeler may be why you struggle with mismanaged emotions. The higher the intensity, the more difficult emotions can be to cope with.

Let's consider depression as an example. We all experience sadness at some point in our lives because we all deal with dissatisfaction and loss, but severe, high-intensity depression is a debilitating and dangerous emotion. It is natural and normal to become sad after a disappointment or a tragic event, but our general perceptions and thought patterns are typically not severely altered by it. We cope with temporary sadness and then move on with our lives. Depression is not so easy to overcome. It is a high-intensity emotion that can severely affect thoughts, feelings, and behaviors, sometimes without any identifiable trigger. Coping with sadness is a difficult but manageable chore while coping with depression is a long-term and complicated journey.

## The Nature of Emotions

Emotions can be tricky. By understanding the mechanism behind emotions, you'll be able to manage them more effectively as they arise.

The first thing to understand is that emotions come and go. One moment you feel happy, the next you feel sad. While you do have some control over your emotions, you must also recognize their unpredictable nature. If you expect to be happy all the time, you set yourself up for failure. You then risk blaming yourself when you 'fail' to be happy, or even worse, beat yourself up for it.

To start taking control of your emotions, you must accept they are transient. You must learn to let them pass without feeling the need to identify strongly with them. You must allow yourself to feel sad without adding commentaries such as, "I shouldn't be sad," or "What's wrong with me?" Instead, you must allow reality to be.

Typically, when someone is described as emotional, this is intended to be taken in a negative light. Emotional people are often regarded as impulsive, difficult to talk to, difficult to work with, unscientific, irrational, loud, or resistant to being spoken to. But this characterization is based on assumptions about emotional people. Indeed, labeling someone as emotional is a simple and almost devious way to neutralize and invalidate someone by immediately labeling them as something which they may or may not be.

No matter how mentally tough you are, you'll still experience sadness, grief, or depression in your life hopefully not at the same time, and not continually. At times, you'll feel disappointed, betrayed, insecure, resentful, or ashamed. You'll doubt yourself and doubt your ability to be the person you want to be. But that's okay because emotions come, but, more importantly, they go.

# Chapter 9: Practicing Acceptance

Acceptance is a key factor in all of this. Everyone has fears in some form or another. We all feel vulnerable at times, we all feel afraid to lose someone we love at times, and we also feel emotionally distraught at times. As human beings, we have to face each of these obstacles in order to grow. Don't look at these fears and emotions as stumbling blocks - but as stepping stones to reach the emotional state that you need to be in.

When we accept a romantic partner into our life, these are the things that we sign up for. It will not all be roses and chocolate. There will be times when you are happy, but there will also be times when you are sad, and there will also be times when you are extremely angry with each other. When these things happen, don't see it as bad. View these events with a more positive outlook. Because we are all different, and have our different opinions and views of the world, they will clash at one time or another. When this happens, this should be seen as an opportunity to grow your bond stronger, rather than tear it apart. This is what should happen in your other relationships also, such as with your friends. Don't fear fights, and instantly think that a breakup will happen because of it. Your bond will always bring you closer together, and it would take a very powerful force to break that bond.

Not only must you accept the differences in your relationships, you must also accept yourself. Accept your fears. Everyone has at some point or another experienced the fear of being abandoned, while some may experience it more strongly than others. We also have to accept the origins of our fears. We can do so by finding solutions, letting go, and finding the beauty in everything that is occurring.

When negative things occur, don't complain. This goes for the things that happened in the past as well. Stop complaining about all the bad things that happened in the past that caused you to be the way you are. It is quite meaningless to complain. By complaining, not only will you drain yourself of energy, but you will drain the energy of everyone around you. The brain often tricks you into thinking you feel better when you complain, but in reality, you actually feel worse. Use the time and energy that you use to complain more wisely. It's like a leaking roof. You can complain all you want, but if you don't go up there and fix it, then it will continue to leak every time it rains. Use your energy to identify and correct the problems that you have or had. Then take the next step in letting it go.

By letting go of certain things, you have accepted that certain aspects of life are out of your control, and that you simply have to do your very best. Life is definitely out of our control, so we can either moan about it for the rest of our lives, or face it with a smile. Accept the way life is, and bit by bit, life will look much more beautiful. There is a lot of beauty in the world. You don't have to go looking for it. Be positive, and you will start to wonder why you were ever afraid in the first place.

# Chapter 10: What rules your emotions

Emotions can be triggered by all sorts of things from people, places, and times of day or even certain objects. How triggers work is that they activate thoughts or memories in our brain and cause us to have physical and emotional responses.

Having emotions is a normal human reaction to our life circumstances, the problem comes when we are unable to evaluate our emotions or consider their impact on our lives. Most people passively accept their emotions; they don't even get to the points we have covered where they choose to identify what the emotion is or what has triggered it.

## How Our Thoughts Shape Our Emotions

During the 1960s, social psychologist Walter Mischel headed several psychological studies on delayed rewards and gratification. He closely studied hundreds of children between the ages of 4 to 5 years to reveal a trait that is known to be one of the most important factors that determine success in a person's life, gratification.

This experiment is famously referred to as the marshmallow test. The experiment involved introducing every child into a private chamber and placing a single marshmallow in front of them. At this stage, the researcher struck a deal with the child.

The researcher informed them that he would be gone from the chamber for a while. The child was then informed that if he or she didn't eat the marshmallow while the researcher was away, he would come back and reward them with an additional marshmallow apart from the one on the table. However, if they did eat the marshmallow placed on the table in front of them, they wouldn't be rewarded with another.

It was clear. One marshmallow immediately or two marshmallows later.

The researcher walked out of the chamber and re-entered after 15 minutes.

Predictably, some children leaped on the marshmallow in front of them and ate it as soon as the researcher walked out of the room. However, others tried hard to restrain themselves by diverting their attention. They bounced, jumped around, and scooted on the chairs to distract themselves in a bid to stop them from eating the marshmallow. However, many of these children failed to resist the temptation and eventually gave in.

Only a handful of children managed to hold until the very end without eating the marshmallow.

The study was published in 1972 and became globally popular as 'The Marshmallow Experiment.' However, it doesn't end here. The real twist in the tale is what followed several years later.

Researchers undertook a follow-up study to track the life and progress of each child who was a part of the initial experiment. They studied several areas of the person's life and were surprised by what they discovered. The children who delayed gratification for higher rewards or waited until the end to earn two marshmallows instead of one had higher school grades, lower instances of substance abuse, lower chances of obesity, and better stress coping abilities.

The research was known as a ground-breaking study on gratification because researchers followed up on the children 40 years after the initial experiment was conducted, and it was sufficiently evident that the group of children who delayed gratification patiently for higher rewards succeeded in all areas they were measured on.

This experiment proved beyond doubt that delaying gratification is one of the most crucial skills for success in life.

## Success and delaying gratification

Success usually boils down to picking between the discomfort of discipline over the pleasure and comfort of distraction. This is exactly what delaying gratification is. Would you rather go out for the new movie in town where all your friends are heading, or would you rather sit up and study for an examination to earn good grades? Would you rather party hard with your co-workers before the team gets started with an important upcoming presentation? Or would you sit late and work on fine tuning the presentation?

Our ability to delay gratification is also a huge factor when it comes to decision making and is considered an important aspect of emotional intelligence. Each day, we make several choices and decisions. While some are trivial and have little influence on our future (what color shoes should I buy? Or which way should I take to work?), others have a huge bearing on our success and future.

As human beings, we are wired to make decisions or choices that offer an instant return on investment. We want quick results, actions, and rewards. The mind is naturally tuned for a short-term profit. Why do you think e-commerce giants are making a killing by charging an additional fee for same day and next day delivery? Today is better than tomorrow!

Think about how different our life would be if we thought about the impact of our decisions about three to five years from now? If we can bring about this mental shift where we can delay gratification by keeping our eyes firmly fixated on the bigger picture several years from now, our lives can be very different.

Another factor that is important in gratification delay is the environment. For example, if children who were able to resist temptation were not given a second marshmallow or reward for delaying gratification, they are less likely to view delaying gratification as a positive habit.

If parents do not keep their commitment to reward a child for delaying gratification, the child won't value the trait. Delaying gratification can be picked up only in an environment of commitment and trust, where a second marshmallow is given when deserved.

## Examples of gratification delay

Let us say you want to buy your dream car that you see in the showroom on your way to work every day. You imagine how wonderful it would be to own and drive that car. The car costs $25,000, and you barely have $5000 dollars in your current savings. How do you buy the car then? Simple, you start saving. This is how you will combine strong willpower with delayed gratification.

There are countless opportunities for you to blow money every day such as hitting the bar with friends for a drink on weekends, co-workers visiting the nearest coffee shop to grab a latte, or buying expensive gadgets. Every time you remove your wallet to pay, you have two clear choices: either blow your money on monetary pleasure or wait for the long-term reward. If you can resist these temptations and curtail your expenses, you'll be closer to purchasing your dream car. Making this decision will help you buy a highly desirable thing in future.

Will you spend now for immediate gratifications and pleasures, or will you save to buy something more valuable in the future?

Here is another interesting example to elucidate the concept of delayed gratification. Let us say you want to be the best film director the world has ever seen. You want to master the craft and pick up all skills related to movie making and the entertainment business. You visualize yourself as making spectacular movies that inspire and entertain people for decades.

How do you plan to work towards a large goal, or the big picture (well, literally)? You'll start by doing mundane, boring; uninspiring jobs on the sets such as being someone's assistant, fetching them a cup of coffee, cleaning the sets, and other similar boring chores. It isn't exciting or fun, but you go through it each day because you have your eyes firmly fixated on the larger goal, or bigger picture.

You know you want to become a huge filmmaker one day and are prepared to delay gratification for fulfilling that goal. The discomfort of your current life is smaller in comparison to the pleasure of the higher goal. This is delayed gratification. Despite the discomfort, you regulate your actions and behavior for meeting a bigger goal in the future. It may be tough and boring currently, but you know that doing these arduous tasks will give you that shot to make it big someday.

Delayed gratification can be applicable in all aspects of life from health to relationships. Almost every decision we make involves a decision between opting for short-term pleasures now and enjoying bigger rewards later. A burger can give you immediate pleasure today, whereas an apple may not give you instant pleasure but will benefit your body in the long run.

### Stop drop technique

Each time you identify an overpowering or stressful emotion that is compelling you to seek immediate pleasure, describe your feelings by writing them down. Make sure you state them clearly to acknowledge their existence.

Have you seen the old VCR models? They had a big pause button prominently placed in the middle. You are now going to push the pause button on your thoughts.

Focus all attention on the heart as it is the center of all your feelings.

Think of something remarkably beautiful that you experienced. It can be a spectacular sunset you witnessed on one of your trips, a beautiful flower you saw in a garden today, or a cute pet kitten you spotted in the neighborhood. Basically, anything that evokes feelings of joy, happiness, and positivity in you. The idea is to bring about a shift in your feelings.

Experience the feeling for some time and allow it to linger. Imagine the feelings you experience in and around your heart. If it is still challenging, take deep breaths. Hold the positive feeling and enjoy it.

Now, click on the mental pause button and revisit the compelling idea that was causing stressful feelings. How does it feel right now?

Now write down how you are feeling and what comes to mind. Act on the fresh insight if it is suitable.

This process doesn't take much time (again, you are craving instant gratification) and makes it easier for you to resist giving in to temptation. The real trick is to change the physical feeling with the heart to bring about a shift in thoughts and eventually, actions. You don't suffocate or undermine your emotions.

Rather, you acknowledge them and then gently change them. When your emotions are slowly changing, the brain tows its line which makes us think in a way that lets us act according to our values and not on impulse or uncontrollable emotions.

### Self-mastery is the master key

According to Walter Mischel, "Goal-directed and self-imposed gratification delay is fundamental to the process of emotional self-regulation." Emotional management, or regulation and the ability to control one's impulses, are vital to the concept of emotional intelligence.

Mischel's research established that while some people are born with a greater control for impulses, or better emotional management, others are not. A majority of people are somewhere in between. However, the good news is that emotional management, unlike intelligence, can be learned through practice. EQ isn't as genetically determined as cognitive abilities.

### Impulse control and delayed gratification

Have you ever said something in anger and then regretted it immediately? Have you ever acted on an impulse or in haste only to regret it soon after the act? I can't even count the number of people who have lost their jobs, ruined their relationships, nixed their business negotiations, and blown away friendships because of that one moment when they acted on impulse. When you don't allow thoughts to take over and control your words or actions, you demonstrate low emotional intelligence.

Thus, the concept of emotional intelligence is closely connected with delaying gratification. We've all acted at some point or another without worrying about the consequences of our actions. Impulse control, or the ability to construct our thoughts and actions prior to speaking or acting, is a huge part of emotional control. You can manage your emotions more efficiently when you learn to override impulses, which is why impulse control is a huge part of emotional intelligence.

Ever wondered about the reason behind counting to ten, 100, or 1000 before reacting each time you are angry? We've all had our parents and educators counsel us about how anger can be restrained by counting up to ten or 100. It is simple, while you are in the process of counting; your emotional level is slowly decreasing. Once you are done with counting, the overpowering impulse to react to the emotion has passed. This allows you act in a more rational and thoughtful manner.

Emotional intelligence is about identifying these impulsive reactions and regulating them in a more positive and constructive manner. Rather than reacting mindlessly to a situation, you need to stop and think before responding. You choose to respond carefully instead of reacting impulsively to accomplish a more positive outcome or thwart a potentially uncomfortable situation.

Here are some useful tips for delaying gratification and boosting your ability to regulate emotions:

**Have a clear vision for your future**
Delaying gratification and controlling impulses or emotions becomes easier when you have a clear picture of the future. When you know what you want to accomplish five, eight, ten, or 15 years from now, it will be a lot easier to keep the bigger picture in mind if you come across temptations that can ruin your goal. Your 'why' (compelling reason for accomplishing a goal) will keep you sustained throughout the process of meeting the goal. Have a plan to fulfill your goal once you have a clear goal in mind. Identifying your goals and planning how you'll get there will help you resist the temptation more effectively.

**Find ways to distract yourself from temptations and eliminate triggers**

For instance, if you are planning to quit drinking, take a different route back home from work if there are several bars along the way. Instead of focusing on what you can't do, concentrate on the activities you are passionate about. Surround yourself with positive people and activities that will help you dwell on your goal. Avoid trying to fill your time with material goods.

## Make spending money difficult

If you are a slave to plastic money and online transactions, you are making the process of spending money too easy for your own good. Paying with cold, hard cash can make you think several times before spending. You'll reconsider your purchases when you pay with real money rather than plastic. Take a part of your salary and put it into a separate account that you won't touch. Make sure that accessing your savings account won't be easy.

## Avoid 'all or nothing' thinking

Most of us think resisting temptation or giving up a bad habit is an 'all or nothing challenge.' It is natural for a majority of normal human beings to have a minor slip here and there. However, that doesn't mean you should just fall off and quit. Occasional slip-ups shouldn't be used as an excuse to get off the track. Despite a small detour, you can get back on the track. Don't try to convince yourself to wander in the opposite direction.

## Make a list of common rationalizations

Find a counterpoint or counterargument for each. For example, you were angry for just five minutes, or you are spending only ten dollars extra. Tell yourself that five minutes of anger is 150 minutes a month wasted in anger or ten dollars extra is $3,000 extra spent throughout the year.

# Chapter 11: How to deal with fear, rejection, criticism

Anxiety refers to the feeling of uneasiness, fear, or worry that you experience when you encounter a challenge, obstacle, or a nerve-wracking situation. This feeling is quite natural and normal in situations that demand it. For instance, you are bound to feel nervous when going for a job interview or right before finding out your examination results.

While feeling anxious occasionally or when the need arises is normal, sometimes we tend to hold on to the anxiety for excessively long and to the extent that it becomes ingrained in our minds. As a result of this, we feel anxious even when there is no need for it.

## How Constant Anxiety Sabotages Our Wellbeing

Feeling extremely apprehensive, pensive, and scared without any solid reason only takes a toll on your mental, emotional, and physical health. You feel scared of taking a step forward worrying it may lead to an unfortunate outcome. You keep thinking of how things will go wrong and stop considering the possibility of things taking a positive turn for once. You doubt your capabilities and incessantly fret over things that may never happen.

This state of constant worry and a racing mind that compels you to imagine the worst-case scenario associated with situations affect every aspect of your life.

Health: When you keep agonizing over what may happen, you are likely to ignore your health. Often people eat a lot out of stress and anxiety, and this unhealthy eating habit coupled with chronic anxiety paves way for health disorders. Some people also stop eating properly at all when they are anxious - this again is an unhealthy approach towards health and nutrition that only weakens you from within.

Relationships: If you constantly fuss over things that may never happen, you only waste the precious moments of the present that you could have otherwise spent with your loved ones. Naturally, when you do not spend quality time with loved ones or are always in a state of panic, you stop giving your loved ones the time and energy they need to bond better with you, and this ends up straining your relationships.

Work Life: Your anxious state of mind directly affects your professional performance. If you remain anxious for days over petty issues, you will only feel distracted while working. This keeps you from attentively working on your projects resulting in frequent errors and low productivity.

Pursuit of Goals: Naturally, when you are panic-stricken frequently, you don't have the ability and courage to believe in yourself and your goals, and thus, let go of them.

If these problems persist in your life, this only makes life more challenging. While this may be the state of your life, it is not what you want, and if you are sure you wish to live a much better life, it is time you work on overcoming your fears and anxiousness by simply training yourself to better control and manage your emotions.

Here is how you can do that.

## Become More Mindful of Your Emotions

You allow your anxiety to increase in intensity and wash you over completely because oftentimes you are not even aware of how you feel. The same applies to all your emotions that lead to unconstructive thoughts that then pave way for problems in your life. Oftentimes, it so happens that you may be doing something physically but are mentally lurking somewhere in the past or future. This state of forgetfulness keeps you from being aware of how and what you feel and triggers your anxiety without you even realizing that.

A good way to thwart this problem is to nurture the state of mindfulness. Mindfulness refers to being completely aware of how you feel without attaching any sort of judgment or label to the feeling. It also encompasses complete consciousness of the environment around you.

When you are mindful of the present moment, you are aware of everything, you feel and experience in that time without worrying about anything else. This enables you to have control of your racing thoughts and the underlying emotions of anxiety and fear easily by bringing back your attention to the present moment.

As you slowly train yourself to live in the moment and not worry about **what may happen**, you overcome your anxiety and fears, one after another and restore peace in your life. Here is how you can nurture the state of complete mindfulness.

When you are struck with anxiety, acknowledge the emotion you experience and sit with it. Do not identify with it or immerse yourself in the experience. Instead, imagine that you have moved out of your body and are now carefully observing the anxiety from the perspective of the third person. Observe the anxiety carefully and see what it is trying to convey to you. If it brings forth any of your fears, acknowledge it, write it down, and dig deeper into it later to find a solution to the problem. For instance, you may feel anxious of meeting people because you feel they will judge you, and if you dig deeper into this thought, you will realize that it isn't people, but you who are judging yourself. When you become more aware of how you fabricate thoughts that trigger unhealthy emotions, you do not become entangled in such emotions and are able to dissociate yourself from them.

Every time you work on a task, pay full attention to every step of the process. While washing clothes, observe how the dryer moves and how the clothes spin in the machine. When listening to a presentation by a colleague, pay attention to every word he/she says and keep bringing back your attention to the task at hand every time you wander off in thought. By doing this, you consciously keep yourself focused on the task at hand and let go of any perturbing thoughts that may trigger your anxiety.

Create a worry period for yourself- a time window wherein you can think of all your worries mindfully. Every time you think of something disturbing, note it down in a journal and remind yourself to reflect on it during the worry period. Keep the worry period limited to 30 to 40 minutes and think of all your problems in that period. Remember to take one concern at a time and then worry about another one, so you deeply analyze it, find the underlying cause, and determine a solution. Also, this makes you more mindful of the problem at hand and keeps you from jumping from one thought to another.

Apart from doing all of the above, make sure not to put any sort of labels to your emotions because often it is these labels that make us hold on to petty thoughts and create a mountain out of molehill for no particular reason. Your anxiety is neither good nor bad, neither is your happiness. They are both mere emotions. It is only your reaction and response to an emotion that makes it good or bad. Therefore, if you stop reacting to your anxiety by isolating yourself from others and respond to it by slowly facing and overcoming your fears, the same anxiety that you earlier labeled as 'bad' would turn into something more 'positive.' Every time you experience a bout of anxiety or feel scared of something, or experience any other powerful emotion, overcome the urge to tag it with a label. Instead, just observe it and accept it as it is. You will be surprised how the mere act of accepting your emotions calms you down helping you break free of its shackles.

Start by working on any of these techniques and slowly add more to your routine so you build habits of these practices. Consistently working on them will help you nurture a state of mindfulness always, which allows you to track your emotions 24/7.

## Take Complete Ownership of Your Feelings

Your feelings are yours to take care of and if you do not take full ownership of them, they are likely to rattle inside you more and make you feel anxious for no solid reason. Every time you feel apprehensive or scared, accept your feelings as they are instead of blaming it on someone else. If you do not feel like going to a social gathering, it is not the fault of the people, but it is your own weakness. If you feel scared of failing in an examination, which is why you don't apply for it, do not take out the anger on your spouse.

Only when you start taking ownership of your feelings are you then able to accept them as your own and positively work towards improving on them. Every time you experience a strong feeling, do not judge yourself based on it and neither blames it on someone else. Instead, write down how and what you feel and accept it fully.

The moment you take accountability of your feelings, you feel a sense of responsibility emerging inside you. This sense of responsibility then enables you to take charge of the situation and do what is right.

## Face Your Fears

You can never completely curb your anxiety unless you face the fears it is rooted in. You can only feel strong when you master your emotions of fear and apprehensiveness, and this can only be possible if you actually face that to which you are afraid.

Now that you are aware of how to control your negative thoughts and be mindful of how you feel, consciously make a list of everything that you are afraid of doing. Things such as confronting your feelings to your crush, starting your own business, publishing your book, trying adventure sports, and anything else that you feel is holding you back can go on that list.

Once your list is ready, pick any one fear that you would like to overcome first and create a plan of action to curb it. If you are afraid of speaking publicly but have always wanted to pursue it, prepare a short speech on a topic you are passionate about and practice speaking it for a minute or two in front of the mirror.

Once you have command over it, speak on the topic in front of 2 to 3 people. You may stumble and make mistakes, but if you do manage to stay strong in that time, you will overcome a part of your fear. Slowly keep speaking in front of more people and soon enough, you will have overcome your fear.

After overcoming one little fear, take on another one, and then another one. Keep combatting your fears this way and thwart them one after another to have better control of your emotions and master them. Remember to record your daily activities and performance in a journal so that you can go through the accounts time and again. This gives insight into your strengths, mistakes, setbacks and accomplishments so that you feel motivated on acknowledging your accomplishments, learn from your mistakes, and improve on them to only do better the next time.

# Chapter 12: How to deal with negative people

People as social beings are influenced by what they hear, what they see, what they smell, what they taste and by what they feel. Therefore, other people automatically always have some influence on you. But what happens if this influence is (constantly) negative? You become passive, depressed and frustrated.

If you have negative people around you, you should still be as positive as possible and not let yourself become infected.

If someone (again) complains about the bad weather, you should not start a discussion with them or try to convince them, but rather change the subject, if possible, towards something that interests them or is their passion.

Another way to deal with negative people is to clearly express your opinion: "I cannot stand your whining and your negativity anymore. You therefore have two options in my presence. Either you are silent or one of us is leaving." You need self-confidence in order to do this and this approach does not work with everyone. But there are some people with whom it works wonderfully to put a mirror in front of their face, because they have never really reflected themselves and been shown how much they play the victim.

If you feel like you are surrounded by negative people it might also be because of yourself, as tough as that sounds. Because usually we attract people who are like us.

Based on the quote above you should always remember that it is easier to change your environment than to change the people around you. You can achieve this successfully if you separate yourself spatially from your previous environment as well and build yourself a new identity in a previously unknown place where nobody knows you. Because then you can choose yourself who you allow to become part of your life and from the very beginning you can allow positive people into your life and avoid negative people and surround you with an environment that is good for you. This may be a drastic measure for some and does not seem easy to implement, but it leads to the desired goal more effectively and faster. Because you cannot change people who all have their own life stories, traits and habits that distinguish them, as long as they do not want that change themselves. Surround yourself with people who give you a positive feeling, who help you, from whom you can learn something, because they are further developed than you. Think well with whom to share your valuable lifetime.

**How you can stop negative feelings and thoughts!**

Here are 5 tips on how to effectively deal with negative feelings and thoughts:

**Tip 1**

Imagine your negative thoughts are like clouds. Just because you can see them does not necessarily mean you need to identify with them. They are there but they will disappear again. It is the same with your negative feelings. Instead of saying you are sad, you could tell yourself something inside of you is sad. That is how you create a certain distance and you do not identify so strongly with your thoughts and feelings.

**Tip 2**

Write down your negative thoughts and feelings as they occur. Try to put into words what you think and what you feel. That also means writing down questions about where these thoughts might come from. Keep writing until you cannot think of anything else and you will realize it will then be much easier for you to better organize and process your thoughts and feelings. You will gain more clarity.

**Tip 3**

Breathe deeply and consciously. Because your breath is the enemy of your negative thoughts. When you breathe and just accept that your negative feelings are there you relax. And once you relax, you no longer fight against your emotional state, making it easier for those feelings to disappear.

**Tip 4**

Whenever negative thoughts and feelings appear remember you are mortal. The very idea that one could theoretically die the next day sets the current emotional state of a person in relation to the worst case that could occur. This usually leads to the doubt whether what you think or feel at the time is really as crucial as you might think? In other words: the negative thought is put in relation to a much worse scenario and thus does not appear as large as before.

**Tip 5**

If you have concrete goals in your life and follow your passion constantly making new achievements you are effectively countering the negative spiral. As you begin to value and use your precious time more effectively, the space for negative thoughts becomes smaller and smaller. Start acting instead of stopping. To take action is a constant process that can be imagined as clean, flowing water. Stagnant water begins to stink after a while due to the spreading of putrefactive bacteria. So plan your day and follow specific goals in your life that you work on daily. This puts your focus back on things that work and give you a sense of success and satisfaction.

# Chapter 13: Stop negative thoughts, feelings

Most of the time, the problems people suffer from come from their minds and not from reality. As previously discussed, there are several negative thoughts that can automatically pop into someone's head, bending reality for the person. Irrational thoughts can transform regular disappointment into something awful. This can make a person less functional in major areas of his life. Since the problem is in the person's way of thinking, then the solution must revolve around changing his or her way of thinking.

The fact that the problem lies in the human mind makes it difficult and easy to deal with, depending on how it is looked at. It is difficult in the sense that negative thinking practiced for a long time cannot be changed quickly. It might require a lot of time before a person can consider he free of the influences of such unwanted thoughts. Time, however, is a luxury some people do not have. Patience is gold and some people are still mining for a piece. Nevertheless, solving problems with negative thoughts is also easy. This is because the solution for this problem does not require a person to move mountains. The person is the one in control of his or her mind, so the person actually has direct control over the issue.

The very first step in combating destructive negative thoughts is identifying them. This is the basic step necessary for most human problems. Only by knowing the problem can a person develop the necessary plan of action to eliminate it? As mentioned in the previous discussion, there are several negative and irrational thoughts that breed in people's minds. They can take different forms and can impact the person's functioning in varying degrees.

At present, it is believed by experts that there are actually thousands of false ideas that cause misery to people. Some of these can be subtle but so convincing, and others are rather obvious and bold. Hence, a person must observe his or her own way of thinking for a certain period of time. 11 of the illogical ways of thinking were discussed, and one can use that list as a guide to decipher his or her unwanted thoughts. Writing every thought observed is necessary. Negative thoughts tend to storm a person's mind, so one can easily lose track of them if they are not jotted down accordingly.

Nonetheless, one should not expect this step to come easily. There are several irrational thoughts the person must have repeatedly experiences to the point that the thoughts became fact to the person.

The next step is identifying the factors that trigger negative thoughts. This can be done by listing the times and circumstances where the negative thought surfaced. Also, one must list the exact feelings that could have generated the unwanted cognitive distortion. Subtle thoughts can be difficult to pinpoint, but by identifying undesirable emotions, one can improve chances of uncovering the underlying illogical idea.

Following this step is the assessment of the possible evidence of the thoughts listed. For instance, a person feels like he is not good at anything at all. Then, the person must write down all the activities he performs satisfactorily or even exceptionally. It is easier to convince the mind to let go of a belief if the evidence disproving the belief are very clear.

Next is to dispute the disruptive negative thoughts. Challenging an illogical way of thinking can take the form of exploring different interpretations of a seemingly upsetting event. For instance, a project proposal made by Mary was rejected by her boss. She felt so bad that she started thinking her boss had never liked her. Instead of dwelling on such a negative interpretation of what happened, Mary must consider other possible interpretations of the situation. It is possible that Mary's boss was only trying to motivate her to give her best in her job. Her boss, perhaps, has seen her better performances at work, and he wanted her to be at her best always.

The event can also be interpreted as Mary's learning opportunity. Experience is the best teacher, after all. By experiencing rejection first hand, Mary became knowledgeable on what to do and not do in order to be successful in the future. It is also possible that her project proposal was out of the budget range of the company. There are several ways to interpret a single event. Hence, it is illogical to stick with the worst or most undesirable possibility.

A person can debate against his or her own negative thoughts. Effective arguments against the cognitive distortions can be created once the person has a full understanding of the ramifications of these thoughts. By continuously asking the question, "Why?" to one, a person can discover more of his impossible demands on himself. At the same time, he or she can see the pattern of his or her distorted reasoning.

Some people are fond of labeling themselves with put-downs. Luckily, there is also a way to turn that habit into something healthy for the self. By restating the negative labels as positive ones, a person can feel better about himself. For instance, the term lazy can be replaced with the words relaxed or carefree.

The next step is creating rational statements to replace the irrational ones listed. Consider the following examples.

I must always perfect the school examinations. If I fail to do so, then I am nothing but a failure. Making mistakes is unacceptable. (Irrational thought)

No one is perfect. Everyone has his or her own weakness. Committing mistakes is a common feature of every individual. Failures, mistakes and faults are all part of the learning process. Only through learning can a person become better. (Rational thinking)

I do not want to try anything. I always fail anyway! (Irrational thinking)

I cannot tell what the outcome of this activity will be. I can succeed at this or I can fail. Either way, I win, for this is a new learning experience for me, a kind of experience that is rewarding in it. Indeed, I cannot control the outcome, but I can control how hard I try. (Rational thinking)

By exploring rational thoughts to counter the prevailing illogical ideas, one frees his mind to consider other possibilities. This is a good start to alter the negative pattern of thinking and to change it using a healthier positive ways of looking at things.

Self-talk can also help in eliminating negative thoughts gradually. However, one must be careful about the content of his self-talk. The power of self-talk lies in the repetition of the idea to the self. The mind has an inclination to believe an idea that is usually present in the person's consciousness, so repetition works well to embed a belief in the mind.

The aim of self-talk is to support a healthier self. Thus, one must avoid halting ideas like, "Don't be emotional" or, "Always be perfect." Instead, one must use self-talk containing allowing messages like, "It is always okay to make mistakes," and, "Nothing is wrong with being emotional. I am a human being capable of feeling, and I have to respect that."

The last step is to be mindful of the occurrence of any negative thought, and attack it immediately before it starts building up. Remember, however, that this method is only effective with repetitive practice. Indeed, negative thoughts can surface anytime of the day, so being alert to these unpleasant ideas is the best way to combat such negative thinking.

Another important consideration to remember is that immediate result cannot be expected. As mentioned earlier, it takes time to eliminate negative ways of thinking. Hence, the techniques and steps mentioned above must be practiced for as long as needed. What is certain is that changing the negative thoughts to positive ones is highly doable. Logical reasoning, however, is hard work. Being rational requires a lifetime commitment. Consequently, some people leave the job undone by giving up early before anything is accomplished.

## Dealing with Negative Thoughts and Memories

In the academic scene, experts do not agree on the most effective means of dealing with negative memories and thoughts. Using the psychoanalytic perspective (pioneered by Sigmund Freud), disturbing emotions must be expressed. For this school of thought, there is no other way for a person to effectively combat unwanted memories except by talking about it – even if it requires a person to dig the bad memory out of his or her unconscious mind.

People have a natural inclination to repress their bad memories. They try to hide them in the deepest part of their brain. However, this is an ineffective way of dealing with such memories. According to psychotherapists, the repressed memories act like a toxin and seep out in more problematic forms like psychological disorders.

However, some research supports the claim that repressing a bad memory actually facilitates forgetting. Once the person has forgotten an unwanted past experience, then there is no way the memory can have negative effects. Nevertheless, this idea needs more research support because most therapy still focuses on decreasing the repression of undesirable memories.

Contrary to this, another research claims that people who deliberately avoid their negative thoughts or bad memories are not making any progress. Instead, they are making the situation worse. The said study revealed that more uncontrollable negative thoughts will be produced by a person who opts to not talk about bad memories. It is likened to what happens if one is asked not to think of a monkey for the next five minutes.

Indeed, science is still on its way to find the best way for people to manage undesirable memories and thoughts. As of now, there are different approaches suggested by various studies that are worthy of trying. Consequently, a person must try the methods to see which works best.

## Acceptance and Moving On

While there are people obsessing over their bad memories or negative thoughts, others enjoy life without trying to forget about their undesirable past experience. It is highly possible that two individuals remember the same event in totally different ways. Individual differences when it comes to perception and the unreliability of the human memory are some factors that could cause such difference in interpretation.

While researchers are still trying to find the best way to deal with this problem, one could start by changing factors within his control. A person's acceptance is a helpful way to effectively deal with unwanted memories. Before one can forget or dig up bad memories, he must first learn to accept it. It could be that a person is continuously bothered by bad memories because a part of him is still resisting the negativity of the event.

With acceptance, a person recognizes that the bad experience took place and that it was indeed painful. A person must accept that the experience affected his life both in negative and positive ways. Most importantly, a person must accept that it is now all over. The experience is in a distant past far from where he is right now. A person must realize that moving on from that negative experience, regardless of how difficult it is, means he is strong enough to carry on with life. A person must accept that he cannot go back to the past. One cannot heal the wounds in the past for that is the task of the present. And the future is for a new beginning.

Bad memories, perhaps, can be likened to a wound. One does not need to rush its healing for it will eventually heal itself naturally. Time really heals, but one must be very patient. What matters is that the person recognizes that the wound exists and is now a part of him. Whether he opts to talk about it or to forget about it, the wound, the memory, the experience is still there. Soon, the wound leaves a scar, and it is up to the person if he sees it as a scar of defeat or a scar of triumph.

### Cultivating the Positive and Eliminating the Negative

It is amazing how people can respond so differently to the same situation. The exact same stimulus can make different people elicit varying responses. Aside from what was previously discussed, attitude is another factor responsible for individual differences in response. Thoughts, attitudes and behavior can influence one another.

Attitude can be better understood by looking at its ABC components – that is, affectivity, behavioral and cognitive parts.

Affectivity is the evaluative part, and it describes a person's feelings about a certain situation, event or person. The behavioral part is the overt response or action taken, and the cognitive aspect talks about what a person thinks, knows or believes about a person or event. Changing one of these components can change the other two. Attitude is dynamic, and it can influence a person's thoughts. Consequently, cultivating a positive attitude can help improve a person's way of thinking.

The first step to improve one's attitude is to be aware of the current attitude. This is possible through self-observation. One can tell if he is more of an optimist or pessimist or whether he is introverted or extroverted through this process. Friends and family can also help a person assess his behavior by sharing what they see in him. There are also scales and tests that give one an objective description of his attitude.

A person with a clear attitude can avoid the phenomenon of cognitive dissonance. This describes a person's predisposition to act and think in opposite manners. If it is clear to a person how he sees, feels and thinks about a certain issue, he can display behaviors parallel to what he believes in.

The second step is to identify desired the positive attitude. A particular attitude that several researches support is optimism. This attitude describes a person's hopefulness and high expectation of the future. Such attitude of hope and positive orientation can protect a person from psychological distress. It is revealed by several studies that having an optimistic attitude betters a person's mental and physical health. In addition to this, optimism was found to be a necessary ingredient for success in almost all aspects of human life.

For instance, a person who thinks negatively of himself always pulls back and avoids trying new things. Consequently, his potentials, skills and talents remain unexplored and underutilized, making him an underachiever for his entire life.

Optimism is commonly mistaken as a kind of attitude that is cheerful no matter what happens. Healthy optimism is not like that. Positive thinkers never deny the existence of their problems, and yes, they do experience problems. They are simply open and ready to address problems in however they can. Optimistic individuals respond actively to their lives, as they are aware that what they do shapes their future.

The third step is to start developing the desired positive attitude. If a person wants to be optimistic, then he or she should practice the attitude. Optimism is not just about being happy all the time. One must learn to face problems and even expect bad times with the aim of solving the issue. Keeping an open mind about the possible solutions is a habit of optimistic individuals. What makes positive thinkers appear constantly cheerful is the fact that they never fail to see the good even in the worst situation. Indeed, being optimistic requires looking at the bright side instead of the depressing part.

To be optimistic means a person is not defeated by his or her negative thoughts. Instead, the person is actively challenging irrational thoughts and is replacing unpleasant ideas with pleasing ones. An optimist also knows how to appreciate life. This gives the person a lighter perspective in life. An optimist is grateful and appreciative even of the rain. No matter how big or small the good in a situation is, the optimist sees it and appreciates it.

Optimism makes a person able to laugh and celebrate life even in the toughest situations. An optimistic person has the ability to control himself. Hence, he or she can adapt better to various circumstances. Accepting that there are things people cannot change is another practice of optimists. Consequently, the optimist rarely complains as he decided not to focus on things beyond his control. What the optimist focuses on instead are his ways of seeing things, manners of performing his tasks, polishing his skills, renewing his energy and spirit, and all that is within his power.

Practicing these specific attitudinal inclinations helps a person cultivate the positive and eliminate the negative

# Chapter 14: Building Healthier Relationships

The biggest thing that kills any kind of relationship is the lack of communication. Or, to be more specific, the lack of **good** communication. If you know that you have a fear and have no idea where it is coming from, you should be willing to open up and talk to your partner about it. Don't see it as just your problem: if you are in a relationship with someone, the problem belongs to both of you. If you have an idea of where it may have originated, talk to him or her about it. Express your desire to overcome it, and change, and that you need their help to achieve that. Don't ever make them think that it is their job to do this for you, though. Their responsibility is only to help through being supportive and understanding where you are coming from. The change itself must come from within you.

The first step in getting rid of the fear of abandonment is to build a life for yourself that isn't entirely entrenched in another person. Do not be so engrossed in the relationship that you give the power to your partner to keep you safe. That's just setting yourself up for disaster. If that person leaves, you are definitely going to feel alone, and maybe even take desperate measures because you made yourself so vulnerable to them. You need to perceive yourself as an individual first, before you can have a healthy partnership.

Ensure that you understand your self-esteem issues, and don't let them get in the way. Try to eliminate any parent-child behavior that may exist between you and your partner. If you depend wholly on your partner for emotional support, take steps to correct that. For example, you should know on your own whether or not you look attractive today, regardless of whether or not your partner complimented you this morning. And if you recently achieved something fantastic, you should be able to feel great about it, even if your partner hasn't yet acknowledged it.

Finally, work towards building trust in your relationship. Trust is built in the everyday interactions we have with the people around us. If there is no emotional interaction, then you cannot build trust with that person. Don't force a person to share with you emotionally, or understand your emotional needs. Trust usually develops over time, through a back and forth of give and take. I tell you a small secret. You tell me a small secret. I make a confession about my feelings. Then you make a confession about yours. Each exchange of these intimate details and feelings gets you deeper and deeper into a relationship of trust. What you might be surprised by though, is how you may be the one holding back for fear that your step might not be reciprocated. My best advice here is to start small, but also start first. Don't wait for your partner to guide you into a level of deep trust, because you never know, your partner may be waiting for your guidance as well. Somebody has to go first, and it might as well be you.

If you and your partner both want to build a stronger emotional relationship, then the underlying assumptions and fears that either party holds must be identified, openly communicated to one another, and then faced and challenged. From a selfish perspective, your feelings may seem a higher priority than your partner's, but you must also make sure that your partner's feelings are secure as well. It doesn't work as a one-way street. When you and your partner tend to each other's emotional needs, a strong trust between you will be formed and your fears of abandonment will be reduced.

# Chapter 15: Identity Crises

As I got older and started to see life from a new pair of glasses. I didn't like how I felt about me and as I took time to really search some things out I discovered I didn't know really who I was nor what I was doing here in the earth. That really bothered me. I was a drug addict that grow up pleasing people and being the giver as well as the taker. I would start something and would self-destruct. I would always hear those voices in my mind that would tell me I was going to fail at it or I would just give up are do something that didn't make sense to cause things to go a totally different direction. I had no understanding of who I really was not what I wanted to be because I was too busy pleasing others. I lost me in the mist of becoming a people pleaser. I started to look in the word of God for answers to my dilemma. I had to find out who I was because I didn't like the person that looked back at me in the mirror. I believed there was nothing good I was going to accomplish based on what was told to me throughout life. Gen 1:27 spoke to me. It said "**So God created man in his own image, in the image of God he created him; male and female he created them.**" This verse change how I looked at myself. I was told that I would never amount to nothing but God said I was created in His image meaning I have abilities that He has so I can do great things with my life. That woke something up within me. I had many wonderful opportunities but couldn't hold on to none of them. I would always do something that would cause me to lose out. But to see that I was created in His image dis-spelled the lies I believed for so many years. I had read this verse many times but this time it spoke to me in a way like never before. I was led to Jer 1:5: "**before I formed you in the womb I knew you, and before you were born I consecrated you; I appointed you a prophet to the nations.**"

This blew my mind because it told me that I had purpose before I was even born and that God knew me. I was important to Him is what I heard in the spirit that brought tears to my eyes. For so long I felt that God didn't love me because of the way my family treated me and talked about me. But He told me something different and I needed to hear it. All these scriptures I had read before but this night I was hearing God and receiving all He had for me. I share with you what took place in me that turned my life around. This was a lonely time for me because I was away from my family my kids everyone I know was on the other side of town. I received no calls nor did people come and visit. I recall saying to myself no one loves me. Then God spoke to me and said I have you all to myself. I have put you into a cocoon and when you come out you will be a beautiful butterfly and you will fly away.

From that point I didn't need to be around anyone but the Father. I found my identity in the word of God. As I read the Lord showed me who I was and whose I was. I felt alive; I wasn't a misplaced nobody with no purpose or abilities. I have purpose; this blew my mind and I begin to feel empowered, like I wasn't scared of people. I began to stand up telling people how I felt about things like I never had before. I know I was called into ministry. I ran from it because I felt who would listen to me. I wanted attention, and the man behind the pulpit seem to get a lot of it; so I thought "that's why I wanted to teach the word of God!"

The Lord showed me myself ministering to a field of people so many people I said yes to the call and my life changed from that point. I had a direction to go and a destiny to reach. It took some time for it to get into my heart that I was going to be used in this capacity. I battled, and even today going around family members can be difficult because those old thoughts bring old emotions and feelings that bring about actions. I don't try to please people today; I please my Father in heaven to the best of my ability and doing that brings peace within me. I'm still not where I want to be but I thank God I'm not where I use to be. I didn't know any other way to write this last chapter but to share with you my story. I hope you can take from it some things that can help you overcome the rejection that has had you bound to a way of living that is not pleasing to you or to the Lord. There is so much more in you that hasn't been tapped into yet. Finding out who you are can only be discovered by seeking God for the answer. His word will tell you many are in an identity crises and have no understanding to who you really are in Christ.

This will lay the foundation of everything else that you will experience as you come to know that true you. Understand we all are born with a purpose there is something that the Lord has for us to do on the earth. That too is found in Him. Matthew 6:33 tells us to **"Seek first the Kingdom of God and all His righteousness and everything thing will be added onto you."**

To move out of the mindset that comes from being rejected we must seek God for restoration of mind body and spirit. We can't do it no other way. He is our source. As we learned about the power of forgiveness in the last chapter that closes the door to many things that has power over us to sway our thinking and actions one way or another. There are those thoughts that overpower us they are called strongmen they must be bound and put away. All this comes from the word of the living God.

As we accept the truth of His word we will feel the freedom that is taking place within. You will have to deal with some people in a harsh loving way because some just won't respect you until you stand up for yourself. Boldness is needed as you take your stand. When people treat and talk to you in a hurtful and disrespectful way there not going to stop because you have changed. In love we must stand up and speak up for ourselves. No one is going to do it for you. This is do or die, and once you walk in this boldness that is in you, you will feel good about yourself because you stood up for you and that is showing that your important and you're somebody that is worthy of respect.

Parents as you have gone through this book you might see where you're feeling guilt for the way you might have been in bringing up your kids. Guilt isn't from God so stop it. I had to go to my children and tell them I'm sorry. If I knew what I know now it would have been different. I felt so bad I did so much and hurt them so bad and even today I see the effects of my actions. All I can do is pray and be the best father I can be as they allow it. Talk to your kids about what you're feeling and why you're feeling it. Live out the words you speak to them and resurrect that relationship and love the hell out of them. And your teens that might have picked up this book understand that you are not what people say you are you have greatness in you.

Surround yourself with people that encourage you and love you and support you and interacts with you. Many parents have been through many things that children have no clue of and it affects their abilities of being all they can be. We all have done, or are doing that best we know how. Young adults love your mother. And if that fathers is trying to come back into your life give him a chance to be the father you need and he wants to be. Rejection had destroyed some really good families and have taken children and send them out into the world with the belief that they will never amount to anything. It's time to come together and unify. We must begin to take time out and spend quality time with our children let them know not by words but actions that they are loved so that this spirit of rejection will have to go back a dry place. I want to pray for you as you completed this book. Take it from me if He can do it for me He will do it for you just trust Him and watch your life transform before your eyes. Lord in Jesus name I pray that as my brother or sister has completed the reading of this book that your anointing will shift their hearts and minds to come closer to you. I speak life not death over them now in the name of Jesus. Release your glory over their lives now Lord and lead them in the direction you will have them to go. I cancel all assignment and break all curses that has kept them bound in a state of rejection. Loose them now in Jesus name. Holy Ghost fire, burn out of their heart everything that is hindering them from becoming who you created them to be. You Lord are a lamb under our feet and a light directing our path. I thank you Lord for what your about to do in the life of my brother or sister. Keep them, protect them, and show them who they are in you. In Jesus' name, Amen.

# Chapter 16: Getting Back to Where it All Began

Just like any other fear, the key in getting rid of this fear is to confront it directly.

You need to dig deep, and try to figure out exactly when and how this all started. With most of us, the fear of abandonment and other fears started in our childhood, the most vulnerable time of our lives. So think back to your earliest memories, and try to pinpoint what may have caused it. Did your parents work a lot, leaving you on your own? Did your old brother join the military and you never knew if or when he'd be coming home? Did you get lost at the zoo during a class field trip and think you'd never find your way back? It could be anything, and it may even be multiple things. Start brainstorming and see what you come up with.

Children are very susceptible human beings, absorbing everything that happens before them in their environment. They have limited experience of the world, and take on everything that is taught to them or happens to them. They have malleable minds like playdough, and the simplest of events can change behaviors in an instance. This is why fears are mostly started in childhood - the adult brain is more developed with its own belief systems, and therefore less susceptible to taking on new fears.

One of the reasons that these fears surface in us sometimes, is the influence our parents had on our development. Not every case of a fear of abandonment is from the parent actually leaving the home. A child can feel neglected and alone, while their parents are right there sitting next to them. These fears often stem from emotional non-support, or else bad communication that occurs between the child and the parent. The parent will either ignore the child when they need interaction most, or discourage the child from coming to them because they are so unapproachable. Basic things like threatening and scolding a child can cause fear and resentment. Most of these issues are simply miscommunications between the parent and the child, wherein the child doesn't understand what he or she has done wrong, and the parent does not understand what exactly the child needs.

Actual abandonment by a parent – when one parent does actually leave the home – tends to have a more significant impact on a child. But then again, in homes where the remaining parent stayed and took wonderful emotional care of the child, he or she may have ended up perfectly fine. But in a lot of cases, being 'abandoned' by even one parent causes great emotional and psychological distress, especially when he or she was close to that parent. The child will feel betrayed, and oftentimes will wonder what they did wrong to make their parent leave. If you've ever thought these things, it's time now to fully comprehend the fact that you did nothing wrong, and sometimes these things just happen. If you had had a parent that raised you alone, be grateful for that one parent. If you didn't have any, be thankful for the person that raised you as their own as well. Gratitude is a powerful tool that can help you to accept what happened in your past in a different, more positive light.

Then, sadly, there are those whose parents died. Death is a very traumatizing event for anyone, especially for children. Do not suppress the memories. Instead, understand what happened, and remember all the great memories you had while they were still here with you. Of course, you will still feel heartbroken from the absence, but you will feel a whole lot better if you keep the good memories close to your heart, and allow the bad ones to fade away.

The majority of our fears develop during our childhood years, but a lot of our fears also develop during our adult years as well. One would think that because we are wiser as adults, we should be able to handle our fears better. However, we often partake in habits and behaviors that, unknowingly, can make those fears even worse. One of the fears in our adult stage that we develop is the fear of rejection. We all want a mate, and in doing so, we go about talking to those of the opposite sex that we like, in the hopes of starting a relationship with them. But at one point or another, we will all experience the feeling of rejection. It is not a nice feeling, and when it happens, our self-esteem can take a nose-dive to an all time low as we ask ourselves a thousand questions about what went wrong. This fear of rejection then feeds into our fear of abandonment, as we fear that the person we do ultimately end up having a relationship with will also eventually reject us and leave.

One needs to understand that when someone rejects us, that does not always mean that something is inherently wrong with us. This is important, and embracing this truth will save you a lot of pain. Think about all the times you were rejected. Then smile, and understand that there was nothing wrong with you. Not everyone will always like you, just as you will not always like everyone. And that's OK. Think about it this way: If everybody likes everybody, then any two people could be in a relationship, which would make being in a relationship pretty mundane and insignificant. What makes a partnership so special is the fact that it can't just be with anybody.

Finally, our fears often stem from us not knowing the future, or even our uncertainty of the present. It seems to be human nature to fear the unknown, and we create objects, legends, stories, and myths in our minds to try and explain them. This lack of knowledge has a tendency to cause intense emotional turmoil. But should we seek to gain knowledge on these unknowns? Should we visit crystal ball fortune tellers or palm readers? No. The beauty of life is such that you simply don't need to know certain things. However, it doesn't hurt to ask your partner about anything that you want to know. If your partner believes you should know, then you will be told. But don't force the issue, and don't let it grow into a bigger problem in your mind.

Whether our fears developed in our childhood, or our adulthood, much of the problem can be fixed by embracing one simple concept: Acceptance. But more on that later

# Chapter 17: Forgiveness Is Key

The traditional family dynamics are quickly becoming obsolete. With less intimacy within or homes we reside under the same roof but have no real knowledge upon who the people in our home really are. With cell phones, texting and social networks being the new means of communication, it makes it easier to hide behind the screens and not share feelings, emotions and ambitions with one another. Parents are also working longer hours, past retirement age due to an unstable economy in the earth. This has a way of keeping people oppressed, working to survive and not being able to enjoy life in the latter years as or great grandparents did back in the 50's and 60's.

As stated in the first chapters of the book, abandonment started to pick up momentum when the economy called for both parents to be breadwinners. Children were left and rejection began to infiltrate the American homes like never before. Children were not nurtured as their parents where. Nor did they receive the quality time needed for bonding, and in some cases attention wasn't shown because of the demand from the job and the need for income to support the growing family of the 60's. Many of those abandoned children entered into parenting without full knowledge and preparation of raising up a child. Most did the best they could with what they seen in their home and some simply couldn't cope with the responsibility of being a parent at all.

Parenting is more than supply a roof over a child's head and putting food on the table and cloths on their back. There are emotional and spiritual needs each child must have and is needed to be whole.

Regardless of age and status, everyone desires love from their parents. The sad truth is some parents are just not capable of giving or receiving love. When you come from a home that love wasn't shown it's hard to give or receive what you never got, and based on what you might think about yourself, it could make it even harder to give love as well. You can' give what you don't have. As the generations continued things didn't get any better, believe it or not it got a lot worse.

Parenting isn't for the selfish, ego driven, attention seeking narcissistic type of individuals, but if we honestly look at it this is what we have become, those of us that grow up rejected and abandoned. We must heal from the past, and that starts with forgiving and seeking the Father's love. Only the love of God can heal your wounds. God's love brings total restoration and will create in you a new heart and empathy for the parent(s) who hurt you and for others. Ps 36:7-8; **"how precious is your unfailing love, O God!"** All humanity finds shelter in the shadow of your wings. You feed them from the abundance of your own house, letting them drink from your river of delight. Forgiveness is the doorway to healing. When we forgive those that have abandoned, abused and hurt you, you give God permission to heal every pain and He will show you the gains from the pain. It is said what doesn't kill you will only make you stronger. In my life I have found that through the painful times I grew and matured in many areas. I couldn't see it in the mist of going through but looking back I can say pain made me stronger. Many find it hard to let go of the things that happened as a child. Don't let unforgiveness from the past destroy your future. Unforgiveness will keep one in bitterness and to be critical of others.

Without God healing your wounds, we may end up being the very person we don't want to be, just like that mother or father we said we would never be like. God has commanded His people to walk in love as He is love, to forgive as we have been forgiven and to live peaceably with others in the earth. True forgiveness can only come when we surrender it all to God. Forgiveness doesn't come to us naturally but when we are in Christ, we are new creatures all old things have passed away behold all things have become new. We also know forgiveness and healing does take time so we have to constantly rely on God. Being human we miss the mark often, but we must stay committed to living our life-like the one who has adopted us.

Heb 4:15 – **"For we have not a high priest which cannot be touched with the feeling of our infirmities; but was in all points tempted like as we are, yet without sin."** Jesus overcame all the things of this world and through Him we can overcome our feelings and emotions also. Jesus suffered rejection from His family and his creation. But through it all He forgave each and every one of those that betrayed Him.

For some time, I had a deep seated anger for my step-father. As I look back, I can see that the more I said to myself that I will never be like him the more I was becoming worse than he ever was. As the unforgiveness set's in it opens the door for rejection and anger and rage. These were the same things that were in my father that led him to be the way he was, and those same ways manifested in me in a greater way. They call this a generational curse. Each generation seems to get worse than the other until we end up with raging kids running around killing each other and their parents. Sounds much like the world we live in today doesn't it? If you are wanting to live a life of total peace and true love you must invite the Prince of peace and the love of God into your life to restore you. This is where it starts with a relationship with Jesus Christ. We must find out through Christ who we are. We all were created with an identity and a purpose but in our trying to fit in and being something we weren't we lost ourselves. We spent much of our lives looking at ourselves and seeing within ourselves what others said about us. Words like your no good, you will never amount to nothing, who would ever want you and so on and so forth. See yourself as God sees you. "**If anyone is in Christ, he is a new creation**" (2 Corinthians 5:17) You are special to the Father and the more you speak His words about you to yourself you will begin to believe it and all those old tapes will start to go away as there being replaced with new words you speak to yourself about yourself. Many people on the earth wonder why they are here and for what reason? This is a question all of us have asked ourselves at one time or another. Knowing your identity in Christ will close the doors to those questions. As the spirit of the Lord reminds you of your true identity that is in Him you must embrace it. God is your

Father - How great is the love the Father has lavished on us, that we should be called children of God! And that is what we are! (1 John 3:1).

You are a child of the most-high God. An heir to the throne. Your father has a kingdom in heaven and you are a prince in it. Your royalty this is who you are. Embrace it. Knowing who you are I mean the true you will free you to walk, talk and live in a way like never before. It is true that the truth will make you free from all the mess you thought about yourself. You are a child of the living God and there is nothing that you nor I can do about it. Once you give your life to Him Sincerely His love will never leave you or forsake you. Many look at God as their parents or people on the earth. God tells us that His ways are not our way's and His thoughts aren't our thoughts He is God and God alone and with a father like that how can you go wrong. Here are some scriptures to recite that will help you know how your Father sees you

• Because of God's great love for us, we are adopted into His family [1 John 3:1], and made joint heirs with Christ [Romans 8:17]

• We are made to sit in heavenly places (of authority over all demons, sickness, etc.) with Christ [Ephesians 2:6]

• We are blessed with all spiritual blessings in Christ [Ephesians 1:3]

• We are the righteousness of Christ through faith, thus being made right before God [Romans 3:22]

• We are entitled to a clean conscience before God because of the Blood and can have full assurance of faith when we go before Him [Hebrews 10:22]

• Our sins have been removed from us as far as the east is from the west [Psalms 103:12],

• And God Himself has chosen not to remember our failures [Hebrews 8:12]

• We are loved with the same love that the Father has for Jesus Himself! [John 17:23]

As your mind is being renewed by the words spoken about who you are in the eyes of God we begin to think about ourselves differently. How people treat us doesn't take us back to a dark lonely place and as our past tries to come to tear us down we're able to stand against it and hold on to the peace and happiness we have from within. In the next chapter we will be looking at implementing new way of living as we begin heal and become who we are created to be.

# Chapter 18: Forgiving and Forgetting the Past

The final step in abandoning your fears is probably the hardest thing to do for any human being. Forgiveness is something we want from others, yet we find it so difficult to give it ourselves. And what could be harder than forgiving someone who probably doesn't deserve it? But for our mental state of mind and our health, we must. Your refusing to forgive the past is fueling your fears of abandonment right now, and if you don't forgive and forget the person(s) or the traumatic event, then you will forever live in the past, which affects your present as well as destroys your future.

To forgive someone, you must first understand that the hate and resentment you are giving someone is not in any way harming them. Actually, it is only hurting you. Nelson Mandela once said that resentment is like drinking poison and waiting for it to kill your enemy. If you really want revenge against your enemies, or the person that hurt you in the past, live a happy and successful life. Be focused, and ensure that your current relationships don't end up like the ones in the past. Live life as if the events in the past never happened.

When you think of all the traumatizing experiences in the past that made you feel lonely, think of what it made you become, instead of how it made you feel. If you think about the person you have become, you will focus more on the positive and less on the negative. Be kind to yourself, and don't blame yourself for anything that has happened. A lot of the time, when things go wrong, we blame ourselves. This shouldn't be the case. Be kind and patient with yourself, and give yourself time to heal. You should also be open to the healing process, as your fears can sometimes cause you to lock up emotionally.

One of the most important steps you can do in forgiving and forgetting your past is to learn to **trust in the future**. You have to remember that not all humans are untrustworthy, and you shouldn't shut yourself away from the possibility of having a great time with someone else. But at the same time, you can't be naïve. Because the reality is, not everyone will have your best interests at heart. So you need to learn how to balance your trust with your instinct and internal wisdom. Wisdom will help you identify the ways in which you can prevent yourself from getting hurt. This is not an easy step, as it is often very hard to balance your wisdom and your trust. But once you have found the balance, you will be well on your way to forming healthier relationships.

The final step in forgiving is to forget. Forgiving and forgetting is often used together, because without forgetting, we often end up not ever truly being able to forgive. Sometimes, you will have to move away from the person to actually do that, and that's fine. But it is important to put the person's actions to the back of your mind. If your parent or guardian abandoned you, sometimes it takes the unthinkable act of thinking from their perspective to understand why they may have left, and forgive them. If they somehow turn up in your adult life, ensure that you talk to them and gain their perspective. From there, you can decide whether to accept them back into your life or not. But it really is important to forgive and forget in order to overcome your fears.

# Chapter 19: Fear of Rejection

As a child that has been abandoned and rejected grows up into adulthood many traumatic things that may have transpired in their childhood can lead them into a protection mode. When the people that brought them into this world can't be trusted, and has hurt them in many different ways as they mature into adulthood doors to fear of rejection can open and have a long lasting effect in their life if not attended to. The bible says in Psalm 55:5 that "**Fear and trembling have come on me, and horror has covered me.**" Fear can become a major problem in their lives of these crippled adults.

Most of their life have been lived in fear of the future and people. In some cases, there are those that are petrified at the thought of meeting a person for the first time or asking a person out on a date. Growing up not knowing what to expect from the people in their lives leaves them in a state of fear, and as they grow up they learn how to cope with the mindsets and emotions in ways that aren't healthy and in some cases aren't legal. Growing into adulthood with a fear of rejection can lead to an unproductive life. Fear paralyzes a person from moving. If you're fearful of being rejected by people there are many things that you will not do, and if you walk through the fear and do them you will find it difficult in some ways because your mind will speak against your movement forward telling you what you heard most of your life. You will never amount to nothing, you're good for nothing, and that word "NO" Don't get me wrong "NO" needs to be spoken to a child and teens in this generation, but when it's used in a negative way like; will you help me with my school project? No ask your dad, or can we have a day for us and no one else? No can't you see I'm busy. No to request like these leave scars that if not dealt with will carry over into adulthood to affect their lives in a negative way that can paralyze and cripple them from prospering.

As a child becomes a young adult and steps out into the world there are many things that they will come against and suffering from rejection and fear of it only makes it worse. Here is a list of areas that fear of rejection can affect. Although not every person experiences every impact, the fear of rejection tends to affect their ability to succeed across a wide range of personal and professional situations. These are some of the most common situations I've come across in my own life dealing with fear of rejection as a young adult.

Dating: First dates, and especially blind dates, are scary for anyone, but those with a fear of rejection may quickly become overwhelmed. Rather than focusing on getting to know the other person and deciding whether they would like a second date, you might spend all of their time worrying whether that person likes them. Trouble speaking, obsessive worrying about their own appearance, an inability to eat and a visibly nervous demeanor are common. People dealing with the fear of rejection try to be someone there not to impress the person their out with.

Doing everything they can to impress them but not understanding that the person they are is being forgotten about and that's the person they expected to see on the date. We can destroy something that could have been a good things trying to be more than what we are because in the back of our minds we feel they are going to reject us and that motivates them to take on another identity instead of the one they were born with. Humans are social creatures, and we are expected to follow basic social niceties in public. Most of the time, idle chatter in the grocery store line or at a festival lasts only a few moments. Occasionally, however, short conversations lead to lifelong friendships. If you have a fear of rejection, you may feel unable to chat with strangers or even friends of a friends. The tendency to keep to yourself could potentially prevent you from making lasting connections with others. This was a hard one for me. Being called into ministry but through the rejection I went through as a child it was hard for me to talk when all eyes were on me. I would just break out in a sweat, what I wanted to say wouldn't come out right because I would be thinking about those words spoken over me as a child; You're never going to amount to anything. Those words have a way of ringing in our mind, and paying attention to that voice will have a negative affect most of the time.

Peer Pressure: The need to belong is a basic human condition. In high school, we tend to be drawn to clicks. Jocks, cheerleaders, nerds, geeks, Goths, preppies, or any number of other small groups. As adults, we tend to draw to those that shared interests, relationship status, and other commonalities. While dressing, speaking and behaving as a group member is not unhealthy peer pressure sometimes goes too far. If your fear of rejection leads you to do things that are illegal, immoral or simply distasteful to you, then peer pressure might be a problem in your life.

Marriage: Married life consists of an unending series of negotiations and compromises. No matter how compatible you may be, it is impossible for two people to agree on everything. Those with a fear of rejection often have difficulty expressing their own needs and standing their ground. You might also develop feelings of jealousy or distrust in your partner as your fear of rejection turns into a fear of being abandoned. This is sometimes expressed in such unhealthy behaviors as checking your partner's phone messages or social network accounts.

Job Interviews: Have you ever felt warm and uncomfortable while waiting to be called for an interview? Sweaty palms, labored breathing, an increased heart rate and trouble speaking are common symptoms of the fear of rejection. They are also potential reasons for an employer to reject a candidate. Confidence and authority are critical in many positions, and those suffering from this fear often come across as weak and insecure. If you have a fear of rejection, you may also have trouble negotiating a work contract, leaving valuable pay and benefits on the table. Now here are some common behaviors in those with a fear of rejection.

Phoniness: Many people who are afraid of rejection develop a carefully monitored and scripted way of life. Fearing that you will be rejected if you show your true self to the world, you may l live life behind a mask. This can make you seem phony and inauthentic to others, and may cause a rigid unwillingness to embrace life's challenges. People-Pleasing: Although it is natural to want to take care of those that we love, those who fear rejection often go too far. You might find it impossible to say no, even when saying yes causes major inconveniences or hardships in your own life. You may take on too much, increasing your own risk for burnout. At the extreme, people-pleasing sometimes turns into enabling the bad.

Passive-Aggressiveness: Uncomfortable showing their true selves but unable to entirely shut out their own needs, many people who fear rejection end up behaving in passive-aggressive ways. You might procrastinate, "forget" to keep promises, complain, and work inefficiently on the projects that they take on. In addition, the fear of rejection often stops them from going after their dreams. Putting yourself out there is frightening for anyone, but if you have the fear of rejection, you may become paralyzed and never take a step. Hanging onto the status quo feels safe, even if you are not happy with your current situation. Whether you want to travel the world, write the Great American novel or ask the girl that sits next to you for a date, the fear of rejection may stop you from taking a step. You might make excuses or even assist the person in behaviors you know are wrong.

Unassertiveness: People with a fear of rejection often go out of their way to avoid confrontations. You might refuse to ask for what you want or even to speak up for what you need. A common tendency is to try to simply shut down your own needs or pretend that they don't matter. The fear of rejection leads to behaviors that make us appear insecure, ineffectual and overwhelmed. You might sweat, shake, fidget, avoid eye contact, and even lose the ability to effectively communicate.

While individuals react to these behaviors in very different ways, these are some of the reactions you might see. Rejection: Ironically, the fear of rejection often becomes a self-fulfilling prophecy. It is well-known in pop psychology that confidence enhances attractiveness. A 2009 study at the University of Florida actually shows that confidence is nearly as important as intelligence in determining our income level! As a general rule, the lack of self-confidence that is inherent in the fear of rejection makes one more likely to be rejected. Manipulation: Some people prey on the insecurities of others. Those who suffer from a fear of rejection may be at greater risk of being manipulated for someone else's personal gain. Expert manipulators generally come across as charming, suave and genuinely caring. They know what buttons to push to make others trust them. They also know how to keep someone with a fear of rejection feeling slightly "on edge," as if the manipulator might leave at any time. Almost invariably, the manipulator does end up leaving once she or he has gotten what they want out of the other person. Frustration: Most people in the world are decent, honest and forthright. Rather than manipulating someone with a fear of rejection, they will try to help.

Look for signs that your friends and family are trying to encourage your assertiveness, asking you to be more open with them, or probing your true feelings. Many times, however, people who fear rejection see these attempts to help as signs of a possible future rejection. This often leads friends and family to "walk on eggshells," fearful of making your fears worse. Over time, they may become frustrated and angry, either confronting you about your behavior or beginning to distance themselves from you. 2 Timothy 1:7: **"For God has not given us the spirit of fear, but of power and of love and of a sound mind."**

# Chapter 20: Relationships and the Fear of Rejection

The fear of abandonment is highly personalized. Some people are afraid solely of losing a romantic partner. Others fear suddenly finding themselves completely alone. Either way, I have found that people with a fear of abandonment often follow one of a few basic patterns. Before we look at the patterns for those with a fear of abandonment, let's look at the way I think a typical relationship may involve. It is especially true for romantic relationships, but there are many similarities in close friendships as well.

Getting to Know Each Other: At this point, you may feel relatively safe. You are not yet emotionally invested in the other person, so you continue to live your life while enjoying time with your chosen person. The

Honeymoon Phase: This is when you make the choice to commit. You are willing to overlook possible red or yellow flags, because you just get along so well. You start spending a great deal of time with one another, you feel peaceful within yourself, and you start to feel secure with your mate.

The Real Relationship: The honeymoon phase cannot last forever. No matter how well two people get along, real life always intervenes. People get sick, have family problems, start working difficult hours, worry about money, and need time to get things done. Although this is a very normal and positive step in a relationship, it can be terrifying for those with a fear of abandonment, who may see it as a sign that the other person is pulling away. If you have this fear, you are probably battling with yourself and trying very hard not to express your worries and fear of appearing clingy.

The Slight: People are human. They have foibles and moods and things on their minds. Regardless of how much they care for someone else, they cannot and should not be expected to always have that person at the forefront of their minds. Especially once the honeymoon period is over, it is inevitable that a seeming slight will occur. This often takes the form of an unanswered text message or unreturned phone call, or a request for a few days of alone time. For those with a fear of abandonment, this is a turning point. If you have this fear, you are probably completely convinced that the slight is a sign that your partner no longer loves you.

What happens next is almost entirely determined by the fear of abandonment, its severity and the sufferer's preferred coping style. Some people handle this by becoming clingy and demanding, insisting that their partner prove his love by jumping through hoops outlined by the fearful partner. Others run away, rejecting their partners before they are rejected. Still others feel that the slight is their fault, and attempt to transform themselves into the perfect partner in a quest to keep the other person from leaving. From the partner's point of view, your sudden personality shift seems to come from out of left field.

If the partner does not suffer from a fear of abandonment, they probably don't have the slightest idea why his previously confident, laid-back partner is suddenly acting clingy and demanding, smothering them with attention, or pulling away altogether. Similar to phobias, it is impossible to simply talk or reason someone out of a fear of abandonment. No matter how many times your partner tries to reassure you, it will simply not be enough. Eventually, your behavior patterns and inconsolability could drive your partner away, ironically leading to the conclusion that you fear the most. In reality, the slight is most likely not a slight at all. As mentioned, people are simply people, and sometimes they do things that their partners do not understand.

In a healthy relationship, the slight may or may not even be acknowledged as such. The partner may simply recognize it for what it is, a normal reaction that has little or nothing to do with the relationship. Or they may feel slighted, but address it with either a calm discussion or a brief argument. Either way, a single slight is not promoted to dominating importance in determining the partner's feelings.

If your fear is mild and well-controlled, you may be able to get a handle on it simply by becoming educated about your tendencies and learning new behavior strategies. For most people though, the fear of abandonment is rooted in deep-seated issues that are difficult to unravel alone. Professional assistance is often required to work through this fear and build the self-confidence needed to truly change your thoughts and behaviors. Although treating the fear is critical, it is also essential to build a feeling of belonging. Rather than focusing all of your energy and devotion on a single partner, focus on building a community. No one person can solve all of our problems or meet all of our needs. But a solid group of several close friends can each play an important role in our lives. Many people with a fear of abandonment state that they never felt like they had any true friends when they were growing up. For whatever reasons, they always felt disconnected from those around them, But the good news is that it's never too late. Whatever your current stage of life is it's important to surround yourself with other like-minded individuals. Make a list of your current hobbies, passions, and dreams. Then find others who share your interests. While it is true that not everyone who shares an interest will become a close friend hobbies and dreams are an excellent stepping stone toward building a solid support network.

Working on your passions also helps build self-confidence and the belief that you are strong enough to cope with whatever life throws your way. Rejection causes people to create defense mechanisms so they can protect themselves. The most important defense mechanism of Rejection is to withdraw like a turtle in a shell for protection. There is a fear of being vulnerable. We don't allow ourselves to trust anyone because we don't want to be hurt again. The reason for withdrawal is Fear; Fear of man, Fear of woman, Fear of God. Some people are more afraid of man than they are of God. We avoid close relationships. There is nothing in life but opportunity. Their security is fear.

Fear of rejection is another defense mechanism that causes withdrawal. You lose the battle in your mind before anything happens. Fear of abandonment comes with Rejection but is easily defeated when you read Isaiah 54. It says the Lord Himself has accepted you. No matter what your problem is. Isaiah 53 and 54 is the foundation for freedom from Rejection because if God be for us, who can be against us? When we feel rejected, we are agreeing with our enemy the devil. Love and acceptance is the antidote to Rejection. The reversal of Rejection is accepting God's love. According to the word of God, you are designed and created on purpose for His pleasure because He foreknew you before the very foundation of the world. Know who you are in Christ. Knowing who you are in Christ is of prime importance. This is the antidote to an identity crisis. The Father has accepted you, but have you accepted yourself? Rejection will not allow you to accept yourself. Self -Rejection, Self-Hatred, Guilt, images, impressions and emotions will tell you that you are not the fairest of them all. He has accepted you through Jesus Christ. John 3:16 tells us; for God so loved the world, that he gave his only begotten Son, that whosoever believeth in him should not perish, but have everlasting life. The Lord had to deal with Rejection. He showed it was possible to defeat it and not make it part of His life. In His strength, as a work of the Holy Spirit, the Lord, the Father and the Holy Spirit will be there to meet you and remove Rejection from your life so that you can be free from it and have peace. The prerequisites for freedom from Fear of Rejection are:

1) Making peace with God once and for all.

2) Making peace with yourself once and for all.

3) Making peace with your brothers and sisters once and for all (even if it is 70 times 7 in your relationship of forgiveness).

With Furious Love, Forgiveness is the key to freedom from the fear of rejection. You must forgive those that hurt you, and the person that hurt you the most was yourself. You must forgive yourself from the hurt you caused yourself. Remember it starts with you. You must also make peace with God. Ask Him to forgive you, ask him to show you how to walk talk and life a life free from rejection. And last but not lest forgive you brothers and sister. This will close port-holes and doors that Satan is using to kill, steal and destroy your life and your purpose. It's time to take back what is rightfully. Are you ready? Let's Go

## Conclusion

Getting rid of your fear of abandonment is crucial. We all want to belong, and if we have these fears, they will affect us for the rest of our lives by how we relate with those around us. Many people who have these issues tend to want to fix the problem only for those around them. Wrong. Ensure that you build a community, and focus more on trusting the world at large. One person cannot solve or fit all our needs, which is why we need to ensure that we build stronger relationships with those around us. If you have only one close friend, try and turn that into a larger pack of friends. This will help you to feel more connected with those around you, and you won't have those feelings of being left out anymore.

Surround yourself with those who enjoy the things that you do. Make a list of the things you love - whether it's sports, reading, gardening, traveling, playing tennis, or listening to music - and find others who share those interests. You don't have to become best of friends, but doing this will ensure that you build a better support network. This will in turn build your self-esteem and your self-confidence. Add that to the steps discussed earlier, and you will be on your way to living a much happier life!

# Book Three
# THE ADDICTION RECOVERY WORKBOOK

## Introduction

*With this highly in-depth, workbook*, I want to inspire and help you to take back control over your own life by not letting addiction be the guiding force of your life anymore. I will share the same simple steps I to go through to quit the worst of the worst bad habits, and addiction. I made it a very practical workbook that will help you instantly. It will guide you into better understanding your addiction and the reasons for it. Most importantly, this workbook will give you the tools to solve the problems your addiction has caused and to be proactive in creating a meaningful, joyful life. A life where you will be strong and secure enough to deal with the inevitable problems of life. And where you will deal with these problems consciously, without hiding in the horrific claws of addiction.

The time indicated under the steps is a mere indication. It could help to follow this timetable, in order to make your addiction process more attainable. If for whatever reason you won't go cold turkey or your goal is only to stop overindulging in your addictive behaviour, I absolutely welcome you aboard. I want to inspire you to take back control of your life. For almost all addicts, that eventually means quitting altogether. But it's up to you. Take your time if you need it.

You could also be the opposite. I've heard from many addicts that they feel an immense power after they've decide to quit all together. If you're one of those, you could definitely speed up the process. I recommend to those people to read the entire workbook at once and start applying the steps immediately.

However, recovery doesn't simply require the fulfillment of some steps.

Especially when accounting for the processes of revealing what kind of feelings you are trying to hide by turning to your addiction, recovery is a procedure that could take months. But even in those months, you can take giant steps to proactively deal with the consequences of your addiction, building up inner strength to combat your addictive cravings. And most importantly you can find meaning in your life by working on your talents, connecting with others and enjoying life to the fullest.

# Chapter 1: Quitting the Pattern

The first step in your journey to a new life without addiction is a simple one. Just don't do it anymore. Don't smoke your cigarette anymore, stop going to the casino, stop overeating. Simple, right?

Simple, yes. Easy, no. Not at all.

Quitting your addiction might as well be one of the hardest things in the world. It means conquering an ingrained habit. It means changing something that you've been doing day in and day out, for a long period of time. It has become second nature. And whatever we say about addiction, it is something that has helped you enormously over the last few years. It has protected you when you needed it most. The addiction numbed your deep feelings of pain. But since you've purchased this workbook, you and I both know that those days are numbered. No longer is the addiction the solution. The addiction is an even worse place, despite its distraction from your deepest pains. Today will be the first step on your journey to change. You have finally woken up from a long nightmare.

Quitting your addiction? Do it smart.

This is really important. As stated in the disclaimer and in the note to the reader, this book is not intended to act as a substitute for medical advice or treatment. Take this statement to heart. Going cold turkey isn't always safe when your addiction has become physical, such as in cases of alcohol or drugs. Keep this in mind. I was a heavy gambler, a true addict. I've tried to lessen my gambling behaviour before, but at a certain moment that simply wasn't helpful anymore. The only solution for me was to quit altogether. Find your way. Be honest with yourself. Quitting your addiction? Do it smart.

**Share, stop and seek help.**

One of the biggest breakthroughs I had during my recovery process was sharing my story. It was just after I had made an attempt to quit gambling altogether. This unfortunately wasn't my last attempt, but the sharing of my story was crucial in eventually conquering my addiction for good. It was on a Wednesday night, just the day before I went through a long and devastating gambling period. I lost almost 2000 Euros, which was a lot of money for me at that time. When I woke up the following day, I decided - no more! That night I called one of my dear friends. After some preliminary chit chat, I was finally courageous enough to share the real reason for my phone call.

"I have a problem, and it's been going on for quite some time now. It's a gambling problem."

I was at my parents' house at the time. Nobody was home. I remember walking through the house while telling the story. My friend listened, as the very best of friends tend to do, and he offered help. It was after one more relapses that I decided to take his help. Yet sharing my addiction story was one of the best feelings I had during those dark years of gambling. It lifted the weight off my back and eventually reassured me that I didn't have to be on this journey all by myself.

That's why my advice is to share your story.

It will take courage, but it will be a huge step to freedom - to breaking down your addiction. If there is someone in your life that you can share it with, someone that won't judge you, than that just might be the person to which you can tell your story. But practice the conversation in your head. This will make it easier when you have to do it in real life. Additionally, discussing the issue over a phone call might be easier than doing it face to face. If you don't have a friend, family member or someone else to call, share it somewhere else. There are online forums or Facebook groups for people with your addiction, where you can share your story either anonymously or not. Alternatively, you could share it with a professional, anonymously with a professional helpline (telephone or chat), or a support group.

This first step, like any other first step, could easily be the most difficult one. Sharing your dark, long-kept secret may be one of the most challenging hurdles you'll ever overcome. And it's worth the struggle. By sharing it, the heavy pressure of your addiction will feel lighter, and all of a sudden you're not alone in your fight anymore.

### Stop.

If you want to quit your addiction, there is no other way than to first say: 'It's over now, I'll quit.' Even if your purpose is only to lessen your addictive behaviour (for example by only gambling once per week with a specific budget, smoking three cigarettes a day, or drinking only two glasses of alcohol and only in the weekend), it's a great first step to stop altogether with your addictive behaviour for a period of time. It's crucial to be one hundred percent behind your decision to quit. If you're a spiritual person, it will help to ask your God for help in this process. If you're not spiritual, ask your Higher Self to guide and guard you in the quitting process.

The conscious decision of quitting your addiction, and actually stopping your addictive behaviour, are steps that are attainable for all addicts (except when it's a physical addiction and you need medical assistance). I absolutely believe that every addict, whether suffering from an addiction to pornography or overeating, social media or gaming, can stop his or her addiction for at least 24 hours. If you do it right, I am quite certain that you'll be able to add another 24 hours.

And another.

"When you make the conscious decision to quit your addiction, don't make it solely about the quitting itself; try to see what you could gain."

Don't make it harder for yourself than it needs to be. Only the act of reaching that first milestone of 24 hours should give you a reason to celebrate. So celebrate if you've made it to the first 24 hours, celebrate again when you make it to 48 hours, and so on. Do this for at least one week. Find a healthy pleasure that isn't your addiction, like watching a movie with friends, taking a walk in nature, or buying yourself a little present. We'll discuss these options further in step 2.

I know the horrors of addiction. That's why the quitting process should be something wonderful. Of course there are lots of responsibilities to attend to after you've quit, like financial consequences, health problems, needing another diet, and deteriorated relationships. And of course, we'll deal with these problems in step 3. But there's more. When you make the conscious decision to quit your addiction, don't make it solely about the quitting itself; try to see what you could gain. A life of freedom, however you define that for yourself. Wearing that beautiful dress with confidence, being able to buy you friends dinner, being in a great condition, having a wonderful night out without being mean, because you're drunk or on drugs, and so on. That joyous and compelling dream or, when you haven't really defined your ideal life yet, at least the absence of addictive horrors will move you forward in the first days of quitting your addiction.

### Seek help.

When you've made the decision to quit, don't be alone. You could share your decision with the friend, family, professional worker or group you've contacted to talk about your addiction. Asking for help doesn't make you weak; it is the only smart way to know your weaknesses and give yourself the extra power of another person to fight something as big as an addiction.

Define for yourself how you want to be helped. For example, the option of calling someone when you're having a really hard time with your addictive thoughts, having an accountability buddy, or simply ask the other person to give a suggest ways for them to could help you. For most addicts, it is one bridge too far to really seek professional help, and yes, there are other ways to do it. But it's going to be hard to do it all on your own. So at least share your story and find courage to ask for help in whatever way suits you best. Like we went over in **Share your story**, you could also do it anonymously, online, or with a professional helpline.

### Cut off resources.

What's critical in the quitting process is cutting off from resources that fuel your addiction. These could mean access to your money, to certain websites, to unhealthy food, alcohol, casinos, etc. By cutting yourself off from these resources, you will make it so much easier on yourself to actually follow through on your recovery. You could do this together with the person or group you've gone to for help.

When I made my final attempt to quit my gambling addiction, more than four years ago, I asked my good friend to take control of my bank account. He took over my banking passes and access to online banking. If you make it difficult for yourself to indulge in your addictive behaviour again, you have a better chance of succeeding.

It's very easy to start blaming yourself during this period. It can be devastating thinking about all the problems you've caused with your addiction... Stop for a moment and consider your achievement of this day.

The day you quit. The day you stood up to your addiction. A new beginning.

You need to be your own best friend in this period (and for the rest of your life). Pat yourself on the back for taking this enormous step to committing to quitting your addiction forever. It's probably the most courageous thing you've done in your life so far. A good way to emphasize this is by putting positive affirmations on sticky notes around your home or on your smartphone. There are countless free affirmation apps for your smartphone that can help you with this! Your life isn't over - far from it. Today is literally the start of a new life.

# Chapter 2: Replace Your Addiction & Find Peace

When you've made the incredible first step of quitting your addiction, you will be left with total freedom. But this freedom is not what we addicts are used to. The addiction was our strongest habit; without this we feel naked. And also probably in pain and bored. It's crucial in the first days and weeks after you've quit your addiction, to replace your addiction with something else. That is what we are going to do in step 2 of this workbook.

## Discover your pattern

A new life is awaiting you. How beautiful... Unfortunately, it's not only sunshine. Apart from the costs of your addictive behaviour, which we will cover in step 3, there is also an undeniable craving to go back to your old habits. These habits, however bad they were, were your ultimate comfort zone. Now, after a hard day of work, you won't allow yourself to drink a glass of wine, smoke a couple of cigarettes, eat a nice, big cheeseburger, or play World of Warcraft for three hours. No, you know for a fact that this addictive behaviour is only making life worse. But instead of taking the glass of wine, what do you have to do now?

You have to understand that our addiction comes from a craving.

I gambled whenever I was bored, irritated, depressed or had financial problems. My own feelings and circumstances lead me towards my addictive behaviour. The first step in replacing your addiction is understanding when you engaged in your addictive behaviour. This is a very practical approach, which will help you prevent relapses down the road or deal with them in a strong and constructive manner whenever they do occur. So take note of the moments when you started engaging in addictive behaviour. Think about circumstances, certain people, feelings and thoughts.

Write down as many details as you can think of. If you want, you could use the notes pages at the end of this workbook.

Next, look at all the moments you've written down and try to find a pattern. Are there certain feelings, thoughts, people or circumstances which led you inevitably towards your addictive behaviour? Write these patterns down. This will give you the golden information: **your addictive pattern.** Whenever this pattern occurs during the first weeks of your recovery process, remember that you can change the end result of the pattern.

In the first stages of conquering your addiction, you probably see your addiction as the enemy. It is important to get to know this **enemy**. Let the following quote guide you during these initial stages of your battle with addiction:

### Replace your addiction

When you know your pattern, you can change the outcome. You can also interrupt in the pattern. Later in this workbook we will go further into interrupting your pattern, but for now it's good to simply know your pitfalls.

To replace the outcome of addiction, find one or two easy alternatives fto your addiction that bring you pleasure. Don't think too hard on this, it should be something you like very much. In my first three weeks after quitting my addiction, I started watching The Sopranos. Besides that, I did an evening walk every day to clear my mind. I recommend to do one truly pleasurable activity where you don't have to be super engaged, and one thing to clear your mind, such as walking, sports, singing or meditation. Also, when you have a physical addiction, such as overeating, cigarettes, or alcohol, replace this habit immediately. So find a diet (which is probably the easiest thing to do nowadays, there are thousand of choices. Just choose one and commit to it. That's the only reason a diet works), an alcohol free drink and something to replace your cigarette, a breathing exercise for example.

This is an interesting story about a fellow gambling addict who also replaced his addiction, right after he decided to quit. He told me that for the first week after he quitted, he felt so tired that he decided to take a one hour nap each day, right after work. Two hours later he went to play tennis with his best friend, who knew his gambling secret. He told me that the very act of scheduling in his nap didn't made him feel guilty, because he knew he needed it. By scheduling it in for a specific time period, he was the master of this little habit of napping. That feeling of mastery, even if for a seemingly silly but necessary activity like taking a nap, was (so he told me a couple of months later) what gave him the confidence to believe that if he could master one action, he could master another. And another. And his addiction.

What is important to understand is that you are already working on being a master on your addiction. You are reading this workbook. You've done or will do the exercise of the earlier paragraph to understand your addictive pattern. So if you work on this process every day, even is it only for ten minutes a day, you absolutely deserve time to enjoy your day, or at least find a little peace. Remember, the addiction isn't over when you've made decision to stop, but you've got to understand that life is still valuable. And that you can choose to make it meaningful, even in difficult times. To deal with all of this, it's important to give yourself some relaxation and peace to charge your battery.

Make sure to do it

When you've chosen one or two alternatives, make sure you do them every day for at least a week. To make sure you do them, plan them in at a convenient time. Schedule them into your agenda. These actions will be something to look forward to in these difficult days and it will be something you could hold onto. By actually planning them in, you will make it real for yourself. Now, it will be much easier to follow through and give yourself some needed distraction and peace.

## Take notes

Take notes during your recovery process. Have one special notebook, or use this workbook as your personal notebook. Write down your thoughts and feelings during your recovery process. It could be as a diary, this way you could track down your changes overtime. By putting your thoughts and emotions on paper, they will get out of your system, at least for a moment. They go from the darkness of your pain, to the light of your consciousness and there, and only there they become solvable. The process of writing will get you a lot of inside in your addictive processes, and in who you are.

# Chapter 3: Take Responsibility & Educate Yourself on Your Addiction

After you've completed step 1 and 2, there is a little distance between you and your addiction. You're not chained as a slave anymore. Your hands and thoughts have freedom. That being said, in no way will this release you from your responsibilities. Most probably because of your addiction, your problems have piled up. Think about financial consequences, health problems, and deteriorated relationships.

It's time to meet these responsibilities and take care of them.

This means taking responsibility for **your** addiction. Besides the problems you're facing, also educate yourself in what addiction actually is, so you will be stronger when your addictive cravings surface again. This way, you will preserve yourself and won't burden others anymore by the consequences of your addictive behavior.

Create the inventory of your problems and make a to-do-list.

When you feel strong enough, it is time to take responsibility for the problems that you've caused with your addiction. It's best to first take care of yourself. Like in any emergency, make sure you yourself are safe. Then it's time to deal with the consequences. I strongly advise you not to wait too long with this. It hurts to confront yourself with the consequences of your addiction, with all the pain you have caused yourself and others, but don't walk away from this suffering.

I am moved and inspired by Viktor Frankl, a psychiatrist who survived Auschwitz in World War II. He wrote a well-known book entitled **Man's Search For Meaning** about his experiences at the concentration camp, which he survived. I want to share an excerpt from his book here:

"The way in which a man accepts his fate and all the suffering it entails, the way in which he takes up his cross, gives him ample opportunity—even under the most difficult circumstances—to add a deeper meaning to his life."

The lesson herein lies, that we as addicts, who've suffered tremendously during our addictive periods, even though we mainly brought it upon ourselves, could make this suffering meaningful when we deal courageously with the consequences. This means, dealing as responsible adults with the consequences of your addiction and finding out why you're addicted, and learning from these sufferings in the past to create a meaningful present and an inspiring future.

Here are the three steps that will lead to more or less solving your problems over time, and more importantly to take ownership of the consequences you've caused because of your addiction. You could start immediately with these steps after you've decide to quit your addiction, and sometimes you absolutely have to because external factors require you to do so. If it is not so pressing, and you first want to come to your senses, you could wait a couple of days to do so. But don't neglect them; I strongly advise to start with these steps no later than seven days after you've quit your addiction.

*The first step* is to make an inventory of the problems you've caused through your addictive behaviour. Write down a list of all the consequences you're now faced with. Think of financial problems, deteriorated relationships, inner conflicts, a messy house, health problems, not taking care of your appearance, etc.

*The second step* is to create one or more solutions for each of these problems. To make it practical, break these solutions down into at least one action item you could do immediately to help solve each particular problem. For example, when you are in financial debt, your ultimate solution could be, **make an extra 500 USD on the side each month**. An immediate solution could then be, **call or email all my creditors and make appointments about realistic installments to pay back my loans.** Or when you are enormously overweight, your ultimate solution could be, losing 50 pounds in 6 months. An immediate solution could then be, **Start exercising 30 minutes a day and choosing a diet.**

*The third and final step* is to take action. Break down the solutions of step 2 into actions and create a to-do-list. Then, schedule these actions in. What will help is to do one action immediately, so you give yourself a reference point that could help combat the consequences of your addiction, however large they are. Like in the example given above, you could make the immediate calls and emails to your creditors, going for a 30-minutes, interval run and buying the foods necessary for your diet.

Educate yourself

Taking responsibility for your addiction means also making the chance of relapsing as small as possible. Make your ability to deal with addictive cravings as strong as possible. You could do this by educating yourself on addiction. You've taken the first step in doing so already, by defining your addictive pattern in step 1. In this workbook we will focus heavily on your inner thoughts, feelings and conditioning regarding your problems, deepest pain and addiction. This is inevitable when you want to tackle the roots of your addiction and bring about lasting change. To make this journey easier, it is important to know at least some basics of addiction, so you know what you're fighting against.

The way to do this is to educate yourself about addiction in general and your own addiction in particular. For example, I read many forums about gambling addiction, read a scientific book about gambling addictions, some other books about addiction in general, and watched Youtube videos about the topic. This really helped me in understanding addiction, but more importantly in understanding my **own** addiction. Every addict is unique, but by taking in information about addiction, you will better understand your own.

There is an extensive list of good resources on addiction online and I've added some at the end of this book.

During the actions of step 3 of this workbook, keep taking notes. During this stage of your recovery process, because you are taking responsibility for your addiction, taking action in solving your problems and educating yourself on addiction, you will have a lot of new insights. These will be worthwhile to write down, as they can help you tremendously in your recovery process. **Knowledge is (potential) power.**

1: What Is Addiction & When You Know You Have A Problem

**Addiction is a disease**! Whether you want to believe this or not, it is the first thing that you need to admit to yourself if you are to have any hope of curing it. Diseases manifest themselves in a number of different ways. A cough and night sweats could be indicative of tuberculosis. A pain in your chest could be an indication of lung disease. A lump under your arm or in your breast could mean cancer.

**Addiction manifests itself in** obsessive behavior, when you crave a substance, or feeling to the point where you have no control over yourself when it comes to that particular thing!

Are you still not convinced about the seriousness of addiction?

Think about this. When you lose control over yourself, for whatever reason, then you lose control over your life. This loss of control inhibits your ability to function normally, and productively, leading you into a downward spiral that becomes increasingly difficult to break free from.

The longer you exhibit addictive behavior, the more difficult it will be to emancipate yourself from this beast, and the chances of a relapse are greatly increased.

Some people successfully beat addiction by going **cold turkey**. This is where you decide one day that you have had enough of your addiction and the destructive consequences associated with it, and you just stop doing the thing that you are addicted to, or taking the substances that have consumed your life.

The success rate of this type of approach is relatively low, however, and the chances of you falling back into the destructive pattern are greater, because you will have convinced yourself that you can do it on your own.

You therefore need to take a systematic approach to beating addiction, because then you will have the constant reminder of the effort it took for you to break free! You remember hard word, and there is no way around it, breaking free from addiction is hard work.

Recognizing the signs that you might be suffering from addiction are sometimes subtle though, so you might not even be aware that you have a problem until it is too late. There are some questions that you can ask yourself though, that will give you an indication of whether or not you have a problem. The following are some of these questions:

Can you go a full day without thinking of reaching for that drink, taking that drug, or performing a certain activity?
Is your ability to function socially and at work impaired by the manner with which you interact with this substance or activity?

Do you find that activities, like drinking or recreational drug use, which you previously enjoyed with other people, are now done in isolation?

Do you find yourself having to explain your indulgence in certain activities or substances, making excuses for these so that you start to avoid the people who are expressing concern?

Is your work or social life negatively impacted by your engagement with these substances or activities?

Have you reached a stage in your life where you cannot live without the substance or activity?

These questions might be hard to ask yourself, and even more difficult to answer. You need to address them however, if you are to have any hope of beating your addiction. You need to know too, that no addiction is less harmful than another, since they all have a crippling effect on every aspect of your life.

Let us now discuss the various addictions out there, the ones that are most common, and the ones that you are most likely to encounter or experience in your own life. If your particular addiction is not listed in the following chapter, you can be sure that you can apply any of the approaches that are closest to the addiction that you are suffering from.

**Know this, however, that while addiction might have a blanket approach, there are** some addictions that require specialized approaches if you are to be successful at beating it!

2: Types of Addiction

There are many addictions out there, but one thing that they have in common, is the **high** that you experience when you partake in these substances or activities. Endorphins are among the chemicals responsible for this feeling, and this **feeling** is at the root of your addiction.

It has been argued that you do not become addicted to the substance or activity, but rather to the feeling that you eventually associate with engaging in the activity. This is an interesting argument, because while you are unable to stop your craving for the substance or activity you are addicted to, you can often replace the activity or substance with ones that give you a very similar high.

Just what are some of the more common addictions out there?

An obvious suspect is **drugs**. Opiates like heroin, cocaine, and even painkillers are top of the list. These offer you an instant high, one that doesn't last too long, so that you have to take them often. This is why you run the risk of becoming addicted to them. Alcohol, nicotine, and caffeine are other drugs that are highly addictive.

Alcohol and caffeine are subtle substances though, because they are freely available, and legal. You can access them easily, so addiction to these substances is relatively easy to maintain. Cigarettes are just as easily available. Even though you are given parameters as to where you can smoke in public, there is nothing that stops you from lighting up in your home, car, or sometimes in your office.

You can also become addicted to **food**! This is a serious addiction, with serious consequences. Binge eating, for example, is an actual condition, and the tendency to overeat is a real problem for many people. Obesity is a problem amongst people who cannot control their eating, and you can experience problems with you weight, to both extremes of this, however.

Anorexia is a problem, where you are severely underweight, and you become obsessed with calorie counting and with your appearance. Bulimia is another extreme, one that results in weight fluctuations, and manifests itself in purging everything that you eat. Food addiction can therefore be a real problem for the sufferer.

Like most addictions, **shopping** addiction can lead to severe financial difficulties. People with this addiction sight it as a stress reliever. They claim that it helps them to forget their problems. Ironically, they also claim that it helps them forget about their money problems too.

Compulsive buying can cause you great distress however, and you will find that the very thing that you think is alleviating your stress is actually adding to it.

**Gambling** has become a huge problem for many people. You can lose control of yourself and your urge to gamble quite quickly, and this is at the bottom of the problem, its root evil. The thrill and risk associated with this activity provides people with an incredible rush. It is an impulse control disorder, and you will find yourself unable to control your urge to gamble.

In this addiction, people tend to become obsessed with recovering the money that they have lost, which usually just leads to more loss. A subject of much debate is **sex** addiction. You become addicted to the feelings associated with intimacy, and not to sex itself, and many people have even claimed to be **sex addicts who hate sex**. While people might be addicted to the high of an orgasm, they might not like the process of copulation.

Low self-esteem, relationship trouble, sexually transmitted diseases and unwanted pregnancies are among the outcomes of this type of addiction. It has been argued that people who claim to be addicted to sex just use this as an excuse to have a lot of it. Given the problems that this caused however, you might want to really think about your viewpoint on this.

**Love** addiction is an addiction to emotional intimacy, and is often referred to as the subtle sister of sex addiction. Most of us are aware of the high that comes with being in love, and some people become addicted to this feeling.

They stumble, therefore, from relationship to relationship, quickly convincing themselves that they are in love with their next partner.

When you work out, you experience a rush of endorphins and adrenaline.

**Exercise** can therefore also become addictive. When you exercise too much though, you can experience physical problems, and you can also find yourself obsessing about your physical appearance to the point that it becomes unhealthy.

**Work** addiction is more common than many might think. It is a real disorder, and resulted in the term 'workaholic'. Regardless of what kind of work you do, you can become addicted to your work. Other areas of your life suffer as a result, including your health and your relationships.

You can actually become addicted to almost anything. Everything that you do to the extreme could be a sign of addiction. **Lying, stealing, rage, fame** and **power** are some things that you can become addicted to. The **internet, pornography, television** and **video games** are others.

Let us now get into the meat of this book, showing you how to overcome some of the more popular addictions outlined above. You will be given tips and pointers for overcoming addiction on your own, but remember, sometimes you need help. You must never be too proud to ask for this help, especially if you are failing to break free from your addiction.

Drug and substance abuse is a real problem. Here is advice on breaking this addiction!

3: Overcoming Substance Abuse

Drug addiction is a serious problem. It affects every aspect of your life, and puts unnecessary pressure on the healthcare system as well. Regardless of how difficult it might seem at the moment though, no matter how hopeless the situation seems, sobriety is very possible.

A systematic approach to overcoming this addiction is very necessary. You can go cold turkey, but as alluded to, this approach has a very low success rate, and your risk of relapsing is very high. There is a systematic approach to drug addiction, and you can break free from this problem by following this approach!

You need to **decide** first that it is time for a change. Deciding to make a change is usually the first step to recovery, and in fact, it is the most important step. Giving up your drug of choice could lead to serious conflict, even though you can see the problems that your drug of choice is causing in your life.

When you decide that it is time to quit, you will need to be prepared for quite a battle though, probably the most challenging in your life. This is a war that you can win, however, just by following through with these steps.

There are some things that you need to consider:

Who do you surround yourself with, and who are the people that you are allowing into your life
How do you deal with stress?
How do you occupy yourself in your free time?
What are your thoughts and feelings towards yourself
Doubt is common, and you might feel that you are not ready to quit. You need to understand though, that addiction recovery is a process, usually a long one, and it requires **commitment, motivation, support** and **time**!

You should start to do the following things:

Track your drug use. How often do you take drugs? How much drugs do you take? You will start to see the impact that your addiction is having on your life.

Think of the things that are important to you. Do you value your family? Is your partner a priority? Do you love your children? Is your career important to you? Then ask yourself, how does you drug use affect these things!

Make a list of the pros and cons that you associate with quitting. Make a list of the costs and benefits, if you continue with your drug use!

What is preventing you from making the necessary change? Ask yourself what things you could introduce into your life that could help you make this change!

Talk with someone you trust, getting their honest opinion on your drug use.

You need to **prepare yourself** for this change too. It is going to be uncomfortable to say the least. Consider these key steps to addiction recovery:

Remind yourself everyday as to why you want to change

Think about what has worked for you in the past, and what hasn't, when it comes to quitting

Be specific about the goals you set. Make them measurable. What date do you intend to quit? How will you limit your drug use?

Remove all triggers and reminders of your addiction from the environments you inhabit and have control over, such as your home and work place

Rally the troops, informing your family and friends of your intention, getting them on board as your support structure

Making the decision to take on your drug addiction will be a challenge. You need to be aware of the treatment choices that are out there for you to take advantage of. A few things to keep in mind though, when exploring your options, are as follows:

**There is no magic one-size-fits-all treatment for drug addiction**. You are an individual, and your needs will be different to anybody else's. Your unique situation should be taken into consideration, and your treatments should be customized to suit your situation and problems. Finding a program that **feels right** is a very important step!

**Focus on treatments that deal with more than just your drug abuse!** Your health, career, psychological well-being and your relationships are all affected by drug addiction. You need to develop new ways of living if your treatment is to be successful. You need to address the reasons why you turned to drugs to begin with. If, for example, you had problems handling stress, then you need to find new and effective ways of dealing with stress!

**You need to commit, and follow through!** Treating drug addiction is no quick process. The longer you have been abusing drugs, the longer it will take you to get off them. Whether it takes you weeks, months, or even years, you need to commit to this long-term, and follow through!

**Know that you can turn to a number of places for help!** You might not need medical help. You might not even need rehab. Your age, drug history, medical and psychiatric conditions will usually determine the level of care you require. Church members, social workers, and counselors can be as useful in your attempt to break free from drug addiction as doctors and psychologists.

So, in addition to seeking help for your drug addiction, you need to address any medical and psychological issues that you may experience as well. Integrating your substance abuse treatment with your mental and physical health treatments will offer you the best chance of recovery. If you can receive combined treatment from the same place, all the better!

Get the **support** you will need! It is possible to do it alone, but this will be considerably more difficult. Having a solid support structure in place will be essential, regardless of the type of treatment that you choose. Your chances of recovery will increase exponentially if you surround yourself with positive influences. Recovering from drug addiction is hard, but with guidance, encouragement, and even just a listening ear, this process will be much easier.

Rope in your **family and friends**. Their support will prove invaluable, and even if you have let them down before, consider couples or family therapy. Expand your network of **sober individuals**. It is important that you have sober friends, friends who will support your recovery, and not feed your previous life of drug use, even if this was social. Take a class, join a group, volunteer, or attend events in your community!

Try a **sober living home** for a while. While you are recovering from your addiction, you might need to remove yourself from your home, which may me riddled with triggers for drug use. These supportive, safe environments provide you with such a place. If your home is unstable, or not necessarily drug-free, that you should seriously consider this option. **Recovery group meetings** are also a good way to get support.

You will be in touch with people who know what you are going through, on a regular basis, and you will find this very healing. The shared experiences of group members will be of great benefit, and you will learn the tricks that others have used to stay sober!

Many people turn to drugs because they cannot handle stress. **Finding meaningful and healthy ways of dealing with stress** is therefore essential. You will likely still have the problems that led to your drug addiction even when you have overcome your addiction.

Numbing painful emotions, calming down after arguments or a bad day, and a whole plethora of problems could lead you to drug use. The negative emotions that you think you dealt with using drugs will probably then resurface, even after drug addiction has been overcome.

You need to therefore solve these underlying issues if you are to have any hope of long-term success. You can cover up feelings such as stress, loneliness, shame, frustration, anger, hopelessness and anxiety with drug use. These conditions will remain in your life even when you do not use drugs to cover them up. Without drugs however, you will be in a healthier position to deal with these conditions.

Drug use is a misguided attempt at stress management. While alcohol and recreational drug use might help you unwind after a hectic day or cover up emotions and painful memories, there are healthier ways to handle the stress associated with these things. Among these ways are:

Sensory strategies
Exercise
Meditation
Breathing exercises, and
Challenging self-defeating thoughts

While these may take time, and you feel that drugs are the quickest way to deal with stress and unwanted emotions, they are not. The following list of quick stress-relief techniques can be helpful. Some will work better for you than others, this depends largely on you psychological, emotional and physical makeup:

**Short exercise** does wonders to relieve stress and promote your general emotional well-being. Walk around the block, jump rope, or even run in place, and you will see what the benefits of doing this just a few minutes a day can bring.

**Fresh air** does wonders for the soul. Sunshine, beautiful views, inspiring landscapes; all these promote your state of wellness.

**Meditation and Yoga** are excellent stress relievers. They also help you to restore your internal balance.

**Pets** are also extremely relaxing. If you have the time or the space, you should invest in one. There are incredible benefits to be enjoyed from just rubbing their fur.

**Music** also has a soothing effect on you general state. Try listening to calming music to enjoy this benefit.

**Scented candles** are a great way to bring you into the moment.

**Other scents** have the same effect. You can breathe in the scent of coffee beans, fresh flowers, even sunscreen if this reminds you of a relaxing vacation that you took.

**Visualization** is a key tool in stress relief. Picture yourself in a peaceful place, like a forest or the seaside, think of your child's first step, or another fond memory, or even a great time that you had with your friends.

**Tea** has long been known for its therapeutic effects. Make yourself a steaming cup.

**Family photos** are also great ways of taking you out of the stress that you a currently experiencing, and taking you to happier times and places.

**Massage** your neck and shoulders. You can do this yourself.

**Take a hot bath or shower,** and use some essential oils like lavender for the maximum benefit.

Another way to break free from drug addiction is to keep track of **triggers**, and keep your **cravings** in check. Sobering up from drug addiction is just the first step in a long process, and you will need time for your brain to rebuild itself, to recover from the changes that it underwent while you were addicted.

You will find that you have intense cravings for the drug during this time, and your best bet is to avoid the people and places that triggered your drug use to begin with.

**Break free from your drug buddies**

Hanging out with people who still do drugs, even if you consider them to be friends, is a detrimental mistake. You should aim to surround yourself with people who support your decision for sobriety, and avoid those who tempt you back into destructive habits.

## Bars and clubs are to be avoided

Even if drinking is not a problem for you, alcohol lowers your inhibitions, and could lead you to a relapse. This is because your judgment becomes impaired. Also, drugs are usually easily available at these venues, and the temptation might be too much for you to handle. In fact, all environments and situations associated with drug use are to be avoided.

## Honesty

Honesty is critical. When you seek medical treatment, be open about your drug use history. Medical and dental procedures usually require drugs before they can be carried out, and you should use practitioners who are prepared to use alternatives or who are prepared to keep prescribed medication to an absolute minimum. This is no time for shame. And if you are uncomfortable with a provider, find another one.

Exercise extreme caution when it comes to prescription medication

These have the potential to become addictive, and could be seen as an alternative to recreational drugs. It is not a safer option, and drugs like sleeping pills, painkillers and anti-anxiety medication could become your new drug of choice.

You cannot always avoid cravings though, and it is important that you find alternative ways to cope with these. The following is a quick list of coping mechanisms that you can set in place to deal with cravings.

Distract yourself. Exercise, reading, engaging in a hobby, or even going to a movie can all be positive distracting activities. The urges will slip away, and you can reward yourself with a healthy snack.

Talk about it. Discussing your craving with friends or family is a highly effective way of pinpointing the source of your craving. Since cravings are nothing to feel bad about, being honest about them can even help to restore your relationships.

Try **urge surfing**. This is a technique where you tough it out, riding the wave of your craving until it eventually breaks.

Change the way you think. Remind yourself of the negative effects that using the drug will have on you, and stop thinking about the positive impact that using will have on you for the moment.

Finally, you want to **build a meaningful life outside of drugs**, and you definitely **don't want to let relapses get you down**. Pick up a hobby, adopt a pet, get involved with your community, set meaningful goals, and look after your health. And when you relapse, you must know that this is just a part of the treatment process. As frustrating as these can be, think of them as the opportunity to learn from the mistakes you are making, and altering your treatment accordingly.

Know that relapses do not mean that your treatment is failing. Instead of giving up, pick yourself up quickly. When you are out of danger again, consider what led to your relapse. Commit then, to doing things differently.

# Chapter 4: Exploring Habits and Their Impact on Self-Control

Habits play a major role in who you are and your level of productivity. To effectively improve your self-discipline, you will need a strong understanding of habit-making and the ones that are in play in your life. This chapter will provide you with comprehensive information about habits so that you are able to make the positive changes you need.

What Are Habits?

By definition, a habit is a regular or settled practice or tendency. They are anything we find routine, and you likely carry out many habits without even really noticing it. For example, for most people, it is a habit to get out of bed in the morning, use the restroom and grab a quick beverage. This becomes automatic, and every time you wake up, you naturally do those actions in that order without even really thinking about it.

Habits can be good or bad. For example, smoking is a good example of a bad habit. Bad habits tend to have a stronghold on you, and they can be difficult to break. This is because there are numerous additional behaviors associated with them, and each behavior needs to change in order to break the bad habit. Procrastination and overspending are two other common habits that have no positive impact on your life but are difficult to break.

Habits that are advantageous can be a boon for your life. For example, the habit of brushing your teeth two to three times a day not only helps to promote greater oral hygiene, it has a statistically positive effect on your overall health.

Why are habits so important to your level of self-discipline? You have dozens of habits that you unconsciously perform each day, but maybe you don't feel disciplined yet. Your level of productivity and discipline are directly tied into the habits you choose to keep up. If you have several bad habits, these are likely taking your productivity away from you. For example, if you are a smoker, think about how many times per day you take a short break to smoke. It likely adds up to an hour or more of not doing anything productive. If you were to eliminate just this one bad habit from your life, you could take this time, this 'extra hour,' and use it to work on achieving your goals. If you regularly lose track of time and are chronically late, you lose the trust of other people over time; how much more effective at achieving goals could you be if people in your life help you out because they knew you, too, are reliable? Instead, a bad habit robs you of both time and trust.

Now, when you're good habits outweigh the bad ones, this allows you to intentionally manage your mind. Ingrained habits free up your mind to focus on a higher level of what is important to you. When people tend to have more good habits, they can think clearer in general, and tasks that once seemed complex are naturally easier to think about and to tackle.

Your habits have influence over all elements of your life. It is easier to develop what we call "bad habits" because these often lead to a sense of immediate pleasure. For example, a person might smoke a cigarette or buy expensive things because this calms them in that moment. However, over time, these bursts of pleasure can cause major problems in your life. Smoking can have negative health consequences, and buying those expensive things can heavily impact your personal finances. This also plays into gratification, which you will learn more about this in a later chapter.

## Habit Loop

The habit loop is a type of neurological phenomenon that governs any specific habit that you might have. There are three elements associated with it, including a routine, a cue and a reward.

The cue element is really anything that causes a habit. Common categories for these cues include:

Location
People
Preceding action
Time of day
Emotional State
For example, if you normally get a coffee at 2:00 pm, once 2:00 pm hits, this is your brain's cue to go and get a cup of coffee. Perhaps you always get an ice cream treat at a certain restaurant, and now every time you go to that restaurant, you crave the treat. The cue can be strong, and can feel almost like an obligation. Cues can become varying levels of positive or negative for your life, depending on the habits that they are associated with.

The routine is the behavior of your habit. For example, you physically going to retrieve the coffee at 2:00 pm would be the routine in this example, or buying the treat you crave at that restaurant.

The reward is the reason that your mind remembers the habit, and why it is worth remembering. For example, that coffee makes you feel relaxed or gives you a boost of energy to get through the remainder of your workday, or the treat tastes like a delicious reward at the end of your meal.

This loop is what can also make bad habits so difficult to break. You have to first be able to recognize your cues. Then, you have to alter your behavior. Lastly, you have to recognize that the reward that you are getting is not as great as it seems. Now, when you are working to build positive habits, you want to use this loop to ensure that they become strong enough to essentially overpower the bad ones.

## Habit Development

In December 2012, a paper published in the **British Journal of General Practice** looked at habits and the psychology behind them. One study discussed in this paper analyzed habit formation and what it takes to make a behavior automatic. The participants chose a behavior that was healthy, such as taking a walk or eating a piece of fruit. They also chose a cue, such as doing the activity directly after breakfast. After approximately 66 days, the frequency of their chosen behavior started to slow. They missed the occasional routine, but overall, this did not slow the ultimate acceleration of the habit. After missing it once, the automaticity of the habit could still be resumed.

This study shows that when you are working to build good habits, it will not be easy to forget about them once the foundation is set. The key is putting in the work to develop the habit to a state of automaticity.

In August of 2014, the Society for Personality and Social Psychology studied people's daily lives and how habits play a role in our day-to-day activities. They estimate that approximately 40 percent of the activities that you do each day are the same and in the same situations. They attribute this to **associative learning**. The research shows that once you find a behavior that makes it easier to accomplish your goals, you seek to repeat these patterns. Associations start to form between response and cues as a result.

The process of habit formation starts within the brain's basal ganglia. This is said to trigger a three-step process, which is the habit loop you will learn more about next. Over time, as the habit-loop continues to be performed, the brain essentially gets involved less and less, making the process of performing the habit one that becomes automatic once the associated cue occurs.

# Chapter 5: What to do and Avoid When Developing New Habits

Now, it is time to know exactly what to do to replace the bad ones that are inhibiting your level of self-discipline. There are common things to try, and also to avoid when you are working on replacing your bad habits. It is important to know what these are so that you are reducing the number of challenges that you might face throughout the process.

## Powerful Methods that Work to Replace Bad Habits

Now you know what to avoid when making habit replacements, but what do you actually do to start the process? This section will help you to develop the specific strategy to make sure that you're bad habits start to fade, and new, constructive ones take their place.

### 1. Fine yourself.

This is to be taken literally, as you will get a jar and actually put money into it when you fall back into your old bad habit. This makes the act of the habit more painful, and once you finally break free of it, you can use the money that you accumulated to help you improve a good habit. For example, if you are trying to break overspending by saving more, put this money into your savings.

### 2. Understand why the habit is bad.

Not all bad habits are obvious. At this point, you need to dig deeper and determine why they are bad, perhaps in how the habit affects your long-term goals. From here, seek out a suitable replacement that is similar in nature to the old habit, but can make a positive impact instead.

### 3. Use a calendar to track progress.

Every time you utilize a good habit to replace a bad one, you want to keep track of this. Set up a calendar that you will use specifically for this purpose and put an "X" on every day that you succeed. As you see more days marked off, this makes it easier to stay on track.

### 4. Give yourself time to prepare.

Take a full week just preparing to make the change from a bad habit to a good one. Make a plan and determine exactly which good habit you will use as a replacement, and when.

### 5. Make a list of positive elements.

Once you determine which positive habit you will use to replace a good one, write down at least five benefits you will get for adopting the good habit.

### 6. Change your environment

You read about this in the above section that your environment, if you make no changes, can make it harder to break a habit. Consider what about your environment needs to change to eliminate the old habit and accommodate the positive replacement. Then, immediately start making those changes.

### 7. Talk to yourself

When you notice yourself falling back into the bad habit, talk yourself out of it, and verbally explain to yourself why the good habit you are working to develop is in your best interest.

### 8. Review your relapses.

If you relapse into your bad habit, take a serious and objective review into why it happened. This will help you understand why it occurred, so that you can make a plan to avoid the same pattern in the future.

### 9. Create a loop.

You want to have a habit loop for your new good habit. Create your cue, routine and reward. Write this information down so that it is easier to remember, and review as needed.

## 10. Retrain your mind

You want to train your mind to see your bad habits as negative and your new good habits as a positive thing. Repetition of these ideas helps ingrain both the mindset and the habit.

### What to Avoid When Replacing Bad Habits

When you are working to replace a bad habit and change your behavior, it is important to recognize the common mistakes at the outset, because then you can work to prepare for them and minimize any issues as you go about your journey of creating new habits. The following are the most common habit-breaking-and-making mistakes:

**Relying solely on willpower.** Willpower alone is not capable of helping you make and maintain long-term changes. It just is not enough. It can help to get you started, but as a mental and emotional resource, it is a limited one. So, if you have strong willpower, use it to spur the breaking of your habit, but know you will need additional resources to go further.

**Creating only the ultimate goal.** All reasonable goals are made up of multiple smaller goals that need to be accomplished first to achieve your ultimate goal. Your ultimate goal of breaking the bad habit needs to be broken down into several small, easier steps that you will plan for and focus on individually.

**Ignoring the impact of your environment.** Your behavior is dependent on multiple factors, including your environment. To change your behavior, you almost always have to change your environment, whether it means taking you out of the environment or changing elements of the environment itself. There is no way around this if you want true success.

**Focusing only on stopping bad habits.** Yes, the ultimate goal is ending your bad habit, but you have to replace it with a good one for the process to work. You cannot just end the bad habit and be done. Intentionally put something in its place and focus on the new habit for the long-term.

**Blaming your lack of motivation.** Motivation is one of many emotional states, and like willpower, it is very limited. Life is not predictable, and as things change, so does your motivation. Because of this, you cannot use motivation alone to make long-term and meaningful changes.

**Not focusing on cues.** You must identify the cues to all of the habits that you are trying to break. These cues must be changed or eliminated in order for you to be successful in altering the bad habits associated with them.

**Thinking that information causes action.** Remember that power comes from both application and knowledge. You have to allow your emotions concerning these habits to influence you to make positive changes. If you only rely on the knowledge that they are bad, you will not succeed.

**Focusing on abstract goals.** Goals are good, and you need them, but you also need a call to action. For example, if your goal is to quit smoking, you cannot just tell yourself to quit. You also need a plan. For example, tell yourself to give up one cigarette per day every four days until you have quit.

**Focusing only on the future.** Creating long-term goals is great and necessary, but you also have to think of the present. When you are looking to change a bad habit, take it a day at a time.

**Making excuses.** Any positive change in life can quickly be killed by excuses, so stop making them.

# Chapter 6: Identifying Bad Habits and Why This is Important

Every person has bad habits. This is inevitable, and a part of life. However, once you have awareness of the habits that are negatively impacting in your life, you can start to make the necessary changes to reverse them and replace them with habits that are beneficial. The first step is being able to determine which of your habits are bad. Once you do this, you want to make note of them, and start following the process necessary to get rid of the habits and their negative consequences.

## The Importance of Replacing Bad Habits

Now you have learned about what it takes to replace the bad habits in your life, so the next step is to determine what the positive effects will be. Once you see the immense benefits of replacing bad habits, it will make it easier to create a replacement plan and stay on track. Remember that you learned in a previous chapter that changing your mindset can contribute to easily altering your bad behaviors and thoughts.

When you replace the habits in your life that are bad with good ones, it can do the following:

You will find it easier to reach your immediate goals

You will find that the foundation of your life is more stable and more conducive to achieving success

You will be able to reduce, or even eliminate, how much time you waste each day

You can more easily create a life plan that allows you to develop reasonable long-term goals

You can develop good habits that allow you not to have to rely on daily or hourly motivation to get things done

You will often find yourself in a better mood with stronger mental health overall
You can take control of your health
It is easier to form relationships that are strong and positive
You will be able to better manage your time and not be late
You will find that it is easier to manage your personal finances
Just make sure that the good habits you do develop are actually good for you. For example, getting more sleep is usually a positive change, but if you are getting too much, it can actually be another bad habit. The key is ensuring that the good replacement habits are within a good balance for your life and goals.

## How to Identify Bad Habits

What causes bad habits in the first place? Pinpointing the source of poor habits will help you to not only curb them now, but curtail forming them later. The following are common causes of bad habits:

Boredom and stress
Seeking gratification
Your environment
Individual needs
Your peers
Here are a few steps you want to take to identify and evaluate your bad habits.

Write down all of the habits you have that you feel could be having a negative impact on your self-discipline and ability to reach your goals.
Be specific about the impact that these bad habits are having on your life. Make sure that you are honest, and that you write down in full, specific details what the negative consequences are.
Consider and write down how any of your habits might be affecting other people around you. This may help you to uncover

how certain habits are bad, even though you might not personally feel their negative impact.

You may also ask yourself these questions regarding each of your habits to determine if a specific habit is bad or not:

Is the habit making it harder for you to reach any goals?
Is the habit causing you to experience negative feelings?
Is the habit making you feel guilty?
Is the habit negatively affecting other people besides you?
If you said "yes" to any of these, the habit is most likely a bad influence that needs to be replaced with something that is good.

## Techniques to Replace Bad Habits with Good Habits

This section will focus on common bad habits and the techniques that you can use to replace them. You likely have at least a few of these habits, so it is important to know about them and the work you need to do to eliminate them and their consequences from your life.

### You watch too much television.

Set a limit on how much television you are going to watch each day. The maximum should be two hours. Next, schedule activities to get you out of the house, doing something more active to occupy your time. Alternatively, take up a hobby that will get you out from in front of the television when you have free time at home.

### You use tobacco products.

This is a habit you want to eliminate completely because of the risks to your health, and it can be difficult due to the element of nicotine addiction. It is best to talk to your doctor. They can help you to determine if a medication might be helpful, or if substitution or cold turkey is the best solution for you.

Chances are, you still have some habits on your list that were not included above. The following process can be applied to any bad habit that you are trying to break:

Identify the reason you have or began the bad habit

Make the conscious decision to address the habit; you cannot just ignore it after identifying the habit, because it will not just disappear without work

Record the details of your habit, including the cue and why you enjoy it

Write down why you want to quit the habit (do not focus on what you will lose by quitting the habit, but what you will gain once it is gone)

Tell yourself frequently that you are going to quit it

Prepare and plan for challenges and mistakes

Change your environment or prepare with alternative actions, to make it so there is no room for the bad habit anymore

If possible, find a friend who is working to lose same bad habit and keep each other accountable so you can both work to eliminate it from your lives

Forgive yourself if you slip up; it can take time to break a bad habit, and this is okay, as long as you regain your focus and keep working toward breaking it.

## You eat when you are not hungry.

There are several ways to stop this habit. First, you can plan your meals and snacks. Create a meal schedule to follow each day. Next, literally ditch the junk food from your kitchen, and make sure what you are eating is healthy. Third, make sure that you are actually feeling hunger before you eat. Lastly, do not continue eating after you feel full.

## You drink too much alcohol.

Most people don't have a problem with the occasional drink, but if you find yourself enjoying several cocktails most evenings, it is time to make a change. Start by evaluating how much you are actually drinking and how much money it costs you. This will make it easier to cut down. Next, choose two days a week when you can have a drink, and make sure that on these days you have no more than two.

## You spend too much money.

It is great to buy yourself something nice on occasion, but you want to balance your spending, or else you can find yourself in immense debt. Start by exploring your finances so that you can see where you are spending. Create a budget of your fixed, variable, necessary, and unnecessary expenses. Next, see where you can make cuts. For example, do you have multiple digital television subscriptions? Start by cutting out at least one. Craft a schedule for **when** you can indulge, versus when to stick strictly to your budget.

# Chapter 7: Build the Intention to Break Procrastination

Every journey to a goal begins with a commitment; a commitment to improve, to have better control of your nerves and to work with dedication and perseverance towards the end goal to eventually actualize it.

Without a strong commitment and a clear intention to achieve a certain goal, you are quite likely not going to move dedicatedly towards it. This is why your journey to breaking procrastination needs to begin with an unwavering commitment as well.

## Set a Clear Goal

Now that you have, a clearer understanding of why you need to overcome your urge to procrastinate and are more determined than before to work towards this very goal, set a very clear goal to actually beat this bad habit. You can have several goals on your list that you would like to fulfill to live a more meaningful, happy life, but it is quite difficult to work on a handful of goals at once.

Remember, you only have a certain amount of willpower to work on a certain task and that willpower depletes with every move you make towards a certain goal. Therefore, if you work for 3 hours straight on creating your company's website, you are likely to feel exhausted after that and will not be able to work on another high priority goal for another couple of hours.

To ensure you don't run short of willpower to work on anything important at all, go slow and steady. Do make a list of the goals you would like to work on to become active, enthusiastic and productive, but pick one important one from the list that you would like to work on first.

Ensure to make that goal as clear and specific as possible so you know exactly what you are trying to achieve. If your goal is to improve your income, think about the amount of money you would like to earn every month and compare it with the amount you are actually earning. If you procrastinate on keeping your house clean, think about how clean you want your house to be and create a specific goal based on it. Once you have better clarity on your goal, write it down on your journal.

You now have a very **strong** reason to overcome procrastination. Next, you need to make an action plan to work enthusiastically towards this goal and battle every temptation that comes your way.

### Accept Your Problem

To build a clear intention to resolve your problem, you first need to admit that you have a problem to address in the first place. Unless you acknowledge your problem, you will not fully realize its effects on your life and will not work faithfully to fix it. Accepting your problem becomes easier when you focus on how it is affecting (read: sabotaging) your life. To do that, do the following:

Analyze your daily routine starting from the time you wake up until you fall asleep and list down all the tasks you actually engage in. Do write down the time you devote to every task.

Now assess the importance of every task on the list and think about what it helped you achieve that day. For instance, if you spent 3 hours researching on your final year philosophy project in college, what outcome did you achieve after that research? Were you able to carry out a meaningful research or were you not so pleased with your findings primarily because you did not devote 3 full hours to researching on the topic? Think about whether or not every task you do daily helps you achieve anything meaningful in the end. If your end goal for the day is to earn $100, is you able to do it considering the time, you spend on your work related tasks? Also, think about how much time you actually spend on the tasks stated on the list and how much of that time is invested in other activities. If you spent 2 hours drafting a 200 word email to a potential investor in your business, think about what you actually did in those 2 hours. Were you actually thinking about the content of the email and researched on it to ensure you draft a well-structured and effective email or did you spend 1.5 hours using social media on your phone and spent only 30 minutes doing the actual task?

Moreover, think about the tasks you plan to do daily, but somehow end up not doing. Write down those tasks and compare their importance and the outcomes they would have helped you achieved with the tasks already put on the list. If you had intended to write a blog post for your blog, email some PR firms, pitch a proposal to a potential client, do some household chores including laundry and preparing dinner and had to spend 2 hours with your family, but you ended up only writing a blog post and doing laundry, why do you think that happened? What went wrong and where did it go wrong that made you mess up your entire plan and not achieve your set targets for the day?

Once you have detailed out all the answers to the questions and have analyzed your routine, go through the account a few times and within minutes, you will realize how prone you are to procrastination and how harmful it is for you. When you compare the results you achieve every day with the desired outcomes, you will automatically realize how your habit to postpone important tasks and engage in something less meaningful but more attractive while you are working on an important task is actually a poisonous habit that is only destroying your life. This realization will help you accept your problem.

It is important to make a verbal and then a handwritten declaration of this acceptance to put things out in the open. Say and write down, "I have a bad habit to procrastinate important tasks and I am going to work to break this habit steadfastly." Your declaration can be different, but the gist of it should be the same.

### Make a Strong Commitment Backed by Compelling Whys

Now that you have acknowledged your problem and committed yourself to fixing it, you need to solidify your commitment and strengthen it by pegging it to a compelling why. You need to have a convincing reason or even several reasons why you need to overcome your bad habit of procrastination so you work with dedication towards your goal.

The whys associated with every goal motivate you to work towards its fulfillment because they are the reasons why you are chasing that goal. If there is no reason why you wish to break procrastination, why would you ever do that? If losing weight isn't important to you, why would you ever hit the gym and focus on healthy eating? To overcome procrastination, you need to figure out exactly why you wish to do it.

Close your eyes or even keep them open if you want and think about the biggest issue you are facing in your life right now. It could be anything that makes you feel discontent, brings you any sort of pain, or is keeping you from living a completely content and happy life. It could be your struggle with losing weight or the obstacles you are experiencing in setting up your business or how you are battling depression and the urge to give in to it or anything else that is seriously adding friction to your life and restraining you from living how you truly wish to live.

Write down your findings and if you recall your work routine and how much time you spend on actually meaningful tasks and those that only make you waste time, you will realize that procrastination is indeed a major reason why you are struggling to achieve your desired goals. Think about how your life would change for the better if you mustered up the courage to fight your temptations and beat procrastination to do actual work for real. Write down those reasons and use them to fuel your motivation to work towards your commitment to beat procrastination.

# Chapter 8: Meditation and Mindset

Before anything, the first step is to believe in you as well as be confident that you can achieve and deserve to have radiant health. You must believe that you can have unlimited energy, because after all you come from it and are made of it. Although the oldest woman on the planet attributes her longevity to her consumption of chocolate, which is considerably valid due to the fact that raw cacao (the plant source from which chocolate is made of) has more antioxidants than any other food; becoming aware of your breathing is probably the next best concept to master due to the fact that it takes your mind away from taxing thoughts which drain you of energy as well as supplies your cells with oxygen which is the most abundant mineral on earth. As odd as this may sound studies have shown that the fewer calories you consume the longer you live.

Whether we are aware of it most of us have dominate thought patterns and habits, which can make it hard for us to break self-destructive routines. Underneath all the chattering of the mind lies silence, once you let go of all thoughts, that will allow you to feel true bliss and peace of mind. If you continue to let your ego run your existence rather than feeling your way through each day then you will continue to get the same results in all areas of your life as well as feel the way you always do.

The first task to optimum wellness is to identify all the matters that are holding you back and write them down, and then come up with a list that will cure you from these ailments. Don't focus on the list that you have trouble with because if you do you will only get more of that. Keep the list of the tasks that you want more of. For example, if you watch too much TV then maybe you might want to walk more. Another issue could be your weight. If you want to lose weight it might not be that you eat too much, but not enough of the right types of food. The right balance of whole foods will get you where you want to be. Write down whatever it is you want to achieve or become. Don't let doubt come into your life. Be all that you want to be and always believe in yourself.

Meditation is something that you can practice everywhere all the time. You can be in a play of peace while still going about your day to day activities. You can allow God to run your life while you sit back and enjoy the show. You are infiniteness. You are God. If you make time to sit and be with your thoughts you will eventually have complete control over them which will help you in all areas of your life. If you start a meditation practice don't set a time frame, as it is just a man-made illusion, but try to do it consistently on a daily basis to ensure ensuring beneficial results.

The ego typically tries or wants to control everything in its path, but you have the power to let go of it. You have control over everything that you do as well as your reactions to everything that happens throughout your stay on this earth. Our ego labels events, material items as situations as good or bad pertaining to what it wants or does not want.

One way to get into a deep meditation is when you eat your food. A lot of people hardly chew their food several times before they swallow it which doesn't allow them to breakdown all the carbohydrates, fats, proteins, vitamins and minerals which causes them to be overweight, malnourished, or results in acne. This used to be a very big problem of mine. Train your brain to think "chew your food" while you eat. The more you chew your food the less you will eat and the more energy you will manifest. Eventually you can get so good at it that you will go into a state of meditation. If you drink smoothies or fresh fruit or vegetable juices then it's beneficial to swish it in your mouth to mix it with your saliva before you swallow to help initiate digestion before it reaches the stomach.

Lastly, I want to talk about sexual energy and I can't emphasize the importance of this enough when it comes to well-being. Master your sexual energy! We are receivers and transmitters of unseen forces. Life is infinite in a physical and metaphysical aspect. Say you give someone a compliment; this in turn sends them some positive energy that they in turn keep sharing to others throughout the day. This is relevant to sexual energy in that if you focus on it you can shift this energy to other areas of your life that need attention. Try going months without exerting this life-force. Focus on true unconditional love which is the love of all of God's creations. A clear picture and a burning desire of what you want must be instilled within your mind so that everyday distractions do not get in the way of its accomplishment. We are meant to create even if it doesn't happen every time we have sex, and it takes a lot of energy to create another living being. If we take our focus off the usual intentional failed attempts at creation we can redirect our energy towards the things we want, and actually manifest them as quick as you imagine them. The following is a list of strategies and tips that will help you achieve the proper mindset for achieving optimal health as well as more energy:

- You are the creator of your reality
- You have the power to change your thoughts
- Your thoughts determine the way you look and feel
- let go of doubtful thoughts
- stay in the moment as much as possible
- become conscious of your breathing
- look at life through your peripherals

# Chapter 9: Exercise and Grounding

A little bit of exercise goes a long way. You don't need to overwork your body at the gym to be in peak physical condition. Simply moving more and walking can be the best exercise protocol. Exercising is one of the most effective ways to boost your metabolism, burn unwanted belly fat, and remove toxins from the body.

I have found that taking regular walks on daily basis keeps the body in peak physical condition. Walking in the morning before you eat breakfast is a great start to getting healthier and detoxifying your body because right when you wake up your body is in the peak stage of detoxification. So if you wait an hour or two before eating you will extend and intensify the detox and fat burning mechanisms of your body.

Grounding and inverting are two exercises that are immensely life prolonging for the human body and incredibly simple as well as free. Ground is simply getting barefoot contact with the earth to recharge all the cells and inverting is putting the human body upside down to alleviate the effects of gravity. If you are not capable of headstands or handstands then you can lean your body over the armrest of a couch. Doing this for ten minutes counterbalances a whole day's worth of the harmful effects of gravity. It also stimulates the lymphatic system which is waste removal pathway of the body. It brings more blood to the brain and makes you feel great!

Aside from taking long walks, my favorite exercise is breathing. The best time to practice this is during times of meditation, while you are waiting for something or someone, or all day if you can manage it. Being aware of your breathing takes you from your thoughts and supplies your body with the with more energy than food or drink. Diaphragmatic breathing allows you to get more oxygen for less breath. The way to go about this is to breathe in through your nose into your stomach. If you take a big enough breathe you can make your belly protrude. Next, breathe this air into your lungs, and then exhale. This method of breathing can make a huge difference in your health.

# Chapter 10: Hydration

A lot of people would agree that they need to drink more water on a daily basis. There really is no particular way to do anything in life, but there is always room for improvement. I weigh around a hundred and fifty pounds and I generally drink at least a gallon of water a day which is a hundred and twenty-eight ounces or sixteen cups. Some experts recommend drinking an ounce per pound of bodyweight per day. I can almost guarantee that if you slowly incorporate more into your diet you will continually have more energy day after day.

So many individuals are dehydrated, and don't know what it feels like to be hydrated because they never have been. The lack of water causes the inside of their bodies to be sticky because of the deficiency of water in the cells. Slowly work your way up to drinking more until you find what works best for you, but don't force anything. Organic coconut water is a great way to speed up the process because they are high in electrolytes which allow your cells to take in the water. If you have access to young green coconuts this can be a great way to take your health and hydration to a new level.

Clean water is what your body craves. I think that many people don't drink enough water because they don't have access to clean water and aren't even aware of it. Chemically treated tap water from your city is some of the most toxic water on the planet. Any filter is better than no filter, or you can gather your water from a reliable spring which can be found at findaspring.com. True spring water is so valuable because it comes from very deep depths, making it very clean and bioavailable for the cells. I prefer spring water but if I don't have access to it I opt for the best water I can find. The three best filters next to Mother Nature are a reverse osmosis system, a water distiller, or a gravity filter. Drink only when you are thirsty. Do what makes you feel best. You may look back one day and realize it was one of the best decisions you've ever made like I have.

There are several ways that you can jumpstart the hydration process which I highly recommend. The first is always drink water before you eat meals, and especially when you wake up. This will also aid in digestion. Without the proper amount of potassium and sodium in your body your body's cells won't be able to intake the extra water you are putting in your system. All raw foods are high in potassium, the common one probably being bananas. Most people get plenty of salt in their diet but it is important to find your balance of potassium and sodium for proper hydration.

Squeezing a half of or a whole lemon into a cup of water when you rise first thing in the morning is another valuable method for achieving optimal wellness and hydration. Every day I consume one lemon and one avocado. Lemon water triggers the liver to secrete bile which helps break down food, resulting in fabulous digestion. Studies have shown that if you use warm water it is more effective. I store all my water on the counter rather than the fridge because it takes unnecessary energy to heat cold water up to your body's temperature. If you can't drink lemon water because it is too bitter then I suggest drinking it with stevia powder or liquid extract. It's an herb that has no negative effects on the human body, making it the safest sweetener known to man. If you desire sugar then opt for organic due to the fact that conventional is made from genetically modified beets, making them very toxic to the human body.

The last, but most effective, cellular hydration technique I want to share with you is juicing. Smoothies are great, and I'll admit that I do consume most of the water I drink in smoothies, but juices are a whole level of health. Consuming fresh homemade fruit and vegetable juices provides your body with truly bioavailable nutrition due to the fact that there is no fiber to break down. If you've never had a juice then I suggest starting with carrots and celery which are high in potassium and sodium. Greens vegetables are some of the most nutrient dense foods to juice, and they mix well with apples to take away the bitterness. Juicing is so beneficial for the body because it is full of micronutrients. Many people are getting plenty of macronutrients which include carbohydrates, fats, and proteins. Micronutrients are all the minerals that your body needs to run optimally. There are around ninety different minerals that the human body needs many of which in incredibly small amounts. However, the conventional food supply only puts three different minerals back into the soil. This causes the body to become unbalanced. If you don't have a juicer you can invest in a cheap one for less than thirty dollars.

# Chapter 11: Non-Toxic Lifestyle

Don't expect to become enlightened in the dark of the night. The sun provides us with food and our bodies with energy. Exposure to it works synergistically with the skin to produce vitamin D, which is actually classified as a hormone. Hormones create our behaviors and moods. The benefits of sun exposure are being more documented as the days go on but it has been known to cure depression and eliminate harmful bacteria from the body. Aim for at least thirty minutes a day but you should spend as much time in the sun as you are able to. Increasing your exposure can greatly improve your overall well-being and longevity.

If you haven't already come to the realization that nearly every conventional product is toxic and disrupting to the body's hormone producing systems, then I'm here to help you become aware of this. There are natural products that you can buy or make at home as I do. I love you use Google to find homemade non-toxic recipes. Making your own is not only cheaper, but way healthier! Baking soda, coconut oil, essential oils for scent, shea butter, vinegars, along with vodka all work wonders in whatever combination your heart desires for deodorants, dish soap, laundry detergent, toothpaste, and any self or home cleansing remedies you might need. Lastly, if you live in a city then I want to recommend a shower dechlorinator. Chlorine is great for the treatment of pathogens but it is toxic to the human. When it reacts with hot water in your shower it creates a gas that is breathed in. You can purchase a high quality one for less than fifty dollars at freedrinkingwater.com.

Sometimes it's necessary to let go of toxic relationships. If you feel as if the people you hang out with are holding you back from evolving spiritually then it's okay to move on because you can always keep them in your heart; if it's what you need then might be beneficial for them as well. Everything that happens in life is necessary for the evolution of consciousness. It may be hard to see sometimes but it is all love.

A good relationship is one that is constantly giving and receiving acts of love. One that is working to rid the body of toxins rather than accumulating them. Although you are responsible for your own inner-circumstance and decisions, until you become fully present it is often easy to become like the people you hang out with. If you are in a close relationship with someone who is self-destructive, and you aware of this then love yourself and move on if you feel as if they are bringing you down.

# Chapter 12: How Habits Influence Our Lives and Success

As you may have derived from our previous discussion, because habits are things we do repeatedly, naturally, we have good and bad habits that have various effects on our lives.

To expound on, and illustrate this, let us go back and use our earlier example where immediately after getting home from work, you plop down into the comforting embrace of your couch, and remote in hand, proceed to watch hours of your favorite TV show. 2 or 3 hours later, you reach for the phone, order take-out, sink back into your couch, and proceed to gobble down the pizza or whatever take-out you fancy as you watch TV into the wee hours of the morning. You do this every day.

In this scenario, what do you think most likely: you have a lean, fit body and your life is a success-laden story, or you epitomize the modern-day American who wages a constant battle with excess weight, lack of success or progress, and struggles with effectiveness or time management: which do you think most probable? The latter is likely to be your case because of one simple thing: you have bad habits.

On the other hand, consider a scenario where after getting home from work, instead of gluing your butt to your super comfortable couch, you head straight into your bedroom, take off the day's clothes, get into your gym clothes, and proceed to engage in any form of exercise.

After this, you shower, plan and compartmentalize your work for the following day. You then read an inspirational book or the bible, follow this up with something that increases your value as a valued member of your workplace or society in general, and after, proceed to make (or order) a healthy meal.

In this scenario, what do you think most probable: that you have a healthy mind and body and successful in every area of your life, or that you are overweight and struggling to achieve semblances of success? The former is likely to be true. That is how habits affect your life.

When you adopt good positive habits that propel you towards the success you desire, habits such as exercising, reading, or personal development, you become highly successful in every area of your life. These hypotheticals vividly paint a picture of how habits influence our lives.

If your life is a series of bad habits (remember: habits define who we are), habits such as procrastination, lack of exercise, negative thinking (yes, negative thinking is habitual), consuming junk, and failing to plan, among others, you are likely to struggle with achieving any sort of success in your life.

On the other hand, if your life is a series of good habits, good habits such as the ones we described above such as meditation, self-improvement, exercise, healthy eating, etc.–you can bet success will come to you as easily as breathing: effortlessly.

To achieve success, therefore, you have to practice success habits, not just for one day, but repeatedly until that thing (activity) becomes habitual and automatic. Unfortunately, while this process seems such an easy one, at least on paper, the process of habit adoption or change is never an easy one.

To help you understand how to create new habits, break bad old habits, and replace them with new positive ones that drive you towards the success you crave, let us discuss the process of habit formation.

# Chapter 13: Secrets That Influential People Use to Stick to Their Habits

Yes, you have learned all about how to create habits and the habits of the effective and successful but what is the guarantee that you will actually stick to them? Have you asked yourself, why these influential people seem to get so much done yet when you try chasing similar goals, it's a wild goose chase?

The difference is that many people do not understand that there is a big difference between wanting to change something and actually changing it. You might adapt and create these new habits but along the way, you lose your motivation and psych due to some negative factors. This in turn discourages you and you end up frustrated with not attaining your goals.

Therefore, sticking to your newly formed habits is important in ultimately reaching the goals you aimed for when you started this process of habit transformation. Creating and sustaining these good habits does not have to be necessarily difficult if you have a good plan to prevent yourself from backsliding. That is why you need strategies to help you stick to them for good. Here are some of the strategies to help you avoid setbacks and instead make sure you stick to your newly formed habits for good:

### Start Small In Your Habits And Progressively Grow

The problem with most of us is that we want to grow rich overnight and that is why instead of working from scratch and progressively growing, we want to become rich as quickly as possible. It is not bad to want more in life but make sure that you do not become greedy because patience pays.

If you quickly jump to bigger and more difficult habits, it will require you to use a significant amount of effort and will power. These two things work like a muscle, when you extend a muscle too much, it becomes tired; that is why you will be most likely to quit and go back to your old habits.

To avoid all this from happening after going through all that hustle, make sure you start doing the habits small before moving up a notch. If you want to change your diet instead of suddenly changing to the new habit quickly, start by adding vegetables to your normal diet and slowly implement other components of the diet. Before you know it, you will have achieved your goal of having your new habit slowly without rushing into it.

Remember always that you should aim on establishing the actual behavior first before moving to the more technical parts of the behavior. Do not increase the effort in behavior before it has become a natural part of you.

## Surround Yourself With Beneficial People

If you are trying to change a bad habit of eating healthy foods and your friend keeps on pulling you to have a bite, you are more likely to give in to the temptation. Therefore, if you surround yourself with people who contribute a lot to your bad old habits then you are definitely going to fail in achieving your goals. You need to surround yourself with people who are only concerned with making sure that you transform and stick to your habits completely i.e. people who are there to help you when you fall down and people who are there to motivate you to keep going by helping you out.

In fact, strive to make these people your accountability partners by declaring your intentions to them (it doesn't have to be a large group of people). In so doing, you will 'feel the pressure' to impress your accountability partners, which means you will do everything in your power to ensure the habit you are striving to build sticks. If you feel that verbal commitments are not enough, you can make money part of your conversation. Give someone a certain amount of money, which you pledge to lose if you do not follow a certain set of habits or activities over a certain period. In so doing, you will be under pressure not to lose your money, which in the end will work in your favor since you will ultimately build your desired habits.

## Make Sure That The Habit Is Implemented

Performing the habit continuously is the first step in making it autonomic. However, how can you keep doing the habit if you forget occasionally? Well, the best option is to make sure that you devise ways to help make sure you do not forget. Remember that these habits are new in your life and therefore, having to keep up with them everyday might be difficult. You need to have clear intentions and that is why poor intentions like "I will try eating a healthy diet whenever I can" will not cut it.

The first step in making sure that you implement the habits is to create an implementation intention. You have to refrain yourself from being pessimistic and disorganized when you use "I will try" to make statements concerning your habits. You have to be sure and optimistic and say "Whenever I'm eating anything, I will make sure that it is healthy and beneficial to my body."

Another good way to make sure you implement the habits is by linking your newly formed habit to an already existing one. Either, you can perform the new habit before the existing one or you can perform it after doing the already existing one. This strategy works best if you link two habits that are almost similar or can lead to the other in a way. For example, after eating a healthy breakfast, you have to eat a fruit before walking out. This way, you will always remember to eat a fruit once you take your breakfast. Make sure you try linking the habits and the first few times, try to observe if it is working out; if not, link the habit to another habit until you get it right.

Implementing scheduling is yet another good way to prevent you from forgetting to do your newly formed habits. Always remember that what gets scheduled gets done. For very important habits, give them space in your schedule so that you can avoid not having time or chance to perform them.

## Prepare For Failure

Man is to error. Nobody is perfect and that is why occasionally we fail in the things we do. This does not however mean that every time you fail, it's due to nature. One thing these influential people do is that they plan ahead for failure because they know everything they do is a risk and there is a probability of it failing.

Once you have formed a new habit and along the way you backslide and find yourself going back to your old habit, don't be hard on yourself. Instead of crying over spilt milk, design ways in which you will stop yourself from repeating the mistakes in the future. Better still; think of possible failures that you may get along the way and think of ways to prevent either of them from happening. This way, you will prevent the likelihood of giving up due to several failures along the way.

# Chapter 14: Living a Healthy Life Through Creativity

Are you one of those people that are really looking forward to retiring, just so you can sit down, put your feet up and rest? Or, are you looking forward to retirement so that you can finally do something you have always dreamed of doing, like taking that photography course, writing your memoirs or going on that trip of a lifetime?

If you can get your mind thinking about things you want to do when you retire, things you will finally have time for, you are more likely to avoid the challenges that affect many people in their golden years – the physical, emotional and mental challenges that come with suddenly not having to go to work, not having to put your thinking cap on all day and actually having to do something.

Research shows that being active and creative as you get older has a direct link to good health, better mental abilities and a much nicer outlook on life than you would have if you spent your retirement sitting in a chair doing nothing.

Back in 2003, a study published in "The Journals of Gerontology" showed that activity of the physical kind in those over the age of 55 helps to slow down the inevitable degeneration of the function of the brain. The year before that, another study determined that people who get together with their friends and chat can also improve brain function.

The director of the Center on Aging at the George Washington University has devoted a good deal of his professional life in studying the effects of creativity in older people. Gene Cohen, M.D., Ph.D, has carried out a number of studies on seniors and the effects on them when they are involved in community art projects.

The control group led a "normal" sedentary lifestyle, the one most of us relate to in retirement, while the second group was more involved in creative lifestyles. He found that the second group fell ill less, didn't need to see a doctor so much and were not prone to feeling depressed or lonely. He also says that the kinds of mental exercises we see in the media are good for making your brain sweat, for keeping your brain function alive – things like doing the daily crossword puzzle, reading and writing.

So, how can an active, creative lifestyle help you stay young at heart and in the brain?

### Be a Trailblazer

On the whole, people are living longer, much longer than ever before. On average, people are living 30 years longer – that's 30 years more you've got to do something with your life in, 30 years that previous generations simply didn't have. Unfortunately, society hasn't really caught up and there is still an awful lot of ageism about, people who think that, once you reach a certain age, you shouldn't be doing certain things. Creativity is all about thumbing your nose at those people and going for it.

Many people simply feel too intimidated to try anything new; they are limited by their own thought processes, thoughts that tell them they really shouldn't take that risk by doing what other people say seniors shouldn't do.

The real trick to an active and healthy life is to go where your creativity takes you, regardless of what other people think or say.

### Look locally first

If you want to learn a new hobby or a new activity, look within your own community first. There are plenty of community programs and you will often find plenty of opportunities to start something new, something you never dreamed of doing before.

And, very often, you will find yourself in an intergenerational class – with both older and younger people learning the same skills.

## Redefine your creative side

It really is never too late to learn something new even if you don't think that you are a creative person. Sometimes, we just don't realize how creative we really are until it's too late to do anything about it. Don't be one of those people who spend their last years on earth saying, "I wish." Instead, be the person who says, "Look what I've done with my life."

Very often, people who bloom late are the most creative of all. But don't make the mistake of thinking that creativity is synonymous with art – it isn't. Creativity is doing something you have a real passion for, no matter what your age or status in life. Yes, music and art are good things but they aren't the only things. Creativity is about so much more than that, it's about making something meaningful out of your life, realizing that, just because you are retired, it doesn't mean you can't hike that trail or take that ride across America.

## Do what you like doing

For those of you who choose a creative and active lifestyle when you retire, I would lay money on the fact that it is because you are doing something you like doing. According to studies, women who are in their 40s and 50s are very often workaholics and not many can find the time to start thinking about when they retire, to start hobbies that they like doing that can take them through their retirement years.

Mid-way through your working life is the time to start thinking about your goals, to start coming up with the ideas for what you are going to do when you are retired. Want to ride your bike across all 52 states? Start planning it. Want to hike the Appalachian Trail?

Start planning it, start getting fit enough to do it and working towards your goal.

There is nothing that says your goal has to be completed in so many days. It can take you 10 years if you want. The important thing is you have that goal and you do something about it.

# Chapter 15: The Awakening

Many of the success stories of beating opiate addiction began with one of two things happening. Most times it required both. One, they hit rock bottom. Two, they had an emotional or spiritual awakening. Unfortunately for many people who hit rock bottom, they still don't stop. They continue struggling with their addiction, sometimes for years, until their own awakening finally graces them.

Whether you are religious or not, this awakening may be extremely important for your success. If you are not religious, look for it anyway. The world will bring it to you - expect it. If you are searching for it and want it, it will happen. If you **are** religious and haven't had your awakening yet, don't pray to God to help you quit drugs. Doing this is pointless without having had some kind of big moment of clarity.

Instead, ask him to bring you your awakening. If you quit taking drugs without it, chances are, it won't last long but this doesn't mean that it would have been for not. It can be very hard to tell which of these moments is **the one**. The only way for you to know for sure whether **this is it** or not, is by quitting each and every time you have one of these eye-opening experiences.

Every big moment of clarity that you have is not the magical one. You may have to quit again and again. This said, if you don't do this, you could be missing out on some very important and precious gifts that you are being given. If you attempt to quit taking opiates each and every time you have one of these eye-opening experiences, eventually you are bound to make it happen and never look back at your old life of addiction again. The only way anyone ever fails is when he stops trying.

I get it, who wants to go through the withdrawals again and again? No one does. But remember, as long as you are on pain medication, there will always be times that you will run out of them. And the longer you take it the more times this will happen to you during the duration of your drug use. You see, you will have to withdrawal over and over again anyway. If we never had to deal with withdrawals, there would be no honest reason for us to even want to quit and read books like this one.

Again, if you take the chance and quite at every opportunity that feels it may be right, you will eventually end up completely clean and therefore not have to deal with or worry about ever having to go through those withdrawals again. You are starting in the right direction. Later in the book you will find ways to alleviate your withdrawals. This will make it easier for you during the quitting process and in turn, will also make it easier for you to want to try again later if the need arises.

# Chapter 16: Frame of Mind

Once you feel that you are ready and make the decision to stop taking pain pills, there is a certain way that you need to set your frame of mind. You need to know one hundred and ten percent that you cannot go on living the way that you have been. If you can still find reasons to continue taking the drug, then you are not ready to quit. If you can't picture your life without them, then you are not ready to quit. See your future as good, clean and happy. Imagine it, and want it without excuses to use.

Make a plan. Set the date that you are going to quit, or begin the process of quitting. Get excited about this event coming up. Pump yourself up about it as much as you can. This is a new beginning you are looking forward to. You CAN NOT see this time in your life as something to dread.

I can't stress this enough. If you are dreading the day your set date rolls around on the calendar, then not only are you going to have a harder time quitting, but your chances of success are going to be very slim. The happiness you feel for your outcome should be stronger than the fears you feel. Constantly focus on your brighter days ahead, not the quitting process.

No, of course it won't be easy. It will be hard, very hard. You will go through some pain. That's okay isn't it? Again, ask yourself this question. Will my new life of freedom be worth the short - term pain I will have to endure? Will it? If your answer is conflicted, then you have some serious thinking to do. If your answer is yes, then you need to use that as a form of excitement.

The more you imagine the way you want your life to be, the easier it will be to be happy about what you are about to do. What you don't want to do is imagine it and sulk in the fact that you are not there yet. You need to visualize your future and be happy that you are finally on your way there.

How the Brain Works

In order to understand habit stacking, we must first have an elementary science lesson in how our brain receives new information. Neurons or cells send messages to the brain as well as receive messages from the brain through connections. The brain trims away connections that are not used frequently and those that are used regularly are built up and become stronger.

An example of how this works is if you spend years studying a particular sport (dance or football for example), your brain will strengthen the connections between those dancing or athletic cells. The more you dance or play, the stronger those connections become. In addition, they will grow to be more efficient and effortless each time you practice. As your brain develops, stronger quicker connections within the cells are built. Your skills will be more evident and you will execute them with more ease and expertise each time you use them. A gradual and natural change will eventually occur that leads to a person's improved competence. These strong cell connections support the new skill development.

Introducing the New Habit

Now that we understand how our mind works, we can easily understand the birth of a new habit. The vast majority of researchers state that it takes 21 days to develop a new habit. While, this may work for some, it is wise to look at both the individual as well as the new habit. People are diverse in many aspects and therefore it is virtually impossible to place everyone in the same development mold.

It is true, that if you repeat an action for 21 days without breaking the chain, you have effectively created a new habit. The critical point upon which to reflect is whether a person can maintain the new habit long term. What will happen when the chain is broken? Or if the routine is switched or changed, is that new habit truly imbedded into your being?

# Chapter 17: Your Support-System & Getting Real

Once are you are ready you are going to need support. You are going to need to tell people of your plan. This SHOULD NOT be your little kept secret. If your addiction has been a secret then this is the time for you to tell everyone of it.

The reason you need to tell people is not because you need them to know you have been taking painkillers just to get through each day. It's not because you need to be accountable for what you have been doing. The reason you need to tell people is because you need to be accountable for what you are going to do. You need to let as many people as you can, in on your venture of quitting opiates.

We're going to use a bit of psychology here. The more who know of your plan to quit taking opiates, the more ashamed and embarrassed you will feel if your plan fails. That is exactly what you want. The more embarrassed you might be of failure, the less likely the chances of failure.

Most people will be happier that you are quitting, than they will be upset at what you have been doing. You know whom you can trust and whom you can't. You know which people will be the most helpful to you.

The most helpful people are the ones who will tell you that you can do it. If you have friends or family members that you have told this to before, who have seen you fail and now they don't believe you anymore, then these are not the people you should tell. Avoid telling them until you have some time of sobriety in. The last thing you need is to hear people telling you that you can't or won't do it.

Tell the right people – the people who will be supportive of you. Tell the people who will be excited for you and whom will show it on their faces. Tell the people who are going to cheer you on. Tell the people who are not afraid to ask you how your sobriety is going later. In fact, ask them to ask you about your sobriety later.

You know who these people are. Tell as many of these people of your upcoming sobriety as you possibly can and avoid telling the naysayers until later. Believe me, after you do this, you will try all the more to make it happen for you due to embarrassment of failure.

Keep in mind that I only use the word **failure** for lack of better word. I could use the word unsuccessful, however, **unsuccessful** doesn't quite have the stigma that it needs in order to make this part of the process work. But anytime that you don't find success it is never **failure**. It is a learning process that you can look back on and evaluate so as to not make the same mistakes the next time.

Now getting back to telling the world of your upcoming endeavor. If you don't want to tell people, here is another question to ask yourself. **What is the real reason I don't want people to know?** Is it because you are embarrassed or ashamed? Or is it because somewhere in the back of your mind, you are hoping that this does fail so that you can go right back to using?

To some, this question may sound ridiculous. But to many, it is an honest question that really needs to be answered. Many people want to quit, but they are so afraid of the unknown that they will subconsciously sabotage their own success. They cannot see the wonderful, life changing possibilities that lay before them. Are you one of those people? If so, the more you recognize this fact, the easier it will be to get over these negative thoughts.

# Chapter 18: Getting Ready for Detox

When you are getting ready for the big day, there are several things you will need to do. Your detox can take anywhere between 5 to eight days, give or take a day. Trust me, you will not want to do anything but lay around your house for most of this time, so taking some time off work in advance is a smart thing to do. If you don't, you can expect to have a lot call in sick days ahead of you. It's better to be prepared. This will be one less worry. If you have made the decision to taper off the drug, then you might not have to take the time off depending on how quick and extreme your taper is. If you are going to taper off slowly, you might be okay. But if you are planning on tapering off quickly, let's say, in a about a week, then you may need the time off as well.

Tell your doctor about your plan. Many people won't want to do this either because they want to ensure that they will still be able to get their meds later if plans change. If this is the case, then again, you need to take a serious look at exactly how serious you are. You could use your doctor's help. He will probably recommend and help you with a taper plan. If that is not what you want then ask him to give you some kind of muscle relaxer or anxiety medication. These medications won't make it all better or make the pain go away, but they will make it a bit easier to get through the next week. I would suggest using these medications whether you are going cold turkey or tapering. Either way you decide to do this, it's not going to be easy.

Some would say that using these medications is not a good idea because of the chance of forming a new addiction. If you go about it the right way, you will lower your chances of this happening. This is where your friends and family come in. You need to find a really close friend or relative who will be willing to assist you. Preferably your friend will be able to stay with you for a while during your detox, especially if you have children at home. If this isn't a possibility you need to at least be able to get in touch with this person every day while you're detoxing. When you get the medications from your doctor, give them to your new assistant. You will decide on a certain amount of this medication per day, and your friend will give you exactly that dose, and no more.

Try this out for a day, and if you need to up the dose and the amount in the prescription permits, then by all means, up the dose. Make sure your friend understands this before you give up the medication for them to hold. Your doctor will have a better insight on how much of this medication you should take, but sometimes doctors underestimate the severity of the withdrawals and give you as little as possible. But some is always better than none.

Your doctor may not be comfortable giving you a muscle relaxer or anxiety med. If not, ask him about Gabapentin, also known as Neurontin. This is a nerve medication that is used for epilepsy and nerve pain. When I slipped my disc I was given gabapentin. But I never took it because I had something much better. I had my Percocet. I wish I could go back in time. I had bottles and bottles of it stacked under my bathroom sink. I got them from my doctor for years along with the Percocet. I saved them in case I ever hurt my back again and didn't have any Percocet. Little did I know at the time, that supposedly it works wonders for withdrawal symptoms too. Although there have been a small number of people who have become addicted to it, those are very unusual and rare cases as it doesn't give a euphoric feeling. It's not a narcotic. Your doctor may be happy as a clam to prescribe this one to you.

Gabapentin has been known to sometimes cure your withdrawals almost completely. This could be the miracle drug that all painkiller addicts have been searching for. If your doctor does give them to you, try it out for a day before your actual quit day. See if it works before you take time off work. You may not even need it.

Now getting back to your detox in case the Gabapentin doesn't work for you as well as it does for others, or you simply can't get your hands on it.

Set up your home to be as comfortable as possible. Try and make sure that it is clean when you begin your detox. Make one big trip to the grocery store. Stock up on canned and frozen foods. You may want to get some fresh fruit and vegetables you can eat raw as well. Make sure you get plenty of things you can whip up quickly. You won't be very hungry, but you are still going to need to eat. The more food you have in your home, the more likely you are to eat something. If you're not hungry and you are trying to force yourself to eat, there is nothing worse than searching an empty refrigerator. Like I said before, once the detox starts, you won't want to do much, including cleaning, cooking and shopping.

Stock up on lots of movies. Comedies are always best for situations like this because they are better at distracting you. Make sure you rent the 1 week rentals if you are not using Netflix. I don't recommend books even if you are a reader. Chances are high that you won't even be able to pay much attention to the movies for the first few days let alone concentrate on a book. This all sounds scary, I know. But remember, you are getting ready for your new beginning. It's all very worth it. I know because I've done it.

## Withdrawal Symptoms

If you are reading this book, you probably already know what symptoms are involved in the withdrawals. But this wouldn't be a book about opiate and pain pill addiction without them. Even though Vicodin isn't an opiate, it still has the same withdrawal symptoms.

Withdrawals are most commonly compared to flu like symptoms. But not just any flu, the worst flu you've ever had. If your addiction is less severe, you'll probably only experience a few of these symptoms, however, if your addiction is heavy, your withdrawals will match the severity. Here is what you can expect.

-Muscle and joint aches

-**Insomnia** (pain pills numb the feeling of being tired so you probably haven't felt truly tired in a while. Because of this, your tiredness will feel more severe)

-**Nightmares** (when you do sleep)

-**Restless legs** (temporary Restless Leg Syndrome)

-Diarrhea

-Hot and cold sweats

-**The feeling of creepy crawlies under the skin** (like Restless Leg Syndrome for the whole body)

-The shakes

-Exhaustion

-Depression

-Anxiety

-Loss of hunger

-Yawning

-Rapid heart beat

-Watering eyes and nose

-Goose bumps

-Pupil Dilation

-Sudden muscle jerks

-Back Pain

-Nausea and vomiting

**-Lowered immune system** (many people get a lowered immune system, which leads to rashes, acne breakouts, colds and infections)

**-Hypnic or Hypnagogic jerk** – Some people have dreams as if they are falling and have just hit the ground (this is how most people describe it). This causes a body jerk, which wakes them right away. Not everyone gets this, but it can be scary if you don't know what it is. This should only happen right before falling into REM sleep.

# Chapter 19: The Kick-off

So far, we have seen how our minds automatically try to derail change, and we now know that there are mental tools to make change less uncomfortable and more directed. With a clear vision of where we are going and a list of smaller steps to take us there, we are now ready to confront the next problem. Between where we want to go and getting started lies a yawning chasm that all of us have to cross. For many people, it is that kick-off, that first small step, which is the hardest to take. They have a vision of where they want to go and a list of progressive strategies for getting there, but still they stagnate. That stagnation can cripple your attempts at moving toward greater things. It can prevent you from becoming the person you know in your heart that you are capable of being. Steering a ship is only possible if that ship is moving forward.

Self-discipline is a choice, and one that only you can make. It may sound trite, but the only way to move forward is to move forward. Planning for it, having a clear objective and focusing on your end goals is all very well, but if you don't actually do something, then all you are doing is setting yourself up to be frustrated and unhappy. Renowned Christian author John Ortberg points out that 'The single most destructive thing we can do is to do nothing; taking one small step can be extremely powerful in robbing failure of its power.'

Being aware of this puts you in a position to take the necessary action. Unfortunately, it also puts the ball in your court and deprives you of any excuse if action is not taken. The world we inhabit saturates us with distractions. Facebook, Twitter, Google and plain old television are just some of the myriad of things we use to avoid doing what it is that is most important. Things we know we really should be doing. One way to overcome all of these diversions is to establish the unbreakable rule of putting your objectives first. With your list in hand and your vision of where you are going in mind, dedicate the first hour or two of the day to doing those things that are most important to achieving your goal. Forget about opening your email or watching the morning news. Instead, dive into the task that you know is more important. Failure to do this will see you constantly surrendering priorities to matters of lesser importance. The result is that you will delay achieving your primary goal, and very often you will abandon the pursuit altogether.

Of course, not all of us have the luxury of scheduling our day in a manner that would be most beneficial. We have children to feed, meetings to attend and commitments that cannot be delayed. If activities of that nature prevent you tackling your goals at the beginning of the day, then build in another block of time that will be dedicated toward your primary focus. Write it into your diary and make every effort to adhere to it. When the time does come around, then dive into the task immediately and don't give your instinct for procrastination time to develop. One of the skills that goes hand-in-hand with self-discipline is time management. In many ways, they are part and parcel of the same thing.

Remember that the delaying and avoidance tactics that your brain suggests are a type of fear orientated around the avoidance of discomfort. In consistently overcoming distraction and excuses, you are going to discover something very powerful. Activity has the capacity to overcome fear and self-doubt.

In her bestselling book, The Five Second Rule, motivational speaker and author, Mel Robbins, suggests that if you have trouble getting started on a task then you should count down backwards from five to zero. By the time you reach zero you must be up and active. She proposes that the act of counting engages a different part of the brain, and that it is then less able to come up with diversions and excuses. This method is a great way to cross that chasm between desire for activity and actual activity itself. You may choose to adapt it or create your own action motivator, but whatever method you use, try to find one that sees you getting into action within seconds. Further delays increase the risk of not getting started at all.

## Reward yourself

There is no doubt, especially in the early stages, that developing self-discipline can be tough. In many ways it is like building any other habit. It requires constant repetition to become thoroughly ingrained in our lives. Highly successful people are those who have developed that act of self-discipline to the point that they are no longer really aware that they are practicing it. Eventually, as you become more accustomed to using self-discipline, you will find it becoming less of a chore and more of a habit. While it may be comforting to know that things will get easier eventually, I imagine you are looking for strategies to get you through the difficult times that you face right now.

A big factor in dealing with these problems lies in how you perceive them. Absorbing any new skill requires a degree of stamina. Self-discipline is a skill. The good news is that skills can be learned and developed. The bad news is that skills have to be learned and developed. You are not simply going to wake up one morning and discover that you have generated a wonderful and life-changing new skill just because you want it. If that were the case, you would already have self-discipline and I would be finishing off a round of golf, having just scored at least three holes in one. If we recognize that we are going to have setbacks and failures, we are better prepared for them and they are less likely to derail our end plan. We need to learn to treat these setbacks as lessons and to examine each of them and see where we went wrong so that we are better able to avoid repeating them.

After making your list of goals for the day, you might have checked your email instead, only to find that several things there required your attention, the net result being you failed to complete your list. When re-examining this setback, you learn that you should have put your goals first and let the emails wait. Alternatively, you may decide that these sorts of issues are important and that your block of time for dealing with personal goals needs to be scheduled later in the day. Either way, you have now examined what was a potential derailment and come away with something positive. Sure, you have slipped back a little on completing what was on your list, but the fact that you have learned from it and not allowed it to cripple your resolve is important.

Because self-discipline is hard, and because we are human, and therefore bound to fail on a fairly regular basis, we need to learn to celebrate the positives. It is too easy to treat ourselves harshly over minor failures and forget to celebrate minor successes. This is one of the reasons we have begun to use lists. They don't only break our vision down into manageable chunks. They also give us a reference we can refer to in order to see how far forward we have come. A classic example of this is when we are watching a politician or big company CEO come under pressure when they are being interviewed for some perceived failing. The interviewer inevitably points to the failing and the interviewee responds with a slight acknowledgment of the problem before launching into a list of his or her successes. In part, this may be because these people have been trained in how to deal with the press, but these are also self-disciplined and highly motivated people. They have had years of training themselves to see the positives even when they are wrapped up in a tangled web of negativity.

That ability to always pick the diamond out of a bowl of pebbles is valuable. Your efforts toward becoming more self-disciplined are going to be dealt a severe setback if, when things don't go perfectly, all your hard work comes undone. Early on in this process you must start to train yourself to recognize each and every little positive and use those as reasons to celebrate.

To augment this ability to see the glass as always being half full, you should also try to surround yourself with positive people who are of a similar disposition. Negativity and a depressive mindset can spread like an infectious disease. Likewise, if you are in the company of successful and optimistic thinking people, that attitude will rub off on you. Some self-disciplined and successful people may be difficult to get on with, but the one thing they seem to share is optimism.

One way of developing a more positive attitude is to keep a gratitude diary. Several times a day, write down little things that have gone well or that you have found pleasing. Don't always search for the grand moments like winning a promotion at work. Instead, focus on the little things such as seeing a flower poking through a crack in the sidewalk or hearing a bird sing. Gradually your mind will tune into these small rewards and you will become better able to see glimmers of light where once all you saw was darkness.

We have looked extensively at the mind and attitude, as they are both crucial factors when trying to develop your self-discipline levels. It should not be forgotten that the human body is an integrated unit. Without wishing to turn this into a book on staying healthy, remember that getting appropriate amounts of nutrition, exercise and sleep are all going to add to your overall strategy. At the same time, as your capacity for self-discipline increases, your ability to exercise and follow a healthy lifestyle are also going to be augmented. That, in turn, will offer you more to celebrate and be grateful for.

## Consistency & Timing

How long does it really take to form a new habit? This is a question that has been the subject of a common misconception. If you do a Google search, the first answer that you get is 21 days, based on a book by Maxwell Maltz called Psycho-Cybernetics, which was published in 1960. According to Dr. Maltz, he observed that his patients had an adjustment period of around 21 days before they will get used to changes in their appearance.

Applying these observations to his own life, the plastic surgeon realized that it also took him around 21 days to form a new habit, which prompted him to name this period as the minimum required before new behaviors and ways of thinking were established. Psycho-Cybernetics was a big hit, selling more than thirty million copies.

However, Dr. Maltz never intended 21 days to be an absolute number, but in the years since his book was published, many self-help gurus have adopted it as a kind of magic number, leading to a misconception that it takes **only** 21 days to form a new habit.

Researchers have since disputed this myth by conducting their own studies. For example, at a study conducted in the University College London, health psychology researcher Phillippa Lally asked 96 test subjects to try and develop a new habit over a 12-week period. Each subject reported on their efforts, which ranged from habitually drinking a bottle of water with lunch to developing the habit of running fifteen minutes a day before dinner.

At the end of the period, researchers analyzed their data and found that on the average, it took around 66 days before a new habit was formed. And the actual time it took each person before the habit became automatic varied based on his or her individual circumstances, taking from a low of eighteen days to a high of 254 days.

What this research basically implies for those who are trying to break a bad habit is that there is no 'one-size-fits-all' period before you can call your efforts a failure. If you were unable to break a habit within 21 days, for example, it does not mean that you can never break it. It just means that it may take you longer to do so, thus, it is important to persist and remain consistent in your efforts.

## Self-Awareness

A habit is defined as something we do automatically as a result of some stimuli. For example, smokers, when they are exposed to stress, automatically reach for a cigarette. People, who are addicted to shopping automatically go to the mall when they feel lonely or depressed, to make themselves feel better. Thus, if you want to break a bad habit, the first step is to develop self-awareness that, first, you have a bad habit, and second, what is actually behind it.

When you develop self-awareness, you become conscious that you are acting automatically and can thus take control of your actions. Instead of automatically shopping, the shopaholic can find a more positive way of dealing with negative emotions. Strive to become aware if you are automatically reaching for something when stressed out, and consciously stop yourself from doing so.

The first step in building self-awareness is to become conscious of just how bad the habit that you are trying to break is. If you are a smoker, for example, keep track of just how many cigarettes you are smoking in a day. You may be surprised at how many sticks you are actually smoking. Or if you are a shopaholic, sit down and take an accounting of how much you are spending per week or month. This will tell you how serious the bad habit is and give you an idea of the milestones that you have to set towards beating it.

The next step is to become conscious of what sets off your bad habit. What are the particular stress points that drive you to indulge in your habit? Write them down so that you become more aware of them so, when you are confronted with these stress points, you can find positive ways to deal with them.

Finally, it helps to become more aware of your feelings. You can do this by learning mindfulness or learning how to live in the moment. When you are consciously mindful, your mind is in the present rather than being distracted by thoughts of the past or the future. You are aware of everything that is going on in your mind and your body.

### Finding the Source

In order to break a bad habit effectively, you need to understand what your particular "habit loop" is. Essentially, there are three steps that lead to a habit being formed:

"Cue" - This is a trigger that causes your brain to perform a particular act or habit, unconsciously. For smokers, the cue may be a stressful day at work or feeling bored. For shopping addicts, it may be a feeling of unhappiness or anxiety.

"Routine" - This is the habit itself.

"Reward" - This refers to the satisfaction or pleasure that you get from the habit. For example, smokers may feel a sense of relief from tension.

The reason why habits are performed unconsciously is because they are formed in an area of the brain called the basal ganglia. This area is responsible for developing memories, emotions and recognizing patterns. Decisions, on the other hand, are formed in the prefrontal cortex, but when a habit is formed, the behavior becomes automatic and the prefrontal cortex effectively goes to 'sleep'.

Hence, to break a habit, you have to identify the cues or triggers that cause you to indulge in a certain habit or behavior. There are five kinds of triggers:

Location - The place that causes you to indulge in the behavior. For example, many smokers may smoke more heavily in the office than at home.

Time - You may feel more inclined to indulge in a particular habit at a particular time of day, such as first thing in the morning or just before going to sleep at night.

Mood - The emotional state you are in when you want to indulge in the habit.

People - Individuals who cause the habit to be triggered. For a smoker, for example, it may be his boss or supervisor. For a shopaholic, it may be a relative whom he/she finds unpleasant.

Action - Many people associate performing a habit with a certain action. For example, truck drivers who spend a lot of time on the road may feel the desire to smoke when they are behind the wheel and driving on the highway.

Hence, to break a habit, you have to identify your habit triggers. You can do this by taking a small notebook with you, then writing down which of these triggers you notice is happening when you want to indulge in a habit. Once you identify your trigger, you can start breaking the habit by avoiding it or learning to deal with it in a more positive fashion.

You can also more easily break a habit by starting when you go on vacation. The reason for this is that when you're in a new location, all of your habit triggers are no longer present, thus, it is easier to form new patterns of behavior.

## Healing & Regrowth

When you're in the process of breaking a bad habit and creating a new one, it is important to accept that you will backslide, make mistakes and give in to temptation. Thus, you should learn to be kind to yourself and not beat yourself up. Doing this will only make it more likely that you will give up on your attempts to eliminate a habit, since you will consider yourself a failure.

Even if you have a long-term plan, you must take things on a day-to-day basis. Celebrate every day that you have succeeded in meeting a milestone. On the other hand, if you fail on a particular day, do not tell yourself that you are a failure.

One particular pitfall you should avoid is the binge. This happens when you slip up, so you tell yourself that you'll do better tomorrow, but you'll indulge yourself today. Thus, let's say you are quitting smoking and you are at the point where you are only smoking one cigarette a day. If you end up smoking three, don't tell yourself that since you already slipped up, you should just indulge yourself for the rest of the day.

Instead, what you should do is try to lessen the damage caused by your backsliding. Thus, if your target is one and you've already smoked three, just stop smoking. Don't indulge yourself.

In addition, you can use positive statements to help you avoid getting discouraged. For example, you can tell yourself, "Yes, I made a mistake but I will do better next time." Or you can say, "I made a mistake but I forgive myself."

Remember that you never really break a habit or an addiction, and that a trigger can easily cause you to fall back into old patterns. So remember to be kind to yourself, but at the same time, remain vigilant.

Once you've successfully used all these strategies to break a bad habit, congratulations! You have learned a lot of new skills that you can use not just to break bad habits, but also to make your life better. For example, being more self-aware can help you find areas of your life where you can improve.

To illustrate, you may notice that at the workplace, you have a tendency to be careless when it nears the end of the working day. You may also unconsciously drive more recklessly when confronted by rude drivers. Once you are aware of this tendency, you can correct it and avoid mistakes that may get you into trouble later.

Also, don't forget to constantly celebrate your new life by rewarding yourself for as long as you are able to avoid your old habits. For example, if you've stopped smoking, you should give yourself a reward at the end of every week that you've successfully avoided giving in to the temptation of a cigarette.

In addition, you may want to start a gratitude journal. At the end of every day, write down in your journal all the things that you have to be grateful for. For example, you can give thanks for something as simple as waking up healthy or making it back home without any untoward incident. Or you can be thankful for having a job when so many people are unemployed.

By doing this, you make it less likely that you will fall back on old, bad habits due to stress or frustration. It will also help improve your outlook in life and make you more appreciative of the things you have, rather than feeling bad about what you don't have.

### Aristotle, the Greek Philosopher

"We are what we repeatedly do. Excellence then, is not an act but a habit." There is much debate over whether this is a quote of the Greek Philosopher, Aristotle or from Will Durant's The Story of

Philosophy. Regardless of whom the true author is, we must take into consideration the message the quote is delivering. Basically, it means we are what we do. Our actions reflect who we are. If we want to be good at something, we have to practice and duplicate our actions until we can do it extremely well.

This is a very poignant statement as it can work for negative issues as well. We certainly do not want to excel in negativity. Therefore, we need to choose our habits wisely and strive for positive results. It literally means that we will excel in our endeavors, as it will become part of our core being.

We are What We Do

Successful people are where they are today as a result of their good habits. Your habits determine 95% of your behavior. Everything that you are or that you will ever accomplish will be determined by the quality of the habits that you form.

Aristotle's philosophy is that the human tendency is to achieve happiness. So whatever endeavor we choose to strive toward we must do it repeatedly until we achieve our personal excellence.

# Chapter 20: Goal Setting and Goal Oriented

Fundamentally, creating good habits and becoming goal oriented is essential to developing habits that you will stick with on a continual basis. A goal oriented person is someone who has a strict mindset of what they want to accomplish. They set goals and will do whatever it takes to achieve their goals, even to the point of taking risks to realize their dreams. They understand it requires hard work and dedication to reach their goals. Goal oriented individuals focus on their goals and the things they hope to acquire. They have a need to be productive and efficient because the goals they set are concrete and detailed.

Being goal oriented means you must be a habitual goal setter and be devoted to working from clear written goals every day. This type of attitude is what drives a person to stay with a positive habit because they want the desired outcome.

## What is Habit Stacking?

Habit stacking or habit chaining is a proven method that allows a person to make necessary changes in their beliefs and behaviors and develop habits that can and will affect their lives in many ways.

Start With What You Know

This technique is a good starting point to maintaining quality habits for years rather than months. As we recently learned, our brain builds a strong network of cells to support our behaviors. The more you do something, the stronger and more efficient the connection becomes. For example, most people are conditioned to brushing their teeth every morning. To stack another habit would be to set a timer for 2 minutes to ensure you are brushing your teeth long enough. You are already brushing your teeth so you are just adding another step to an everyday ritual. It will be surprisingly easier to develop this new habit because your brain already has developed a strong connection to this task. Over the years they have built a strong connection in that area. The technique of habit stacking is simply "stacking" a new habit on top of a current habit. This method works because your old habit is already strongly connected to your brain. By adding a new habit to an already established and efficient thought process enables you to quickly adjust to the new habit.

Using the key words "before" or "after" is important when defining new habits. Examples of habit stacking:

Exercise Habit: Before I shower each morning, I will run on the treadmill for 20 minutes.

Diet Habit: Before lunch each day, I will eat one apple.

Working Habit: After I turn on my work computer, I will review all new emails and keep my inbox up to date.

Inspirational Habit: After I fix my morning cup of coffee, I will review the daily inspirational quote.

Make the Connection

Habit stacking works in any aspects of your day to day routine. Since your current habits are already connected or wired to your brain, your new habits are more easily linked to an already effective system. Therefore, you are more likely to stick to the new behavior.


The Three Components of Habit Stacking

There are three preliminary components to learning to effectively habit stack. Your first step should be to identify positive habits that you do every day. Don't discredit everyday mundane habits that you don't think twice about as these habits can play a critical part in establishing the foundation for habit stacking. Secondly, you need to identify habits or behaviors that you would like to begin to include in your day-to-day activities. Thirdly, you will need to be aware of the size of your new habit. You will want to start off somewhat small and eventually escalate and build upon your new habit gradually. Success is not immediate and neither is discipline. It will take time to get from where you are today to where you want to be tomorrow. In our busy life, forming positive habits can be difficult to say the least not to mention keeping and maintaining them and instill them in our daily activities.

# Conclusion

There will be days when all that we covered, all the work you've put in and all your good intentions may seem useless. Times when it will be difficult to sit down and do what you have to do.

To put on your running shoes or to say the kind words you want to say to your loved ones. Hours where you want to close the curtains and lock the door. You are going to make mistakes and different problems will arise. There will be fresh tears and unhappy moments.

Lasting recovery won't change that.

But it will give a new perspective and hope in the beginning, and it will give purpose and energy later on. Then you will feel the strength, deep within you, to deal with the storms and the rain as **you**, a strong, resilient and caring person. You will feel peace of mind, courage and an undeniable feeling of self-confidence and love for life.

And there will come a moment, when you fully enjoy the fruits of your work and the safety of your outstanding character, a moment where you dance, have one of these rare, great conversations, or walk on a magnificent island with your loved one… There, glancing over the blue water and feeling a tingling breeze in the sunny afternoon, you will stop for a moment. Realizing, without a single doubt, that all of the struggle, all of the pain and all of the tears have been worth it.

# Book Four
## COMPLEX PTSD, TRAUMA AND RECOVERY

## Introduction

This book will shed light on the topic trauma. Trauma is a disorder, which makes a person depressed and agitated about certain events. Trauma can be of many types. It can be psychological trauma, physical trauma and physiological trauma. Trauma has symptoms as well and it can be cured through proper medication and a flexible routine of exercises. The longer we live, the more unavoidable it is that we will encounter injury. Injury is the reaction to a profoundly upsetting or upsetting occasion that overpowers a person's capacity to adapt causes sentiments of defenselessness, reduces their feeling of self and their capacity to feel the full scope of feelings and encounters.

It does not segregate and it is unavoidable all through the world. A World Mental Health overview led by the World Health Organization found that in any event 33% of the in excess of 125,000 individuals studied in 26 unique nations had encountered injury. That number rose to 70% when the gathering was restricted to individuals encountering center issue as characterized by the DSM-IV (the arrangement found in the Diagnostic and Statistical Manual of Mental Disorders, fourth Edition). Yet, those numbers are only for occasions that have been accounted for; the genuine number is most likely a whole lot higher.

While there are no target criteria to assess which occasions will cause post-injury side effects, conditions normally include the loss of control, selling out, maltreatment of intensity, defenselessness, agony, disarray as well as misfortune. The occasion need not ascend to the degree of war, cataclysmic event, nor individual attack to influence an individual significantly and adjust their encounters. Awful circumstances that reason post-injury side effects differ significantly from individual to individual. Surely, it is exceptionally abstract and it is imperative to manage at the top of the priority list that it is characterized more by its reaction than its trigger.

## Regular Responses and Symptoms of Trauma

Reaction to a horrible accident changes fundamentally among individuals, yet there are some essential, basic indications.

Enthusiastic signs include:

bitterness
outrage
forswearing
dread
**disgrace**

**These may prompt:**

bad dreams
a sleeping disorder
trouble with connections
**passionate upheavals**

**Normal physical side effects:**

sickness
discombobulation
changed rest designs
changes in hunger
migraines
**gastrointestinal issues**

Mental issue may include:

PTSD

sorrow

uneasiness

dissociative issue

**substance misuse issues**

## Intense Stress Disorder versus Post-Traumatic Stress Disorder

Few out of every odd damaged individual creates post-awful pressure issue (PTSD). A few people build up certain side effects like those recorded above, however they leave following half a month. This is called intense pressure issue (ASD).

Sorts of Trauma When the side effects last over a month and truly influence the individual's capacity to work, the individual might be experiencing PTSD. A few people with PTSD don't show indications for quite a long time after the occasion itself. What's more, a few people manage PTSD side effects of an awful encounter for an amazing remainder. Indications of PTSD can heighten to fits of anxiety, sadness, self-destructive considerations and emotions, medicate misuse, sentiments of being detached and not

# Chapter 1: Defining Depression

There are many people all over the world who suffer from some form of depression. There are many disorders that fall under the umbrella category of depression. In this chapter, we will discuss what exactly depression is, as well as who it affects. We will also outline the various types of depression and the process of how depression is diagnosed.

What is Depression?

Depression is a common mood disorder. It is perhaps the most commonly diagnosed mental illness. However, although it is common, it can also be quite serious. Depression can be the cause of many severe symptoms that a person experiences. These symptoms can affect a person's daily life in the way that he or she thinks, feels, and even how he or she goes about his or her daily activities in life. Even the most mundane of daily activities such as eating, sleeping, and going to work or school can be affected by the disease of depression.

Depression is commonly diagnosed as clinical depression or as major depressive disorder, but these are just the two broadest terms used in the world of psychiatry in diagnosing depressive disorders. In order to receive a diagnosis of depression, the symptoms a person experiences must be persistent, nearly every day, for most of the day, for a minimum of a two week period of time. Symptoms and signs that may point to a diagnosis of depression include persistent anxiety or feelings of sadness or emptiness. This can include feelings of loneliness, low self-worth, and apathy. Feelings of intense pessimism or lingering hopelessness can also be a part of depression. A person who is depressed may lose interest in activities that he or she previously enjoyed or might no longer feel pleasure from spending time in previously much-loved hobbies. A depressed person may find that he or she is struggling with feelings of guilt, has become more irritable than normal, or feels helpless or worthless. A patient with depression may begin to talk and move in a slower manner than he or she did previously. This could be due to fogginess of fatigue that has enveloped the person or because of decreased levels of energy that have occurred. This can be related to the fact that many people suffering from depression have difficulties associated with sleep. These patients may experience insomnia, may often wake in the early morning hours, and often oversleep past the time they need to be up and functioning for work or school responsibilities. On the other hand, a person who is experiencing depression might have difficulty sitting still or feel restless and move about much more than what is normal for him or her. Another symptom that shows up commonly in cases of depression is the development of a mental fog that causes the person to have difficulty in remembering things, often lose his or her train of thought in conversations, have trouble concentrating, and unable to make even the most inconsequential decisions. A person with a depressive disorder often experiences changes in their appetite and therefore can have weight gains or weight losses. Some people lose their appetite altogether and find that they are only picking at their food if they even remember to eat and may experience weight loss, while others might eat more out of emotion or feelings of anxiety and so will see an increase in their weight. Both of these instances, although at extreme opposite ends of the spectrum, can be seen in people who have depression. Achiness and a variety of pains such as cramps, headaches, and digestive system issues are often found to be complaints of depressed patients. These pains often occur with no clear cause in a physical sense and often are not successfully treatable. Some of the most troubling concerns that may occur in patients with depression include uncontrollable thoughts of suicide and death, that in some cases can even lead to attempts of suicide.

Major depressive disorder or clinical depression is a diagnosis that is given when the symptoms discussed above cause distress to the person or cause a significant impairment in occupational or social functioning. The symptoms cannot have a relationship to the use or abuse of drugs and alcohol. There is a high mortality rate associated with major depressive disorder. The majority of these deaths are a result of suicide. It is of the utmost importance that anyone who thinks that he or she may have symptoms of depression is seen by a doctor, therapist, or psychiatrist in order to receive treatment for his or her condition. Depressive disorders are one of the most commonly diagnosed mental illnesses and in most cases are highly or completely treatable. Cognitive behavioral therapy is a short-term treatment that is highly effective when utilized to treat depressive disorders. The tools and strategies that are developed and learned in therapy can help a person to manage his or her mental conditions for a lifetime.

## Depression in Daily Life

Over 15 million people suffer from depressive disorders worldwide. Depression has been cited as one of the most common disabilities. Sadly, however, only approximately 10 percent of the millions of people who suffer from depression will receive adequate treatment.

One-quarter of adults in the United States live with a diagnosis of clinical depression also known as major depressive disorder. Although depression is a disorder that affects mental wellness, it can also take a toll on physical health. The cardiovascular system is especially vulnerable to the added stress placed upon it as a result of depression. The risk of suffering cardiovascular issues increases with a diagnosis of depression. This is mostly because the stress of depression causes the blood vessels to constrict, which makes the heart to work harder. People who have depression are also more likely to die as a result of a heart attack than their counterparts who do not have depression.

Depression can have a direct impact on nutrition especially in the form of fluctuations in appetite. Some people with depression do not eat enough, although it may seem an unpleasant side effect, it can actually contribute to anorexia nervosa, an eating disorder that can often time be quite severe. Many times, people who experience depression also have deficiencies in at least one of the following categories: B vitamins, amino acids, minerals, and omega-3 fatty acids. Without adequate amounts of these nutrients, the brain is unable to work as it is supposed to. In other cases, people with depressive disorders tend to overeat, even binging. This can lead to extreme weight gain, along with other physical health disorders such as the onset of type II diabetes, high blood pressure, and other illnesses that are a direct result of obesity. It may be difficult, but for these reasons, it is essential to maintain a healthy and nutritious diet while experiencing depression and while undergoing treatment for depressive disorders.

There are many factors which lead to worse overall health in those people who have a depressive disorder. These include poor sleeping patterns, poor eating habits, and a lowered immune system. It is just as important to receive treatment for one's physical health as for one's mental health when suffering from a depressive disorder.

Depression has an impact on every aspect of an individual's daily life. It affects your ability to eat and sleep. You may not be able to sleep well, you may have insomnia, or you may sleep away your entire day. All of these can be symptoms of depression. As far as eating goes, a person with a depressive disorder may eat too much or too little. Depression can rob a person of the ability to understand when they need to eat. Due to these factors, as well as the suppression of a person's immune system, depression can also have a negative effect on your health.

Depression can also take its toll on your relationships. The correlation between your moods and emotions and the health of your relationships is strong. When dealing with a mental health disorder such as chronic depression, it can be difficult to manage relationships. When your mood is often low, your behaviors can cause distance to occur between you and those with whom you have relationships. You may not even realize that you are behaving in a manner that can cause issues within your relationships. This is one way in which learning replacement behaviors through the use of cognitive behavioral therapy can be of great benefit to people who are suffering from depressive disorders.

There are multitude ways that depression can affect a person that may not be visible to others. One of the most common and extreme feelings that a person with depression may experience is guilt. Too often, a person with depression just does not feel the ability to do the things that need to be done. This includes showering, eating, cleaning his or her home, walking his or her dog, and more. A person with depression knows that these are things that should be done, but may not have the ability to complete them. The resounding feeling that follows the inability to complete these daily tasks is often guilt. Studies have shown that due to variances in the brain, people with depression feel guilt in a much more intense way than people who are not depressed.

Some people with depression have a much more difficult time dealing with their lives in the morning than at any other time of day. This is when it can be a tremendous struggle just to make it out of bed. Frustration, fatigue, anger, and extreme sadness are some of the feelings that can compound so-called morning depression when the mornings contain the most severe depression symptoms.

People with depression are often good at hiding things from the outside world. This can be due to the guilt that they feel. A person with a depressive disorder may actually be totally exhausted at any time, yet be able to pull himself or herself together in order to prevent causing distress to others. Some people who are experiencing depression might be great at acting like they are alright, even when they are not. This is why it is not always possible to look at a person and decide if he or she is depressed.

A behavior that is often displayed by people dealing with depression is canceling plans. This is especially common in cases of bipolar disorder. Many times a person feels that they can go through with the past when the time comes, however, when dealing with depression, once the time comes, the person is unable to participate or even to leave his or her house. Just the thought of preparing for a scheduled activity can be too much to deal. Entering the outside world, where it appears that everyone else is able to easily function can be extremely stressful for a person struggling to deal with the side effects of a depressive disorder.

One of the most difficult things for a person with depression to understand is that even though he or she knows logically that his or her life is great and he or she thinks that he or she should be happy and grateful, is that it is not always possible to use logic in terms of feelings. Even if a person does not think that there is any reason to feel depressed, the feelings are not necessarily on board. Feelings are not something that can be controlled and this can be one of the most frustrating circumstances a person with a depressive disorder must endure.

What Causes a Person to be Depressed?

In the United States, depression remains one of the most commonly diagnosed mental conditions. There are many factors at play in how a person can have a diagnosis of depression. These factors can be singular in nature or occur in a combination for the cause of depression in any one individual person. Depression can be genetic, meaning that it can be found in a person's DNA to have a higher risk of developing a depressive disorder. In many cases, a diagnosis of major depressive disorder is not merely a psychological effect, but may also be linked with biological factors as well. In some of these cases, a biochemical background of higher depression risk can contribute to the development of the disease of depression. Environmental factors can also be at play in the onset of depression. This is most commonly seen in cases of seasonal affective disorder which will be discussed in depth later in this chapter but can also include events like divorce or the death of a family member. Lastly, psychological reasons may be a causation of depression in some cases. In this case, pessimists and people who already carry conditions such as having low self-esteem may develop depression.

Some people develop depression as a comorbid diagnosis, along with another serious physical or mental medical condition. It is not uncommon for patients who experience cancer, diabetes, heart disease, or Parkinson's disease to develop depression as well. Any of the previously listed diagnoses can completely change a person's life and limit daily activities, which in turn, can lead to depression.

Some people carry higher risk factors for developing depression than the rest of the general population. As stated above, experiencing major life changes can predispose a person to be at a higher risk of developing depression. This can include anything from a job change or a move to a different city to the death of a loved one or going through a divorce. Trauma and stress can also cause depression to more easily occur in some people. Even high levels of stress on the job can contribute to a diagnosis of depression. People who experience post-traumatic stress disorder have a very much increased likelihood of depression. Post-traumatic stress disorder is often seen in soldiers who have been in active duty. It can also occur in other situations such as after an abduction, assault, or car wreck. Depression and post-traumatic stress disorder are often co-diagnosed in individuals. A patient who has a personal history of depression is more likely to have concurrent relapses of the disease, especially when medication or therapy has been discontinued. Likewise, a family history of depression allows for a higher incidence of depression to occur in an individual with this background.

Many medications carry potential side effects that include a possibility of predisposing a patient to become depressed. In addition to this, as discussed previously, certain diagnoses of physical illnesses can cause a person to more likely to develop depression. Sadly, in many of these cases, not only does the disease itself lend a higher incidence of depression, but in addition, the medication prescribed to treat or control the disease can carry depression as a potential side effect as well.

Depression often co-exists with the abuse of substances such as alcohol or illegal drugs. Since the two diseases share many of the same symptoms, sometimes it can be difficult to discover whether a person began to abuse substances because he or she was depressed or if the substance abuse led to depression. A propensity substance abuse is quite similar to that of depression. There can be a genetic link, as both depression and substance abuse tend to occur generationally in families. Issues with mental health can at times be found as the reason that a person began to abuse substances. Conversely, substance abuse can be a cause for later mental health issues to develop. Both depression and the abuse of alcohol or other illegal substances have an effect on the human brain. They both affect the same portion of the brain which is the one that is in charge of a person's response to stress.

This combination of depression and addiction is often referred to as a dual diagnosis. A dual diagnosis can be any form of mental illness that coexists in combination with any form of addiction. The instances of dual diagnoses in the US are rising in number. Another worrying fact is that both mental illnesses and substance abuse can down a person's immunity, causing them to more easily become susceptible to illnesses. One safety measure that can be taken is to avoid the use of alcohol and medications that have not been prescribed for you if you have depression or any other form of mental illness.

Depression can become so severe that it can be considered a disability. Depending on how well a person with a depressive disorder continues to function in daily life or how much impairment it creates will determine whether or not it is a true disability. Both major depressive disorder (or clinical depression) and bipolar disorder are considered to be disabilities by the social security administration.

## Types of Disorders Found Under the Umbrella Term of Depression

Anyone can potentially have a depressive disorder. Depression is not a disease that occurs only at a typical age, to a standard stereotype. Age, fitness level, wealth, race, or religion makes no difference in who can develop a depressive disorder. Depression can be mild or major. Mild depression typically has less severe symptoms and it mostly interferes with motivation. Major depressive disorders as previously stated is also called clinical depression is the most commonly diagnosed form of depression. It interferes in a person's daily life and with his or her daily activities.

Under the diagnosis of depression, many forms of the disease exist that have some degree of variance from each other. Some types of depression may be slightly different from each other, while others will develop only under certain unique circumstances. In addition to clinical depression and major depressive disorder, here we will discuss five other forms of depression that exist under the umbrella of the depression diagnosis.

The first type of disorder we will look at is a persistent depressive disorder. This is also termed as dysthymia. A persistent depressive disorder is a mood of depression that persistently lasts for a period of at least two years. This is a continuous, chronic, and long-term type of depression. Although the level of depression may not be as deep as it is with some other types of depressive disorders, the key component with the persistent depressive disorder is the length of time that it lasts. Similarly to clinical depression, the patient may experience symptoms such as feelings of inadequacy, hopelessness, and a lack of productivity. The person may lose interest in their typical daily activities and even in completing personal hygiene tasks on a regular basis. People who have a diagnosis of this disorder often feel gloomy and down, finding it difficult to be happy even in circumstances and occasions that would typically warrant higher spirits. This particular depressive disorder can cause impairments that range from mild to severe.

Next, we will discuss postpartum depression. This is a type of depression limited only to women who have experienced pregnancy or delivered a child. Postpartum depression is viewed as a complication of giving birth. It is a separate phenomenon from the typical "baby blues" that many women experience in the first few weeks after giving birth that includes difficulty in sleeping as well as some mood swings. Although this disorder has a certain event of causation, women who experience postpartum depression have full symptoms of a major depressive disorder that begins at any point during the pregnancy or after the delivery has occurred. The woman may experience anxiety, severe feelings of sadness, and extreme exhaustion. Many women who experience postpartum depression have a difficult time bonding with their new baby. Due to these symptoms, the woman experiencing postpartum depression may find it difficult to care for themselves or to complete daily care for their newborn babies. Many women with postpartum depression feel intense emotions of anger, sadness, and irritability. They may feel that they are not or are unable to be a good mother to their child. In some of the most severe cases, the new mother can have recurring fantasies of hurting either herself or her baby. This can include uncontrollable thoughts of suicide and death. There are cases of postpartum depression that can occur in new fathers as well as new mothers. Men experience the same symptoms as women, but they are typically focused on the lack of sleep they now endure, feelings of being unworthy as a father, and a lack of energy. Other symptoms may include insomnia, difficulty in bonding with the baby, and a withdrawal from friends and family members.

The third disorder we will outline is psychotic depression. This term is used when a form of psychosis is present in addition to the diagnosis of severe depression. It can also be referred to as major depression with psychotic features. Depression with accompanying hallucinations or delusions qualifies for this diagnosis. A delusion is defined as holding a false, disturbing fixed belief. Hallucinations can be auditory or visual in nature. Auditory hallucinations occur when a person hears things that are disturbing that no one else is able to hear. Likewise, visual hallucinations occur when a person sees upsetting things that are not seen by anyone else. Typically, the theme of the hallucinations and delusions are of a depressive nature. An example of this is a person with depression who experiences delusions of illness, poverty, or guiltiness. This is what occurs when the psychotic features are mood congruent. This means that they comply with typical depressive features. When the psychotic features are termed mood-incongruent, it is considered more dangerous for the patient and the other people in his or her life. With this type of hallucinations and delusions, the risk of suicide, harm to others, and self-harm are much increased. The hallucinations and delusions not only cause people to hear and see things that are not real but also to believe in them. Approximately one out of every five people who have a diagnosis of depression also has a psychotic diagnosis as well, making this disorder far from uncommon. This type of depressive disorder is more serious than some other types. Behavior, mood, sleep, and appetite are among the many areas of a person's life that this depressive disorder can affect. It typically requires immediate attention from a doctor and immediate medical treatment.

Seasonal affective disorder is a type of environmental depression that is commonly experienced to some extent by many people, particularly in the northern hemisphere where there are prolonged seasonal periods of darkness. This disorder is most commonly characterized by depression symptoms that have an onset in the winter months while lifting in the spring and summer months. The onset generally occurs due to the lessened availability of natural sunlight. Symptoms of seasonal affective disorder include an increased amount of sleeping, a withdrawal from social activities, and weight gain. Seasonal affective disorder usually has a predictable return each year as the months grow colder and darker. Some reasons that may potentially be behind the cause of seasonal affective disorder include a disruption of the body's natural circadian rhythm and an imbalance in the hormone melatonin which is caused from the decrease of natural sunlight.

The last type of depressive disorder that we will discuss in this chapter is bipolar disorder. This illness was previously named manic-depressive disorder, referring to the extreme highs and extreme lows that the patient could reach. People who experience bipolar disorder have extreme shifts in mood. On end of the spectrum, extremely sad moods that meet the diagnosis criteria of major depressive disorder. These low moods are labeled as bipolar depression. On the other hand, patients with bipolar disorder also go through periods of extreme highs, called mania. These moods are unstable and can cause the patient to feel either irritable or euphoric. Manic episodes of a lesser severity are called hypomania. Some of the symptoms that people with bipolar disorder experience include changes in activity levels and sleep patterns, unusual behaviors, and intense emotions. While displaying signs of depression or mania, the moods and behaviors are quite different from what would typically be expected from the person. Manic episodes can consist of increased levels of high energy, feelings of elation, difficulty in sleeping, speaking very quickly, having difficulty staying on topic, being jumpy and irritable, engaging in risky behaviors, and thinking that many things can be handled at the same time. Periods of depression can consist of decreased levels of energy, feelings of hopelessness, sleeping too much, sleeping too little, forgetfulness, difficulty concentrating, eating too much or too little, and thoughts of suicide or death. Bipolar disorder is actually able to be divided into four distinct subcategories. All four of the categories have commonality in that mood, activity, and energy levels are variable. The first of the subcategories is bipolar I disorder. Manic episodes lasting for at least one week are a characteristic of this category. Sometimes the manic symptoms can be so intense that the person will require hospital care immediately. The time frame for depressive episodes can last for as many as 14 days. Some patients with this diagnosis can experience mixed features during their depressive episodes which means that manic and depressive symptoms can exist at the same time. Bipolar II disorder is quite similar to bipolar I disorder. The main difference is that instead of reaching the intensity of the manic period that can be experienced in bipolar I, bipolar II is consists of hypomanic periods, along with periods of depression. Cyclothymia which is also known as cyclothymic disorder is quite an interesting category. With this diagnosis, symptoms must last for a period of a minimum of at least two years. There are depressive and hypomanic symptoms present, but they are not at a level of severity as to be diagnosed as either bipolar I disorder or bipolar II disorder. This is because the diagnostic requirements have not been met to see the episodes as truly depressive or hypomanic. The last category of bipolar disorder is labeled as "other specified and unspecified bipolar and related disorders." This serves as a category for people whose symptoms of bipolar disorder do not meet the requirements to be diagnosed as any of the other three categories. In some cases, people who are having switches from depression to mania may not notice the shifts themselves, but they can be picked up on by family members or friends. Bipolar disorder is famously difficult to diagnose due to the similarities of symptoms it shares with types of psychosis and other mental conditions.

Depression can take on many forms. A similarity among each type of depressive disorder is the theme of feeling low, sad, empty, or sad. Due to the similarities of symptoms and the number of diagnoses that fall under the umbrella term of depression, finding the right diagnosis and treatment option can be difficult. However, in most cases, if a person has a diagnosis of depression, cognitive behavioral therapy can be a key to successful treatment.

At this point, you can skip ahead to chapter four if you wish to find out how cognitive behavioral therapy can help you to overcome your depression.

# Chapter 2: How to Avoid Becoming Part of the Problem

Working with clients reporting memories of abuse and trauma is a potential minefield for the client and the therapist. The formation of the False Memory Syndrome Foundation (FMSF) in the United States in 1992 led to a political and legal storm across the trauma and abuse field. Many lawsuits resulted against alleged perpetrators and the therapists of alleged victims. Clients faced additional stress and trauma as a consequence of sensationalized media stories about sexual and ritual abuse, child pornography, and sex rings. These stories frequently alleged that high ranking public officials, including politicians, judges, lawyers, police, doctors, teachers, and others with access to children, were among the perpetrators. The predominant position taken by the media, often without any conclusive evidence that a crime had or had not been committed, was that claims by alleged victims were false. Furthermore, according to the media, such memories were the result of suggestion from charlatan therapists and questionable therapy on vulnerable clients. The term **Recovered Memory Therapy [RMT}** was coined by the media. While there is no doubt that there have been cases of questionable therapeutic practices, that have caused harm to clients, alleged perpetrators and the trauma field, to the knowledge of the authors, there is no actual therapy called RMT.

Some clients present reporting continuous recall or partial recall of abuse. Others may seek therapy due to common life experiences, such as unsatisfactory relationships, addictions, generalized depression, or dissatisfaction with life. A major life-changing event, such as a birth, death, marriage, separation, job loss, or a serious accident or illness may be the precursor to entering therapy. While these events can be experienced as traumatic in and of themselves, they may also be the catalyst for dissociated memories to begin to surface.

Clients may have diverse reactions to the veracity of their memories of abuse and this may change throughout the initial phases of therapy, including during the processing of traumatic material. This can occur regardless of whether the memories have always been intact, have been partially conscious, or have surfaced years after the events. Some clients are convinced of the truth and accuracy of their memories. Others are racked with doubt, erring on the side of disbelief. These clients will search for some other cause or reason for the mental images, physical sensations, or intense emotional reactions they experience, including a preference for believing they have a "mental illness" or for some inexplicable reason are simply making it up. Oscillation between belief that memories are real and recanting is common.

At some point during therapy, a client may seek from the therapist, directly or indirectly, validation of her memories. This is the, "Do you believe me?" question. It is a question asked at a time of great confusion, uncertainty, and vulnerability, and out of a need for something or someone to hold onto. Depending on how the therapist answers this question, it can have far-reaching consequences for the client and the progress of therapy. Preempting the question through educating the client about the principle of therapeutic neutrality can avert a great deal of misunderstanding, minimize the potential of the client externalizing her conflicts and ambivalence about memories through polarizing with her therapist, and help keep therapy on track.

## The Principle of Therapeutic Neutrality

As therapists, we identify ourselves as people with a great capacity for compassion and empathy. Indeed, these are important traits in our work, as well as life in general. This is why the word "neutrality" in reference to therapy can sound counterintuitive. Neutrality seems to conjure a lack of empathy, even indifference. To be non-empathic and indifferent would be damaging to the client and limit the potentials of therapy. The essence of the principle of therapeutic neutrality is **"supporting the client through ambivalence, conflicts, and intense emotions about her memories and alleged perpetrator."**

Transference describes the process whereby a client projects conflicts about himself and significant people in his life, the issues he is in therapy to address, the therapist and therapy process, onto the therapist. Counter-transference describes the therapist's reactions to her client's projections, as well as reactions toward the client's personality, behaviour and the material he brings into therapy. During the course of therapy both client and therapist may have genuine reasons to be upset, angry, or hurt by the other's behaviour. However, it is always the therapist's responsibility to manage these reactions with a clear understanding of the unequal power relationship, and the context, boundaries, and triangle dynamics in operation.

In any therapy situation the possibilities of transference are limitless. The nature of trauma, abuse, and dissociation amplifies the potential for complex transference reactions. It can be almost guaranteed that, in varying degrees, two of the biggest internal conflicts a trauma client will grapple with are the "reality" of his memories and his relationship to the alleged perpetrator. This is true even when a client is high functioning and has a clear understanding of the dynamics of attachment to the perpetrator and the locus of control shift. The ability to understand concepts does not immediately translate into a shift in the emotional "reality" of the client.

## FACTORS INFLUENCING CLIENT RESPONSES TO MEMORIES OF ABUSE

Attachment to the Perpetrator
Locus of Control Shift
Age and duration of abuse
Intervention and support
Level of functioning and stability

Most adults who report a history of abuse do not have independent corroboration, such as police, hospital, or school reports, or verification from a witness. It is for this reason we often refer to the "alleged perpetrator." This term may seem cumbersome, and as if we are casting doubt on clients' reports of abuse. The intention is to assist clinicians to approach clients' uncorroborated reports of abuse with an open mind and avoid the risks of making assumptions about true or false memories.

Taking the position of believing or not believing a client's memories, where there is no corroboration, sets the client up for greater conflict. For example, if the therapist says she believes her client, she takes away the possibility for him to disbelieve, which is an important avenue that he needs left open as he works through painful and conflicting feelings. If the therapist disbelieves the client, he will feel unsupported, not validated, and limited in his ability to explore all the issues he needs to deal with, whatever the truth of his experience may be.

Lacking corroboration, it is possible that the client's memories may not be accurate in part or totality. The client needs to explore what is coming up for him and what it means, for himself. If the therapist takes a position of believing or not believing, this process is hindered.

The memories are a source of great conflict and ambivalence. This is a struggle in which the client needs support to find his way through. The therapist who states a belief or disbelief in her client's memories becomes a player on the Victim-Rescuer-Perpetrator triangle. The client will either feel rescued or victimized by the therapist's position. Whichever the client feels, the therapist has also become the perpetrator.

If the therapist believes and the client recants or it becomes apparent the memories were in part or total not true, then the therapist has contributed to his suffering by encouraging him to believe. If the therapist doesn't believe, she has hurt the client, whether the memories are ever found to be true or not. She has become another person who has let him down and not validated his experiences. Whatever the truth of the memories may be, the therapist who states a belief or disbelief has hindered the client in his own journey of discovery and its potential for healing and growth.

In stating a belief or disbelief in client's memories, the therapist is in fact "suggesting" that abuse did or did not occur. In addition to the conflicts this creates for the client as already outlined, it leaves the therapist open to potential lawsuits by the client and/or his alleged perpetrator.

REASONS TO REMAIN "NEUTRAL" ABOUT UNCORROBORATED REPORTS OF ABUSE

To minimize the client projecting the conflict of believing or disbelieving onto the therapist
To not become part of the problem through taking on the polar position in the client's conflict
To allow the client the space to work through conflict and ambivalence
To keep off the Victim–Rescuer–Perpetrator triangle

Where there is no corroboration of a client's accusations the therapist can never know what did or did not happen. There will be exceptions, such as a client in a state of psychosis. For example, a client of one of the authors, during a psychotic episode, claimed that she knew that there were tunnels underneath the therapist's' office building and that she had seen one of her therapists colleagues exit the building through these tunnels to meet secretly with secret service agents in a nearby coffee shop.

Another client, who was not psychotic at the time, had a memory that she had given birth to piglets. The therapist knew that neither of these events had occurred. However, it is important not to dismiss such claims as delusional and therefore, meaningless. The therapist may choose, depending on his knowledge of the client, to remain "neutral." It may also be equally valid in some instances for the therapist to state that these events didn't occur (in the first instance) or couldn't have occurred (in the second instance). Whichever approach the therapist takes, such material can be explored (once a psychotic episode has subsided) in the same way other memories and issues that are brought to therapy are explored.

Of course, a therapist will form opinions about a client's memories over time. These opinions may or may not be accurate. While it may appear to be supportive and empathic, stating an unequivocal belief or disbelief in memories will typically create more problems. As with many things in life, "never say never." There may be times, with some clients, when stating your beliefs may be helpful to therapy. We recommend that if you think you have such a client and it might be helpful to state your position that you explore this thoroughly with your supervisor or case consultant.

### "Taking Sides"—Conflicted Feelings Toward the Alleged Perpetrator(s)

Linked to the delicate issue of believing or not believing a client's memory is managing your client's and your own feelings toward the alleged perpetrator. Ambivalent attachment to the perpetrator is to be expected. The client may mostly express idealized love, outrage, and hate, or seemingly total indifference. It is common for an individual to oscillate among these states. When the client has DID or DDNOS, other parts will hold the polar position to the one that is being expressed, creating additional internal conflicts.

Horror, disgust, anger, and outrage are some of the feelings as therapists we experience when we hear about the atrocities committed against others. These are normal and healthy reactions. When we are working with clients we need to monitor these reactions in sessions. We are not suggesting that it is inappropriate to show or express any feelings in front of clients. It can be validating and a pivotal point in therapy for a client to witness another human being—their therapist—expressing sadness and anger on their behalf. It is the timing and degree of such expressions that may either help or hinder a client's process.

Conflicted feelings about the perpetrator will be present throughout all stages of therapy, including end stages. Clients generally need a great deal of assistance in learning how to manage and express their feelings in healthy ways. Learning to hold conflicting and intense feelings safely is an integral part of therapy and will be discussed in a later chapter.

It is important that our own feelings toward our client's experiences do not cloud our judgment or pressure clients to take a particular position toward their perpetrator. We have consulted with clients where they have felt their current or a previous therapist was pressuring them to take a particular course of action, such as legal processes, ceasing contact with particular people, making contact with someone, or forgiving their perpetrator. Clients have reported they were getting the message from their therapist, implicitly and at times explicitly, that they should or shouldn't be feeling a particular emotion, such as anger, hate, or love. Clients have expressed feeling they were "wrong" to feel or not feel something. Similarly, we have consulted with therapists who were either pushing too hard in a certain direction or colluding with their client to avoid unpleasant feelings and reactions. In general the process the therapist was trying to initiate may have been correct but the timing was inappropriate for the client.

When the therapist "takes sides" regarding a client's alleged perpetrator, not only is he making a statement about the accuracy of the client's memory, he also becomes a player on the Victim-Rescuer-Perpetrator triangle. The client will either feel rescued or victimized by the therapist's position. As with the memory issue, whichever the client feels, the therapist has also become the perpetrator. When the client gets in touch with the polar position of the therapist she may feel she is "wrong" or "not allowed" to express these feelings. She may fear rejection or disapproval from her therapist and so hide what she is feeling, which will hinder her progress and create further conflicts.

When the therapist takes a one-sided stance toward the alleged perpetrator, it deprives the client of the important process of learning to hold and manage her conflicting feelings, which will eventually lead to a place of resolution. Resolution does not mean "happily ever after," it means the client can sit with whatever feelings she has at any given point in time and make healthy choices about her actions and relationships. When the therapist is overwhelmed by his feelings and they are left unaddressed, they interfere with therapy. It is important to take such feelings and reactions, which are part of the territory, to supervision or personal therapy.

## HANDLING CLIENTS' FEELINGS TOWARD THE PERPETRATOR AND NON-PROTECTING PARENT

Clients typically have strong and ambivalent feelings toward their perpetrator and non-protecting parent.

It is common for therapists to have strong feelings about a client's perpetrator; these should be processed in supervision or the therapist's own therapy.

Allow the client to experience and express all feelings: anger, hate, fear, love etc.

Be careful of explicit or implicit messages regarding contact, no contact, forgiveness, etc.

### Communicating the Principle of Therapeutic Neutrality

A client may come into therapy reporting a history of abuse. Further memories may emerge or be recalled for the first time during the course of therapy. At the point your client raises a known or suspected history of abuse, it is important to explain to him what he may expect working with such issues. This includes information about the nature of memory, some of the difficulties he may experience and encounter along the way, and the principle of therapeutic neutrality. An outline of the concepts of attachment to the perpetrator and the locus of control shift can also be useful to help him understand your "neutral" position in relation to his memories and his relationship to his alleged perpetrator.

As well as providing a verbal explanation, it is also helpful to provide handouts and/or an informed consent form. As with any psycho-education, timing is key to when and how much information you give in any particular session. These things will depend on your assessment of your client's emotional capacity as well as his current level of functioning.

## PROVIDE INFORMATION TO HELP NORMALIZE FEELINGS AND REACTIONS

Information on memory, traumatic memory, and dissociation

Informed consent explaining some of the issues that will come up as part of working with a history of trauma and abuse

Information on Attachment to the Perpetrator and the Locus of Control Shift

Therapy is never clear sailing and it generally doesn't run along the neat lines laid out in manuals and books! Other issues come up out of the blue that require attention; the best therapy plans don't necessarily flow smoothly. For clients with a history of abuse, therapy is usually long term and the same ground is covered many times. A client may disclose abuse without your having any idea this is where he was heading, and he may ask if you believe him or ask for your position about his perpetrator before you have had the opportunity to explain the principles behind therapeutic neutrality—so be prepared!

Most clients are eager for any educational material you can give them that can help them understand their experiences. Education about memory often eases the pressure clients place on themselves to believe or disbelieve their memories. Education can assist in developing tolerance for ambivalence and uncertainty. It helps to normalize confusion and fluctuating emotions. It helps to prepare for some of the difficulties clients will encounter along the way.

However, providing information does not mean that clients will necessarily welcome this position in the midst of working with difficult material or grappling with intense feelings toward their perpetrator. These are times when you may expect your client to express anger, frustration, and feeling that you are not supporting or validating him. A "neutral" stance can be misinterpreted as you saying you don't believe. Remember, these are conflicts that your client needs to navigate with your help. Let him know you understand why he is angry, remain emotionally present and empathic, and reinforce to him that you know his distress is real and that something has caused him to feel this way. Your role is to help him work out what the cause of his distress is, for himself. Remember that you are working "as if" his memories are true.

## When It Is Important Not to Be "Neutral"

Therapeutic neutrality is a fundamental principle in Trauma Model Therapy. As explained above, therapeutic neutrality does not mean lacking empathy or warmth. Therapeutic neutrality is about **"supporting the client through ambivalence, conflicts, and intense emotions about her memories and alleged perpetrator."** This requires the therapist to be empathically attuned to the struggles and conflicts within the client.

Explaining the principle of therapeutic neutrality to your client allows the therapist to be free to respond compassionately, and validate her client's distress and feelings, without compromising the therapy. By explaining that you are not in a position to believe or disbelieve the reality of memories (where there is no corroboration) but that you can see that something has caused your client to be experiencing such great distress and difficulties, you can proceed while working with memories and material "as if" your client's memories are factual. The client and therapist should remain open to all possibilities.

WHEN NOT TO BE NEUTRAL

Make clear statements that abuse of any kind is never OK

Make clear statements that it is never the client's fault he/she was abused

Follow professional guidelines regarding mandatory reporting

Express concern if client is in a current abusive situation; explain that working on safety is a priority

Assess and take appropriate action regarding threats of violence toward others and suicide risk

Equally crucial to humane and ethical therapeutic practice is making clear statements that abuse of any kind—emotional, physical, sexual, or spiritual—and neglect are never OK and are never the fault of the client. This will need to be reiterated throughout therapy as the client works through issues of attachment to the perpetrator and the locus of control shift.

If a client reports knowledge of the abuse of a child occurring in the present, therapists are required to follow their professional guidelines regarding mandatory reporting. If your client is currently in an abusive situation, it is important to state that what is happening to her is not OK, and that you are concerned for her current well being and safety. Working with a client on how to increase her safety is crucial. Clients are rarely ready to immediately exit an abusive relationship or cease contact with a perpetrator who is still abusing them. However, stating concern about her safety, and reminding that this needs to be a primary focus of therapy, is vital.

Therapists need to respond when a client makes threats of violence toward another person that they believe could be acted upon, and when suicide is assessed to be an imminent risk. Seeking supervision or case consultation in such situations is recommended.

Finally, being compassionate and empathetic to a client's struggles with the long term and ongoing impact of trauma is central to effective therapy. Similarly, offering encouragement, praise, and humour where appropriate are the golden threads that weave together the intricate and complex tapestry of a strong therapeutic relationship. While knowledge and skill in working with trauma provide the foundation of effective therapy, it is the "relationship" between client and therapist that provides the framework for healing to take place.

# Chapter 3: Dealing with category D symptoms

Sufficient endurance conduct is a vital "endowment of nature." Humans have been genuinely effective in lessening the danger to life. All things considered, going across a road or driving a vehicle requires expanded readiness so as to endure. Cataclysmic events, for example, the ongoing tidal wave and man-made calamities, for example, war, fear monger assaults, slaughtering, looting, sexual and physical maltreatment, and plane accidents show how helpless we are. In the wake of enduring such an occasion, individuals need nuts and bolts—nourishment, cover, therapeutic consideration, and encouragement. These days mental consideration has been added to this rundown of fundamental requirements for certain individuals.

Specialists should know whether and when mental assistance is vital. The new rule on overseeing post-horrible pressure issue in essential and auxiliary consideration from the National Institute for Clinical Excellence (NICE) fantastically outlines the encounters of sufferers and carers and gives proof and exhortation on intercessions for grown-ups and children.1 The rule gives extraordinary thoughtfulness regarding "debacle arranging"; the requirements of ex-military staff, casualties of abusive behavior at home, and displaced people and refuge searchers; and the job of the non-statutory segment, underscoring the expansive effect of injury in present day society. Giving more regard for the nature and importance of post-awful pressure issue in a social and recorded setting would have made the rules total.

At the point when manifestations, for example, flashbacks, rest issues, trouble in concentrating, and passionate lability are gentle and have been available for under about a month after horrible mishaps, the rules suggest beginning attentive pausing. Behind this shrewd counsel lies the proof based end that early mental intercession, frequently called questioning, has no impact in anticipating post-horrendous stress issue; for sure, regardless of detailed high fulfillment, it may even be harmful.2-4 Clearly the standard practice of questioning after debacles and fiascoes should end. In any case, for dealing with the bedlam, material misfortunes, misery, and outrage—for instance, after a fear based oppressor assault—no indisputable proof is accessible yet on how a fiasco stricken network recovers control.

As per the NICE rule, treatment is essential when, in the outcome of injury, post-horrible pressure issue, misery, suicidality, compulsion, restoratively unexplained physical side effects, or dissociative issue emerge. The danger of creating post-horrendous pressure issue after injury is 8-13% for men and 20-30% for women,5 with a year pervasiveness of 1.3% to 3.9%,6 making a colossal weight on society.

Post-horrendous pressure issue is essentially a deregulation of the dread framework. Dread is an essential feeling on occasion of peril, and is trailed by a stress reaction—battling, solidifying, or escaping. This endurance framework relies upon evaluating dangers so as to start endurance behaviour.7 Once the risk or injury is finished, the dread framework ordinarily quiets down following a couple of days or weeks. In post-awful pressure issue this framework neglects to reset to typical, keeping the sufferer hyperalert, filtering for hazardous signals as though the occasion may happen once more.

The turmoil is subsequently described by automatic, tireless recalling or remembering the awful accident in flashbacks, striking recollections, and intermittent dreams. The individual attempts to abstain from recalling the injury, by dodging its area or TV programs about it. Diligent manifestations of expanded excitement, for example, hypervigilance, overstated frighten reaction, dozing issues, peevishness, and trouble concentrating, are a piece of the turmoil. Comorbidities, for example, misery, substance misuse, and other nervousness issue are the standard instead of the exemption. Passionate desensitizing, for example, feeling isolates from others, is likewise observed—for instance in officers subsequent to peacekeeping missions.

The NICE rule deliberately audits the proof for both mental and pharmacological mediations. As first line treatment NICE suggests injury centered mental treatment. Both distributed and unpublished information demonstrate just constrained viability for few pharmacological intercessions, so NICE prescribes not utilizing drugs as first line treatment.

The best treatment for resetting the dread framework is psychological conduct therapy.8 By fanciful presentation to the horrendous accident the dread response will diminish in time. Ideas about the self that are provoked by the occasion, for example, feeling "frail," liable, or insusceptible, are supplanted by progressively sensible perceptions. The rule likewise underpins, yet not as unequivocally, treatment with eye development desensitization reprocessing, which uses a distractive move of respective incitement after presentation to diminish the passionate lability identified with the injury.

An unanswered inquiry remains whether the elevated feeling of dread in post-horrendous stress issue is identified with the occasion or to the concealment of bizarrely compelling feelings of despondency and animosity realized by the awful experience.9 Like Summerfield we accept that more consideration ought to be paid to the significance of shocking encounters, breaking the sufferer's perspectives about life,10 in spite of the fact that proof on this viewpoint is deficient. We additionally concur with the rule about focusing on the regular comorbidities of post-awful pressure issue, (for example, misery and uneasiness), however the proof is still very limited.1

Regardless of the presence of powerful psychosocial medications, 33% of patients won't recuperate fully.11 Comorbidity, chronicity, and the aggregation of intense and ceaseless pressure may disclose the restricted reaction to treatment. Additionally, from a developmental perspective one can perceive how "the endowment of nature" of recollecting and gaining from peril may confine what is achievable in treating post-horrendous pressure disorder.12 We can't erase the memory of injury.

# Chapter 4: How to deal with the trauma

It's normal to be apprehensive in the wake of something frightening or hazardous occurs. At the point when you feel you're in risk, your body reacts with a surge of synthetic compounds that make you increasingly alert. This is known as the "flight or battle" reaction. It causes us endure perilous occasions.

Be that as it may, the cerebrum reaction to terrifying occasions can likewise prompt constant issues. This can incorporate issue dozing; feeling nervous habitually; being effectively alarmed, on edge, or jittery; having flashbacks; or maintaining a strategic distance from things that help you to remember the occasion.

In some cases these side effects leave following half a month. However, now and again they last any longer. On the off chance that indications last over a month and become serious enough to meddle with connections or work, it might be an indication of post-awful pressure issue, or PTSD.

"There are genuine neurobiological results of injury that are related with PTSD," clarifies Dr. Farris Tuma, who directs the NIH awful pressure research program. NIH-supported scientists are revealing the science behind these mind changes and searching for approaches to counteract and treat PTSD.

What is Trauma?

"A great many people partner post-awful pressure side effects with veterans and battle circumstances," says Dr. Amit Etkin, a NIH-subsidized emotional wellness master at Stanford University. "Notwithstanding, a wide range of injury occur during one's life that can prompt post-horrible pressure issue and post-awful pressure issue like manifestations."

This incorporates individuals who have experienced a physical or rape, misuse, a mishap, a catastrophe, or numerous different genuine occasions.

Anybody can create PTSD, at any age. As per the National Center for Post-Traumatic Stress Disorder, around 7 or 8 out of each 100 individuals will encounter PTSD sooner or later in their lives.

"We don't have a blood test that would let you know or inquiry you can pose to someone to know whether they're in the most elevated hazard bunch for creating PTSD," Tuma says. "However, we do realize that there are a few things that expansion chance by and large and a few things that secure against it."

Science of Traumatic Stress

Analysts are investigating what puts individuals in danger for PTSD. One group, drove by Dr. Samuel McLean, an injury master at the University of North Carolina, is examining how post-horrible pressure side effects create in the cerebrum. They will pursue 5,000 injury survivors for one year.

"We're enlisting individuals who visit injury focuses following an injury since proof proposes that a great deal of the significant natural changes that lead to steady side effects occur in the early fallout of the injury," McLean says.

They're gathering data about existence history preceding injury, distinguishing post-awful side effects, gathering hereditary and different kinds of organic information, and performing mind filters. The examination is additionally utilizing keen watches and PDA applications to gauge the body's reaction to injury. These devices will assist scientists with revealing how injury influences individuals' day by day lives, for example, their action, rest, and state of mind.

"Our objective is that there will be when injury survivors come in for consideration and get screening and mediations to avert PTSD, just similarly that they would be screened with X-beams to set broken bones," McLean clarifies.

## Adapting to Trauma

How you respond when something awful occurs, and in the blink of an eye a short time later, can help or defer your recuperation.

"It's imperative to have an adapting methodology for overcoming the awful sentiments of a horrible mishap," Tuma says. A decent adapting methodology, he clarifies, is discovering someone to converse with about your emotions. A terrible adapting system would turn liquor or medications.

Having a positive adapting procedure and taking in something from the circumstance can assist you with recuperating from a horrible accident. So can looking for help from companions, family, or a care group.

Chatting with an emotional well-being proficient can assist somebody with post-horrendous pressure side effects figure out how to adapt. It's significant for anybody with PTSD-like side effects to be treated by a psychological well-being proficient who is prepared in injury centered treatment.

A self improvement site and applications created by the U.S. Branch of Veterans Affairs can likewise offer help when you need it following an injury.

"For the individuals who start treatment and experience it, an enormous level of those will show signs of improvement and will get some help," Tuma says. A few drugs can help treat certain indications, as well.

PTSD influences individuals in an unexpected way, so a treatment that works for one individual may not work for another. A few people with PTSD need to attempt various medications to discover what works for their manifestations.

Discovering Treatments

"While we right now analyze this as one issue in psychiatry, in truth, there's a great deal of variety among individuals and the sorts of side effects that they have," Etkin says.

These distinctions can make it hard to discover a treatment that works. Etkin's group is attempting to comprehend why a few people's minds react to treatment and others don't.

"PTSD is extremely normal. In any case, the assortment of ways that it shows in the mind is huge," Etkin clarifies. "We don't have the foggiest idea what number of fundamental conditions there are, or particular mind issues there are, that lead to PTSD. So we're attempting to make sense of that part."

His group has recognized cerebrum circuits that show when treatment is working. They've discovered a different cerebrum circuit that can anticipate who will react to treatment.

His gathering is presently trying a procedure called noninvasive cerebrum incitement for individuals who don't react to treatment. They trust that animating certain mind circuits will make treatment progressively compelling.

A great many people recoup normally from injury. Be that as it may, it can require significant investment. In case you're having indications for a really long time—or that are excessively extreme—chat with your medicinal services supplier or a psychological wellness proficient. In the midst of emergency, call the National Suicide Prevention Lifeline at 1-800-273-TALK (8255) or visit the crisis room.

"PTSD is genuine. This isn't a shortcoming in any capacity," Tuma clarifies. "Individuals shouldn't battle alone and peacefully."

# Chapter 5: Trauma treatment Exercises for Self-Therapy

If you feel your daily life is a blur, that you aren't achieving your goals or excelling in your tasks and that everything is mundane and slow, it's time to change that attitude because the only thing that is stopping you from enjoying a fulfilling, successful, and worthwhile life is your negativity!

Yes, negative attitudes and mindsets are one of the biggest obstacles that disable creative thinkers, movers, and shakers from achieving success beyond their wildest dreams. If you want to change the way you look at the world, engage in healthy activities, increase your productivity, strengthen your relationships and pave the way to higher success, then the first thing you need to do is change your perspective and outlooks on how negative and positive emotions play their different roles in our lives.

In this chapter, we look at the various exercises that therapists often use in trauma treatment and how you can employ some of these therapies on your own safely.

1. Journaling

Keeping a journal of thoughts and moods is one of the most fundamental aspects of trauma treatment exercises. In doing this, therapists look for certain dominant patterns that they can take relevant steps to change.

2. Challenging thoughts

With trauma treatment, the main goals are to find and change disruptive and negative thoughts.

Therapists specifically look for automatic thoughts. These thoughts are the ones that occur without any intention.

When therapist finds these negative thoughts and patterns, they challenge them. For example, a child who thinks that they are stupid because they are not getting straight A's, therapists can find counter-arguments and find ways to tell the child that he's actually intelligent and to erase any negative thoughts that the child has.

## 3. Changing behavior

This type of behavior is usually used for those suffering from OCD. For this type of exercise, therapy usually use intentional exposure to situations in which they will respond negatively in repetitive ways. The therapist will also intentionally re-create a scenario and encourage the patient to react in a different or alternative way.

## 4. Introspective exposure

For this type of exercise, therapy is usually used for those who have panic attacks and anxiety.

In this situation, therapist intentionally recreates bodily sensations that patients will respond negatively to. They then deliberately make the patient react in a different, new and healthier way. This exercise trains the patients' mind to stop reacting to sensations that would cause anxiety and panic.

## 5. Following Fear to the End

Most of the time when a person feels fear, they stop all their thoughts or start thinking irrationally. For example, if patients fear heights, therapists usually work towards helping the patient push aside their feelings of fear. Using this exercise, therapists usually allow the fear to manifest and continue until it is over. They will then recreate a scenario that enables the patient to feel this fear but then helps them to get on with life after the episode is over.

This will then train the patient to realize that even if the worst happens, things will probably not end up that bad as how they imagine it in their head.

6. Changing behavior experiment

For this exercise, therapists usually use it to test how a patient's different and irrational thoughts and beliefs lead to different and irrational actions. For instance, if patients believe that being hard on themselves makes them work harder, the therapist will experiment with the opposite reaction. Patients will be encouraged to stress less and be a little kinder to their own selves and see the kind of reaction they get and the results that come with it.

7. A change of perspective

With this type of exercise, therapists employ the technique of thinking the other way. Take for example a child that keeps getting bullied and then ends up failing their exams. They begin thinking that they are a failure and just stupid. What can this child do? The therapist will first ask the child to write down all the reasons or evidence that points out that they are failures.

Next, the child is asked to write down all the reasons or evidence of why he or she is a success. This gives this child a better and clearer perspective. They are now vividly aware of their shortcomings and also acutely aware of their strengths too.

8. Looking for positives

This is a favored exercise among trauma treatment therapists. It has been proven that positivity makes people healthier. But how do you train your mind to be more positive?

You can:

Make a habit of scheduling positive events that you can look forward to

Always look at the positives from past experiences.

Always look at the positive aspects even at the present time and focus on all the good things that are happening around you.

Do all of those things above, just not one of them. These are all some of the small things you can do to object a little bit of positivity.

9. Facing Fears

For this trauma treatment technique:

You need to write a list of your fears or of negative things that worry you.

Compile a list of events from the good ones to the bad ones.

Go through each event, beginning with the easiest and working towards the hardest. And actually face those fears.

This will build your tolerance for unpleasant experiences and trains the mind to overcome fear.

10. Turning negative to positive

For this trauma treatment technique, it is simply about writing a positive reasoning for every negative thought that comes out of the patient's mind. For example, when a patient thinks "I'm ugly" so adversely, they just write "I'm beautiful". In this technique, it is all about remembering positive things that happened yesterday and even today.

12. I hate that, but I love that

This final technique is about turning our negatives into our positives. Whenever a negative situation arises, we pinpoint and focus on the positives. So even if you are in a burning building, you focus your mind into looking at the positives. Is there an open window? Can you find the door? Is your phone with you? Can you call the fire department? Do you have a blanket that you can wet and cover yourself with? A bathtub, maybe?

Training our mind to not dwell on the negative enables us not only to see the positives but also respond reactively.

Try These Mindfulness trauma treatment Exercises

13. Three-Minute Breathing Space

The primary mindfulness trauma treatment exercises are called 'Three-Minute Breathing Space'. It is an easy and quick mindfulness-of-breath exercise. This breathing exercise is also called 'a practice for approaching experience from two intentional lenses, both narrow and wide' according to Zindel Segal.

This three-minute exercise is broken down to:

The first minute is dedicated to observing how we feel, and we describe those feelings in words

The second minute focuses on practicing the awareness of our breathing

The third minute is the continuation of focusing on breathing but then bringing back the awareness to the entire body.

14. Body Scan

The body scan meditation is a popular meditation technique and you have probably come across from some YouTube video or even through meditation apps. This type of meditation has a great way of enhancing a person's happiness and at the same time reducing any symptoms related to depression and anxiety.

15. Mindful Stretching

Both body and mind health is crucial, and if the body can benefit from some stretching, surely the mind can have those same benefits too. Mindful stretching is exactly what it sounds like, it stretches the mind. There are different types to this technique and this includes:

• Pandiculation: While sounding ridiculous, this technique refers to a type of stretching that we do when we yawn. To do this stretch, we do exactly what we do when we yawn, palms on shoulders, elbows raised, mouth open.

• Proprioceptive Neuromuscular Facilitation: This technique is a stretch that is normally used by sports persons especially footballers who have cramps in their legs.

• Gomukhasana (cow-face pose): For this technique, which is sort of a yoga post, you sit cross-legged while interlocking your hands behind your back. This move expands the chest.

• Side-to-side neck stretch: You probably would have done this stretch a few times during gym class. You simply put your hand on one side of your head, tilting it to the right and left.

• Eka Pada Rajakapotasana (One-Legged King Pigeon Pose): For this technique, you place your hips to the mat, with one leg in front of you, perpendicular to the mat whilst your other leg stretches out straight behind you. This is a more complex pose that beginners may struggle with. For a more comprehensive guide, visit YogaOutlet guide.

• The Scorpion: This technique requires you to lie flat on the ground on your back, and keep your arms on your side. Lift your right foot high up and press out your right hip. Next, stretch the right foot to the outside of the left leg. It's important to keep your chest and the arms on the flow while doing this. This technique is a modified version of Vrischikasana (Scorpion Pose).

16. Trauma treatment Stop Technique

In this technique, you basically stop all negative thinking and thoughts in its tracks. trauma treatment therapists use this technique to intercept bad thoughts when a patient starts thinking it and immediately aids the patient in changing them.

Here's how the stop technique is conducted:

Take note of when you have negative thoughts.

When this happens, STOP. Take a deep and mindful breath.

Make a mindful observation of the thoughts going through your mind.

Notice what elements or topics that you are focusing your thoughts on.

Notice any sensations in the body.

Pull back and examine the thoughts.

What's the overall picture of the thought?

What's another way of looking at the situation?

How important is the thought?

What would you say to a friend who had this thought?

What is the first thing you could do right now to help yourself? Do it.

17. Trauma treatment Downward Arrow Technique

This downward arrow technique can be used to uncover core perceptions and beliefs that disrupt our normal life, and it is usually conducted with the help of a licensed therapist.

Here's how the trauma treatment Downward Arrow Technique is applied:

It starts with the choosing one negative thought from the patient's journal. This could be anything from meeting people, swimming, or having to do a presentation.

The therapist asks the patient "Why would it upset you if this happened?"

The patient answers the question. "If my presentation is bad, my boss will be angry."

The therapist then asks why that would matter, "If my boss is angry, I may lose my job."

This keeps going until the therapist and patient come to a core self-defeating belief: "Because if I lose my job, I won't be able to support my family."

18. Creative visualization

Creative visualization is a mental technique that harnesses our imagination to make our goals and dreams a reality. When used the right way, creative visualization has been proven to improve the lives of the people who have used it, and it also increases the success and prosperity rate of the individual.

Creative visualization unleashes a power that can alter your social and living environment and circumstances, it causes beneficial events to happen, attracts positivity in work, life, relationships, and goals. Creative visualization is not a magic potion. It uses the cognitive processes of our mind to purposely generate an array of visual mental imagery to create beneficial physiological, psychological or social effects such as increasing wealth, healing wounds to the body or alleviating psychological issues such as anxiety and sadness.

This method uses the power of the mind to attract good energy and really, it is the magic potion behind every success.

Mostly, a person needs to visualize an individual event or situation or object or desire to attract it into their lives. This is a process that is similar to daydreaming. It only uses the natural process of the power of our mind to initiate positive thoughts and natural mental laws.

Successful people like Oprah and Tiger Woods and Bill Gates use this technique, either consciously or unconsciously, attracting success and positive outcomes into their lives by visualizing their goals as already attained or accomplished.

The Power of Thoughts and Creative Visualization

So how does this work and why is it so important to us?

Well, our mind is a powerful thing. With only the power of our mind, we can reach amazing success, or we can also spiral out of control. It swings both ways. Our subconscious mind accepts the ideas and thoughts that we often repeat, and when our mind accepts it, then your mindset also changes accordingly, and this influences your habits and actions. Again, a domino effect happens where you end up meeting new people or getting into situations or circumstances that lead you to your goal. Our thoughts come with a creative power that can mold our life and attract whatever we think about.

Remember the saying that goes 'mind over matter?' When we set our mind to do it, our body does what our mind tells us. Our thoughts travel from mind, body, and soul but believe it or not; it can travel from one mind to another because, it is unconsciously picked up by the people you meet with every day and usually, most of the people you end up meeting are the ones who can help you achieve your goals.

You probably think and repeat certain thoughts every day pretty often, and you probably do this consciously or unconsciously. You probably have focused your thoughts on your current situation or environment and subsequently, create and recreate the same events and circumstances regularly. While most of our lives are somewhat routine, we can always change these thoughts by visualizing different circumstances and situations, and in a way, create a different reality for you to focus on new goals and desires.

Changing Your Reality

Honestly, though, you can change your reality by changing your thoughts and mental images. You aren't creating magic here. All you are doing is harnessing the natural powers and laws that inhibit each and every one of us. The thing that separates normal, average folk with wildly successful people is that the successful ones have mastered their thoughts and mental images while the rest of us are still learning or trying to cope. Changing your thoughts and attitude changes and reshapes your world.

Take for example you plan on moving into a larger apartment and instead of wallowing in self-pity such as the lack of money, do this instead, alter your thoughts and attitude and visualize yourself living in a larger apartment. It isn't difficult to do because it's exactly like daydreaming.

Overcoming Limited Thinking

You may think daydreaming about positive things and money and success and great relationships are nothing but child's play but in fact, creative visualization can do wonders. Though, it may be hard for different individuals to immediately alter their thoughts. Limits to this positive thinking are within us and not the power of our mind. We control it.

It might sound like it's easy to change the way you think, but the truth is, it takes a lot of effort on your side to alter your thoughts at least in the immediate future. But never for a second doubt that you can't. Anything that you put your mind to work on, it can be done.

We often limit ourselves due to our beliefs and our thoughts and to the life we know. So the need to be open-minded is an integral part of positive thinking. The bigger we dare to think, the higher and great our changes, possibilities, and opportunities. Limitations are created within our minds, and it is up to us to rise above all these obstacles.

Of course, it takes time to change the way we think and see things and broaden our horizons, but small demonstrations of changing our minds and the way we think will yield bigger results in due time.

Guidelines for Creating Visualization

Concise Guidelines for Creative Visualization:

Step 1 - Define your goal.

Step 2 - Think, meditate, and listen to your instinct. Ensure that this is the goal you want to attain.

Step 3 - Ascertain that you only want good results from your visualization, for you and for others around you.

Step 4 - Be alone at a place that you will not be disturbed. Be alone with your thoughts.

Step 5 - Relax your body and your mind.

Step 6 - Rhythmically breathe deeply several times.

Step 7 - Visualize your goal by giving it a clear and detailed mental image.

Step 8 - Add desire and feelings into this mental image, how you would feel, etc.

Step 9 - Use all your five senses of sight, hearing, touch, taste, and smell.

Step 10 - Visualize this at least twice a day for at least 10 minutes each time.

Step 11 - Keep visualizing this day after day with patience, hope, and faith.

Step 12 - Always keep staying positive in your feelings, thoughts, and words.

Staying positive can be easy. It is all about training your mind. When you do feel doubts and negative thoughts arise, replace them with positive thoughts. Also, remember to keep an open mind because opportunities come in various ways so when you see it, you can take advantage of them. Every morning, or each time you conclude your visualization session, always end it with this 'Let everything happen in a favorable way for everyone and everything involved.'

Creative visualization will open doors but it takes time and whenever you feel you are in a position of advantage, take action. Do not be passive or wait for things to fall on your lap. Perhaps, you've met someone who can put yours in a position of advantage to reach your goal or perhaps, you've landed a job that has the possibility of enabling you to travel. All these things come into your life, and if you have an open mind, you can see the possibilities more vividly.

When you use the power of imagination for you and the people around you, always do it for good. Never try creative visualization to obtain something forcibly that belongs to others (like someone else's husband or wife or a managerial position someone else rightfully achieved but you want as well). Also, don't harm the environment.

Most visualized goals happen in a natural and gradual manner, but there can be times that it can happen in a sudden and expected manner too.

Be realistic with your goals, though. Don't visualize a unicorn and expect it to turn up. If money is what you desire, you know that it just will not drop from the sky. You may or may not win it in the lottery. But the chances or possibilities are higher when you go through life with a new job, or you get a promotion, or you end up making a business deal. It is always better to think and visualize what you actually want because you do not want to attract situations that are negative, in your quest to fulfill your goals and desires.

# Chapter 6: Trauma treatment and Mental Health

Trauma treatment might be a rather new term to some, but too many common. Cognitive behavioral therapy is a type of mental therapy that helps or enables one to deal with their thoughts and balance their daily mental state. This involves one's surrounding in terms of their societal constraints as well as actions and how they affect them in one way or other or their feelings. This is a study that will help you keep a profile of some of the things that trigger you emotionally as well as how to manage and contain them.

Just as the name entails, it is therapy done to treat mental conditions that are caused by past experience or situations that impacted one's well being. That is conditions or ailments such as depressions or even anxiety. Yes, depression is an ailment. As we all know that when someone is depressed beyond measures they can handle they are prone to self-destruct or self-inflict injuries or mostly common abuse drugs. TRAUMA TREATMENT is not only for mental but also physical wellness as well.

This has always been a study under review and many have benefited from it in the society. It zeros in majorly on the challenges in the society or community at large that are not necessarily treatable through medicating or normal hospital appointments. Many have mental or behavioral distortions unknowingly but when addressed and carefully decrypted you'll find that there's always one thing that can o does trigger a person not to be or act themselves. Trauma treatment help improves and uplifts one's personal emotional as well as social or even physical regulation by providing lasting and long-term solutions and strategies that add up to solving and diagnosing conditions.

The main aim of trauma treatment is to help an individual with previous problems, boost happiness as well as get rid of sadness and upgrade and treat dysfunctional and wrecked emotions one may harbor in them. As we all know, emotions affect our every move as well as influence them in one way or another. That is our behaviors, actions as well as thoughts. Trauma treatment is mainly rooted on providing and implementing effective solutions that will help an individual outgrow previous toxic habits and traits as well as uplift and encourage them to change destructive norms they take value in as well as uphold.

The thought of emotions influencing a person comes out strongly as we know that distinct circumstances or situations bring out a rare and authentic part of us all raw, authentic and original and could either be negative or positive. So trauma treatment identifies problems, possible roots of the problems as well as how logical or realistic they are and how or what degree and extremity bring one to their breaking point.

Trauma treatment as well know is a practice done on every one that is all ages and races and has no limitations in terms of the level of mental advancement or development. I mean, anyone can be depressed, anyone can feel extremely anxious due to haunting thoughts or even pas negative experiences. It's an efficient task that can be carried or conducted around not only physically but also mentally but with that said it requires one's devotion as well as consistency and discipline levels to be checked, it's a practice for one's well being and there's no better doctor that oneself since they know where the shoes pinch the most.

In trauma treatment there are various tools used. These are not physical tools but rather ideologies that are believed to have worked over the years in successfully treating patients or clients. These include identifying and disputing unhelpful, toxic or even unrealistic thought as well as coming up with problem-solving solutions and skills that are both compatible as well as a diverse range of metal/psychological ailments. Trauma treatment is one of the most if not the only efficacious modes of verbal therapy if only inducted into our day to day lives. This form of interest brings out one's attention to getting insight into their behavioral and cognitive processes and turns them into effective and constructive methods that incorporate gradual practice for success and full recovery. If one fully corporates and stick to the course they are most likely to have fewer sessions as well as more productive time.

Trauma treatment helps people moderate their thoughts. That is, these people tend to overthink situations and tether then on the wrong directions, there are unhelpful ways or means that people direct their thoughts that end up leading to psychological problems. Our own thoughts either elevate our moods or send you on a roller-coaster of thoughts. The same behaviors and traits that develop as a result of the toxic thoughts and emotions that manipulate us. Psychological issues just don't originate out of nowhere, it starts as small ideas that grow in due time and develop roots in our day to day life. As it becomes tailor made in us, it also changes our personalities into darker and more mentally disturbed individuals.

When it comes to an individual's modes of thinking and reasoning out, they do according to previous experiences or how the norms of things around them obliges them to. As we all know our minds are weapons that if used rightfully and effectively could impact the society in major ways positively. However the same mind, when affected in one way or another or, is not in its rights state could ac out and just like normal working machinery around could act faulty, distorted and rather inefficient, inefficiency comes in when one's moods are low or feelings are no right therefore affecting a person's performance and output in the society. Output in the sense of socializing or even interrelating with people and handling situations and responsibilities around them.

Trauma treatment introduces newer or rather older but more advanced ways that improve one's behaviors as well and their thinking. The introduction or adaptation of new ideas and habits can greatly heal or relieve someone of mental or physical symptoms and conditions and lead people to more manageable and better ways of conducting themselves and acting in much better ways

How trauma treatment works

Trauma treatment, when followed and packaged properly, can help get over overwhelming problems as well as make sense of them by segmenting them or breaking them into small bits. It's primarily broken down into:

Situations

These are the predicaments or state an individual finds themselves in that force them to yield to mental instability. Situations may be the triggers that occur, probably an action that takes place that reminds someone of something or that bring forth certain emotions or feelings. It may be out of our own creation or some that we just find ourselves in unknowingly.

Thoughts

Since it's all in the mind, it's often a time tailored in us to follow how we feel and the judgment that it outlays for us. Our thoughts after the key primary cause of mental issues since it's in the mind that we process stuff that is either blown into proportion or things that alter our resultant behavioral traits in relation to the surrounding. Being overwhelmed by thoughts is something not easily controlled and this is often the best place to address as a root source of the mental issues.

## Emotions

Emotions are triggered by thoughts. Emotions are also reflected by our physical states. That is, if we are sad, we frown or show in our facial expressions. Emotions in trauma treatment are a key factor that leads towards the cause of many ailments. One's emotions show a deep or profound connection with things or situations and therefore could be able to lead one to the relation they have with the root cause. Trauma treatment focuses on emotions since its well know that emotions cannot be manipulated since they are always in their original and authentic form. How one's emotions are during different situations and around certain people help a lot to arrest n issues.

## Actions

Our actions reflect on our emotions and thoughts. What we do as reflex actions show or rather express our true intent and feelings towards things. Think about it, when you see something and immediately start trembling or shaking, it may depict fear in which will be simply related to past experiences that you might have had that brought about the trauma. As they say, actions speak louder than words then it is. The genuine intent or motive as generated in the mind is what comes out in the respective body parts or physically and communicate what words couldn't have expressed.

Well trauma treatment is concentrated in the above aspects then are filtered out carefully using specialized methodologies to come up with the actual and factual information or diagnosis as well as analysis. One's thoughts and feelings about specific things directly affect and influence how they feel and react both emotionally as well as physically. So trauma treatment incorporating all these to help and provide quick diagnosis and arrest issues by finding quick or dominant pointers that tether or lean more on a specific aspect. It may seem simpler read but the real deal is quite more on the ground.

The difference of trauma treatment from other therapies

Since it's all under the same room of therapies, most people dismiss it to be as common as any other. What they don't know is that all this deal with different solutions as well as issue as much as they are connected or related to the human body they serve different purposes. Trauma treatment is unique in its own ways from other psychotherapies since it's:

Highly structured

This means that instead of narrating your whole life history so as to look for loopholes or certain problem causing issues it helps your therapist focuses on specific problems their relevance or influence in your life as well as set up achievable goals and checkpoints to mark progress in the healing or treatment journey.

Collaborative

If truly you're seeking help you ought to be cooperative and disciplined. You don't expect your therapist to always be on your case getting you to do normal self-responsible tasks. Remember this being an interactive session it requires you and your therapist to lock heads, brainstorms and help each other come with solutions. In some cases, it is the therapists that have consistency issues but rarely will you find such a case. Since it's you who is in need you're required to be collaborative as well as instrumental in this journey since it's all for your own good. Attend all session as supposed to. Observe the dos and don'ts as well as keep in mind that you're not doing it for anyone but yourself.

Tethered on current issues

Trauma treatment may at some point dig inter your past for some few pointers or root causes but it never focuses on your then mental or emotional state. It focuses on the here and now state where your actions and reactions are fresh and under the current reign of emotions or feelings in play. The current issue is the one which is to be diagnosed and addressed as it affects your wellbeing as well as those that surround you. Yes, your past may be important but what you felt and did back then can't be treated or worked on by real-time solutions.

Pragmatic

This is simply put as pointers that point directly to problems. You may be having all a thousand and one issues on your back and some filled up in your head but there are those specific ones that when zeroed in on they'll help bring out the issue at hand and even point out on which route to healing to take. Focusing the energies on one problem helps an individual get the best of the therapy sessions on the thing that affects them most as well a full exposure to the solutions and what they have to offer in full extent.

Stopping and reducing negative thoughts

The ways we address things around depending on how we think of them. Often at times, we take into serious considerations some of the things that happen to us due to our own doing. We take them as final verdict of our happenings and even future possibilities of them happening again. Some of these things leave us sad, hopeless, helpless, depressed or even tired with life. This traps someone in a negative cocoon that if filled with regret and a trail of loneliness. Instead on is supposed to learn from previous mistakes and I think this is what becomes hard for a lot of people. Accepting failure and seeing it as a mode of learning and a possible push to a higher pedestal in the future.

Trauma treatment main aim is to help individuals facing such issues break out from the negative cycles they are in that keep on haunting them and keeping them hostage. This sheds more light on your problems and makes them more manageable. Trauma treatment will arguably help you come out of the cycle as well as come to terms with your conditions or situation as well as change the negativity patterns and uplift you as an individual and your wellbeing. In the first stages, it requires help from a specialist but once you're out of the woods and capable enough you can even get too much greater heights of self-care by your own as well as tackle issues without a therapist.

Trauma treatment session being the main form of appointments can either be physical or online. The physical is best considered since there is a bond or relationship that is developed first hand. It may be a one on one basis or just a group of people with the same issues and experiences seeking help. The period of time taken to see a therapist in terms of personal or individual basis depends on your current issue and how cooperative you might be in the process. In group sessions, you can really count on time because your understanding rate and abilities are all not yoked the same. However, trauma treatment is essential and everyone deserves proper mental healthcare.

# Chapter 7: Understanding anxiety and the anxious mind

## Historical Treatment of Anxiety

The World Health Organization (WHO), reported that 300 million people worldwide suffer from depression. That is almost 1/5th of the world's population. Depression is also believed to be the No.1 contributing disability in the world. Anxiety disorders ranked at 6th. These statistics make sad reading. The US has one of the highest rates of anxiety. With 8 people in every 100, suffering anxiety disorders in some form WHO (2017).

Studies are also showing that common mental health disorders occur at a higher rate in the lower income sectors. Even more disturbing is the fact that anxiety disorders are treatable. Why then are the figures so high? Is it a modern epidemic?

In medieval times treatment consisted of blood leeches and bathing in freezing water. It was a real breakthrough when psychologists such as Sigmund Freud, started treating sufferers more as patients. Such patients began to undergo the "talking" therapy. It was not until as late as the 1980's that the American Psychiatric Association recognized "anxiety" as a mental health disorder. Before then, anxiety was simply classed as a "woman's problem." Sufferers became stigmatized and labeled as depressives. Women are twice as likely to suffer from anxiety disorders, but such conditions are by no means restricted to females only. Today, anxiety may be treated with medication as well as therapy.

## What is Anxiety?

In days gone by, our ancestors risked their lives whenever they hunted live food. Luckily, these skills are no longer needed, but it brings us to how the body reacts when facing danger. This is a time when we instinctively make the decision of "fight, flight or freeze."

It's not a choice brought on by conscious thought. Rather, it is set in motion by the release of chemicals in the part of our brain known as the limbic system. The chemical is cortisol, which is a steroid hormone released through the adrenal glands. One of the side effects from raised levels of this hormone is anxiety. If you feel this type of anxiety too often, the high levels of cortisol can damage cells in a part of the brain known as the hippocampus. This is an area that helps process memories. Such damage can lead to impaired learning and loss of memory. McAuley et al (2009 )(2a). de Quervain et al (1998) (2b).

## Symptoms of Anxiety

Anxiety is now separated from the condition of depression. Although many who suffer from depression also have anxiety issues. Patients who suffer from depression tend to dwell on the past and feel very negative about themselves, and life in general. This is not typical in the case of patients suffering from anxiety. They will worry excessively about the here and now, or the future. Their lives are full of "what ifs," in the eventuality of a disaster. Symptoms of anxiety can vary in individuals, but here are a few to look out for:

Feeling tense for no reason, on edge and almost nervous.
The sense of dread and impending doom.
Unable to sleep because of worry.
General restlessness and fidgeting, unable to relax.
Lack of concentration.
Irritable for no reason.
Breaking out in a cold sweat.
Shaking.
Feeling nauseous.
Digestive and intestinal upsets.
Panic attacks can come as a result of feeling one or many of these symptoms. When someone has frequent anxiety attacks, it inevitably leads to ill health. This is because of the cortisol levels

remain high too often and for too long. One of cortisol's roles is to increase blood sugars. Unbalanced and this can result in insulin resistance. In turn, this may lead to the late onset or type 2 diabetes. Hackett et al (2016) (2c).

In a modern fast-paced society with access to social media, many people are feeling more and more anxious about the world around us. This can start at an early age. If young people are not diagnosed and treated, their anxiety attacks will follow them into adulthood.

There are also various stages throughout life that can lead to feeling over anxious:

Education
Learning and education should be an enjoyable experience. All too often children are pressured to meet certain academic targets. Those who don't meet them may very well consider themselves a failure. The burden of being successful lays heavy on the shoulders of young people.

Family life.
This is a worrying time, particularly if you have never had responsibilities. Women are expected to raise families and go out to work at the same time. Such pressures create huge stresses in their daily lives. With the increasing break up of marriages, the pressure of anxiety reflects on both parents, and on the children.

Materialism
People who live in wealthy industrialized countries are bombarded with a heavily commercialized culture. Advertising constantly prompts us to buy the newest and seemingly greatest ever products. Such deviant tactics imply that their goods will improve your life and make you happy. It seems we must keep up with all the latest gadgets to have an attractive home, and wear the latest fashion labels to look good. All increasing the pressures of life as we attempt to earn more money to keep up.

The Anxious Mind

Whilst it might seem to be stating the obvious, worry plays a key role in anxiety. People who suffer from anxiety attacks are likely big worriers. Often, the only way a worrier will stop panicking over a specific problem is if they have moved on to a different one. Worry leads to anxiety until the released chemicals mean the person cannot think rationally. At this point, they will jump to conclusions of their own making. Unable to focus on reality because their minds are highly aroused, the problem is no longer solvable. They cannot see any solutions which then leads deeper into anxiety.

Simple Coping Techniques
For those who experience the build-up of burdening pressures and suffer anxiety attacks, there is help available. We will look at this in more detail later in this book. There are lifestyle changes that can be put into practice, using techniques to nip the anxiety attacks in the bud. A sufferer may find that these techniques are all they need to alleviate the experience of anxiety. Such as:

Discussing your anxiety issues with your doctor. Doctors can prescribe medication to help you initially, and then refer you to a trauma treatment therapist.
Look at the foods you eat and what you drink. Caffeine and alcohol can both affect anxiety levels negatively. Take the general advice and at the very least cut down on the intake of foods known to cause such effects.
Exercise is beneficial, but it doesn't mean you must work-out like crazy at a gym. Go on walks in calm and soothing vistas, if possible. Learn relaxation exercises that you can do sitting at a desk or watching TV, such breathing exercises and muscle relaxation.
Try and keep active so you tire yourself out naturally during the day. That way sleep will come easier at night.
Stress and anxiety are closely related conditions. Though it is possible to suffer one without suffering the other. For both, you should seek help but there are many self-help techniques that you can do to ease some of the immediate pressures.

Anxiety can include phobias and is often only triggered in certain circumstances. Stress is more a build-up of worry because there is too much pressure in your life. Something has to give. We will look at ways of helping yourself to cope with anxiety. Many of the coping methods are ways to ease the pressures, are similar to the stress self-help approach. It could be that stress is what has brought on your anxiety in the first place. Deal with one and the other may ease as well.

Recognizing that you are suffering from anxiety is the first stage. Events such as employment interviews will naturally cause anxious feelings, these are normal. You should not worry about anxiety when associated with common stressful events. Having adrenaline coursing through your system when under such stress, is a way your body copes with the situation. When you come out of the interview, the anxiety should lift to be replaced with relief that the stress is over. Of course, you may then stress while you wait for the results but try not to be over anxious in such situations.

It is when you are anxious over too many things, especially every day and maybe even all day. This is unhealthy as you will be producing those hormones we mentioned earlier, in high amounts. If you find that stress is affecting your everyday life, then it is time to seek help. The stress will mount up causing triggers to anxiety attacks. Hopefully, you will recognize the dire situation before it gets to that point.

If you have suffered anxiety attacks for over 6 months, this is known as Generalized Anxiety Disorder (GAD). Our next chapter will help you to assess yourself and recognize if this is you.

# Chapter 8: Developing your anxiety profile

Matching Anxiety Types with Anxiety Programs

Self-diagnosis is not encouraged when it comes to health issues, but anxiety can be eased with self-control. To do this, you will need to think about "when, where and what" triggers your own symptoms. Because there are various types of anxiety, it could be helpful to recognize which one you are suffering from. Learning the various types of anxiety and seeking the correct treatment for it, is important in the process of self-help. We will go into detailed treatment options later in this book. This chapter will look at ways you can identify your anxiety type and outline possible options for self-help treatment.

Let's start with some of the more serious profiles for the onset of anxiety. Post-Traumatic Stress Disorder (PTSD) is not as prevalent as generalized anxiety. The rarer types are usually brought on from specific events. By learning the various anxiety types, it will help you categorize your own anxiety profile. Once you understand your own profile, you will be better able to know which treatments might help you.

PTSD

**Situation:**

This relates to people who have experienced a traumatic incident that is out of the ordinary. It is usually an event that is not considered the norm, such as:

Soldiers in combat.
Childhood abuse.
Rape or physical attack.
Witnessing a murder.
Natural disasters.

This list is only an example, but it shows the unusual circumstances that someone suffering PTSD may have gone through.

**Symptoms:**

They will suffer symptoms such as:

Reliving the experience as if in a daydream. The event will play out in their minds with a feeling that the experience is happening right here and now.
Reliving the experience in a nightmare when they sleep.
Bad dreams will lead to broken sleep.
Broken sleepwalk lead to irritability.
Trigger points can set off the memory and lead to a panic attack.
They may begin to avoid places and people. This is because they become frightened of any reminders of the traumatic event.
Anger issues can set in as they are always on guard.
Sufferers may become easily startled and have difficulties concentrating.
PTSD sufferers may find their minds focusing on the traumatic memories more and more each day. This can lead to the inability to cope with the normality around them. Sadly, they may try to forget by taking drugs or alcohol.

The onset of PTSD symptoms can be delayed by months or even years after their experiences. It can be a gradual process before the patient finally breaks down. Anxiety symptoms may not be diagnosed until it comes in the form of panic attacks. It is likely that they will suffer the symptoms of depression first. PTSD does not only affect victims of traumatic incidents, it can include anyone who witnesses such an event.

**Treatment:**

Self-help alone cannot treat the symptoms someone with PTSD will suffer. Only when a PTSD patient can control their maladaptive thought process, can they begin their self-help process

Medication can be an important first step and a valuable tool in the beginning of their treatment.

Attending group sessions with other PTSD suffers can help them to talk about their experiences. Support groups will consist of fellow sufferers, so the patient can see that they are not alone.

Family counseling can be helpful to allow those closest to them to understand what they are going through. This also helps families to realize their loved one is suffering an illness. Then they too can provide that all important support.

## Phobias

This is when a person feels afraid of a particular sight, smell or situation.

**Situation:**

It could come in the form of seeing insects, blood or even certain smells.

Or it could come from an experience of heights or being enclosed in an elevator.

Symptoms:

When in that situation, they begin to imagine extreme consequences; What if I fall and die and nobody finds me? What if the spiders go inside my body? What if the elevator gets stuck and no one knows?

Feelings will be a sense of dread, shallow breathing, dizziness, cold sweats, nausea.

It can bring on a panic attack.

They will begin to avoid any situation that might entail such fears. Someone with a fear of spiders may no longer enjoy working in a garden, even though they loved to before their phobia took hold.

**Treatment:**

It may be a combination of self-help exercises similar to stopping a panic attack.

Plus, there will be an element of exposure therapy which we cover in another chapter.

<u>OCD</u>

**Situation:**

Someone suffering from OCD may have spent many years with generalized stress and anxiety.

They may have suffered a terrible experience that brought on their anxieties in the first instance.

It could be a build-up of many situations as to why an OCD sufferer becomes obsessed.

**Symptoms:**

Everything around them is exaggerated and distressing in their minds.

They feel that the world around them is intruding upon them all the time. To overcome this, they may pray over and over or repeat certain words of comfort to themselves.

Other forms of OCD can lead to obsessive cleanliness and everything must be orderly.

One OCD symptom is that of hoarding, in case they need it later.

They will probably be aware of their irrational behavior, but cannot stop.

Some have intrusive and disturbing thoughts. Thoughts such as, if I don't spin around to the left 3 times, then someone in my family might come to harm. Or they may imagine they will get a disease if their home is not clean and tidy.

For some, everything must be placed in a particular order.

For others, they must carry out their rituals in a certain order.

OCD is how they relieve their anxieties.

When it takes an extended time to complete rituals, it can take over their lives and become debilitating.

**Treatment:**

Medication may be an option.
Support from family members will be encouraged.
Group therapy means sharing their worries and admitting their obsessive behavior.
Exposure therapy is a good option for those who avoid certain situations. Learning to confront their fear and seeing that all is still well in the world.

## Panic Attacks

**Situation:**

This type of profile is more one of sudden intense fear.

A sufferer may, or may not, know the reason for the reason for the onset of sheer fear.
It is almost always a reaction to a bodily sensation, such as increased heartbeat or tightness in the chest.
Symptoms:
Heavy and fast breathing.
This can lead on to a tingling sensation.
Dry mouth causing and you may have difficulty swallowing, or even feel like they are choking.
Hot and cold sweats.
Lightheadedness and dizziness, believing they might collapse.
Impending doom that something bad is about to happen.
Imagining horrible scenarios, such as:
- "I'm going to die."

- "Someone is going to attack me, I don't feel safe."

- "There's going to be a disaster and I won't be able to get away.

- "I've lost all control."

The sufferer has started to feel anxious for some reason, and it has led on to a full-blown panic attack.

For example: You are sat in your car on the freeway in a huge traffic jam. Normally you're patient in such situations, but you have a meeting to get to. Already the stress is setting in because you have no control over the situation. Then, you hear a car backfire and it triggers off an anxious thought. You start thinking, "What if someone's running lose with a gun and we all think it's just a car backfiring?" Now you won't get out of the car because you're imagining bad things. This makes you feel trapped so your anxious thoughts take control of you. You can't breathe and you're all alone in the car. You start to imagine that you're going to have a heart attack. You start to breath quick and shallow breaths, which leads onto a tingling in your fingers. That's it, now you know that today you are going to die. All the signs are right. You are now in a full-blown panic attack.

Can you see how this happened?

- Clearly, this person is already suffering stress.

- They must get to the important meeting on time.

- Frustration is setting in as the delay increases their stress levels.

- This could play out in many ways. Perhaps, in the same scenario, the driver gets out of the vehicle and starts shouting and swearing at no one in particular. Then, if someone responds, the driver abuses them as they have now become the focus of their target.

The entire scenario has been caused by stress.

- Do you recognize any of these feelings happening to you, whereby you blow a situation out of proportion?

- See how easy stress can lead to feeling anxious, which can bring on a full-blown panic attack?

**Treatment:**

- Self-help treatment will be learning how to recognize and deal with the symptoms before they blow out of proportion.

- It may also involve medication initially, to help with relaxation.

- Learning simple relaxation exercises, such as mindfulness and deep breathing.

### Generalized Anxiety

**Situation:**

We have looked at many anxiety conditions. Yet, being over-anxious can happen to anyone who is overloaded with stress. The main problem with generalized anxiety is that it never goes away. Everyone has everyday worries to contend with.

**Symptoms:**

- The first signs you are not coping is when you are constantly worrying until the worry is on your mind all the time.

- It will be a build-up to lots of small worries, such as will you get somewhere on time? Who's doing the school run? How can you pay bills?

- You may find yourself not eating breakfast because you woke up worrying.

- Suffering constipation because your body is to tense.

- Constant headaches.

- The situation escalates until you feel physically ill.

**Treatment:**

- Recognize that you are suffering anxiety.

- Self-help treatment begins with mindfulness. Recognizing; Acceptance; Setting out a plan of action to ease the stresses in your daily life.

# Chapter 9: Why Some People Are More Prone to Depression Than Others

According to surveys, about 7% of the population experiences depression. With 7 billion people on the planet, that means 490 million people battle depression every year. Women are more likely to develop depression than men. In fact, about one and a half to three times more likely.

Why do you think that happens? Could it be attributed to the impossible standards that Society sets upon women? Could it be that females worry more about the house and caring for the family and putting their own needs ahead? Men experience stress just as much as women do but they are taught to keep their emotions inside and not show it.

Are we more depressed as a society that we were 50 years ago? Or is it that we are learning how to talk about it now as to where our parents and grandparents weren't? It wasn't something you did back in the day to discuss your feelings. Many times people dealt with their problems and depression behind closed doors. Now we have services to help us express ourselves, but it seems like we're becoming more depressed.

People don't have the same reactions when it pertains to stress and depression but there are several factors that do affect and cause depression. It may be a combination of two or more of the following factors that induce depression:

Neurotransmitter Defects

Neurotransmitters are mood-regulating chemicals in your body. Research says that it plays an important role as when these chemicals change in function and effect, it leads to depression.

Genetics

Unlike other genetic diseases such as Huntington's chorea or cystic fibrosis, depression doesn't seem to have an exact explanation or link why it exists on a person with a family history of depression.

Even if your family has a genetic predisposition towards depression, it doesn't guarantee that you will automatically have it, although there may be a possibility that you are prone to it as it also includes other factors as well.

Hormones

You have more possibilities of depression if you are susceptible to hormonal changes or imbalance. People who undergo hormonal changes like women who gave birth to children or those who have certain thyroid conditions experience symptoms of depression.

Abuse and Early Trauma Those who have experienced trauma and abuse in their early part of life are more prone to depression during their prime years or later part of their life.

Prescription Medication

Are you taking prescribed medications? Medicines such as sleeping pills, corticosteroids, Accutane, and interferon-alpha increase risks for depression.

Drug Abuse

It may be hard to determine why some people use drugs. It may be because they want to treat their depression by starting up with self-medication or they had previously started using drugs abusively. It's the same with prescription drugs. Certain illegal drugs can also cause you to have depression symptoms and its effects are seen.

Pain and Illnesses

There are two main reasons why pain and illnesses are related to depression. The illness itself causes biochemical changes in the body that causes depression.

People with illnesses tend to be depressed as they experience prolonged pain, normal body function is limited or incapable and sometimes facing the possibility of death. They become depressed because of their health.

Death and Loss

Don't be surprised if you see somebody depressed after experiencing extreme losses whether it is in finances, properties or even lives of their loved ones. These events may have triggered their tendencies of depression.

Personality

Check this out if you've got some of these traits on your personality.

Overly dependent on others

Low self-esteem

Self-critical

Pessimism

If you have any of these traits, you are more prone to getting depressed.

Interpersonal Conflict

Family and friend conflicts also contribute to increased stress. Undergoing conflicts such as these will tend you to develop depression.

**Stress**

You can have stress whether your life is uphill (getting married) or downhill (losing your job). When you are under attack by stress, your cortisol levels rise to the point that possibly affects the transmission of serotonin, a mood-regulating molecule.

In other words, depression is a complicated situation wherein certain factors are involved, e.g. biologically based differences in brain function. The more you are faced with various factors, the more tendencies and possibilities to develop depression.

# Chapter 10: Treating Depression with Cognitive Behavioral Therapy

Life isn't one big party as you've learned. You've got your good days and you've got your bad days. The trick is not to let your bad days linger into bad weeks or months or years. And to keep that from happening, sometimes it's necessary to see someone professionally.

It's normal to feel down occasionally. It's a common feeling shared by all of us in society. Major Depressive Disorder affects 14.8 million adults in the United States today according to the Anxiety and Depression Association of America. The stressors of working more for less pay, dealing with a scarcity mindset and reality, or having problems in your relationships can all contribute to depression. Piled on top of that with battling addictions and it's no surprise more Americans are feeling the effects of depression.

However, if that feeling keeps you from doing the things you once loved to do or sucks the motivation out of doing anything at all and you can't seem to get out from under it, it could be a sign that you are suffering from depression.

Depression sucks. It's isolating and lonely. It can make you feel like you've lost your mind. It can make you feel confused about who you are and what you want in life. It may make you believe there is something permanently wrong with you. Worse, it can make you feel like you will never be able to face the world in your present situation. When at this point the low feeling of despair has taken hold of your life and just won't shift, you could be suffering from depression. Depression can be incredibly isolating. It can make you feel like you're the only one in the world who feels the way you do. It's no wonder why many people turn to drugs and alcohol to numb the pain of depression. Very often those things can give a short term comfort. But it's simply a mirage. They only cover up the problem and not directly deal with it.

If you're feeling hopeless and down, there is light at the end of the tunnel, and you don't need to suffer in silence.

Notice that each session is a collaborative effort between you and the therapist as you get into a deep conversation. You both have to decide what to go about and how to go about it.

With help from the therapist, the problems you have are going to be analyzed and broken down into smaller parts. The therapist we asked you to keep a journal or diary to help you identify and assess your feelings and thoughts.

Together you and your therapist will evaluate your behaviors, feelings, and thoughts to see how they affect you and other people around you. You both will determine whether they are unrealistic or unhelpful. Then your therapist will be assisting you in changing any negative behavior by replacing them with more realistic and positive ones. Expect your therapist to give you homework to do on your own time. Usually, your homework will allow you to practice the techniques you learned so you can personally witness any change in your behavior.

When meeting your therapist, you'll have an opportunity to talk about your progress and what happened since your previous session. You'll both discuss what works and what didn't. From there, figure out where to go.

No one will make you do anything you don't want to do. You are in charge of the pace on which your therapy progress has. You can also take the skills you learn and practice them long after you stop seeing your therapist. This is encouraged because it can help you live a long healthy life.

The great thing about having a therapist is that they will work with you to establish a set of treatment goals to help you feel less depressed and to cut out such negative habits as drugs or alcohol. The goal isn't to concentrate on your past or your personality. Your therapist will likely help you turn your focus toward how you think and feel in the present and ways in which you can change it. Treatment length can last anywhere from 10 to 20 sessions. Many can go to therapy for over a year, while others can go a handful of times. Your therapist may also give you homework to do at a self-study pace.

If your therapist is worth their weight in gold, they will show you some skills to help prevent the return of your depression. Should your depression return, it's a good idea to pick up therapy again. You can also do it anytime you feel bad or need to work through a tough problem.

A good therapist will equip you with several skills to prevent your depression from returning before your therapy ends with them. The goal is to keep you functioning at a healthy level long after you graduate from therapy.

The key here is to work only with trained therapists. Those who have been in the industry for some time and can competently diagnose and treat you. You can tell a qualified therapist by the degrees they hold and the number of years of experience they've had success treating clients with depression. Most have a master's or doctoral degree with a focus on counseling. Check their certification and license in your state and make sure their area of expertise lines up with your needs. This would be some of the qualifications you'd want to take a look at before picking a therapist.

A trauma treatment therapist's first action when treating all disorders is to educate their clients about their patient's diagnosis and how trauma treatment will be applied to it. They will also help clients set goals in their treatment program and will train clients on how to cope by using behavioral and thinking skills.

Typically, the type of interventions that trauma treatment therapists conduct is centered on reminding the client of all the activities they used to do before they became depressed. They help them find ways to re-engage in those activities and find their joy again. Which if you think about it, when you are preoccupied with other things, you turn your attention away from your own problems. This is especially true when helping others.

A trauma treatment therapist will also do the hard work with the client of helping them face and acknowledge their negative beliefs about themselves, their environment, and their perceptions about the world.

The type of trauma treatment training can be tailored to the client depending on the client's characteristics. For example, when a therapist counsels children, they may incorporate parents by showing them new behavior skills that specifically help with the child's depression.

When talking about adults, the trauma treatment therapist may turn the focus of treatment toward engaging in a fulfilling and active life, questioning negative and/or false beliefs about getting older and learning how to deal with issues of health.

trauma treatment therapists can also help clients who have health problems that lead to depression by assisting them in what it means within their life while making sure they're still engaging in activities that mean something to the client.

So you can see that regardless of the age of the client or health issues they face, the key is to re-engage in social and physical activities to treat their depression. Not only that but to be able to identify what's engaging in those activities means knowing who they are and their importance in the world.

## Effects of Untreated Clinical Depression

When most of us are facing depression at some points in our life, neglecting can be a serious issue. Untreated depression increases the possibility of developing risky behaviors such as drug and alcohol addiction which can lead to breaking relationships, cause problems in the workplace, and making it difficult to overcome chronic ailments.

Clinical depression which is likewise known as major depression is an illness that affects the person's thoughts, body, and moods. It can affect even the way you sleep and eat, the way you feel and the way you think.

It's hard to pull yourself together when you are depressed. However, when left untreated, the symptoms can last for weeks, months, or even years. Appropriate treatment, however, like trauma treatment can help people suffering from clinical or major depression.

## Major Depression Affects Physical Health

Mounting pieces of evidence are now being uncovered that major depression can take a serious toll on one's physical health. In most recent findings of health and major depressions which are focused on stroke and coronary disease patients, people recovering from heart attacks and strokes finds it difficult to make health care choices, follow doctor's directives, and to cope with the challenges that their illness presents. A separate study further discovered that patients with major depression have a higher risk of dying in the first few months after the heart attack.

## How is Sleep Disrupted by Untreated Depression?

When a person is suffering from major depression, one of the most apparent symptoms of clinical depression is the change in sleeping patterns. Most of the sufferers find themselves dealing with insomnia or the difficulty to get adequate quality sleep. They would feel the increased need to sleep while experiencing excessive energy loss. Lack of sleep can also bear the same symptoms as that of depression such as extreme fatigue, loss of energy, difficulty to make decisions and to stay concentrated or focused.

In addition to disrupted sleeping patterns, untreated depression may also result in either weight gain or weight loss, feeling a sense of helplessness and hopelessness, and also, irritability. Treating the sickness of major depression can help the sufferer gain control over their depression symptoms.

# Chapter 11: Cognitive Distortions

Whenever you feel stressed or worried, do you notice the kind of thoughts that occupy your mind? Usually when we go through stress or sadness, worry or fear, our thoughts are filled with negativity.

What are Cognitive Distortions?

There is a strong relationship between what we feel and what we think. Whenever we feel challenged or unhappy, our thoughts become dramatic and absolute, and it usually goes along the lines of feeling 'I am stupid and unworthy' or 'I don't fit in' or 'nobody likes me.' These types of thoughts are recognized as 'cognitive distortions,' and it is a term in psychology that describes the way we are thinking about something that doesn't match up to the extent of the reality that is going on.

Why Are Cognitive Distortions So Important To Understand?

Cognitive distortions are an element of extreme thinking, and they often lead a person into a negative cycle. This can make anyone spiral further and further down into a whole series of negativity, until they feel there is no way out or no solution or end to their problems. Distorted thinking is very common among people who suffer from negative issues such as low-self esteem or mood swings and anxiety.

When a thought affects your bodily sensations and your feelings, this combination then dictates your behavior. Your behavior then triggers your next thought which then creates another cycle of negativity.

It is an ongoing loop that goes on and on, and each cycle leads to an even more destructive negative thought. For example, you go to a party and see the girl you want to talk to. Before you can even approach her to say hello, you are already processing the many different things that could go wrong. You start thinking 'What if she doesn't like me' or 'What if she snubs me.' This negative thinking then makes you start feeling anxious and self-conscious (feelings), and then it makes your body react by excessively sweating and your heart beating fast (bodily sensations). Because these negative feelings have overcome you, you abandon all desire to speak to that girl. You retreat to a quiet place and don't talk to anyone. You feel left out of the party and alienated which then produces another negative thought, "Is there something wrong with me? Why doesn't anyone like me?" (Behavior)

This starts the cycle all over again.

Cognitive distortions determine the number of trauma treatment therapists that work with you to change your moods and alter the way you think. Trauma treatment therapists help you to recognize the moment when you think distorted thoughts, and they also help train yourself to replace these thoughts with more balanced and positive thoughts. While this sounds simple, the process to get there is not. Negative thoughts are a strong habit, and it is deeply rooted in a person's unconscious mind that it sometimes can be perceived as normal.

Changing negative thinking is a robust process of focused work and attention, but with the therapist's help, a patient is steered in the right direction.

How to Recognize Cognitive Distortions

It may be you or someone you know who have these distortions, so it would help to try to recognize these signs. Here are ten of the most common distortion traits:

Mental Filter

Mental filtering relates to how a person focuses, whether consciously or subconsciously, to the most negative and upsetting feature in a situation. When they think this way, they filter out positive aspects of that situation. For example, you had a night out with friends and the very next day, suffer from a hangover. Your entire mood goes downhill because you are too focused on your hangover even to think that it is a result of a fantastic night out with friends. You convince yourself that you feel too sick and that you will not participate in future events. This levels you not recognizing the fun times of last night and the enjoyment that you felt.

Disqualifying the positive

This happens when we continuously dismiss and discount positive experiences that we encounter and instead, choose to dwell on details that are negative. We decide that the positive experiences are not important or don't count. For example, an acquaintance comes over to your work table and compliments you on the sweater you are wearing, and instead of feeling good or pleasant, you decide that they are nice just to get something out of you.

Always or Nothing

This type of thinking is when we view things only in black and white. It is either a never, an always or an every. Everything you see is either good or bad or a failure, and more often than not, it is usually the negative perception that is pushed forward, whereas everything in the gray area is discounted. For example, you score 90 percent on your driving test but get sad and think you are a bad drive because you didn't score 100 percent.

Over-generalization

Over-generalizing refers to how we often perceive a single unpleasant incident or event as proof that everything else will be the same awful and negative experience, and how it is a sign that everything around will go wrong. For example, if you fail at an exam, you immediately think that you are never going to pass. Or you might even go for a job interview and fail badly at it and think you are never going to get a job.

## Jumping to Conclusions

A person that jumps to conclusions is very inclined to make a negative prediction that the worst is yet to come even though there is no evidence to support their assumption. This thinking materializes from what we think other feels towards us. People like this often act like mind readers. They assume the thoughts and intentions of others or they also act like fortune tellers anticipating the worst.

For example, you are giving a pitch presentation, and you already know (fortune-telling) that you'll end up failing. Or you are going to a party and do not like the dress you are wearing, because you think everyone is going to hate it (mind-reading).

## Magnifying or Minimizing

Thinking either in a minimizing or magnifying way is a kind of thinking where we exaggerate the importance of negative events and downplay the positive events. People who are depressed often exaggerate the positive characteristics of other people and the negative ones are downplayed. It is the reverse when we think of our own selves. When we exaggerate a situation, we are unable to see other ways or outcomes except the worst one. For example, you wrongly sent an email out to a client, and you exaggerate the worst by thinking 'I'm about to lose my job now. My house and car won't now be paid. I'm going to lose my house. I will no longer have a place to live.'

## Personalization

Personalization in the cognitive disorders refers to a situation when a person automatically thinks a bad thing or negative event has happened because of him or her. They assume responsibility and blame for things that are above and beyond their control and they feel guilt, shame, and inadequacy. For example, there was a burglary in your house, and you immediately assume responsibility and say it is your fault because you didn't install proper locks or can't remember if you ever locked your gates and doors when you went out. You'd probably be thinking 'if only I installed professional locks' or 'if only I subscribed to the neighborhood watch.'

Should Have, Must have or Ought to have Thinking

Individuals who think this way often have a very rigid view and a set of rules that can arouse the feeling of anger, resentment, frustration, guilt as well as disappointment with their constant thinking of 'Should' 'Ought' and 'Must.' For instance, your daughter doesn't like playing the piano, but you put her in classes anyway because you feel that she should learn it and when she makes mistakes, you think that her teacher 'ought' to be stricter on her.

Emotional Reasoning

This kind of thinking relates to when we assume that our feelings reflect the fact, whether or not there's evidence. The basis of this is 'I feel it, which means it has to be true.' This kind of thinking often leads to self-fulfilling prophecies and our thoughts often end up promoting the very behavior we predicted, all because we changed our behavior in line with that specific thought. For example, if you think 'I feel stupid and useless, therefore I must be stupid and useless.' This might cause you not to learn new things or read more books even though you are a bright person and very resourceful.

Labeling

An individual with this kind of thinking usually assigns a negative and very emotive label on themselves and even others, with no room of change. This label is automatically given the minute something goes wrong or is done wrong.

For example, you send out a newsletter, and there is a spelling error. Immediately, you think 'I am so stupid and careless' instead of thinking 'It's a mistake and I will not let it happen again'. This person can also label someone else automatically. For instance, your friend made an error in a computer program and you quickly say 'You are so incompetent'.

Do you suffer from Cognitive Distortions?

Sometimes, we all end up becoming negative, especially when we are not focused or become too stressed. It is a normal human behavior to experience these emotions but people with cognitive distortions often exhibit these behaviors too often and is usually destructive to themselves and the people around them. If you feel you or someone you know has any of these types of thoughts, don't panic. Instead, realize that you can overcome this pattern or thinking. Realization is halfway to the path of change. It would be good for you to monitor when and how often you experience these distortions and in what kind of situations do they occur.

# Chapter 12: Common Mental Health Issues

Mental health has always been a vital topic of discussion in society. One's mental abilities and potentials are dependent on their wellness mentally and health. This is quite obvious because one of insane mind cannot be trusted in judgment and in making decisions. However mental health is not all about mental illnesses or ailments that require medical attention. Some of the issues that cause illnesses or issues in one's health commonly come about as a result of the things we engage ourselves or involve ourselves in our day to day lives. The people we interact with the impact of our mental health greatly. You could be asking as to how your friend does this but it's not really rocket science to understand that how they talk or treat us or rather relate to us affect us in one way or another.

Just as people have physical health and are greatly concerned about it so does one's mental health prove to be important. We should look after ourselves we a lot of care and consideration to the things that affect or influence us either in term of behaviors or even making decisions. We need to look after ourselves and glitter around what we bring in into our lives. I know that this might be hand; controlling things in our lives but there's always something that is within our power. Some things happen as a result of our choices and we end up facing the repercussions whereas some come about obviously and affect us the same way. At the end of the day, we cannot escape our mental responsibilities or try suppressing them or manipulating. They'll always come out as they are. Question is, are they going to be of positive impact to those around us or we'll be spreading out negative vibes.

Possessing a good and healthy mental state means that one is able to reason out, think, react and feel their surrounding as per how you'd want or desire to be living your life. Every day as you walk the streets going about your business or interacting with people, what you don't notice or have at your attention is their state of mentality or mental health. Once you interact or relate with them Is when you'll notice some of the things that could be disturbing an individual. Most at times, people mask their feelings and mental ailments in a bid to look strong, brave and indestructible were in real sense their inner self is crying for help. This kind of cry could be the urges that one may have to do the thing that they'd like to do but because of past negative experiences or certain toxic feelings or principles that could have been imparted into them over time.

Looking at yourself as an individual, there are points in your life that you've noticed a state of poor or questionable mental state. This are situations that make you realize that your reactions to things or feelings towards specific aspects of your surrounding are becoming or rather seems so impossible and difficult to get along with. Some react to the extent of even bringing about a physical effect of illness or even worse conditions. You've seen people before becoming bedridden due to the stressful situations around them. Some end up sick and hospitalized in the same way. Mental issues are also a matter of concern in the society that if not handle at an early stage and effectively it could cripple one's wellbeing.

Mental issues arise about in almost everything that we engage ourselves in. yes, everything. Don't you use your mind to think in situations? Making decisions? Speaking? Conducting and relating to people? Well now imagine if all that is compromised manipulated and distorted, how life will be for an individual. That is what mental issues is all about. With such tragic results when an individual is unattended to, it leaves one with no choice but to seek help. Coming out and asking for help won't make an individual weak, rather it makes them stronger than someone who is living in denial and pretending to be alright. Accepting your flaws and imperfections help one go a long way to be a much better individual personally as well as it puts them at a pedestal where they can influence others in the society in an advantageous manner.

Mental issues vary and are brought about by many situations and causes. Some of the mental issues we all suffer from are anxiety and depression. Well, at least those are the most commonly experienced and dealt with in society. And no one can ever say they've never experienced them to some specific point of their lives. However, there are some rarer issues that are also important to note and be on the lookout for. These are bipolar disorders as well as schizophrenia. Having to understand the mental health spectrum could be rather a bit complex and confusing. That is, you wouldn't really know where you stand as an individual well unless you're examined or observed and later brought to attention. To some bits, the experience could be frightening especially during your denial stage where you're thinking that things are just temporary and will soon go away.

There is never anything like being weak when you accept your conditions. One might think they are losing their mind but that is not the case. It's all normal to be unwell and fall in the unfortunate pits life has dug for us. The fears one develops overtime when their deteriorating thoughts are reinforced by the negative and unrealistic way people package mental health experiences and problems in society. Often at times, this stops individuals from opening up and seeking help or counsel. In the same isolating and solitude one gets only much worse as well as an increment in their degree of distress and ailments. Looking at it from a medical point of view, for instance, having a wound not attended to for a long time only opens more doors of resultant illnesses or even infections. In the same analogy so does mental issues bask in.

Ignoring a serious issue that is affecting you will only leave you vulnerable to more problems in the same way.

However to treat such problems one require a combination of support, i.e. from a counselor or people around you, self-care(treating yourself right and knowing what is good for you and your mental state) as well as treatment that has to be followed to the latter for a successful journey towards healing and a sane wellbeing. Don't wait till you are having breakdowns so that you may consider yourself viable for help or wait till it's serious enough. The following are some of the mental issues explained and characterized by people's daily experiences and can as well be present simultaneously:

Depression

This is arguably one of the most common conditions impacting almost half of the people in our community. It has no specific gender or age group that it attacks and so anyone can be presented with such a condition. Depression is brought about by general sadness, the feeling of little to no self-worth or guilt. It has symptoms such as reduced activities especially if someone used to be very active and instrumental in their surroundings. Sleeping habits, as well as eating habits, are also affected. One is always in constant thoughts that never end and also drain from their personality. From their daily routine or patterns taking a sudden or gradual shift, there is also exhaustion that is always present since the entire time they feel like doing is sitting and go deep in thoughts and this in return derails a lot in their lives as well as brings setbacks.

Depression at times presents itself either as long term or recurring. This affects one's ways of life as well as their surroundings. That is their work, school, social life as well as their functionality in relationships. Depression is quite dangerous when not noticed and addressed fast because at its extremity its leads to suicidal thoughts as well as regrettable thoughts that most at times are tragic or gruesome. Some of it could be self-inflicted whereas some may affect their people in their surrounding or people they relate with. To treat such an ailment that requires immediate attention in certain cases, trauma treatment is essential, physiotherapy as well as in some special cases antidepressants may be advocated for.

Anxiety

Depression goes hand in hand with anxiety. It's quite unheard of to find some who are suffering from the latter lacking depression somewhere in their trail. Anxiety can come about as a result of several factors such as life events, constant thoughts, and genetics all the way to brain chemistry. Anxiety at times is considered normal in the society and that is where people go wrong, self-diagnosis conditions. Whereas some may be temporary, some have a lasting effect on an individual and could affect their wellbeing. Being anxious in the same situations someone finds themselves in constantly should raise an eyebrow and prompt the subject to seek treatment. In treating anxiety, medication comes in handy but not self-medicating. Seek help from a specialist who'll know what exactly the problem is and recommend the right drugs to use. A psychotherapist as well as one who'll effectively help in such conditions and help control as well as manage the situation or symptoms that come out strong.

Schizophrenia and psychoses

The name might be unheard of but its actions and ripple effect is seen in the community at large. It is brought about by distortions in one's ways of thinking, their emotions, perceptions of things in their surrounding their behavioral traits overall as well as their self-sense. The effect of such a condition is hallucinations as well as delusions. Such like conditions make one quite unreliable since they'll be constantly blowing things out of proportion as well as making up situations and issues in their own mental state do not exist. Interacting with such characters becomes harder especially when they see you as a source of distress or even conflict. They'll gradually create their own profile of you with added and exaggerated traits that could be negative.

Such as people in the society are often discriminated and secluded since they are seen as "mad". This stigma leaves them in their own cocoons in which the same condition will keep on deteriorating. In the discriminative community at large, you'll notice that these people don't have any access to social amenities and help that would help diagnose as well as treat their disorders. And alteration of thoughts and manipulation of them is not something that should be taken lightly. If you've ever been under some drug (prescribed or not) and experienced hallucinations then you now know what an individual suffering from such has to get along with on a daily basis.

Dementia

This is a chronic condition in nature and is all about the deterioration of one's cognitive functions beyond their normal aging rate. This affects one's brain completely. That is from one's thinking, calculation, and reasoning out, comprehensions of things around them as well as their language at large. Unfortunately, there is no cure available for dementia patients and this has been sad since one's brain is impacted in ways that they cannot control or prevent. On the flipside here might not be a cure in hand but there are some palliative treatments that have been designed and formulated to ease the confusion and suffering inflicted to the subject with the condition. One with dementia or one thinking they could be developing from it should seek medical attention so as to arrest the situation early in its development stages and avoid further damage. This is a condition that as well does not have a specific age group or caliber that is attacks. One's memory deteriorating could start at any age whether from school or even while you're working. All this affect one's social and emotional control and could affect you tremendously.

Bipolar disorder

Bipolar has been a socially affecting condition. This is one where people experience a series of extreme heights or degrees of emotions that quickly shift to their opposites in no time. Someone might find themselves in both depressive and manic episodes and sometimes stabilized or normal moods. These types of people with manic episodes are easily irritable as they as their attention shifts just by a small effect or alteration in their surroundings. They are often at times hyperactive as well as have a form or inflated or off the scale self-esteem as well as insomniac to some extents. On the other hand, depressive just as the name suggests are those with series of hopelessness, extreme sadness as well as little to no energy at all (don't confuse it with laziness).

The major causes or root sources of bipolar are not really known but some specialist tethers its origin around genetics, neurochemicals as well as some environmental factors that play major roles in the budding of the condition. Bipolar, however, can be treated through a series of therapy session as well as medication that can be provided. So in case of such a condition budding, seek help at an early stage.

Anger

We all get angry at some different times as we are minding our business. This may be as a result of one thing or the other. Either people around us cause it or just things not working to our favor. I mean it's all part of a normal human. Its shows firm stand and belief in principles or perspectives. It's something everyone must feel like a normal emotionally healthy person. It's never always negative as we all know it but also a way for us to understand ourselves better in terms of what we dislike and how we react to them, the motivations that push us beyond our limits as well as equip us and act as protectorates in during aggressive situations. Anger can be managed as well as control but it now becomes a problem when out of bounds and unleashed.

Anger becomes a serious problem when it now tends to harm people around us as well as offend them. We might get angry at very little irrelevant but our anger goes overboard when we constantly express it in destructive or unhelpful behaviors. It is also considered a problem when it impacts you negatively in terms of your physical and overall mental health. When someone always runs to their anger "protectorate" it blocks out all other emotions and makes one numb to other feelings that could be used or considered or ought to be experienced in place of anger. So find healthy and meaningful ways and means to be expressing your anger. Possible signs of extreme anger issues are increased aggression, slamming of doors, banging hitting or even throwing things but it also takes a much worse turn to self-hate as well as inflicting injuries to yourself i.e. by cutting yourself or denying yourself essential in your life in a bid to punish.

Hearing voices

I don't know if you've heard voices before in your head or just heard someone call you out yet you're alone. Well, you could be having a mental issue, or maybe just a normal day that you're tired. This is however considered a problematic condition when it gets overboard. It might result in a form of hallucination brought about by anxiety or depression. People may find their "voices" distracting and quite irritable whereas some don't mind them after all. To some extreme extent, some find them as intrusive and frightening and this could lead to madness since it's only you who is hearing this strange voices and you are rather distressed and fed up since you cannot mute or stop them. Such like conditions, in the long run, lead to self-destruction.

Some of the causes of such like condition could be lack of sleep, hunger, abuse of drugs, stress or even a series of traumatic experiences. All this, when combined, could bring out mental disorder. Other confuses instincts for a disorder but at the same time distinguishing is not easy. If it persists and becomes a brother that is when one should seek help and at least some counseling.

Loneliness

Loneliness comes about as a form of missing something that used to give you a sense of belonging and value. Experiencing loneliness is quite normal but when it persists for a long time it could affect your wellbeing. It detracts from a person rosy personality and even the radiant self that had remained faced away. Loneliness may come about as a result of the loss of a loved or friend or even an item that used to occupy your time and gave you a sense of accomplishment. Feeling lonely and tolerating it for long affects one's mental health as well as their productivity. Having a mental disorder or issues that separate you or rather makes you want to seclude yourself from the public leaves you lonely and could bring about negative effects.

Loneliness may require a specialist if it's an extreme condition but this time can be self-treated. To cope with loneliness one first has to accept their current state and shun way denial that could be wrapped up in a word like "I'm laid back". We all have a social circle no matter how small it is. That social circle is the perfect treatment for this condition. But what happens when nothing happens or we cannot connect with them? Develop new social contacts. Yes, it might be hard at times but a little compromise would help you a great deal. First, you to address the elephant in the room, first, get to know what makes you lonely, try and make new connections and be open as you take the process slow. You should as well be careful as you try to uplift by doing comparisons and majorly get some help. It never really hurts just to reach out and get you a helping hand and support.

# Conclusion

At the completion of this workbook, you will have learned everything you need to know to create your own program which should last for a minimum of two months and can last as long as half a year. This is probably one of the few anxiety disorder books that has covered this much information for a beginner that is interested in self-treatment.

The next thing for you is to take out your journal for one last exercise from this workbook. Write down how you feel about the information here. Does it relate to you in any sort of way? How did these principles make you feel about you and your condition? Are you more confident of your ability to overcome depression and anxiety disorder?

Using a combination of these techniques, along with remedies you might have learned elsewhere, you can create a customized program that will help you overcome your own depression and anxiety disorder. You can either work with a licensed therapist with whom you can bounce your ideas, or you can work alone and fully personalize your approach.

Take note that this workbook isn't an exhaustive source of every technique and method used in trauma treatment. Over the years, trauma treatment has acquired many changes and adaptations that have made it the very flexible program that it is today. It is a constantly improving method that is refined just as much as it is critiqued.

As you conclude this book, walk away with the notion that this is not the end of your learning and self-practice. As with any other therapeutic approach, trauma treatment is not perfect and has its own list of flaws.

In time, more developments will be made to trauma treatment to overcome these flaws and improve the overall effectiveness of the program. As a practitioner, you should also be on the lookout for these developments.

Experts and therapists from around the world are always researching and experimenting on new ways to complement trauma treatment in order to make it better. A good place to start research next would be the hybrid form of trauma treatment mixed with heavy hypnotism principles.

Another thing you should remember as you walk away from this workbook is the notion that you are now a source of relief and comfort for other people that are suffering from the same afflictions you're now able to conquer with ease. As a human being, you have a calling to reach out to these people and share with them what you know. You never know who among your social networks could be in dire need of help.

# Book Five
# EMDR AND SOMATIC PSYCHOTHERAPY

## Introduction

Frightening and trauma invoking experiences come in many forms however, their impact if not addressed in time can be devastating to the human life. Assume that you're involved in a near car accident as you drive towards the intersection of a busy road. Such an experience is more likely to leave you frozen and in a state of shock. As a trained somatic psychotherapist who understands the impact of such an experience, you are more likely to engage in moving your body so as to centralize the body awareness by taking deep breaths as you focus on releasing the fear that you are likely to be feeling at the moment.

After several months, you might notice anxiety gripping your heart whenever you're approaching the intersection of a busy road as you drive and you may notice your stomach tightening and your breath also quickening. The experience can lead to intense feelings of trauma and deep anxiety that can be immobilizing if not addressed. This is just an example, however, there are numerous causes of trauma, depression and PTSD. Somatic psychotherapy and EMDR therapy helps with addressing the conditions, identifying the root causes, the emotional and behavioral impact and treating the conditions effectively.

Somatic Psychotherapy and EMDR therapy offers a structured and comprehensive approach that effectively treats trauma, PTSD, alongside the associated sensations, beliefs and emotions. The synthesis of somatic psychotherapy and EMDR therapy provides such an advanced treatment to mental health and are considered as per the various research findings as two of the best models of trauma treatment that are available. Integrating the two therapies helps with enhancing their level of effectiveness.

**Somatic Psychotherapy and EMDR Therapy** is a book that's fully packed with valuable insights, techniques and strategies that helps with addressing and treating trauma. The book provides an in-depth guide to mastering the integration of the two and how both can be effectively used in addressing traumatic experiences and behavioral issues. The effectiveness of somatic interventions can greatly improve the effectiveness and results of EMDR therapy. This book is ideal for therapists who desire to realize tremendous success in their engagements and also individuals looking for ways to enhance their performance by learning the strategies they can use to stay centered and emotionally whole.

Take your time and read the book all through to the end for a deeper understanding of how you can not only use the strategies to alleviate your own pain and trauma but also gain some professional insight on how you can help others as well.

# Chapter 1: Understanding Somatic Psychotherapy and EMDR Therapy

The body has several ways of manifesting the different types of trauma and fear that people face with many opting for talk therapy as a way of coping with the various symptoms of emotional distress. Talk therapy is a type of psychotherapy that's generally based on verbal processing of thoughts, experiences and feelings. Somatic psychotherapy and EMDR therapy is quite different from talk therapy as they shift the paradigm from that of talking to feeling. The approach helps with providing a new way of healing trauma through engagement in body-centered techniques.

## What is Somatic Psychotherapy?

Somatic psychotherapy which is also referred to as body psychotherapy mainly focuses on the profoundly powerful and complex connections between the mind and the body and how the connections tend to affect processing and recovery from the various forms of emotional distress and trauma. In somatic psychotherapy, practitioners tend to use the mind-body exercises alongside other physical techniques to help clients release the held up tension that seem to negatively affect their physical and emotional well-being.

Somatic psychotherapy stems from the fact that human beings tend to engage with others and the world at large through movement, expression and sensations. When responding to any situations and all kinds of stimuli, the core response network of the body gets activated. This network consists of the limbic system, autonomic nervous system and other regulatory body functions that influences the organizing and generation of an immediate response to the challenges that gets presented by the environment that one finds themselves in like the fight, flight or freeze way of response to the perceived dangers and stressors.

Somatic psychotherapy is ideal for those suffering from anxiety stress, grief addiction, and depression alongside issues related to abuse and trauma. Humans tend to struggle with recovery after undergoing a traumatic experience and those who experience ongoing of sudden trauma alongside other distressing events lack ways to clear their systems of the arousal, survival and the energy that gets produced in response to such experiences. The energy ends up lingering in the body and if it stays unresolved for long then it might lead to conditions such as depression phobias, posttraumatic stress disorder (PTSD), muscle aches, irritable bowel syndrome, insomnia, pain, digestive issues, and autoimmune disorders.

The main purpose of engaging in somatic psychotherapy is to help with resolving issues that trigger physical and emotional distress. Unlike approaches such as cognitive behavioral therapy that focuses on helping people to talk about their experiences so as to gain insight into the patterns of negative thinking as they identify harmful behavioral patterns; somatic psychotherapy starts with the body and identifying how the trauma is being experienced physically. It then progresses to finding ways of safely discharging the energy that's related to the trauma. While talk therapy encourages those with the challenge to think about the traumatic experience as they express their feelings in words, somatic approach mainly focuses on feeling the body sensations fully and the emotions that come along with such feelings. People are then encouraged to engage with their body's responses to experiences, memories and their surroundings.

### What is EMDR Therapy?

EMDR refers to Eye Movement Desensitization and Reprocessing. This is a form of therapy that enables people to heal from trauma or other forms of distressing life experiences. It is an integrative psychotherapy approach that has been proven to be effective for trauma treatment. EMDR consists of a set of standardized protocols that entails elements from diverse treatment approaches and involves use of bilateral stimulation through tones, eye movements or tapping.

The human brain has a natural way of recovering from traumatic events and memories and the process entails communication between the amygdala which is like the alarm that signals the brain on stressful events; the hippocampus which majorly assist with learning and also includes storage of memories on danger and safety and the prefrontal cortex which analyzes and also controls human emotions and behavior. As much as several traumatic experiences can be solved or managed spontaneously; it's normally difficult for the condition to be processed without help.

Stress responses are generally part of the natural fight, flight and freeze instincts. So when is stuck with some distressed experience, the upsetting thoughts, images and emotions can create feelings of being overwhelmed or being frozen in time or back in the moment. EMDR therapy helps with processing such memories through engagement of the brain and in turn allows for the normal healing to resume. The person might still remember the experience but it will not lead to the fight, flight or freeze response once it's resolved.

EMDR unlike other forms of therapies doesn't require engagement in detailed talking about the distressing issue. It instead focuses on changing the thoughts, emotions or behaviors that result from the distressing issue and in turn enables the brain to resume the natural healing process. EMDR therapy is majorly designed to help with resolving the unprocessed traumatic memories within the brain. Part of the therapy entails use of sounds, traps and alternating eye movements.

EMDR therapy has helped millions of people to relieve different types of psychological stress and traumas and the model is based on adaptive information processing. This type of therapy is ideal for those struggling with mood disorders and depression, generalized anxiety disorders, panic attacks, PTSD, somatic problems such as image issues, gastrointestinal issues, chronic pain, vicarious trauma, performance enhancement and more.

## Basic Concepts of Somatic Psychotherapy and EMDR Therapy

Effective treatment of trauma requires a holistic way of addressing issues such as emotional, cognitive and somatic symptoms. The traditional therapy majorly focuses majorly on the emotional elements of the traumatic experience and the somatic experience is normally left out in most cases. EMDR makes use of a structured protocol to address post-traumatic stress and the related beliefs, emotions and sensations. The therapy entails somatic awareness and interventions that help with enhancing body awareness during treatment.

Therapists that have been trained in effective use of EMDR and somatic psychotherapy as a combination have advanced tools that they can work with. Trauma is considered by somatic psychotherapists as an event that takes place in the whole body, so in order to address the physiological components of psychological distress alongside cognitive component is quite vital when engaging in therapeutic process. Trauma experts believe that the human body can reflect on past traumas through body language, body posture and in the physical manifestations of the diverse ways of nature such as digestive problems, chronic pain, and immune dysfunction among others.

Somatic therapy integrates the mind and body by focusing on how the autonomic nervous system which is also part of the nervous system that's responsible for controlling the body functions that are not consciously directed such as heartbeat, breathing, digestive processes and also reflects traumas that had been experienced in the past through expression of instability. It also helps those who are traumatized to regain mastery when going through difficult experiences by regulating the nervous systems.

Somatic psychotherapy is a body oriented therapy that helps with healing trauma and other related conditions. Those affected gets to release survival energy that has remained stuck in the body and body awareness gets induced that enables those affected to tolerate some of the difficult bodily sensations and emotions through greater body awareness and touch. The physical, emotional and cognitive processing are all vital for working through trauma where the physical sensations gets tracked as a step to recovery.

Somatic psychotherapy helps with the resolution if trauma and PTSD related responses. Human beings can't think their way out of traumatic experiences as one is more likely to feel trapped with the physical and emotional states. Such feelings heightens the feeling of anxiety and causes panic and thus makes it difficult for the body to calm down. There are times when one just feels unmotivated and depressed without the ability to accomplish even simple tasks. The great thing about somatic psychotherapy is its ability to intervene directly by developing new neural pathways and behaviors that provide one with alternative ways of responding to the environment without being stuck in the past habits.

The synthesis of RMDR therapy and somatic psychotherapy is such an advancement in mental health and are considered as two of the best trauma treatment models that are available. Integrating the two therapies helps with enhancing the effectiveness of both of the therapies. Somatic psychotherapy focuses on body awareness as a way of intervention in psychotherapy.

Somatic interventions tend to address the connections that exist between the brain, the mind and behavior of the body. Therapists who only focus on talk therapy only tend to appeal to the mind as a way of influencing psychological health, however, somatically oriented therapists tend to use knowledge of the basic functions of the nervous system as a way of enhancing the therapeutic process.

Some of the basic concepts of somatic psychology include;

## Grounding

This concept is at the basis of all body based psychotherapy. The concept was introduced by Alexander Lowen who was the developer of bioenergetics. Grounding refers to human's ability to experience embodiment. It's where one gets to feel their feet as they step on the earth, they get to sense the body and also calm the nervous system.

## Cultivating Somatic Awareness

Somatic psychotherapy promotes body awareness where one can work with tension patterns and brain constrictions that are held beneath conscious awareness. It's achieved by simply bringing to the physical sensations that in turn creates change.

## Staying Descriptive

As much as the early somatic psychotherapists made interpretations that were based on posture patterns and tension, the modern day somatic psychotherapists are more focused on the somatic experience of the client. This is a concept that you can as well try to your own as you take note of the sensations. Try making use of descriptive words such as tingly, hot, cold, sharp, or dull.

## Deepening Awareness

Once you are aware of the sensations, or the tension pattern, you can deepen the experience by amplifying the sensations gently. Focus your breath into the sensations by making some sound or even adding movements. The key is to deepen your experience at the pace that doesn't make you feel overwhelmed and also honors your timing.

## Resourcing

When helping clients to develop resourcing, you should focus on increasing safety and a sense of choice. Identify time, people, and places that reinforce a sense of safety, peace and calm. How do they know when they are feeling relaxed and peaceful? How does their body feel?

## Titration

When the attention is turned to traumatic events, the centered awareness of the body enables one to become conscious of the physical tension patterns. Titration is the process of experiencing small amounts of distress and is done with the intention of discharging the tension. It's used in somatic psychotherapy and is normally achieved by pendulating or oscillating attention between feelings of distress and that of calm.

## Sequencing

When somatic tension begins to release or discharge, therapists can report on the movement of sensations and emotions. When tension is experienced at the belly it's more likely to move to the chest and leads to tightness in the forehead and the throat. At times, you can see the hands or the legs shake or even tremble. The tension can then get released at times in the form of tears or by breathing freely and a feeling of lightness.

## Movement and Process

Somatic psychotherapy taps into the innate healing capacity and invites one to listen to the story of the body. From the body postures to gestures and use of space, therapists are provided with insight into what the client is experiencing. For example, a client that might be experiencing an impulse to cower, hide or crouch should be led to mindfully engage in the defensive movements.

After doing that you might notice a new impulse emerge that cause them to kick the legs or push the arms. As the client reengages intuitively, the protective movements resolutions may emerge with some new found sense of calm in the body.

## Boundary Development

When you allow the somatic experience to guide the pacing of your therapy process, you should consider working in the here and now. Focusing on the present moment makes it possible for you to stay responsive to the clients changing needs and makes it possible to develop clear boundaries. A boundary makes it easy for the client to not only recognize but also speak your yes and no in a way that makes them feel stronger and protected.

## Self-Regulation

The modern somatic therapies integrates the research obtained from neuroscience on how humans respond to trauma and stress. The research emphasizes on the importance of mindfulness to the body while experiencing big emotions or sensations. When you create awareness of the body sensations, you get into a position where you are very much able to effectively respond and even regulate the emotional intensity. This helps one to stay connected and supported while experiencing the intensity of healing trauma.

By practicing mindfulness, the body gets to access the prefrontal cortex through use of interception as a way of recognizing what's taking place inside then re-interpreting the danger by either moving together, synchronizing voices or the respiratory systems. This can be done by either singing or breathing together which then activates the bidirectional communication system that exists between the nervous system differently.

## Discovery and Development of EMDR

Eye Movement Desensitization and Reprocessing (EMDR) is a therapeutic approach that's normally guided by adaptive information process. It is an integrative psychotherapy approach where the dysfunctionally stored memories becomes the primary basis of clinical pathology. The processing of such memories and their integration within the larger adaptive networks creates room for their transmutation and reconsolidation.

Over the past 25 years, sufficient research have been gathered for EMDR therapy which makes it to be widely considered as being effect for the treatment of trauma. The history of EMDR therapy, AIP model, the clinical applications and the procedural elements are also clearly described. EMDR is an integrative and therapeutic approach that has procedural elements that are compatible with somatic psychotherapy and other procedures. The therapy is normally guided through AIP model and emphasizes the role of the brain's information processing system within human health development and pathology.

AIP model focuses on the insufficiently processed memories of the traumatic or disturbing experiences as the primary source of all the psychopathology that's not caused by organic deficit. EMDR is an eight phase treatment that focuses on;

The memories that exists beneath the current problem
The present situations alongside triggers that must be addressed in order to bring the client to a state of robust psychological health. The integration of the positive memory templates for reinforced future adaptive behavior.

One of the key characteristics that distinguishes EMDR from other therapies is the use of bilateral stimulations such as the alternating hand taps, auditory tones that are applied within the standardized procedures, side-to-side eye movements and protocols that address all the facets of targeted memory networks.

## History of Somatic Psychotherapy

Somatic psychotherapy originated in the 1940s with Wilhelm Reich. Reich perceived that the human's life force energy flowed all through the body as primal expressions of human emotion and needs. He identified the body's holding patterns which were areas that had emotional tension as the abdomen, pelvis, chest, diaphragm, neck, forehead and jaw. He identified the habitual tension patterns ended up developing into symptoms such as the grinding of teeth, headaches, and sluggish digestion.

Mr. Reich identified that the needs that were left unmet all throughout early development stages became the root holding patterns. The approach that he used for releasing the bound energy ranged from pushing, kicking and screaming so as to release the physical tension and emotions from the body.

In the 1950s, Reich worked closely with Alexander Lowen and branched off into developing bioenergetics that could help with resolving what was referred to as the body mind conflict which is such a key component of the treatment that involves body reading. This type of treatment is where the therapists observe and also interpret the client's breathing, physical and muscular tension patterns. These patterns are referred to as character strategies and associated with core beliefs that are learned during childhood.

Bioenergetics brings clients into stress positions where the body gets to stay in long holds and even uncomfortable holds at times so as to evoke physical shaking and vulnerable emotions. The ultimate goal of this therapy is to release both physical and emotional tension so that one can feel connected and grounded to self and the world.

## History of EMDR Therapy

The development of EMDR started in 1987 when it was recognized by Shapiro the effects that eye-movements had in disturbing memories. It led to her developing a treatment protocol that was referred to as Eye Movement Desensitization (EMD). Since she was coming from a behavioral background, the perceived the impact of the eye movements to be similar to systematic desensitization and knew it was based on an innate relaxation response.

The initial research by Shapiro assumed that END process was to an extent related to Rapid Eye Movement (REM) sleep phenomenon and the effects. The initial research was more of a random one that showed promising results with treatment of war veterans and sex assault victims. She continued to develop and also refine the procedures that were used in EMD beyond the behavioral paradigm. In 1991, she changed the name to EMDR with the R meaning reprocessing. It came for the understanding that desensitization was just an outcome of the therapy and the broader aspects of the therapy would be understood better through information processing theory.

EMDR therapy has so far been proven as an effective treatment that has led to the realization of results much faster for many clients. Shapiro felt that it was her ethical obligation to teach other therapists and clinicians so that those struggling with PTSD could be helped to find relief. However, EMDR therapy was still experimental since it had not received any independent confirmation through the controlled studies. She opted for controlled training that was only focused on the licensed clinicians.

She ensured that everyone who learned EMDR approach did it within the institute and in the same model as that helped with safeguarding what was taught. By 1995, after publishing the controlled studies, the raining restrictions were then removed and text books published. Shapiro has been intensely criticized on her dissemination method and the restrictive way of training; however, critics tend to ignore APA ethics code that mandated responsibilities of an innovator to be able to determine the training practices and the fact that there had not been effective treatments for PTSD that had been well established and well validated.

Various studies have been published so far that have demonstrated the effectiveness of EMDR in treatment of PTSD and EMDR has been recognized as an efficacious in treatment of PTSD. IN 1995, a professional association that was independent from Shapiro and the EMDR institute was established to help with setting the standards for EMDR training and practice. The EMDR International Association (EMDRIA) with the primary role of establishing, maintaining and promoting the highest standards of excellence and integrity in EMDR practice, education and research was formed.

## World View and the Values of EMDR and Somatic Psychotherapy

Substantial research studies have shown that adverse life experiences contribute to both biomedical and psychological pathology. EMDR therapy is a form of treatment for trauma that has been empirically validated. The positive therapeutic outcomes that have been achieved rapidly without detailed description provide the medical community with an efficient treatment approach alongside a wide range of applications.

EMDR has the ability to rapidly treat psychological trauma and other negative life experiences in such an effective way. The ability to treat unprocessed memories of diverse experiences tend to have great implications for the medical fraternity. The clinical application of EMDR entails a wide variety of psychological problems that affects family members and patients. The frequent way in which EMDR brings about substantial improvement within short periods of time has brought relevance to some of the major problems that exist within the medical practice such as an increase in patient load and the cost of medical care.

One of the key components that have been used during the reprocessing phases consists of dual attention to stimuli through bilateral eye-movements, tones and taps. The eye movements is a subject that has generated great scrutiny and have been called into question previously as the studies evaluated treatment effects with and without the component.

EMDR therapy is guided by adaptive information processing model which was developed in the 1990s. This concept focuses on the fact that, apart from symptoms that are caused by injury, toxicity of organic deficits, the key foundation of mental disorders are the memories of earlier experiences that stay unprocessed. The high arousal level that arises as a result of distressing life events cause the memories to be stored with the original emotions, beliefs and physical sensations.

The nightmares, flashbacks and the intrusive thoughts of PTSD are examples of symptoms that result from the triggering of such memories. As shown in AIP model, a wide range of traumatic life experiences can be stored in a manner that's dysfunctional and that provides the basis room for diverse symptoms to emerge that include the negative effective, somatic and cognitive responses. Sufficient processing of the memories that have been accessed within EMDR therapy protocol brings about an adaptive functioning and resolution.

Processing the targeted symptoms transfers them from being memories that are implicit and episodic to those that are episodic and semantic. The negative emotions that had been originally experienced alongside beliefs and physical sensations gets altered as the targeted memory gets integrated with some more adaptive information. Whatever that's useful the gets learnt and stored with the appropriated somatic interventions and makes the disturbing experience to become a source of resilience and strength. Clients that experience anxiety, hypervigilance, depression, frequent anger and such like emotions needs to be evaluated for the adverse experiences that contribute to the current dysfunction that they are experiencing.

There are two RCTs that have demonstrated the effectiveness of EMDR towards treatment of distressing life experiences. Both the trials reported some positive results within three sessions. The ability of EMDR therapy towards treatment of the unprocessed memories of the distressing life experiences has numerous applications within medical practice since such memories have been identified as the cause of diverse clinical symptoms. Exposure to some of the diverse stressful events has always been linked to the socioemotional behavioral problems and cognitive deficits.

Before opting for EMDR therapy, a client should be evaluated for the adverse life experiences. When treating children, the therapy should be focused at identifying interpersonal experiences, bullying, household dysfunction, humiliation, and other symptoms that might be contributing to the feelings of anxiety, angry outbursts, lack of focus, inattention, and impulsivity issues that might have been diagnosed incorrectly as PTSD. EMDR therapy can help with alleviating the effects of experiential contributors and to evaluate whether medication is necessary or not.

Conditions such as night terrors, traumas, and insomnia should be evaluated since the processing of memory alone is capable of improving sleep quality. Rehabilitation services can equally benefit from EMDR therapy in order to support the client and family members. The traumatic impact that results from dealing with life-threatening and incapacitating conditions can be mitigated by combining few memory processing sessions in addressing the medical experiences, the current situations and fears of the future. Use of such approach can help with;

Facilitating the processing of traumatic events with the client and whole family.
It can help with establishing an interpersonal context that's secure between the client and the caregiver by reducing the high level of arousal.
It can help with transforming the health service into a very effective support for the client and their family by providing the help needed in managing the emotional vulnerability that's connected with the physical vulnerability and that in turn prevents the impact of worsening clinical conditions.

EMDR therapy can be used as a way of providing support to family members that are dealing with death of a loved one. There are trauma symptoms that come with the sudden death or prolonged debilitation of a loved one. It can make it difficult for the grieving family member to retrieve positive memories of the deceased and that can further complicate the grieving process.

# Chapter 2: The Neurobiology of Stress and Trauma

The period of development tend to also bring along a higher probability of the emergence of some mental health disorders and can lead to intensifying of childhood behavioral and emotional concerns. Neuroscientists are committed to understanding what takes place in the brain that increases the human's vulnerability to mental health challenges. Factors such as genetics, childhood adversity and behavioral concerns are some of the significant influences of mental conditions.

Chronic stress that's experienced during childhood and also referred to as childhood adversity have been associated to be a factor that contributes to mental health difficulties in later adulthood. The brain areas that are notably involved in responding to traumatic experiences all through one's life are the same ones that undergo significant developmentally based changes during the transition to adolescence and through the 20s.

Trauma is the word that's commonly used in describing a range of everyday experiences however, not all the stressful experiences tend to a change an individual's neurobiology or their ability to feel safe emotionally. Psychological trauma is a form of traumatic stress that's felt both physically and emotionally and tends to affect the brain networks including altering the stress response system. Traumatic experiences tend to differ with individuals and is influenced by a person's subjective perception of what's considered to be traumatic.

Some of the key factors that influence such a variation include; prior traumatic experiences, severity of exposure to traumatic experiences, social stressors that come as a result of interpersonal relationships. Taking time to recognize the underpinnings of psychological stress and trauma can be helpful towards identifying of what needs to be addressed. The classic way in which humans respond when faced with perceived threats is the fight or flight which is generally a reflective nervous phenomenon that generally has survival advantages.

However, the systems that lead to the trigger of reflexive survival behaviors that normally follow exposure to the perceived threat can at times lead to functional impairment in some people who may get psychologically traumatized and in turn suffer from PTSD. There are numerous research studies that have shown neurobiological abnormalities in those struggling with PTSD. Some of the studies have provided an insight into the pathophysiology of post-traumatic stress disorder and the biological vulnerabilities of some when it comes to developing PTSD. Psychological trauma can occur from having witnessed an event that might have been perceived to be life-threatening or a situation that pose bodily injury to self and others.

Such experiences are normally accompanied with intense fear, a sense of helplessness, and horror that can lead to the development of PTSD. The response of trauma doesn't depend only on the stressor characteristics but also on certain factors that are specific to the individual. For the vast majority, trauma that comes up as a result of some profound threat can be limited to an acute disturbance, such reactions can be unpleasant to a great extent and are normally characterized by reminders of the exposure to intrusive thoughts or nightmares, activation of an irritating or agitating experience, or deactivation that leads to withdrawal or a numbing experience.

As much as these reactions are self-limiting, they tend to provoke minimal functional impairment over a period of time. The psychological trauma that come up as a result of such experiences often lead to a longer syndrome that has been defined and validated clinically as PTSD, a condition that's normally accompanied by a devastating functional impairment. Post-traumatic stress disorder is characterized by the presence of symptoms and signs that reflect a persistent abnormal adaptation of the neurobiological systems to stress that's related to a witnessed trauma.

The neurobiological systems that helps with regulating stress responses include neurotransmitter pathways, certain endocrine alongside a network of brain regions that helps with regulating fear behavior at both conscious and unconscious levels. Various research studies have focused on exploring these systems in more detail and have helped with addressing the changes that take place in clients that develop PTSD. There still continues to be ongoing efforts that link neurobiological changes that are identified in the patients that suffer from PTSD to the clinical features that constitute PTSD such as altered learning, heightened arousal and intermittent dissociative behavior are some of the relevant examples.

## Neuroplasticity and Adaptive Coping Strategies

Neuroplasticity refers to the brain's ability to adapt or coping strategies that tend to emerge in response to some traumatic experience or adversity. It's rooted in the biological ability to survive the life-threatening situations alongside ability to cope with the consequences of traumatic experiences. As much as they are formed during childhood stages, these adaptation strategies are embedded in the neural networks that normally function outside of human's conscious awareness and continues to operate eve after the traumatic experience has ended.

The human brain tend to store traumatic memories as a protection strategy and when memories begin to intrude into the present moments through upsetting emotions, thoughts, sensory memories, flashbacks and bodily sensations the original fear that had been experienced during the past traumatic experience and the survival strategies gets activated. Adaptive behaviors such as spacing-out, aggression, distrust, and avoidance become automatic responses to any slightest cue of anger. For example, trauma survivors could be sensitive to the loud noises, physical proximity to other people and touch where such experiences has the potential of activating adaptive reactions.

Neuroplasticity is vital for the healing and recovery from psychological trauma. The body and the mind has the ability to learn how to feel safe again after undergoing a traumatic experience. When therapists identify traumatic stress responses as neurobiologically- embedded adaptations and coping instead of identifying them as symptoms of mental health disorders, they can successfully help their clients to revise the coping strategies so as to better meet their current psychological needs.

The stress-response system that's referred to as hypothalamus-pituitary-adrenal (HPA) gets initiated by an actual or perceived threat. The amygdala is normally the first responder that receives information from the incoming sensory information known as thalamus which rapidly screens for danger and has the potential of activating the pituitary gland that releases hormones. The hippocampal memory system helps with the assessment by providing amygdala with the information that exists in the past threats database.

It works in tandem with the prefrontal cortex which is quite critical for decision making and the regulation of hormones. The memory storage structures which is also referred to as the hippocampus are also essential for deactivating the HPA axis when threat subsides. Once the alarm gets triggered by the amygdala, the HPA axis gets to release a cascade of chemicals alongside hormones that enables the individual facing the traumatic experience to survive by either fighting or fleeing. When survival through mobilizing is not possible, automatically survival through immobilizing gets triggered and gets to slow the individual's life sustaining systems such as breathing and heart rate.

Such reactions takes place instantly and normally bypass any of the thoughtful decision making that one can engage in. Once the real or even perceived danger has passed, the HPA axis then returns to the original pre-threat status. However, when their traumatic experience is an ongoing one, the HPA axis continues to flood the body with the stress hormones that gets released from the adrenal glands. The overproduction of hormones creates a very toxic state of stress within the body and that I turn changes the function and physical structure of other hormones.

As much as the intention of the brain is mainly to promote a higher survival possibility through engagement in constant vigilance it can lead to a compromise in other capacities such as ability to manage feelings and think clearly. The release of high levels of cortisol and the inability to emotionally regulate the overproduced hormones leads to engagement in risky behaviors and the onset of some of the physical health issues. Youths who have had traumatic childhood experiences are more likely to get stuck in the fight or flight mode where they tend to feel anxious, jumpy, hyper vigilant and some can even feel disconnected, numb, disconnected and foggy.

Such feelings and the resulting behaviors can be confusing and might also end up disrupting the daily activities and relationships of an individual.

### How the Brain Works and the Impact of Trauma on Health

The brain areas that are implicated in stress response include the hippocampus, prefrontal cortex and the amygdala. Traumatic experiences can have lasting impact in the brain areas and is normally associated with increased cortisol, norepinephrine responses and other subsequent stressors. Through use brain imaging techniques in research, various changes have been recognized in the brain structure or certain areas that might be connected to the impaired functioning of those suffering from PTSD especially the hippocampus, amygdala prefrontal cortex and other brain areas.

To understand how the traumatic stress that takes place at the different stages of life interacts with the developing brain it's important that one gets clear understanding on the normal brain development. The normal human brain normally undergoes changes in function and structure all through the lifespan of an individual right from childhood to the later stages of life. Understanding the various stages is critical in determining the difference that exists between pathology and the normal development alongside how both interacts.

It's therefore understandable that trauma that happens at different stages in life can have adverse effects on the development of the brain. Various studies have suggested that there are differences in the effects of trauma on neurobiology and that highly depends on the stage of development at which the trauma takes place. Symptoms of PTSD such as nightmares, sleep disturbances, intrusive thoughts tends to represent behavioral manifestation of the stress induced changes that takes place in the brain function and structure.

Stress arises from the acute and chronic changes within specific brain regions and neurochemical systems with then leads to long-term changes in brain circuits that involve stress response. Trauma has such a powerful ability to shape the physical, emotional and intellectual development of the brain especially when experienced at an early age. Traumatic experiences has the potential of altering an individual's life and ability to diminish their resilience. Continual exposure to threatening situations is capable of making a young person's brain to be prone to flight, fight and freeze response and that makes it difficult for one to build meaningful relationships or reach out for help.

Traumatic experiences tend to overwhelm an individual's coping capacity and normally has long-term effects on the functioning and well-being of the individuals. There is a connection between traumatic childhood experiences and the greater chance of experiencing physical and behavioral health challenges. Before children reach 5 years of age, their brain tend to be in a critical development stage and positive experiences are more likely to lead into healthy brain development however, negative experiences can lead to unhealthy development.

Prolonged traumatic experiences can impact on the cognitive functioning of the brain such as having short term memory, emotional regulation and such like. Children with exposure to trauma tend to develop coping mechanisms that enables them to overcome the feelings of hurt as a result of the trauma. The strategy can in most cases evolve into health risk behaviors such as overeating, drug and alcohol abuse. When the childhood traumatic stress goes untreated, the coping mechanisms are more likely to lead to anxiety, social isolation or even chronic diseases.

# Chapter 3: The Principles Somatic Psychotherapy and EMDR Therapy for Trauma Treatment

The human body needs to process events that are stressful through movement and breath. When a therapist fails to include body awareness, conscious breathing and movement into trauma treatment, it limits the body's ability to work with the innate healing capacities. Somatic psychotherapy engages the awareness of the body as an intervention and also addresses the connections that exists between the mind, brain and behavior.

The field of somatic psychotherapy encompasses a broad range of treatment modalities that has to a great extent evolved overtime. EMDR therapists that have training in somatic interventions uses advanced tools to work with dysregulation of the nervous system that's associated with post-traumatic stress. Both somatic psychotherapy and EMDR therapy was endorsed as one of the best approaches that was ideal for treatment of PTSD by Bessel Van der Kolk, a trauma treatment researcher.

Somatic psychotherapy has evolved through the years from the cathartic approaches. The early therapeutic modalities used some approaches that were intense and even invasive such as deep pressure massage, stressful positions, primal screams and deep pressure massage that were held overtime. As much as the therapies created room for rapid change, they also in a way re-traumatized the client and as a result the modern day somatic psychotherapy and EMDR therapy helps as they incorporate mindfulness that helps with somatic release in a safe and well contained fashion.

The brain as covered earlier is such a powerful organ that constructs human experiences from diverse channels of sensory inputs then regulates the responses through the thoughts and emotions of humans and also controls actions. Human beings should be able to learn from their experiences so as to effectively adapt effectively and meet the challenges that exist in our environments. The human brain has a unique dual perspective and while the neuroscientists still grapple with the workings of the physical brain, from an external viewpoint as they examine the brain's neural firings, the psychologists are focusing on their study from the position of what being in such a system feels like.

The dual view of the brain also applies to the body. While the traditional medicine focuses on evaluating and investigating the functions of the body in an objective way and treats them, somatic psychotherapy focuses on the subjective study that takes place from the position of experience. Understanding the biological nature of perception, thought, feeling, memory, learning and consciousness has become such a central challenge in the field of biological sciences. In order to approach psychotherapy in a more effective way, there is need for a multifaceted paradigm and this is due to the fact that the body's neural memory is the ground in which the life experiences gets imprinted and psychotherapy treatment starts with tracking the experience.

A therapist should start treatment by investigating how a client experiences the world by focusing on the primary diagnostic inquiry and not by asking how the client feels but how he perceive and comprehend the world. Memories gets created by the physical firing of the neurons and therapists should focus on the emotional surface feelings first as they consider their biological cause and effect since the body's communication extends beyond the symbolic verbal expression.

People's belief is normally bound in body posture, breath, and movement while the inner realities get masked, emphasized or even betrayed by the facial expressions. Emotions on the other hand gets revealed by the rate of breath. In somatic psychotherapy facial expression, posture, movement, breath and vocal tone tend to provide important clues about the congruence that exists between the inner experience that has been embodied and the outer expression.

In somatic psychotherapy, the body is never separate from self and from the perspective of the body; therapeutic objectives seek to elicit a sensory dialogue that stirs up a meeting point and in turn establishes conscious unity between the mind and body. The main focus of therapy should be towards helping clients to develop the ability to observe the bodily activities that exists on the layers of sensory awareness and that might be difficult to express in words. Such can be expressed through diverse body experiences such as body heat, muscular contractions, skin sensitivity, and organ vibrations.

Body centered approaches tend to focus on the sensory experiences as they rise from diverse realms. Somatic methods tend to use sensory tracking alongside recognition of the movement impulses so as to access interactive links or the lack that exists between behavior, sensation, affect and cognition. Somatic psychotherapy encompasses the experiences that are processed in the neocortex and those experiences through the limbic and the mid and lower brain centers.

## Sensorimotor Psychotherapy

This approach focuses on use of the basic tools of body-mind integration such as movement, body awareness, and breath in providing a framework for understanding the fundamental connection that exists between the mind and body in reference to psychological development and growth.

## Mind-Body Psychotherapy

The basis of body-mind psychotherapy lies on physiology and the early motor development. The psychological forces tend to use physical energy. Mind and body tend to function in mutual feedback loops where the state of the body reflects that of the mind with the state of the mind also reflecting that of the body. This principle is vital towards integrating somatic and cognitive processing within a therapeutic context. The recognition of the connection that exists between mind and body is also the basis for somatic self-discovery that focuses on the exploration of the relationship in posture, sensation, and movement to the emotional and mental states.

The early motor development forms the basis for the later development states and is normally nonverbal. The body therefore, provides direct access to the early developmental and the implicit behavioral issues. All human beings have the capacity to read each other's signals however translating nonverbal bodily states into verbal consciousness can be a challenge. With more evidences accumulating that support the mind and body idea and how they are closely connected, therapists are gradually embracing the different types of treatment alongside somatic psychotherapy.

Doctors understand the impact that mental health can have on the overall physical wellbeing. The body is linked quite closely to mental health and both can be healed if complete victory is to be realized. The principles of somatic psychotherapy explains the fact that the mind, body and spirit together with emotions are all connected. Emotional events therefore impact the body in several lasting ways including facial expressions, body posture and body language. Therapists who are trained in somatic psychotherapy are capable of recognizing the physical changes and can help with treatment for improved physical and mental health.

### Benefits of Somatic Psychotherapy and EMDR Therapy

Various independent studies including controlled ones have shown that EMDR therapy is quite effective for treating PTSD. The therapy is even used by the Department of Veterans Affairs and is strongly recommended for treating PTSD. The benefits of somatic psychotherapy and EMDR therapy are diverse, however, having knowledge of them can be of great help;

### Therapeutic touch links the body and mind

As much as human beings are whole, they hardly operate as one. For example, when experiencing a panic attack, you might feel like just being in a body while unable to breathe. Combating fear with logic is never possible and it's also advisable to intellectually understand the impact that trauma can have in one's life.

Therapeutic touch helps with bridging the gap that exists between the mind and body. Through somatic psychotherapy, one can become increasingly aware of what's actually happening in both their mind and body. Engaging in top-down thinking helps one to even heal much faster.

### Helps work through attachment issues

Most people have attachment issues emanating from their childhood experiences that keep showing repeatedly all through their adult life. There are various methods that can help with working through the issues however somatic psychotherapy and EMDR therapy has been proven to be some of the most effective tools. Therapeutic touch goes way back to the first attachment that was entirely nonverbal. The primary caregiver or mother conveyed emotions that were understood through tough and the child understood senses.

### Learn skills to rebalance the body

Somatic psychotherapy and EMDR therapy helps with bringing back the body into balance. Trauma has a way of impacting the body and when the trauma lasts for a longer period of time, the remnants of that traumatic experience can get stuck in the body. Somatic psychotherapy incorporates a rage of techniques that helps one to regain their physical and emotional health. Through the therapy, one can learn new methods on how to soothe self, get entered and grounded as they connected to the mind, body and spirit.

The techniques are helpful whether one considers themselves to be a trauma survivor or not. Such people can reduce stress, increase mindful awareness, quell a number of anxiety and stress related issues.

### Helps improve resiliency for the future

Some of the skills that you get to learn during somatic psychotherapy and EMDR therapy may not help you immediately but are more likely to help you improve resiliency for the future. Regardless of what you get to face in the future, you will likely be at a much better state to work through the challenges. One of the techniques used in somatic psychotherapy is referred to as pendulation. It is a structured way of moving from a state of stress within the body to that of calm and back again to a state of stress.

As you engage in pendulation, you will realize how the body feels like when in different states. You will also learn the process and how to bring the body back to that calm state. Learning this technique can be quite helpful for all of the future experiences. As a result, you will be able to reach greater goals as you are more likely to feel confident that you have the potential to handle whatever life throws your way.

### Re-empowers you

After taking time to study trauma responses across survivors of sexual abuse, war veterans and other populations, Dr. Bessel van der Kolk came to the understanding that the most paralyzing aspects of trauma is the feeling of being completely powerless. The brain's amygdala tend to respond to danger with either fight or flight response. However, there are times when the wires get crossed and instead of engaging in fight or flight you get to freeze. It means that the brain becomes desperate to get out of danger but it can't and that leads to a feeling of being disempowered.

Through working with the mind and body system, it's possible to regain the feeling of empowerment that you might have lost in the past.

### Increased engagement with life

When the mind and body are in a state of disconnect, it's possible to feel disengaged from life. One is more likely to feel as if they are just going through motions and it feels as if you're present but not fully there. Somatic psychotherapy helps clients to regain that sense of engagement with all the areas of life. As one becomes free of physical psychological and emotional pain, they also get to increase their ability to feel freedom, joy, and an increased range of positive emotions.

### Chance to try a new therapeutic approach

Many people have gone through a number of therapies in the past and still can hardly have feelings about such experiences. Therapy is capable of triggering trauma especially with those struggling with PTSD as just sitting around and talking about traumatic experiences that had happened may not be quite helpful for some.

EMDR therapy works optimally with clients who are motivated about change. They should be willing to detach themselves from the past traumatic life experiences without carrying along their problems. Secondary gains when focused on can be a great impediment to successful processing of EMDR. EMDR also works well for those willing to experience feelings that are uncomfortable and thoughts that are disturbing. Once the processing starts, troubling memories can be intensified by eye movements.

The therapist that's practicing EMDR should be well trained and with sufficient skills as lack of sufficient training can to a great extent cause damage. EMDR is more like a power tool that when wielded with a person that lacks sufficient training can in a great way cause harm. EMDR therapy in most cases opens up a client in ways that are unexpected and that might require the intervention of a therapist with advanced skills for guidance purposes. The therapist should be very skilled and capable of assessing each moment as they care for the client.

Since the use of EMDR therapy is likely to exceed the ability of a new therapist that has few skills and very little experience, sufficient training is therefore recommended. EMDR therapy can make it possible for clients to break through very defensive barriers that in turn results into the feelings of being overwhelmed with traumatic emotions and images. Therapists should therefore be aware of how they can work with highly charged clients. Shapiro reports that inappropriate use of EMDR therapy can cause clients to be re-traumatized. Apart from being well-trained in EMDR therapy, therapists should also have some basic clinical skills.

The therapists should be comfortable with the process while also being aware of what's likely to happen next with every process. If a therapist is uncomfortable with the intense experiences and the forbidden thoughts the discomfort can easily be felt by the client who may in turn not feel free to accept the material that's perceived to be difficult. Therapists should also be quite aware of their personal beliefs as unawareness is more likely to limit the possibilities of healing for the client. EMDR therapy starts with the desire by a client to heal from a traumatic experience, overcome any performance problem that they could be facing or the willingness to deal with a troubling aspect of life.

# Chapter 4: Embodiment in Trauma Treatment

Human beings live in a culture that is disembodied where more time is spent in entertaining the boredom with short attention spans given to information and media and very little time is spent in feeling and sensing the body responses to what we actually spend time consuming. These results into a sense of emotional and physical disconnection that range from having a numbing dissociation to apathy alongside other experiences. In the process humans get to lose that connection with embodied self-awareness. Embodiment is vital as it helps with reducing numbing that does occur.

When people are embodied, they tend to feel others and can easily connect with others through and become more active in showing empathy and protecting those perceived to be vulnerable including the surrounding environment. Getting into a state of disconnection from our embodied self leads to disconnection with the larger body and the world around us. Embodiment helps with ensuring survival and is the direct feeling of oneself without having that constant narration or the interpretation of the thinking mind.

Traumatic experiences tend to defy all manner of subjectivity as it is with mind and body dualism. The physical traumas hardly keep to the boundaries of the body but also progresses to impact the mind and in most cases the psychological traumas often manifest in the body. In most cases, events that just seem to be physical may not be physical and even those that hardly leave any scars can to an extent manifest in physical symptoms. Trauma then reveals that actual issue to be foundationally embodied and one whose body and mind coexist in such a dynamic and interconnected relationship.

When dealing with embodiment, the mind tends to be of great importance since it's the actual seat of the matter and the body becomes the object. Which should be clearly observed and analyzed. If all you have understanding of is the traumatic experience then the mind becomes the framework for analyzing the human experience. It then leads to systems that are based on belief that it's only by intellectual reflection and detailed examination that one can gain access to the actual truth that exists in such a scenario. The underlying principle then is that human condition highly depends on their reflection of the issue at hand rather than the actual existence of the issue.

Instead of viewing life just as it, there should be an attempt to analyze the behavior so as to understand the context from which the trauma rose. The challenge however, lies in the fact that the body can either perceive correctly or incorrectly so it takes working with a therapist if the truth is to be established. Embodiment entails focusing on your sensations and awareness of the body works more like a guiding compass that enables people to feel more in control of their life. Somatic psychotherapy creates a foundation for empathy and enables people to make healthy decisions as they provide important feedback concerning their relationship with others.

How people think and feel tend to influence how we operate in the world. How humans operate in the world also impacts on how they feel and think. The representation, processing and perception of bodily signals play such an integral role in regards to human behavior. Several theories that embody cognition identify the fact that higher cognitive processes tend to operate on perceptual symbols and the concept us entails reactivation of sensory motor states that takes place as we experience the world. This type of bi-directional loop to a great extent shapes the perceptions of people and how they experience the world.

It focuses on family, cultural and social norms as guiding patterns to expression of emotional behavior. Embodiment is therefore culturally and socially determined and is cultivated through engagement in reflective awareness of sensations within the present moment. Embodiment entails integration of sensory feedback systems such as exteroception, interoception and proprioception.

## Exteroception

This is sensory experience of external environment that gets facilitated by the sensory neurons that normally travel from the areas of the body such as eyes, ears, nose tongue and skin all the way to the brain. The sensory experience may also include sounds, sights, smell, tastes and the sensations of touch such as having a feeling of clothing touching the skin.

Humans tend to perceive feelings from the body in relation to the internal and external state of the body which in turn provide the body with a sense of our physical and psychological condition. This is based on the fact that humans have a body that we are embodied. The familiar feelings often lead to the intuitive notion that bodily sensations are normally tied to life and do represent the relevant signals for well-being and survival and beneath all that underlie the emotional state, mood and the fundamental cognitive processes.

As much as bodily response and its perception are vital processes when constructing emotional experience, the fact that bodily processes might be of great importance for most of psychological functions including decision making or cognition is quite important. For example, imagine experiencing a very frightening situation where you're left alone in a dark hall or park and all of a sudden you begin to hear footsteps coming towards you. The mental processes seems to be quite embodied when we are experiencing such situations and the strong emotions can turn out to be overwhelming.

The influence of bodily interior signals on experience and behavior have been investigated for over 100 years and has to a great extent influenced how humans understand self.

## Proprioception

Proprioception refers to sensory feedback about the position of the body in relation to gravity. These form of awareness entails having knowledge of how you are sitting whether it's upright, maintaining balance while walking, standing or leaning to the side. Proprioception gets facilitated from the body joints and inner ear all the way to the brain. The influence of bodily interior signals on behavior and experience has been investigated for over 100 years and has to a great extent influenced the human understanding of self.

## Interoception

Interoception Interoception entails sensory experience of the inner body and it consists of feelings of sleepiness, hunger, alertness, thirst, pain, tension and restlessness. It has two forms of perception such as proprioception and visceroception. Feelings such as those of thirst, hunger and other internal sensations are to a great extent less distinct and also less discriminated which makes them different from the ones that have been associated with exteroceptive somatosensory system such as temperature, itch and pain. The foundation of emotional feelings depends on neural representation of the body's physiological condition with the somatic elements evoking feelings that influence behavior and feelings.

Interoception helps with providing feedback about the inner emotional experience that's facilitated by the sensory neurons that in turn bring information from the organs, muscles and the brain's connective tissues. Theories of embodied cognition tend to hold higher cognition processes that operate on perceptual symbols and the concept use involves reactivation of the sensory motor-states that normally take place during a person's experience with the world. The three sensory feedback systems tend to create a sense of self. With the help of somatic psychotherapy, embodiment can be developed by engaging in mindfulness practices that also includes body awareness.

A central component of somatic psychotherapy is that felt sense which is actually embodiment and it means bringing awareness inside the body as the ever-changing energetic, sensory and emotional landscape gets evaluated. Embodiment removes the focus of the therapist from the actions of the client and other things that are happening in the outside world to the qualities of the present and internal experience of the client. It focuses on sensations, textures and colors. Being in the body when undergoing trauma can be quite challenging. One has to be helped to re-learn how to stay present while they also sense some of the basic things in a positive step.

Embodiment is such a powerful exercise that can help with recovery from PTSD as it helps with encountering hypervigilance and dissociation. When engaging in EMDR therapy or somatic psychotherapy, the client should be help in developing the ability to of being in tune with both their mind and body and be able to describe the embodiment, and the sensations that are taking place in a subtle as well as overt levels in all of the areas of the body. Therapists should however, take caution when engaging in such an exercise so that if in case they encounter a traumatized part of the body when engaging in the exercise, they should bring their awareness to a neutral or positive part or engage in an action that brings resources to that very part.

Human beings have the habit of overriding their natural behaviors and it therefore means that when experiencing a traumatic experience, the nervous system is more likely to become stuck on alert. To an extent, one becomes oriented to danger even if the traumatic experience has passed. It's possible for the nervous system to remain struck in that chronic state where the traumatic experience gets activated easily. It ends up draining one's energy and creating patterns of tension that become habitual within the body. Over time, one gets to construct their lives based on a very complex foundation of complex defenses that are designed to protect and also keep them safe from danger.

Once the patterns are established within the body, the person may start avoiding people and situations that to an extent represent a potential threat. It's possible for one to be found in a loop of some self-perpetuating stress without having any idea on how to break the cycle. Somatic psychotherapy contends with the fact that it's not actually the original events that normally cause traumatic symptoms to emerge, but the inability on the part of the client to be able to discharge the fight/flight /freeze responses that gets generated so as to cope with the crisis. Such an experience that leaves the body in a state of suppressed high activation and causes the chronic tension to keep appearing alongside other physical and the psychological symptoms of ill health that the person might experience.

The aim of somatic psychotherapy is to help with bringing back the nervous system into regulation. One of the ways that this can be achieved is through felt sense which also means embodiment. It entails creating a deepening awareness of emotions and the physical sensations as they continue to arise within the body and that makes it possible for one to navigate more skillfully as they go through states of high activation and stress. Somatic psychotherapy makes use of techniques that's referred to as titration which is also commonly used for trauma treatment. The therapists uses the technique to dive straight to the heart of that traumatic experience during treatment and the client gets encouraged to work at a pace and level that they find to be manageable.

As the session progresses, the therapist gradually increases the capacity of the client to bear the sensations and the feelings as they arise while also building safety and confidence as they progress. This in turn helps with integration however, there are a number of somatic psychotherapy techniques or strategies that can be used.

### The Phases of EMDR IN Trauma Treatment

EMDR (Eye Movement Desensitization and Reprocessing) is a therapeutic treatment method that initially addressed treatment of post-traumatic stress disorder (PTSD) but is presently being used in diverse therapeutic sessions such as in treatment of phobias, anxiety pain disorders, and dermatological disorders amongst others. EMDR therapy enables clients to heal from symptoms and the emotional distress that comes with experiencing some disturbing life experience. It uses detailed procedures and protocols that are learned during EMDR therapy training sessions and therapists can help clients by activating the process that allows for natural healing to take place.

Complex PTSD happens due to longtime exposure to some unrelenting stressors, attachment injuries and repeated traumatic events that majorly take place during childhood. In most cases, the traumatic experience is interpersonal which means that an individual might have experienced some chronic neglect, exposure to domestic violence or abuse at an early age. It's also important to also note that chronic trauma can also take occur due to ongoing experiences such as bullying, undiagnosed or unsupported disability or such like. In all forms of PTSD, the injury is normally repetitive, cumulative and prolonged.

In most cases, trauma takes place when one is in vulnerable times and the experiences tend to shapes the identity of an individual. The purpose of engaging in EMDR therapy for trauma is so that clients can develop an embodied self that one can compassionately hold on their emotions including the vulnerable sensations. The embodiment process requires that therapist develops skills on how to work with nonverbal and preverbal memories that are stored in the body and mind as motor patterns, affective states, sensations, and psychological arousal. It's advisable that the therapist focuses in the relational exchange.

EMDR therapy is an eight-phase treatment process where eye movements alongside other liberal stimulation are used during the treatment process. Once the therapist has determined the actual traumatic experience that should be targeted first, he or she can then ask the client to hold in view different aspects of the experience or thought in their mind as they use their eyes to track the hand of the therapist while it's being moved back and forth across the client's view point. EMDR therapy is believed to be connected with the biological mechanisms that are similar to Rapid Eye Movement sleep.

While engaging in the exercise, internal associations arise as the clients begin to process the memory of some of the disturbing feelings. EMDR therapy helps with transforming the painful and traumatic events on an emotional level. For example, a victim of rape can shift from feelings of self-disgust and horror to that of holding a firm belief that they survived the rape and therefore they are strong. Unlike engaging in talk therapy, the insights that the client gets to gain during EMDR therapy results not quite much from the interpretation of the therapist but from the accelerated emotional and intellectual processes of the client.

The client is therefore more likely to conclude the therapy feeling empowered by the very same traumatic experience, that which debased them before. The natural outcome of EMDR therapy phases is that where the thoughts, feelings and behavior of the clients become the indicators of the resolution of emotional health. It all happens without engaging in form of speaking or engaging in homework as used in other therapies.

## The EMDR Therapy Phases

EMDR therapy entails focusing attention into three time periods, the past, present and future. Focus then goes towards the memories of the past that can be disturbing and the related events. It also focuses on the current situations that causes emotional distress and towards developing the attitudes and skills needed for positive future actions. With EMDR therapy the specific items can be effectively addressed using an eight-phase approach of treatment.

### Phase 1 – History Taking

The main purpose of this initial phase is to help the therapist with gathering a thorough history of the client's life including both the positive and traumatic life events. The first phase of EMDR therapy involved history taking and treatment planning. Having a detailed history helps the therapist to identify how ready the client is and the secondary gains that might be maintaining the current problem. The therapist can take time to analyze the behaviors that appear to be dysfunctional alongside symptoms and specific characteristics. They can decide on an ideal form of treatment that is suitable for the analyzed situation.

When identifying possible targets, the therapist should also focus on related traumatic incidents that might have happened in the past. Initial EMDR processing can also be directed towards childhood events instead of adult traumatic experiences. It can be realized in the process that the client might have had some problematic childhood. As clients continue to gain insight over their situations, the emotional distress gets resolved and they are more likely to start changing their behaviors.

The length of EMDR treatment highly depends on the number of traumatic experiences and the period the client has experienced PTSD. Those that only have a single event of adult onset trauma can be treated and be free within 5 hours. Those struggling with multiple trauma may require longer treatment time for resolution of trauma. Therapists should be able to observe the capacity of the client for somatic awareness and also assess for dissociation. They can review the individuals early childhood history so as to understand how their somatic or core patterns and the pervasive negative cognitions are conceptualized.

## Phase 2 - Preparation

The second phase is referred to as the preparation process and it's where the therapist and the client moves towards creating that therapeutic relationship. The therapist helps the clients on how to develop the necessary resources that can help them face the difficult challenges or memories without feeling overwhelmed. The preparation process can be accomplished through engagement in resource development installation where the client is encouraged to practice feeling and imagining being connected to a positive emotional state. As you commence the second phase of treatment, the therapist should take time in ensuring that the client has diverse ways of handling the emotional distress.

He or she can train the client on some of the self-control techniques that they can use to close those sessions that appear incomplete and also maintain stability between and during the treatment sessions. The therapist can also instruct the client on how they can use metaphors to enable them stop signals and also provide a sense of control during treatment sessions. The client can also be taught a range of imagery and stress reduction techniques that they can use during the treatment process. The goal of EMDR therapy is to be able to produce effective and rapid change while the client maintains some element of equilibrium in between and during the treatment sessions.

## Phase 3 - Assessment

The third phase is the assessment phase where the therapist and the client gets to jointly identify the traumatic memory that is targeted during that specific session. The phase involves engaging in target development where the therapist helps the client to identify some of the disturbing feelings, body sensations, images and emotions that are associated with the traumatic experience. The client can then be instructed to recognize a salient image that's associated with the memory and the therapist can in the process help with eliciting negative beliefs that is associated with the memory so as to provide some insight about irrationality of the specific event. Positive beliefs that suit the target can also be introduced especially those that contradict the client's emotional experience.

The therapist should be able to evaluate the validity of cognition scale and the subjective units of disturbance scale. Such are normally assessed so as to understand how appropriate the positive cognition is considered by the client to be true a true statement that addresses the target memory. Both of the assessments can be used by the therapist as baseline measures. In the assessment phase, the physical sensations and emotions that are associated with the traumatic memory also gets noted down.

EMDR therapy gets modified when working with nonverbal and preverbal memories through development of targets about the childhood events and body sensations that might be having unknown origin or some pervasive cognitions that don't resolve after the traditional EMDR therapy.

## Phase 4 - Desensitization

The fourth phase incorporates use of dual awareness state where the client maintains awareness of both the present moment experience while recalling at the same time memories of the traumatic event. The desensitization phase is the stage where the disturbing event gets evaluated so as to change the trauma related sensory experiences and their associations. This process helps with increasing for the client that sense of self-efficacy and also elicitation of insight. The client can be asked to focus on both the eye movement and the target image at the same time as they get encouraged to be more open to whatever takes place. After engaging in a set of eye movements, the client can be directed to take a deep breath as they blank out the material to which they were focusing.

Depending on how the client responds, the therapist can then direct their focus of attention alongside the length of time, speed and the type of stimulation that they get to use. In addition, the client can also identify a positive belief in relation to the experience. They can then get asked to rate the positive belief as well as the intensity of the negative emotions. The client can then be asked to go ahead and focus on the negative thought, the image, and body sensations while at the same time engaging in EMDR processing through use of bilateral stimulation.

Dual attention stimulation gets amplified through bilateral eye-movements, tones and pulsars that gets alternated between the right and the left side of the body. EMDR therapy for complex traumatic experiences involves focusing careful attention to the dissociative symptoms during the treatment process. The emphasis should be towards keeping the client regulated with tolerance while processing. This can be achieved through engagement in somatic psychotherapy interventions such as titration or pendulation.

## Phase 5 - Installation

This is the installation phase that focuses on strengthening the positive beliefs so that they can become more available after the process of desensitization is accomplished. It's where the therapist attempts to intensify the strength of positive cognition which is supposed to be used in replacing the negative experience. Until the validity of cognition scale reaches to about 7 or up to the desired ecological validity, some of the most enhancing positive cognition can be paired with what was previously dysfunctional during this bilateral stimulation stage.

For example, once the client can no longer hold on to the misconception that they are not lovable, they can then start to develop and also integrate a new positive belief that they are worthy of being loved. In most cases, there will be a new embodied experience where the client can attend to their emotional parts with great acceptance and compassion.

## Phase 6 - Body Scan

This is the body scan phase where body is brought into therapy process as a way of assessing any of the lingering tension or distress while also enhancing the good feelings that the client might be feeling after completion of desensitization and installation phases. The client gets asked so as to be aware of any somatic response that can be considered as residues of the tension related to the traumatic event that's still remaining. If in case there is a residue then the therapist should target the specific body sensation for some further processing.

## Phase 7 - Closure

This is the closure phase is quite essential for the successful treatment and also helps with ensuring that the client is quite grounded before leaving the session. It's where self-control techniques that the client had already been taught are used whenever reprocessing is considered incomplete. It helps with bringing back the client to that state of equilibrium. The therapist can explain to the client what they are likely to experience during the sessions and how they can maintain a record of disturbances that are more likely to arise during the sessions through use of the targets if in case necessary.

During this phase, the client can be asked to keep a log through the week where they can document any specific instance that's related to the process that might arise. It also helps with reminding the client of the self-calming activities that they had mastered in phase 2. During the process, the therapist instructs the client that they can function in between sessions.

## Phase 8 – Reevaluation phase

This phase entails reevaluation where review of the process is carried out so as to attain optimal treatment while also checking out for additional targets. During this phase, therapists can also examine the progress that has so far been made. It's important to note that all of the EMDR treatment processes are related to historical events, and the current incidents that tend to elicit feelings of distress and what is required if the future events are to be different.

During reevaluation phase, the embodied EMDR therapist takes time to review the previous sessions as they also look for any lingering cognitive, somatic and emotional distress that is likely to lead to further traumatic experiences. Early childhood and attachment trauma require ongoing therapeutic support so that the psychological arousal can be integrated accordingly since such states such as emotions, beliefs and sensations have been in place for longer periods of time.

Therapists should help clients to develop awareness of the various parts of the body that hold memories of the early trauma. There are times when a part of the body may have some resistance to trauma work and can in the process sabotage therapeutic intervention. There are also times when the part of self could be holding traumatic memories. So in EMDR therapy, vulnerable parts should be sourced together with the allies so as to create safety. Resourcing such parts may take time, however, when the client has ideal resources, processing of the traumatic memories can be quite effective and much gentler.

When dealing with EMDR therapy, it's important to note that the process is not in any way linear. Early developmental of trauma is generally a process which might be slow and dies require ongoing stabilization alongside resource development. Successful treatment outcome should therefore focus towards building tolerance for the emotions together with the body sensations that normally accompany traumatic experiences. The client should increasingly be able to access their whole wise self as they get to attend to their while also upholding the responsibilities that they get to experience.

The symptoms of PTSD that once seemed overwhelming can be resolved as the client gets to learn how they can turn toward the parts of themselves that hold such pain and suffering as they experience greater compassion and awareness.

# Chapter 5: Use of Somatic Psychotherapy and EMDR Therapy with Clients

Several theories have emerged on how EMDR therapy works based on the observed clinical effects. It could be that it ignites stimulation of the brain's hemispheres which then causes the reprocessing effect to take place. There are also theories based on the fact that eye movements tends to be linked with the hippocampus which is in a way associated with the consolidation of memory. Another theory states that the dual attention that the client gets to maintain during somatic and EMDR therapy enables them to focus on their inner feelings and the eye movements makes them to be more alert in the brain and that helps with metabolizing whatever they are witnessing.

Therapists use eye movements that are patterned with somatic psychotherapy techniques to help with clearing physical, emotional, and cognitive blockages. In theory, traumatic experiences tend to leave unprocessed feelings, thoughts and emotions that can either be metabolized or processed through engagement of eye movements and other techniques. The same way in which rapid eye movement or dream sleep works, the eye movements similarly helps with processing the blocked information which then allows for the mind and body to release it.

In some cases, the strong dreams that we get to experience in relation to the past events are attempts made by the body-mind to heal the past trauma. The challenge lies in the fact that when one awakens during such disturbing dreams, they end up disrupting the eye movements and interferes with the recovery process. It's important to note that rapid eye movement alone cannot complete the task of healing the trauma, engaging a therapist that assists the clients with maintaining the eye movements while also guiding them on how to focus on the traumatic experience is quite important. It then allows for the traumatic event to be reprocessed and also integrated.

During the trauma treatment process, the therapist can engage in other acts such as tapping of hands or sending of sound to the client's ears can also help with stimulating the reprocessing of the traumatic experience.

### Trauma Treatment with Accelerated Information Processing

Traumatic experiences has the potential of causing one to develop beliefs that are erroneous about themselves or the world. For example, a child who has been molested may come up with a negative belief about themselves that they are bad, and that the world is always unsafe. Such experiences are more likely to become fixed in their body and also in their mind in the form of blocked energy, irrational emotions, and physical symptoms. Traumas are in two forms, there are traumas that assaults one's sense of self-efficacy and one's self confidence.

Traumas are more likely a perceptual filter that keeps narrowing and also limiting one's views of self and the world. For example, you can come across a person who was teased as a child due to some attributes they had such as being overweight and such like. Such people may find themselves struggling with low self-esteem issues and with a deep irrational feeling that they are not good enough deeply embedded into their psyche. Even if such a person claims that they are smarter than many people, they are still more likely to feel inferior to others.

Such false beliefs if not well addressed has the potential of dictating their self-concept and how they get to approach life. Traumas can affect a person in dramatic ways and has the potential of interfering with one's perspective on life while also making them to question themselves and their world. Such traumas normally lead to debilitating symptoms of PTSD such as having nightmares, flashbacks, phobias, anxieties, and fears including difficulties at work and at home.

Traumas tend to lock into one's memory network what was actually experiences with the physical sensations, images, smells, tastes, sounds, and beliefs as if frozen in time within one's mind and body. That's why a person who has experienced a train crash will continue in having fear of trains. He will end up panicking at the sight or even sound of a train since all the memories related to the accident are still lodged within their nervous system and he's unable to process them. Both the internal and external triggers of the traumatic memory brings the experience into their consciousness just as it took place in its original form.

Just like a recording, traumatic experiences are more like a recording as they get trapped and forms a perpetual blockage and they keep repeating themselves in the body. Nightmares could be the attempts made by the mind to metabolize the trapped information, however, the traumatic experiences tends to last beyond the dream time. When engaging in therapy, a client might be asked to focus on the target which is related to the trauma such as a dream, a memory, a person, a projected event, and an experience and such like. While using the target, the therapist tries to stimulate the memory network where the traumatic experience is stored.

Simultaneously, other stimuli or eye movements can be used to help with triggering a mechanism that stores the restores the mind-body system's information processing capabilities so as to enable it to draw onto the information from a memory network that's different and that which will give the client insight and understanding. Accelerated information processing then takes place when there is rapid free association of information between the memory networks. Each set of eye movements helps with further unlocking the disturbing information and also helps in accelerating it towards an adaptive path until those negative feelings, thoughts, pictures and emotions have dissipated and replaced spontaneously with an overall positive attitude.

As shared early somatic psychotherapy and EMDR therapy works quite successfully with clients who are motivated to change. The clients should show the willingness and readiness to detach themselves from their past as they get to experience life without previous problems. Secondary gains if focused upon can act as an impediment to successful processing of therapy. Clients should be ready to experience disturbing thoughts and uncomfortable feelings. As the therapy process begins, the troubling memories can be intensified through engagement in eye movements and other techniques. The therapist can then instruct the client to stay with the feelings or to refrain from doing anything that can make the feelings go away. Occasionally, the intense emotions and feelings can become overwhelming and that might cause the client to black out or be in a state where they are unable to proceed with the process. The therapist can then ease the client through such obstacles by helping them move to a resolution that is adaptive.

There are times when a client can fail to process a memory and that might be as a result of an existing neurological problem, deep rooted personality disturbances, and some obsessive –compulsive disorder. A client might be very willing to engage in therapy but such conditions can in a way hinder them from connecting with their emotions and going past the blockages. There are also times when a client's traumatic experienced may not be possibly traced to a specific target. Clients with problems that stem from deep conditioning of abusive fundamentalist religious orders or punitive parents may have difficulty when lowering their psychological defenses so as to allow for EMDR and somatic psychotherapy.

## Structure of EMDR therapy Processing Session

Therapy processing typically starts with the therapist taking a thorough history and also establishing an alliance with the client. The step normally takes a few sessions however, it can still last longer. It's vital for the client to establish a feeling of connection with the therapist as that's when the process can effectively begin. EMDR therapy can last for about 90 minutes depending on the problem that the client could be faced with. For example, a client that has issues with a traumatic child abuse can be advised to follow ninety minute of EMDR session with fifty minutes of somatic psychotherapy within the same week.

It can help the client to integrate the information raised within the first session well with that of the second session. There is a client who might also benefit from engaging in EMDR therapy in succession. During therapy, the therapist acts more like a facilitator or a guide to the process with the client. The therapist should help the client to identify and also focus to the target that's related to the trauma they are dealing with. For example, a person who has been involved in a traumatic car accident can picture being in their car and seeing another car hitting them from the side.

In the next step, the client can verbalize a life limiting belief that can be associated with the incident that the client might have carried over to the present time. The therapist can verbalize beliefs such as I'm not safe when driving at night, and since that negative belief is emotionally charged, it can end up affecting the person in his/her everyday life. The therapist can then ask what it is that the client desires to believe for themselves when such an image is evoked. A positive cognitive in such a case would be I am safe when driving any time.

The therapist can then question on the physical sensations that they are feeling when image of the accident is recalled. The client might mention feelings such as stomach tension, knot in the throat or any other type of sensation.

Lastly, the therapist can ask if at all any other thing also surfaces when the client think of the sensations. The client can report of hearing the sound of the impact or gasoline smell. Remember the goal of asking such is to aid stimulation of memory network where the actual memory is locked so that the various components of the memory can be reprocessed. By using subjective units of disturbance scale, the client can then report on how disturbing the experience is on a scale of 0 – 10. The client should be encouraged to recall the disturbing image together with all its related sensations, sounds and the negative cognition.

The client should follow the therapist finger with their eyes while allowing everything that comes up the surface without censoring it. Clients may experience images, a range of emotions, insights, body sensations and ordinary thoughts or even nothing much at all. Since everyone processes they're experiences differently, the feelings that gets revealed should not be labeled as wrong or right. Therapists should in the process pay close attention to the experience of the clients as they keep moving the client's eyes until they obtain a clear indication that the client is through with processing the information.

If in case the client is highly emotional, the therapist should ensure that the client eyes are kept in motion until they are able to stay calm and has cleared fully the traumatic experience. However, a client can also signal the therapist to stop with the process for some time. Each client may refer a different number of eye movements which can either be 10 or 15 while some may continue to hundreds. After engaging in a few rounds of eye movements, the therapist can then ask the client "What's happening now" or "what are you getting now". Once the client has answered, they can proceed with the eye movements.

During the eye movements clients tend to go through a multidimensional free association of feelings, thoughts and body sensations. People go through a range of experiences including horrific images, intense sensations and strong emotions such as overwhelming terror, homicidal rage, love, grief, forgiveness and terror. There are times when memories and descriptions that suggest prenatal as well as infancy experiences arise. Very rich and detailed dream like imagery alongside symbolism also arise. Throughout the experiences, therapists can tell the client to stay with that, let it pass through or they can even reassure that the experience is an old stuff.

Engaging in EMDR therapy has a way of evoking a thorough and immediate re-experiencing of the past just like it was locked within the mind and body. A witness awareness can the take place that enables the client to let the unfolding experiences continue with minimal interference. The process of eye movements and the check-ins should be allowed to continue until the session comes to an end. During the time, the initial image should be reassessed with SUDs. For example, the therapist can ask the person with traumatic car experience the following question; "when you bring up the accident picture, how disturbing is the image? They can then respond on a scale of 0 to 10. When the client responds to being free of the emotional charge with a scale of 0, the therapist can then ask what it is that they believe to be true at the moment.

Eliciting a positive cognition towards the end of the process is such an important step that should not be ignored. When the level of disturbance is entirely reduced and the client is free from feelings of distress, the therapist can then ask them to express their new way of understanding verbally and in view of themselves. The positive cognitions should only come from the client and should also fit their subjective experience. The client can say that they are safe. The client can then install the positive cognition by asking the client to join the statement together with the image that was distressing which might have so far changed by becoming dimmer, smaller and less threatening.

As they combine the experience with the positive cognition, they can also engage in a few sets of eye movements. It will make it possible for the client to experience new orientation to the traumatic image. The therapist can then check if in case a new material has emerged that might require reprocessing. If there is a new material then it can be cleared during the same session or it can be carried forward to the next session. When doing therapy, creating a sense of closer is quite vital for the well-being of the client since engaging in therapy brings up materials that are highly charged and has the potential of leaving one feeling vulnerable and open.

If in case client's don't arrive to a good close, they can end up feeling overwhelmed with emotions that can be quite depressing and such can make it difficult for them to function well both at work and at home. They can also be scared of continuing with therapy. The processing material should be allowed to progress on its own during therapy sessions. The process should be facilitated naturally by recording the dreams and insights that come up in a journal as well as painting, drawing or engaging in any kinds of artwork.

## Somatic Psychotherapy Approach

Somatic psychotherapy can be integrated easily with EMDR therapy or any intervention that one is already using. The key aspect is that you have to not only inform but also include clients into the decision that you are making when using such techniques. Somatic psychotherapy is a body oriented therapy that's designed for treatment of trauma and PTSD conditions. The focus is majorly on physiology and instinctual biology in regard to what happens when the body is exposed to extreme threat. The approach is based on the knowledge that PTSD and trauma symptoms in most cases the result of the nervous system being overwhelmed by the speed and intensity of a threatening and violent event.

The nervous system cannot manage to process the traumatic experience and that makes the event to get stuck in two patterns; hyper-arousal which is the fight-flight response or the immobility response. When the stuck energy isn't released the traumatized person may end up experiencing all manner of symptoms such as nightmares, flashbacks, alongside physical symptoms such as chronic pain tension in different parts of the body and stiffness. Because of the neurological impact that trauma has, resolving it should also take place at the physiological level before the person starts processing the thoughts and emotions about that event. This is due to the fact that the emotions of a traumatized person makes it difficult for them to interact effectively at an emotional level or even to benefit from the empathy that's shown by a therapist until they are able to regain some element of self-regulation to their nervous system.

Somatic psychotherapy focuses on the regulation of the nervous system where the client gets guided on how to become aware of and also experience the bodily sensations. Traumatic experiences tend to trigger self-protective mechanisms within the body, however, a traumatic experience such as being involved in a car accident tend to interrupt the completion of self-protective mechanisms which then leads to destabilization of the nervous system. Through use of the various body-oriented techniques that encourage clients to complete the self-defense orienting responses, clients can be able to regain pleasure in the body as they also reach the various stages of relaxation that allow for the progressive gentle releases of energy that in turn induces self-regulation to the nervous system in a great way.

Sensations of goodness can then get triggered in the client's body and that in turn allows them to reconnect with the outside world and also be able to regain a sense of independence in life until they reach that stage where they can process the trauma at a cognitive and emotional level.

## Evaluation and Preparation

Here are some of the building blocks to somatic psychotherapy approach;

### Create a relatively safe environment

Before getting started with therapy, ensure that the therapy room promotes those feelings of calm and enables the therapist to stay present, centered, and calm. There are key things that should be taken note of such as the positioning of the therapist in relation to that of the client. The therapist should be able to assume a neutral stance that's easily acceptable to the client and not just at a cognitive and emotional level but at a bodily level as well.

### Support the initial exploration and comfort with the bodily sensations

Since trauma survivors tend to view their body as the enemy, the therapist should focus on helping them in making friends with the body again by helping them experience positive sensations.

### Pendulation

This is a technique that helps with encouraging the coming into contact with an intrinsic rhythm in the bodies that keeps alternating between states of expansion and relative contraction. Those facing traumatic experiences are more likely to react with fear to the contractions that they might be experiencing and try to stop them which just intensifies the experiences and in turn leads to increased feelings of fear.

Somatic approach is aimed at helping the client to experience the rhythm so that they can learn through their body that the contraction is followed is followed by an expansion. Such an awareness provides the client with a tool that can help them feel relaxed.

## Restore the active defensive responses

Human bodies tend to instinctively react to danger by trying to protect us. When traumatic experiences take place, the protective responses get thwarted and that in turn causes the nervous system to get overwhelmed and in turn collapses. The completion of such protective reflexes helps in enabling the normalization of the traumatized body.

## Titration

When working with traumatic experiences, it's advisable that you get to work with one feeling or sensation at a time so as to avoid getting the nervous system overwhelmed. Since the client nervous system may not be able to distinguish between the original traumatic experience and the feeling of being overwhelmed by re-experiencing the trauma again.

## Uncoupling fear from immobility

The immobility response normally gets engaged when the fight-flight response fails to resolve the situation. The body ends up collapsing and becomes frozen which causes the sensations that are perpetuated by fear to keep continuing. This process helps the client to experience the physical sensations that are associated with immobility when fear is absent and that in turn causes the immobility to dissolve.

## Encourage energy discharge

The discharge of energy that gets accumulated during the traumatic experience takes place through various reactions such as trembling, shaking, vibrating or changes in breathing and temperature. This experience usually takes place in cycles and allows for hyper-arousal states to be brought right to equilibrium.

### Restore balance and equilibrium through self-regulation

The discharge of energy in cycles helps with resetting the nervous system. Clients are then more likely to be calmer as they experience a sense of hope, goodness while they also feel more empowered to regulate themselves.

### Reorient to here and now

The ability of the client to re engage with their environment gets to increase as their nervous system regulates. The therapist should encourage this orientation to the environment so that the client can get the sense of coming alive to what the outside world is like.

When engaging in somatic psychotherapy, the consent and also involvement of the client is very critical. You can begin by asking a client questions such as "Would you like to try out some experiment" "How about we try this exercise". Asking such questions is not just an expression of respect but also helps with placing the client into an experimental frame of mind and one that can be adjusted and improved upon for success. Somatic psychotherapy entails engagement in experiments that are aimed at helping the client to take time and find out for themselves what really works and what doesn't.

The therapist should be willing to explain ahead of time what the practice or exercise is like so as to make them feel safe as they access the practice. The therapist should also be open to any suggestion made by the client in regards to the exercise. Majority of somatic techniques are normally aimed at increasing the client's level of self-awareness as they get invited to discover what it is that they can do differently for the traumatic conditions to change. Lasting and sustainable change or recovery normally takes place when the client reaches a state where they can discover for themselves what they need to do so as to realize the desired change.

To initiate a process with a client, a therapist can do the following;

Suggest the exercise to the client
Get their consent to try something new
Follow the process through by asking some questions
Summarize the outcome to be realized.

As you incorporate somatic techniques, you can ask questions such as;

Would you like to try out this exercise?
How about if we try this other one?
Let's find out if we can help you try this out with this next exercise
Are you ready to try out the following experiences?

As a therapist, when working with the body, it also means that you are working with how the mind perceives the body. So you should keep in mind the fact that mind and the body are actually connected. You should therefore be aware of the following principles about the body;

The human body tend to respond to a traumatic external experience with blockage, constriction, imbalance, and muscle tension. The body also tend to be drawn to unhealthy habits when physiologically and emotionally stressed, threatened or misused.

The body tends to remember feelings, memories and sensations implicitly when touched, triggered, vulnerable or emotional. It's also important to note that the body changes at all times, it's quite flexible and also moldable.

The experience of the body is transient and therefore doesn't last so even the traumatic pain can subside.

The body is capable of experiencing healing at any time. When the body is treated with kindness, curiosity and patience, it yields wisdom on what it needs.

The body is also the most important place where healing and transformation can take place.

## Tools and Techniques

For successful delivery of somatic interventions, the therapist should have a clear understanding on how to assess for body cues and symptoms in relation to the traumatic experience. For example, you might hear a client claiming to be having severe shoulder pain as a result of sleeping in bad posture then brush it aside as the ideal truth. The therapist can instead respond by saying, "Let's pay attention to the shoulder right away so as to see what you can feel or sense in the process. It can bring forth some increased and meaningful level of body awareness.

Learning of a client's individual expression is such an important factor in regards to somatic psychotherapy. Pay attention to how the client moves, how they talk about the body and how they respond in the body whenever increased emotional material surfaces. The goal is to understand what the client is saying in relation to how they make the expression in their body. When you keep hearing a client consistently mentioning of the body parts that are paining, it could be an indicator of something that require more attention. Learning and carefully observing the nonverbal language is quite vital and matters a lot.

Here are some of the guidelines to follow when working with the body;

When working with the client, the therapist should inform them when they intend to include the body oriented interventions. Avoid surprising the client with new techniques but instead explain the technique that you are including so that they are in the picture.

As a therapist, you should always ask for permission so as to explain the exercises and interventions that you are doing. Consider providing the client with a range of options that they can choose from.

Safety is of great important and the therapist should find out what the client needs if they are to feel safe. For example, you can help the client to identify part of the body where they feel strong and also good then have the client guided on how they can periodically connect with the place by having them imagine the safe place that they can go to.

Resource for strength and wellness by identifying somatic places within the body, imagery or therapy room where the client can associate with wellness and strength.

Track the client on how they are doing and get to identify if there is any disassociation, or whether they are feeling overwhelmed. If you identify something then take time and slow down, resource or even stop. You should still continue with verbal contact but if in case the client feels uncomfortable with the body work, you can stop then provide some alternatives. Never insist in providing interventions that the client is not interested in.

Track the client for signs of physical safety such as any existence of self-harm threads, suicidal ideation and such like then follow the professional ethical guidelines as you provide therapy.

Consider being trustworthy. Ensure that you work within the ethical codes, honor the set boundaries, and avoid coming up with any surprise to the client.

Phrases that can help facilitate body trust;

How are you experiencing these feelings?
Where are you sensing?
How are you recognizing these experience right now?
Are you feeling....what do you sense
How does the body experience of tension appear to you in this moment?
What is it that you need to stay with this feeling?
What are you curious now about?

One of the vital aspects of somatic psychotherapy is to prepare the mind and the body for the work that's ahead. The therapist should be able to understand the techniques from inside out so as to understand the power of the techniques and how they can be applied with the client. Evaluate yourself as a therapist by having clarity about how you feel, the sensations in your body at the moment, and your level of balance. Having knowledge of how you feel before you start working with your client will not only give you a measure but also that evidence that you actually know what you need to do to stay balanced.

It is an important self-assessment that will help you get to understand what it is that makes you experience a burnout and that which rejuvenates you. Even as a therapist, you should consider making awareness as a practice so that you get to know how you feel in your body, mind and heart as being part of the practice to becoming a somatically-oriented therapist. You should consider cultivating a body-questioning vocabulary as part of your somatic psychotherapy work.

Some of the tools and exercises to use for the therapeutic interventions are;

## Taking a snapshot of the body

The goal of this exercise is to help the therapist establish how they are feeling in the present moment. They should be able to take a quick inventory of how they are so as to establish that somatic baseline that can help you compare on how you are when working with clients all through the day.

A body snapshot should be a moment of awareness that is inwardly directed and focuses on the moment. Having knowledge of what goes within is critical as it helps the therapist to be aware of when they are off balance and how they can get their balance back. With such knowledge, they will be more aware of when they are getting overwhelmed, triggered or when they are getting flooded emotionally.

Therapists can choose to take the inner snapshot in between therapy sessions so as to help them with staying tuned into themselves.

## Body awareness for therapy readiness

This is a technique that helps with grounding the therapist as they get ready for a therapy session. It helps the therapist to return back to their inner balance when feeling thrown off balance after a session. The goal is to help the therapist attain that inner balance and alignment so as to access strength and balance. You can do that by taking some five or seven minutes in quietness. Engage in this exercise at the beginning of the day as you prepare to start the sessions.

You can either sit on the floor as you assume an outer posture by sitting upright and having the shoulders aligned with the hips. Ensure that the head is also in alignment with the chin not protruding. Ensure that you align your posture so that you feel upright. You can then evoke an image that ignites that relaxed quality. Consider practicing this body awareness for therapy readiness after every session so that it becomes a healthy habit.

## Grounding through the body

When you learn how to ground your body as a therapist, you can be able to overcome any challenge that the client raises during therapy sessions. Grounding through the body is such a vital and basic tool and should be often used so that it becomes a habit. As a therapist you can arrive in the body with your awareness regardless of how you feel whether activated, disconnected, tired or triggered. Learning how to have yourself grounded as a therapist is a health and wellness practice that will help you as a therapist in sustaining your work.

Grounding through the body makes it possible for you to engage in that regular self-check that helps you with being aware of how you are doing. The goal of grounding is so that you can reconnect with the joy that comes from engaging in your work, having a calm mind and heart despite the chaos that you might experience during the sessions. You can ground yourself through the body by sitting, standing, lying down or modify the body posture to what feels right for you.

## Shaking it off

Shaking is that natural body process that helps with restoring the body to that natural state after experiencing some shocking or frightening experience. This body response can be used in a conscious way so as to help with restoring body awareness and equilibrium. Shaking helps with restoring the body to its inherent self-restoring capability. It is a tool that teaches one on how to safely release tension or anxious feelings that exist within the body.

The exercise enables one to interrupt that mental chatter that might be going on at the moment so as to refocus the body. Through shaking, the body regains awareness and can be applied to a client especially when they report of feeling upset, ungrounded or shaky. If as a client you feel ungrounded after helping in facilitating a client's process then you can consider the exercise. The exercise can take about 5 minutes with the focus being relaxation and grounding.

## Calling internal support team

This is an exercise that helps a therapist to get ready for work. It entails visualization that centers both the mind and body and also reminds the therapist of the resources that they already have available in their life. When one is connected to the internal resources, they become more present and available for the client. This exercise is ideal when you require some extra grounding for the sessions that you anticipate to be a bit challenging.

You can practice visualizing the exercise anytime you feel stuck and unaware of the next intervention to make. You can do the exercise by sitting comfortably in a quiet place then closing your eyes so as to establish that centering breath to the body. You can then allow yourself to calm down as you reflect. Visualize yourself as having a supportive people around you that are more like a physical team sitting right around you. You can then notice what happens to your body posture, as the team sends strength to you.

## Self-Resourcing

As a therapist, there are times when you will have difficult sessions and there are times when you will feel exhausted and in need of quick rejuvenation before you commit to seeing more clients. The quickest way of self-resourcing is by connecting with the ground and the movement through your body. All you have to do is to take about fifteen minutes then slow down as you synchronize your movement with your breath. Begin by finding a comfortable spot on the floor then take time to feel the floor that's beneath you as you let your weight drop on the floor.

Exhale as you let out any tension you might be feeling. You can then begin moving the body in a twist while leaving the lower body where it's located and only rotating the upper part of the body and your arms. Repeat the motion several times as then rest on the side once you are through with the exercise.

## Somatic inventory on signs of burnout

Burnout or feelings of fatigue is a common occurrence when working closely with stress and trauma related clients. This exercise will help you to evaluate your burnout level from the inside out. Burnout is normally a condition where as a therapist you get both physically and emotionally drained due to the therapy process that you perform. You can identify the symptoms by paying attention on how your body responds.

You can undertake the exercise by tuning in to your level of somatic level and burnout distress. Some of the symptoms of burnout include;

Excessive blaming and feeling of being resentful
Isolation from others
Feeling of being easily overwhelmed
Being stuck in emotions that you can't express
Feelings of irritability and having a tendency of aggressive outbursts
Misunderstandings and frequent troubles with others
Compulsive behaviors
Flashbacks of client's traumatic stories, and nightmares

# Chapter 6: The Procedural Steps in Trauma Treatment

As a comprehensive approach, all somatic and EMDR therapy procedures and protocols should be geared towards contributing to the positive treatment effects through an interaction with the client in a way that enhances containment and processing of information. Every treatment effect entails an interaction with the client, the therapist and the method being used. Therapists should have a clear understanding on how to prepare the clients appropriately as they also stay attuned to their specific individual needs while still keeping the information processing system activated so that treatment and learning can take place.

Therapists should begin by taking a comprehensive history so as to identify the appropriate targets for developmental and processing deficits that might have to be addressed. Various studies have proven that the early traumatic experiences of all types have very similar long-lasting effects that are negative. For example, if the mind is allowed to scan back to childhood days and bring up some depressing incident, many people will realize that they still feel the flush of some negative emotion when such memories are brought up. You May realize that your body still flinch when such thoughts come up.

As per adaptive information processing model that's used in guiding EMDR therapy practice, it would mean that the traumatic experience was insufficiently processed and that the automatically arising emotions, thoughts and physical reactions could be coloring one's actions and perceptions inappropriately and in a way that's similar to the present circumstances. You may realize that such a person trend to react negatively to new learning, groups, authority or whatever the aspects that are contained in that memory.

Those are actually not conditioned responses but are responses that are inherent within the stored memory. When a traumatic event has been processed sufficiently, one can remember it but they don't experience the old sensations, or emotions in the present moment. We should be informed by our memories and not be controlled by them. For therapists a clear distinction between dysfunctionally stored events and the adaptively processed events is that in adaptively processed event, the required learning has taken place and it's already stored with the appropriate emotions that can help with guiding the individual in the future.

The dysfunctionally stored event still has some of the thoughts and sensory perceptions that were present when the event took place. When childhood perspective of traumatic memories is locked within the mind and body, it causes the person to perceive the present from a vantage point that's defective such viewing themselves as not good enough/unlovable and that in turn makes them to feel a lack of control or lack of safety. Therapists should be able to observe such in their practices. As much as clients know that they shouldn't be feeling powerless, hopeless and unlovable, they still do.

When speaking of their childhood experiences, they can slip into using the same intonation. The therapist should therefore identify the events that have been stored dysfunctionally by the client, those that are coloring and stunting the present perception of the client and then assist them accordingly.

Somatic psychotherapy and EMDR therapy facilitates learning on multidimensional emotional, physiological and cognitive levels. The processing of traumatic events that are dysfunctionally stored enables clients to become free from such feelings. For most clients, by simply processing the childhood experiences allows for appropriate emotional and cognitive connections to be made adaptive behaviors can emerge spontaneously alongside positive self-concepts, and insights. For clients who might have been neglected badly and even those who got abused in their childhood, it's vital for a therapist to take time in determining the developmental windows that might have closed before the development of important infrastructures were in place.

The therapist should take time and find out about the following so as to ascertain the extent of neglect or abuse;

1. Did the child learn anything about object constancy or will it have to be taught during therapy?
2. What will the therapist need to model for the client?
3.What experiences will have to be engendered for healthy relationship patterns to emerge?

Once the therapist has established such positive interactions within therapeutic relationship, they too should be stored in memory and can then be enhanced through therapy process. Therapists should be careful and be able to view clients as very complex people that functions at all the levels of thinking, feeling, sensing, acting and believing.

Example 1

As a therapist, you can test your psychotherapy skills by working with those who are struggling with traumatic memories. As a therapist, you should consider the following when engaging with a traumatized client;

Ensure that you don't re-traumatize the clients. Therapists can end up doing such when they keep prodding for too many details or when they come out as someone interrogating the client.

Consider the fact that getting traumatic history in a chronological order might be impractical or unsafe due to how the memories are stored. Taking time to determine the presenting issues and the corresponding themes is of great importance.

Remember to as open ended questions, questions that start with words such as "what" and "how" as they allow the client as much information as possible with very little detail.

Avoid being judgmental and it doesn't mean that you have to endorse any unhealthy behavior, however, it does mean that you should respect the client's dignity at all times.

Be genuine and work towards building rapport from the first encounter. When engaging in the therapy sessions, let the clients know that they can opt out of answering to the questions.

Have closure strategies in place. You can allow for about 10 minutes to close down then consider teaching some brief coping skill towards the end of the session.

Remember that assessment should be an ongoing process and not just for getting client's history.

## Procedures and Checklists

### History Taking

Begin by asking the client some general information about themselves. The session should take about 5 minutes and should allow for some rapport building. Here are some of the questions to ask;

What are some of your assets, strengths, and resources? You can also ask an alternative question such as "What are some of the things you have been going through both internally and externally?

What do you want to work on during these sessions? General themes and memories can be worked on.

What result do you expect to have out of this session? Get the expected goals and outcomes.

It might not be possible for the client to give a detailed chronological history, and recounting a detailed history can be a challenge if one has not processed the memories or they may not feel ready to share the details. You can instead ask if there are themes that the client can identify in relation to the issues that the client is presenting.

**Theme: Negative Cognition**

First float back memory
Worst float back memory
Most recent float back memory

As a therapist, you can then present a list of negative cognitions for the target selection then let the client select the negative beliefs that they still hold in the present. If the client checks over three negative beliefs then you can ask them to go over the list again and rank the beliefs on the basis of most charged or less charged ones.

Once they have identified the negative beliefs, ask them some three float back questions for example;

1. Looking back at your life journey, when was the first time you believed (I am not good enough.....I cannot... or I don't have.......

2.Looking back over your life journey when is the worst time you believed...................

3.Looking back over your life journey when is the most recent time you believed...........

**Step 2:** In this resourcing phase you should make a list of existing adaptive coping skills and the resources that the client can use to address both internal and external issues.

Review the resources/skills and how they can be used then let the client try them if they can help. For resourcing and stabilization, come up with coping skills and exercises that the client can practice in every session. You can also come up with coping skills and exercises that will work after the session.

**Step 3:** Target memory or Incident

Let the client identify the image or worst part by asking;

1. Looking back on the event now, what image represents the worst part? If in case there is no image available or that which exists doesn't carry much charge then you can guide the client to think about the target or use another sensory channel that carries more charge like sound.

2.To identify negative cognition you can ask the client this question. "When you bring the image or that worst part now, what is that negative belief about you that seems to go with it?

3.For positive cognition you can ask the client, "When you bring the image or the worst part of the event, what would you like to believe about yourself at the moment?

4.For validity of cognition you can ask the client, "As you look back on the image or the worst part now, what is your feeling on how true the positive belief is right now on a scale of 1 – 7 with 1 being false and 7 being true.

5.For subjective units of disturbance ask the client, "What is your level of disturbance as you bring up the image or worst part of the even, the negative emotions and beliefs together on a scale of 0 – 10 with 0 being no disturbance and 10 being the worst you can imagine?

6.Location of body sensation, "What are you noticing within your body now as you bring up the image or worst part of the event with the negative emotions and negative belief together?

**Step 4:** Encourage the client to bring up the body sensations together with the negative belief of _____ and the image or worst part of the event memory. Encourage the client to notice all that happens as the stimulation begins. You can check for tones, eye movements and tactile stimulation.

Try to stay out of the way as much as possible and after each set, you can invite the client to take a breath and also ask questions such as "What are you getting? What are you noticing at this moment? The question is quite broad and that invites free association.

When the client reports of what they are noticing, you can move on to the next stimulation. Encourage that by using statements such as "Just notice" that or "Go with that". If in case the client brings up an image, ask for SUDs rating so that you can check on their progress as the responses become more adaptive. You can use statements such as "When you return to the event image or the worst part of where we began, what is the level of distress that you feel now with 0 being no disturbance and 10 being the worst you can imagine.

**Step 5:** This is like the installation phase where you get to check for positive cognition. "When you bring up the image, does that original positive belief of "I'm good enough" fit or is there another positive belief that fits better now?

Check VoC of the positive cognition that you have arrived upon then ask"What is your feeling of how true that positive belief is right at the moment as you look back at the image with 1 being completely false and 7 being completely true. You can then keep going on with that until VoC is 7 or as close as is reasonable. You can then ask the client to place that positive belief together with the original image.

**Step 6**: Now that the client has installed the positive belief, you can ask "What are you noticing as you scan your body? If in case there are some residual disturbances then let the client notice them as you continue with the fast sets until the identified residue is neutralized. When the client's body become clear/adaptive you can ask the client to "Hold that body scan together with the original target and the positive belief.

**Step 7**: This is the closure phase and in case you realize that the session is not complete then it means that you might have jumped from step 4 or step 5 to step 7 and that's still permissible. During closure, you can make use of the resources built and strengthened in step 2 to reduce any form of residual distress as you ensure a safe departure. You can also engage the client in general debriefing about the session and also be mindful of addressing any concerns that the client might have. Remember that processing may still continue after the session ends so you should review with the client a plan for safety, stabilization and even contact to support in need arises.

| List of Negative and Positive Cognitions | |
|---|---|
| Responsibility: | Responsibility: |
| I should have known better | I did the best I could |
| I should have done something | I did the best I could with what I had |
| I did something wrong | |

| | |
|---|---|
| I am to blame | I do my best |
| I cannot be trusted | I am blameless |
| My best is not good enough | I'm not at fault |
| | I can be trusted |
| Safety: | Safety: |
| I cannot trust myself | I can trust myself |
| I cannot trust anyone | I can choose who to trust |
| I cannot show my emotions | I am safe now |
| I am in danger | I can create my sense of safety |
| I am not safe | I can show my emotions |
| Choice: | Choice: |
| I'm not in control | I am in control |
| I have to be perfect/please everyone | I have power now |
| I am weak | I can't help myself |
| I am trapped | I have a way out |
| I have no options | I have options |
| Power: | Power: |
| I cannot get what I need | I can get what I want |
| I cannot stand it | I can handle it |
| I cannot succeed | I can succeed |
| I cannot let it out | I can stand up for myself |
| I am powerless/helpless | I am powerful |
| Value: | Value: |
| I'm not good enough | I am good enough |
| I'm worthless/inadequate | I'm a good person |

| I'm insignificant/I'm not important | I am whole |
|---|---|
| I deserve only bad things | I'm restored |
| I am stupid | I'm special |
| I do not belong | I deserve to live |
| I'm alone | I am special |

# Conclusion

Traumatic experiences can be quite devastating and can have such a huge impact on one's overall health and wellbeing if not well processed. **Somatic Psychotherapy and EMDR therapy** is a book that has shared in detail valuable information that therapists can use for treating clients that are faced with traumatic experiences. The valuable information shared in this book not only helps with promoting trauma awareness and understanding but also provide valuable tools and techniques that can be used to address diverse cases of trauma.

It enables therapists to view trauma in the context of the client's environment and other related factors. Once the recovery from trauma has been identified as the primary goal, therapists can provide the necessary support as they create collaborative relationships with the clients that helps with minimizing the risk of re-traumatization. As shared earlier in this book, therapists should have in depth understanding of somatic psychotherapy and EMDR therapy if they are to provide the much needed help to the clients.

If any part of this book is not well understood then I would like to encourage you to take your time and read the book again for better understanding.

Thank you for purchasing the book and make the best use of the information learnt from the book.

# Book Six
## SOMATIC PSYCHOTHERAPY

## Introduction

Many people accept that as you age your body becomes stiffer and you will be less able to do the tasks that you currently take for granted. However, there is a study which suggests this is not the case. Somatics is the study of movement; it is believed that the modern, Western, way of life contributes too many posture and stiffness issues. These can be improved by altering the way you perceive your body and completing some key exercises as you move around.

Somatics was touched upon as early as the beginning of the twentieth century by the philosophers John Dewey and Rudolf Steiner; they both advocated the advantages of experiential learning. However, it was the work and study of Moshe Feldenkrais in the 1970's which was to lead to a wider knowledge and understanding of this field of research. These studies came to the attention of the Chairman of Philosophy at the University of Florida; Thomas Hanna. Moshe's research and theories fitted in with the work that Hannah had been doing; his introduction to Moshe Feldenkrais shaped his life and reinforced his belief that that attitude towards your body can be changed to improve posture and movement; no matter how old you are.

Thomas Hanna had a good understanding of the rules of biofeedback; he added this understanding to what he had already discovered and to what he learned from Moshe. For several years in the early 1970's Hanna studied Moshe's techniques and principles, by 1975 he had managed to get the first Feldenkrais training program established in America. At this stage he was the

Director of the Humanistic Psychology Institute; during the same year he and Eleanor Hanna founded the Novato Institute for Somatic Research. It was thanks to his studies and teachings that people started to become aware of what somatics was.

He continued to study Moshe Feldenkrais theories and added his own knowledge and research t them. It became increasingly apparent that many people developed the same postural difficulties, regardless of their age or vocation. Groups of people had the same characteristics although this was far more pronounced in Western civilisation than elsewhere in the world. This naturally led to the development of a variety of exercises which helped anyone to improve their mobility and flexibility. As his theory evolved these exercises would become known as Hanna Somatic Education.

Hanna has been described as a philosopher, a theologian, a professional writer and, even, as a revolutionary thinker. His studies led him to discover that there were far more people with movement issues and chronic pain in the Western world than there was in the less industrialized parts of the world. It was this belief that drove Hanna to find a new way of approaching aging; to return mobility and flexibility to those who followed his teachings. He spent several years studying the neurophysiology of development and control before he went on to develop what is now known as Clinical Somatic Education.

Clinical Somatic Education is designed as a teaching method; it involves a student learning to move in slow, precise ways. The movements must be a product of your conscious, not your subconscious and, with the aid of the instructor you will quickly discover a vastly improved range of mobility, flexibility and movement. Most people can master the basic techniques within twelve sessions; providing you continue to practice what you have learned, you should enjoy a far greater range of movement than what you thought was possible; for the rest of your life. In fact, the principles behind this are so easy to learn that it is possible to learn and understand the movements without a professional teacher.

Sadly Thomas Hanna died in a car accident two thirds of the way through his first somatics teaching course; thanks to the dedication of Eleanor Hanna, his students and the skill in which he organized his work and teachings, clinical somatic education has become available to anyone who wishes to improve their mobility and flexibility.

The guiding principle behind somatics is based on the understanding that a person is a whole individual; you are not a separate mind, body and soul. You are one entity, which is capable of growing, learning and evolving; as such anything is possible and healing is simply an extension of this; you are capable of healing yourself.

Somatics is based on a sound understanding of the human body and the neurological pathways that operate inside you. Every function you perform is controlled by your brain. Even sitting still your body will constantly be sending messages to your brain, via your nerves; this will be regarding how you are feeling and how you are moving. This information is processed by the brain and returned to your muscles and tendons via the same network of nerves.

Most movements you make are termed 'voluntary'; this is because you are thinking about them, even if you are barely aware of it. Making yourself a drink is a conscious, voluntary decision. However, if you repeat the same process too many times your brain will see a habit developing and stoop processing the information. It will accept that you sit in a certain way, or walk a certain way. It can even recognize the weakness of a leg in plaster and accept that you will always walk more gently on the leg. This process is known as habituation and it is an essential part of your life. It allows your brain to handle all the mundane tasks without using any real effort, saving your brain power for the more important things in life. However, it is also this habituation which can become an issue. If you strain a muscle and continue to use it while it is healing you are likely to develop a new way of moving; this will compensate for any weakness or loss of movement while the part is healing. However, once it has healed, your brain will not automatically return to its previous, subconscious, way of moving, it will continue to operate in the new way. This will limit your movement unnecessarily. For example, if you break your leg and it is in plaster, you will be unable to bend it for several weeks. You body will remember this and, even when the cast has been removed, it will continue to resist bending it. For you to gain active and full use of your leg again, you will need to tell it to start bending again. This is one of the techniques which can be taught by clinical somatic education.

In effect, habituation is the body's way of coping after trauma, however, this leads to tight muscles which are tight because habituation has taken effect and not because there is anything wrong with them anymore. It will quickly reach the point where your muscles are tight and will cause pain if you move a certain way. At first you put up with this pain, ultimately, you stop moving that way to prevent the pain from occurring. At that point your movement, flexibility and probably posture have all been compromised; your body will become stiffer and less mobile, just as you expected it to! It is a self-fulfilling prophecy!

# Chapter 1: General Uses of Somatics

Understanding that your muscle is tight and causes pain because of an old injury is only part of the story. You then need to figure out a way of getting your muscle to relax. It is possible to use the services of a masseuse or a chiropractor; they are highly likely to give you some relief from the pain of your muscle tightness. However, they are also likely to last for a limited time only, the main reason for this is habituation; your brain will still be telling your muscle to contract and it will do so as soon as possible. Of course you can repeat the massage or other treatment you undertook every three or four days, however, this is a time consuming and expensive way to deal with the issue. It is also only successful as long as you keep up the treatment.

The inability to voluntarily contract or relax a muscle is known as Sensory Motor Amnesia (SMA), learning to regain voluntary control will stop your brain from sending a message to your muscles telling them to contract. This is the main use of somatics, the prevention of pain by relearning how to control your muscles voluntarily. The emphasis is on learning how to feel everything you sense; you can then change the way you move and control your own body.

There are several key benefits from practicing somatics:

**Flexibility**

Learning somatic techniques is essential to improve the range of flexibility, movement and posture. It can also be used to help with managing pain; in part because it will deal with stiff muscles and body parts, but also because it can help you to control the nerves and the brain's response to various stimuli.

Flexibility is an essential but relative part of everyone's life. A professional athlete will probably need to be exceptional flexible; especially if they are a gymnast or similar. Golfers may require an improved range of flexibility in their shoulders while people practicing karate will need good flexibility in their hips and legs. People who are work in an office environment and live a fairly sedentary life will only need a good general flexibility. Of course, the more flexible you are the better you will be able to adapt to any situation and the less likely you will be to suffer from injuries or any stiffening as you age.

Being flexible is also the basic requirement if you are looking to correct your posture or improve your movement range. This is because if you are flexible your muscles will be loose enough and relaxed enough to learn new ways of doing things. If this is not the case then you will be unable to effectively move individual body parts without risk of injury. Stretching properly is an essential part of keeping your body ready for anything.

**Posture**

Somatics has been shown to be beneficial for posture in several ways. The most obvious benefit is that, by learning to control your own muscles you can stop any strain being placed on your spine by tight muscles and tendons. Stresses and strains on your spine can lead to poor posture and either a bent spine or to it shrinking. In turn this will increase the likelihood of vertebral degeneration; where the discs supporting the spine are no longer able to do so.

Problems with your spine can also cause constrictions to blood flow or even nerves; both of which can cause serious issues in other parts of your body.

Your spine is one of the most important parts of your body; the central nervous system passes through and is protected by it. At the same time it keeps your body upright and capable of a variety of tasks. Looking after it is essential to your long term health and enjoyment of life.

## Movement

Fluid movement, in any direction necessary is the result of good posture and a good range of flexibility. Movement is essential to life, the more you move the better the heart responds and the easier it will find it to pump blood around your body. A good range of movement will ensure a good blood flow to all vital organs and a plentiful supply of oxygen.

If you have issues with your range of movements then you are likely to have reduced function and be less willing to push your body past any movement or pain issue. A reduction in movement will result in you doing less out of a fear of making an injury or movement issue worse. Unfortunately, this is the exact behaviour which does make the movement issue worse and ultimately results in you having very little mobility.

In order to ensure your ability to move stays as good as possible, you should practice somatics for as little as five minutes per day. You will be amazed at the benefits which can be gained from such a short brain retraining period!

## Pain Management

Pain is often the result of trauma; an accident, no matter how big or small, can damage muscles and tendons in your body. After the accident has happened you are likely to discover pain in one of your muscles or tendons. The muscle is contracting to deal with the injury; it may have been damaged itself or it may be reacting to protect another part if your body.

Many people will treat muscle injuries with hot and cold compresses; attempting to decrease the blood flow and minimise swelling whilst sending fresh, oxygenated blood to the muscles to aid healing. The risk is that the muscle will continue to contract after treatment and cause pain. This is often treated by taking painkillers and not dealing with the actual issue; the result is that the injury is masked, your muscle remains contracted and your brain learns to deal with the issue by operating in a different way. Unfortunately, this is avoidance instead of recovery and, in the long term, the injury is likely to return to haunt you! Clinical somatic education can help you to learn how to control the muscle, whilst ensuring it relaxes and stretches so that you body can return to more mobile, active state.

By taking voluntary control of your muscles you will also be able to alleviate any pain associated with the injury and repetitive use of your muscle whilst contracted.

Although the main uses of somatics are to improve flexibility, posture, movement and to assist with pain management, it is also an excellent technique to target a wide range of ailments with the human body:

### Sciatica

The sciatic nerve can become trapped, pinched, or occasionally damaged. This will result in a shooting pain down your leg, usually starting from your hip and extending as far as either your knee or even your toes. In extreme cases this can cause a loss of feeling in your leg and the pain can cause a rapid reduction in movement or a dependency on painkillers.

Fortunately, somatics can help with these issues by teaching you to stand correctly and control the muscle in your back. It is usually this which is contracted and putting pressure on the sciatic nerve.

By learning to take voluntary control of the muscle you can ensure it is relaxed and the pressure is removed from your sciatic nerve. Movement and pain release can be provided very quickly!

## Hips, Knees & Leg Muscles

This is a common area of concern for those who spend much of their day sitting at an office desk. It can also be a matter of concern for those who run or perform similar exercises regularly.

The issue will usually arrive through either injury or incorrect posture, leading to habituation of your muscles. These tightened muscles will imbalance your movements as your joints tighten due to the pressure being placed on them by your muscles. To correct this issue and relieve any pain and mobility issues you can learn somatic techniques which will relax your muscles and allow you to stand correctly again. This will alleviate the pressure in your hips, knees and even your leg muscles

## Plantar Fasciitis

This is the pain and inflammation which many people get in their feet. In fact, this is caused by the tightening of your muscles in your legs and your feet. These may be a result of trauma, bad posture or just years of bad habits. Somatics will teach you how to stand and even to move, using conscious thought which will, ultimately, replace your subconscious actions with a new set of actions. The new ones will be far more beneficial to your health, posture and muscles.

## TMJ Pain

TMJ pain occurs in the face and is usually linked with stress. Many people react to stress by grinding their teeth, alternatively you may simply clench them. It is simply a way of dealing with an issue and getting the job done within the confines of the timeframe available. Sadly, it is an increasing issue as the modern, technologically advanced world, places more demands on everyone.

The cause of this pain is a tightening of the muscles in your face and jaw, to relieve this pain for the long term you will need to learn how to relax your facial muscles and, preferably, stop clenching your jaw or grinding your teeth in the future!

In fact, it is possible that almost any muscle in your body could become contracted and remain that way. This is because every muscle in your body is used to some extent and has the potential to be either injured or used incorrectly for an extended period of time. Once it has learned to function incorrectly it will continue to do so until you train it to do otherwise.

Training your muscle is not difficult, it simply requires you to perform a series of exercises daily which allow you to focus on your muscles and control them better. Every exercise must be performed slowly and deliberately; this is the only way for your brain to learn a new method of doing something instead of continuing with the old way. Somatics should also help you to focus more on your own body, how it operates and how you can help it improve the way it moves and deals with exercise and trauma.

As well as the issues listed above, somatics can help deal with the following conditions:

• Carpal Tunnel Syndrome

• Tendonitis

• Bursitis

• Thoracic Outlet Syndrome

498

- Scoliosis

- Chronic headaches

- Myofascial Pain

Treatment sessions are usually short and an entire course of treatment is usually over within between ten and twelve sessions. However, unlike some alternatives, it is a highly effect, long term strategy.

# Chapter 2: Exercises

Somatics can be learned by anyone and can be used by anyone. Obviously, the exact exercises which will benefit you will depend upon the injuries and issues you have.

Before you start these activities it is essential to understand the concept of pandiculation. It is this concept and way of exercising that is fundamental to somatics. Instead of just stretching you are doing three things in one exercise:

• The targeted muscle group is already contracted, or tight. Your brain has become used to it being this way and accepts it. The first stage of this process is to tighten the muscle more; this will remind your brain that the muscle is capable of different levels of contraction.

• Next, you will need to lengthen the muscle or muscles as much as possible. The amount you can lengthen them will rapidly increase. The opposite side of this step is releasing the muscle. Again, this is a way of reminding the brain the full range of movement every muscle has.

• Finally, you need to relax completely, the brain will associate complete relaxation with the state that the muscle should be in and start to refocus its efforts on using the muscle correctly and not in the way that habituation has shown it.

It is these three stages which make a somatic exercise so effective; you will go through the complete range of physical movements and reset your brain to accept the possibilities. One of the greatest parts of starting somatic exercises is that you will feel a difference straight away and within a few weeks develop a much better range of movement than you had thought possible.

There are an abundance of options available but the following exercises can be beneficial to almost anyone; it is essential to remember that these exercises are designed to be completed slowly:

## Body Awareness

This exercise should help you to become more aware of your body, which points are tight and which need to be worked on. Start by lying on your back and bend your knees so that your feet are flat on the floor. Next, you need to spread your arms out as far as you can; keeping them on the mat. You should have your right hand with its palm downwards and the left with its palm upwards.

The slowly roll your arms, moving both at the same time roll them in opposite directions, three times. You can extend this movement by putting your knees towards the side which currently has the palm facing down and your head towards the other side. This exercise should be completed between five and ten times; keep the pace slow and focus on how your coordination changes.

## Lower Back

Lower back pain affects the majority if people at some point in their lives. In fact; many people live with their back pain for many years as they believe it is simply the way things are. Fortunately, it does not need to be the case forever! The following exercise can loosen and relax your back muscles and provide relief from pain as well as improving your posture.

Lie flat on your back with your legs extended out in front of you. Then, with your eyes shut, twist your right leg outwards; your lower back should arch. Hold this for a few seconds before twisting inwards, your lower back should flatten to the floor. You should then repeat this with the other leg. You will need to focus on how this exercise affects your lower back. Once you have done each leg several times you will need to do both legs at the same time outwards and then inwards. Repeat the exercise five times keeping your focus on what your lower back wants to do. Do not try and stop it from arching or flattening; simply pay attention to which it does.

## Right and Left Back

This exercise is a natural extension to the lower back one you have just completed. Still laying on your back with your legs extended, bring them up slightly towards your body and bend them a little at the knees. Then, roll your legs together to the left, followed by a movement to the right. You will feel the movement on the right and left sides of your back. You can obtain a more subtle feeling in your back by doing this exercise with your legs extended.

You should repeat the exercise between five and ten backs, focusing on the way your back moves.

## Spinal Freedom

Again, lie in your back with your knees bent and your feet flat on the floor. Start with your left leg and bend it to bring it towards your chest. Use your left hand to hold it in place. Next put your right hand behind your head and lift your head towards your left knee. Exhale while lifting; you will feel your spine lengthening. To finish, inhale as you lower yourself back down, arching your back as you do so. Once you have repeated this exercise between three and five times you will need to switch sides and move your right leg whilst your left hand holds your head.

## Hamstrings

Start by sitting on the floor with your legs out in front of you. You will then need to bend your right leg so that your foot goes towards your crotch. Your thighs should extend to the side of your body although it will probably not naturally touch the ground. Next, hold your left leg which is still extended out in front of you. Then bring your head down towards your knee. Repeat this between three and five times before switching legs.

It is also possible to stretch your hamstrings by sitting as above, instead of taking your head towards your knee, hold your extended leg and pull it towards you. Focus on keeping your back straight and your head up. This will provide a deeper stretch of the hamstrings and strengthen the lower back muscles.

**Side Stretch**

This exercise starts in a standing position. Your feet should be shoulder width apart and your hands clasped behind your head so that your elbows stick out to each side. Take a breath in whilst lowering your body to one side, as the weight of your body pushes down you will find it impossible to continue breathing in. After a few seconds straighten and repeat between three and five times. You will then need to lower your body to the other side.

Alternatively you can stretch your sides by standing with your legs shoulder width apart and lift your right arm and shoulder straight up. To get them straight you body will need to bend to the left. You should breathe in as you move your arm upwards and then breathe out as you start to bend. Your body weight should be lifted and the pressure on your lungs will not be felt in the same way.

**Stretching the Thighs**

Start by standing up, again, your feet should be in line with your shoulders. Then lift one leg off the floor and bend it at the knee, placing your foot behind your buttocks. You will need to use your hands to hold and support your foot! Next, pull the top of your foot towards your buttocks. You will feel your thighs gently stretching.

Alternatively you can Push you foot away from your buttocks whilst pushing your pelvis forward. This will increase the stretch potential for your thigh and avoid any overarching; which can often happen when first trying this exercise. Again, repeat between three and five times, slowly.

## Neck and Shoulder

This exercise is started by lying down flat on your back, with your legs extending away from you. Lift both arms straight up towards the ceiling. Then, choose one arm and stretch it up further, as though reaching for something approximately another foot higher. As you do this your body will naturally roll slightly to one side as your shoulder and upper body on the other side lift off the floor. Your waist should stay on the floor.

Hold the position for a few seconds before bringing your arms level again and repeating the move twice more. You will then need to switch sides and do the arm on the other side. Repeat the entire process two or three times, according to how you feel.

There are many different exercises which can be learned to assist with you your recovery from a life of pain. The above are a few ones which will get you started but all the exercises are as simple and effective as this. Somatics is not designed to force movement or place any additional stress on your body. It is a method by which your body can relearn the balance and full range of movement which you were born with and are still capable of. Old age or accidents do not mean a lifetime of pain; these simple exercises will give you a new lease of life!

# Chapter 3: What are somatic symptoms?

Pain

Pain is a sensation of extreme discomfort and abnormal hypersensitivity. It appears as a signal and a warning that something in our bodies is damaged. This could be caused by inflammation or trauma. Pain is the most common symptom. When pain indicates on an injury or inflammation in the body and lasts until the injury is healed, it is helpful and purposeful. However, when the pain lasts even after the injury is healed and becomes chronic, lasts for weeks, months, years, it becomes troublesome and needs treatment. Sometimes we can't find out where the damage is or with which mechanism the pain is induced, especially when there is no damage to any organ. There are different kinds of pain: somatic, visceral, and neuropathic.

Visceral pain comes from internal organs when they are stretched, damaged, or under inflamed. Nerves that surround these organs bring the sensation to our brain, and this pain is deeply aching, difficult to localize, and may increase in intensity and then abate before reappearing. It is difficult to find out where the pain is coming from. Abdominal organs can be the source of visceral pain.

Neuropathic pain appears when there is damage or inflammation of the nerve itself. It sends signals of pain associated with tenderness and numbness. There is no real damage to the surrounding tissue, just damage to the nerves. This can happen in facial neuropathy or in people with diabetes. It is difficult to treat.

Somatic pain is triggered when there is damage to the body surface, joints, tendons, blood vessels, or muscles. This is the most common type of pain. We can say that there are superficial and deep somatic pain. For example, if you cut your hand or finger, you would feel the pain on the certain localisation of the hand, but if you hit your hand on something firm, you experience deep somatic pain, because your joints, muscles, and tendons hurt, and your whole hand hurts as well.

Pain in somatic symptom disorder can't be explained by any known medical condition, even though a doctor has to first exclude somatic and visceral pain aetiology. Pain can affect personal, professional, love, and family life. The mechanism of pain appearance is in somatic disorder due to stress, which triggers the nervous system that stimulates adrenal glands and the sympathetic system, which induces bowel activity. It can be presented as pain or can cause muscular tension, which then hurts. Our perception of pain and the way we notice and bring attention to pain may also play a role. If one has increased sensitivity to pain awareness, he/she may become intensely worried that pain can be in fact a sign of damage in the body. Worrying only increases the intensity of pain.

Pain in somatic symptom disorder is usually located symmetrically, and the most common places are the face and mouth. This pain may be time-related to some stressful situations in a person's life and may prevent him/her from doing some activities. It can also affect the work and personal life.

The most commonly reported pains that are medically unexplained are:

Generalised pain

Face pain

Leg pain

Back pain

Joint pain

Pain when urinating

If pain appears in the last couple of weeks and up to three months, then it is considered as acute pain. Chronic pain lasts more than three months and can be present for years. It can be either constant, which is rare, or amplified along with some stressful situations. Even though they are considered to come "from mind," they are indeed real sensations and can affect a person's life greatly. Other people may not understand it, and a person may experience stigmatised behaviour from others. A person may have some psychological issues that make him/her more sensitive to some sensations, or according to other theories, there may be damage that happened before but didn't completely heal and thus the pain comes from it, but amplified. It is rarely possible for pain to develop entirely from emotional factors.

## Generalised pain and/or fatigue

Generalised pain is pain that spreads all over the body without a proper way to localise the source. Pain can be sharp or dull, depending on the location. It can include distant parts of the body that have no connection to each other, or in places close to each other. A person may complain about pain in the abdomen, one leg, and the head. This pain is usually chronic, and he/she has symptoms for months that induce trouble in their professional and personal life, stopping them from participating in various activities.

In general, all over body pain can be a sign of increased body temperature, chronic fatigue, or some illnesses that affect many joints and/or muscles. When these are excluded from the diagnosis, a doctor will consider fibromyalgia. Generalised pain is characteristic for fibromyalgia. It is an illness of unknown origin, but includes pain all over in various parts of the body. These locations experience pain with just the touch of a finger. It is known to have psychological disorders as a background. The pain they are experiencing is deep, sharp, or dull and can come and go.

However, fibromyalgia doesn't satisfy the criteria for somatic disorder, because there is evidence that in this illness, the nerves are abnormal, and in somatic disorders, there are no anatomical damages at all. This is why when a person comes in with this complaint, he/she should be excluded from all of these illnesses and problems. If the diagnosis is still uncertain, the doctor will consider a different approach.

Generalised pain is most likely caused by stress and increased with anxious thoughts. It can present as pain in the legs, arms, and head simultaneously without any announcement or known pattern. It comes and goes and it can last up to several months. A person may feel pain on various localisations: for example, the chin, arm, leg, or lower abdomen. These couldn't be otherwise explained by any known illnesses. A mechanism of how this happens would be known after the talk with the person. It can be very common with young people, especially women, who find themselves in conflicts with themselves or other significant people, and also, that time may be a transient period when major goals are already achieved or on the way to be achieved. Either way, a person can find himself/herself in a situation under great pressure from others and surrounded with rejection and feelings of being a failure. This can lead a person to have anxiety issues and problems with adjusting. These feelings may last for a long time and are expressing themselves through various ailments. The pain may appear anywhere - in the head, arms, face, back, and can also be associated with some bowel discomfort and pain in the pelvis (in women this is especially in uterus). A person has difficulty in pointing out the exact location of the pain or the situation when it is magnified.

Generalised pain may be associated with known illnesses as aggravating factors. It may worsen the illness itself. It decreases a person's will and ability to participate in activities.

Generalised fatigue or weakness can appear with generalised pain. This fatigue is characteristic for persons who first complained about their symptoms when they were under the age of 30 and have lasted for months or even years. There is confusion between chronic fatigue syndrome and fatigue caused by somatization. Chronic fatigue syndrome has clinical signs (on lymph nodes) that indicate the diagnosis, which can't be said for the latter. Somatization fatigue is present along with other somatization symptoms such as gynaecological or abdominal discomfort. Fatigue itself isn't a symptom of somatization disorder. (14) Generalised or localised weakness may also be a part of conversion disorder in young people.

## Face pain

Face pain appears very often in the population (12%). Face pain usually spreads in the area of the upper, middle, or lower part of the face. There is a term that doctors refer to as atypical facial pain (persistent idiopathic facial pain). It is present in the same prevalence in men as in women. The pain often crosses the midline of the face and is described as stabbing, throbbing, or burning. It lasts more than three months and usually, a person would complain about numbness, pain, or tingling in one particular part of the face. It gets worse in stressful life-changing events. The first professional they turn to is usually a dentist. After diagnostic procedures and an exam, the right cause isn't found.

There is also a condition that is referred to as myofascial pain dysfunction syndrome. It is the pain around the teeth and in the jaws, pain in the jaw joint, and sensations in the mouth. It is very common for pain to be localised around the mouth area. Myofascial pain dysfunction syndrome is associated with pain in the jaw joints, pain while chewing and speaking, or moving chewing muscles in any way. This disorder is strongly related to depression and somatization and can appear along with other somatization symptoms. (15) A person may be very concerned about the pain because it appears so frequently during the day and with almost every movement of the jaw. A person may also experience trouble sleeping. The stressful component in causality is the tension of the muscle in people who are more sensitive to stressful events because of certain mild or severe psychological traumas previously experienced. Face and jaw pain are also related to stress and anxiety.

## Back pain

Back pain is very common in our population. It can be caused by muscle injury or inflammation, spine malposition, illness of kidneys, pancreas, gallbladder, or nervous system problems. People who experience back pain have difficulties in everyday working life and find it as stressful and frustrating as the job itself (16). This is due to stress and its effect on the muscles of the back and neck that can't relax properly. These people often visit the doctor's office in search of a reason for back pain, and they regularly have other signs of somatic symptom disorder as well, like arm pain, headaches, chronic fatigue syndrome, etc. Usually, they have already been to physical medical specialists and have been given exercise samples to strengthen the muscles, even though that didn't help. With some of them, there are signs of depression and anxiety, but that isn't necessarily obligatory for somatizers. Back pain in somatization is atypical. Between 10 and 20% of all people who suffer from somatization have back pain problems. Back pain is related to anxiety and depression. Neck and back stiffness are more reported in persons with post-traumatic stress syndrome and phobias of open spaces. There is a type of personality in which back pain is more common than others. People that are well-organised, responsible, hard-working, and are self-critical tend to be under great stress, even though they tend to push it to the subconscious. Some of them have some repressed memories or troubling issues from early development. The relation between them is inexplicable. Back pain is very resistant to treatment, and a lot of work needs to be put into the therapy. A person also needs to organise activity and rest since they are very important in treatment. Also, a healthcare provider will try to find out about some emotional issue that might be bothering the person. They too need to be resolved in order for treatment to work.

Back pain can vary from mild to severe. If touched or pressed, certain muscles are stiff and painful. A person may also feel numbness, tingling, or burning pain.

In somatic symptom disorders, back pain (previously referred to as tension myositis syndrome) is caused by tension and stressful situations. Tension myositis syndrome is a psychosomatic pain disorder. The sympathetic autonomic system is activated with stressful events that induce emotional reaction and then stimulate muscles of blood vessels. As a response, it constricts and blood supply begins to lower. This affects massive muscles of the back and their function since they don't get enough oxygen and nutrition. This leads to the accumulation lactic acid, which is responsible for pain.

People usually complain about back or neck pain that moves from one spot to another. Pressing some spots on the back may be followed by intense pain all over the muscle. Because of the pain, people frequently change their sleep position. Thus, they become chronically tired. (17) This type of pain is similar to myofascial pain, where the pain originates from the fascia (outer layer of the muscle) and muscles. Pressure on certain spots on the back triggers pain in the whole area. Myofascial neck pain spreads pain to the face (temporal region) after putting pressure on the back of the neck. There aren't any clinical studies that differentiate myofascial back pain from somatized back pain, and it might be that they have a mixed pathophysiology.

### *Leg pain*

Leg pain can be in one part of the leg or in the whole leg, as well as in both legs. Also, it can appear while doing nothing i.e. sitting or while standing or walking. Various illnesses of the internal organs can be followed with changes in the leg. Pain in the leg is mostly neurologic (diabetes, ischialgia) or from varicose veins or joint pain. Pain in the leg can be in the form of cramps, deep pain, pain when walking that is sharp, dull pain, etc. In conditions that may be considered as somatic disorder, leg pain is caused sometimes by anxiety. The mechanism of this pain may seem unbelievable, but negative and worrying thoughts can actually increase sensitivity in the legs. This condition isn't rare. The pain can be caused by anxiety attacks, when muscles of blood vessels contract and deprive the legs of oxygen and tighten the muscles of the leg, which causes pain. In somatic symptom disorder, these symptoms last longer than the anxiety attack. It is hard distinguishing between the two. Pain in the leg may be disabling and last for months and years without a known cause.

Numbness, tingling, or even paralysis can appear as a symptom of conversion disorder in young people. In some cases, after an accident that's been avoided, they sometimes convert the stress and emotional shock into actual symptoms.

### Joint pain

Joint pain may be associated with inflammation or injury. It may also be associated with muscle pain. When declared as a somatic symptom disorder, it is very difficult determining what the main cause is and is often associated with other somatization symptoms. Knee joint pain is the most often reported somatic symptom that affects joints. Most of the studies actually proved that pain in the jaw joint can be affected and influenced by psychological disorders.

## Unexplained menstrual symptoms

First, menstruation occurs when all the body factors are set to specific parameters, which depends on the height, weight, production of hormones, percentage of fat in the body, as well as a normal, unimpeded psychological structure. This is all regulated by hormones in the pituitary gland, which is regulated by the hypothalamus in the centre of the brain. As for later functioning and regular menstrual cycles, they too are controlled by the pituitary gland and the hypothalamus, but they receive various stimuli, including environmental and stressful factors. It reacts when a person is under huge stress, which impairs the production of hormones (estrogen and progestin), which then leads to irregular menstruation and even absence of it. Factors that can also affect menstrual disorders can be: over exercise, weight loss, and eating disorders, which all have some psychological background and induce exhaustion. Chronic stress as well as short term worrying and having anxious thoughts of one particular event/subject may have all the same effect on menstrual bleeding.

Other menstrual problems may be excessive pain during menstruation such as dysmenorrhea and irregular bleeding between two menstruation cycles. Even pain during menstruation can be influenced by psychological issues and can be a form of expression. It develops similarly as other types of pain. Usually, a person may amplify the pain perception because of some subconscious anxious or depressive content, and menstruation becomes more painful. Painful menstruation related to stress is linked to 75% of adolescent girls. Irregular bleedings may also be explained with somatization. This, however, happens with great pressure and stress on the person, and happens rarely. The bleeding isn't usually profuse.

Menstrual symptoms are often associated with other somatic symptoms like gastrointestinal symptoms as well as with back and joint pain. Some sexual difficulties may be a part of the complaints. Menstrual symptoms may vary from mild to severe.

## Unexplained sexual symptoms

It is more and more a subject of various discussions how the psyche affects the sex life. Usually, there could be some obvious life problems that put pressure on both of the partners, or there is a body complaint of any kind that brings discomfort to both of them. The key to a happy relationship is good communication between two partners, even if problems about different topics and not just within the relationship are making a person more stressed and frustrated. He/she may not be aware of the large amount of stress he/she struggles with, but with more deep talk, he/she discovers that sexual problems have begun or are in some way linked to certain events or feelings.

Sometimes, a person is already having trouble but considers it to be just the way things are, or the partner doesn't understand the situation. A lot of people bring their frustrations and insecurities into this delicate part of life. The negative background expresses itself through the inability to relax and through anhedonia, not just in sexual life, but also in the professional and family life. A person becomes unmotivated and unhappy, which turns the cycle around. The problems that are frequently reported are pain during intercourse and erectile dysfunction.

## Pain during intercourse (dyspareunia)

Dyspareunia is pain associated with vaginal intercourse. It can appear in women as in men, but in men, it is just recently discovered that the problem exists. Women are frequently confronted with this problem, which then brings other problems as well. Pain during intercourse appears in between 10 and 20%

of the female population. However, the reasons for this could be infections, sexual indifference, problems with lubrication, and vaginismus. Most of them except infections are caused by psychological factors: anxiety, worry about performance, fear of pain, etc. The severe type of dyspareunia and pain in the pelvis comprise a smaller part of those women. These women, not surprisingly, have sexual intercourse less frequently and have more interpersonal problems with their partners, which may lead to discord in marriage.

Vaginismus has already been proven to be directly linked to a woman's psyche. Vaginismus is the appearance of pain because of involuntary muscle spasms inside the vagina, which causes problems during intercourse. It appears when a woman is anxious about sex or inserting tampons or medical objects during a gynecological examination. Pain can appear during entry or deep inside. It is unexplained or simply called dyspareunia when we exclude vaginism as a possible diagnosis. Most women actually don't report this problem to their gynaecologists, which raises a question of how often does it actually appear in the population. Psychologists have found a particular attachment and self-confidence problems with women who complained about pain during intercourse. Some inner frustrations and tension are expressing in a way of pain in the lower pelvis. (28) The reason may lie in inner or external conflicts as well as stress and tension of sexual intercourse. Somatization pain may be different from vaginismus, such as persistent Kegel's pelvic exercises. In vaginismus, women, particularly gynaecologists, can feel the stiffness of the vaginal wall due to muscle spasms. Dyspareunia seems to be unfit for any other similar diagnosis and requires psychological evaluation. Women usually say that the symptoms are present for more than 6 months.

Women are affected by this as well as their partners. They may have problems with self-image and motivation to conceive, and often they feel incapable or unfit. Continued and unsuccessful attempts and high expectations make it even worse, and sometimes a man may, as a consequence, develop some sexual issues such as erectile dysfunction.

Pelvic pain is the pain in the lower abdomen that is frequently noticed in women who had suffered sexual abuse. When they feel real pain, they may not necessarily consciously link it to what has happened in the past. Also, unresolved depression and anxiety problems cause the problem to stay persistent.

### Unexplained headaches

Headaches are the most common severe symptom in adults. Half of the population has some kind of a headache with mild to severe characteristics. Headaches are actually often left unexplained or developed from the influence of many factors combined. It is unsurprisingly the most bothering symptom. A person can't function properly at work and can't control his/her emotions. They'll have problems in general, day-to-day functions such as concentrating, driving, etc.

Headaches develop from cardiovascular, neurological, psychological, or some other body problem such as dehydration or high fever. If all other organ functions are fine, we still have many possible causes. Exact mechanism of the development of a migraine is unknown, even though cardiovascular factors and chemical imbalances are found to be responsible. A person may complain of headaches that happen with explainable reasons and in certain situations (after too much chocolate, cheese, caffeine, or alcohol). Others have headaches once or twice every month, with tendency to chronicity. Localisation of pain may vary. Some complain of pain on one side, or back of the head, forehead, or in the whole head. Localisation may suggest the type of headache. Psychological factors have proven to be responsible in pathogenesis.

It has been known and proven that when a person struggles with pain, he/she can't take their minds off the pain. When this happens, the effect of medication might not be able to help them because of their expectations from the medications. From the early days of medical history, doctors have been practising the placebo medication treatment with such patients, and they proved to be valuable. Nowadays, new studies suggest that we would expect the pain to go away at the exact moment as we ingest it, but thinking that way only makes the pain stronger since pain is a sensation created by the brain as an alarming sensation of damage of the tissue. Same but opposite, we may not think that the medicine is going to work, so we lower our expectations and stop thinking about its effect, which then leads to less pain relief. These mechanisms seem complex and not well-known for now. However, psychological and voluntary influences are able to modify pain, or even create it.

Somatization of psychological issues is often the explanation for a headache. A certain type of personality is more likely to develop somatization headache. These people are responsible, busy, and under great emotional stress. Some personalities are subconsciously creating an image of something worse that would happen, or have fear of pain itself, so they subconsciously create or enhance pain. Scientists again can't accept the theory about emotional factors creating the pain, so there could be more factors included. For psychologists, a problem seems easier.

People struggling with headache have no knowledge of when a headache might strike, and so they have big problems when it does. With lack of concentration, patience, and attention to environment, a person may have difficulties at work or at home and may injure himself/herself. Episodes of headaches usually have been present for more than 6 months. Headaches with a psychological background are a pain in the entire head, with pressure or tension (this is why sometimes it may be called tension headache), light or sound nuisance. Anything opposing to migraine criteria for diagnosis is better explained as somatization, if it's associated with other symptoms as well, and otherwise, we can call it tension headache. Somatization disorder may include headaches associated with gastrointestinal symptoms or abdominal pain, with pain in the back, arms, or legs. A stressful situation may be the onset of the headache, and if the temporary situation becomes chronic stress, the headache becomes chronic too.

Somatoform headache in children and adolescents appear in every tenth person. It usually follows the pattern of pain observed in their parents, which tells about parental influence in the pathogenesis.

# Chapter 4: Be Aware

## Mind what You Put into Your Body

Living mindfully means bringing yourself to a full sense of awareness about you and your body. And if you've been living the same busy lifestyle as so many others, chances are you haven't really given much thought to the types of fuel you've been living on.

This isn't going to be some sermon on how you should be living like a vegan or cutting out red meat or restricting your carbohydrate access. But the food you eat should be nourishing. Read the packaging carefully to see what vitamins and minerals each is providing you, care less about calories and more about chemicals and avoid as many as you can and put together a meal that can meet the energy demands of your lifestyle. There are several websites and smartphone apps that can help you determine what each food is providing you with. Use these to your advantage to create a diet that will nourish you, not just fill you up.

Of course, some junk foods, treats, desserts and even drinks may still find themselves lingering around your kitchen. And that's okay in moderation. This isn't about condemning particular food groups, or about judging you for not being the healthiest person on the block. Rather, this is to make you aware of the food you eat and aware of the way the food fuels your body.

## Eat and Drink Slowly

If you're like most busy professionals, breakfast is something of a blur, lunch is probably nonexistent and supper is a blend of storytelling, last minute cleaning, and checking on tasks still left over from work. It's time to stop all of that. Eating mindfully means savoring each bite. Relishing every sip. Appreciating every breath you hold to swallow and the feeling of satisfaction as the food makes its journey down your esophagus. It means taking the time to really enjoy your meal and the nourishment that it is bringing to you. Additionally, listen to your body. Stop eating once your body is satisfied and nourished. No more worrying about whether or not you've cleaned your plate. No more eating so much food you feel sick and bloated.

Stay in the moment with each bite. Your body will feel better for it and so will you. Feel the textures bump against your tongue. Breathe in deep right before you take a bite and savor the aroma of each ingredient. Having a burger? Close your eyes and concentrate on each and every topping: the way the pickles dance against the beef. The way the cheese sticks briefly to the roof of your mouth. The way the buttered roll crunches slightly when you bite down into it. The way the acid in the mustard teases at your senses and sets the nerves at the back of your tongue on fire. Savor every moment of your bite.

### Take Your Day One Step at a Time

Multitasking is a wonderful and often desirable skill to have. However, without proper discipline, multitasking can quickly take over your life. When was the last time you sat down to eat and just ate? When was the last time you did anything without also either thinking about the past or planning out a bit of the future? Ever take a shower in the morning and not try to also map out your day? Ever take a bath at night and not think about everything you tried to do that day? To live mindfully means that while you are brewing yourself a cup of coffee, for that moment, that is all you are doing. No running to grab the paper real quick, no stepping over the cat to shove some bread into the toaster, and no sorting out the day's to-do list in your head as you stir in the creamer.

**Just brew the coffee.**

Have you ever seen a coffee commercial on television before? Are the people in the commercial ever enjoying their coffee while they run around, dodging each other's briefcases and tossing kisses at their children? No. In those moments of chaos and pandemonium, it's hard to even recognize what good can come from a cup of coffee.

But then the moment comes. The music slows down. The steam wafting up from the cup of coffee tickles the person's nostrils, and he or she smiles and closes his or her eyes. Then, the sip. They hold the coffee in their mouth for a moment, then swallow and lick their lips.

That is the epitome of mindful living.

Once you've finished brewing the coffee, move on to the next task, whatever that may be.

### Move Slowly and Deliberately

Rushing through the task at hand is a sign of multitasking: you're trying to hurry so you can get to doing something else. For example, maybe you're speeding on the drive home so you can hurry up and get supper started. Rushing through one task in hopes of starting another task isn't staying in the moment. It's allowing the future to try to take over your thoughts again, and bring with it anxiety and stress.

Stick with one thing at a time, and give it your full attention. Make sure every second you spend on that activity is planned and deliberate. Doing this will help you to keep from rushing and possibly making mistakes.

During that drive home, try to monitor your breathing. Stuck at a red light? Rather than tapping your fingers anxiously awaiting the green signal to carry about your trip, try taking in a deep breath and thinking about how comfortable your seat is. Take a look around you and try wishing each person also stopped at the light a nice day. Concentrate on how the steering wheel feels gripped between your fingers. How the gum you're chewing feels as you gnash your teeth.

Take in each moment of the drive. Make each moment purposeful and meaningful, and you will find the drive to be more enjoyable.

# Chapter 5: Meditation and Psychiatric Conditions

More and more studies are being done to see what link there is between the different types of meditation and psychiatric conditions and what is being found is very interesting indeed. The kind of meditation that has proven popular with people who are looking for peace of mind or may have been anxious or depressed are mindful meditation, transcendental meditation and Buddhist meditation and all have been found to be beneficial for different reasons.

However, the basic premise of these being beneficial is gleaned from the same reasons. One is able to slow down the mind, to take control of the thoughts and in the process of doing this is more capable of coming to wiser conclusions. These types of meditation have been used in substance abuse centers for years and help those with problems to get their lives back on track. Since meditation is long term, it means a changing of ways, and the changes that are made during meditation really are important to those who would previously have been treated by psychiatric care:

●One becomes more focused in life

●The cognitive skills are improved

●Panics are less likely to occur

●Fears can be overcome or controlled

●Life's crises can be put into perspective

●Practitioners of meditation are less likely to self-abuse

You can see from this that people gain a better perspective of their lives and that they are able to overcome many obstacles using this method, rather than traditional methods of psychiatric treatment.

Thus, this helps them to gain better control of their lives. Since this is long term, it also means that people become more aware of the needs of the body and mind and are able to see things from a much healthier perspective. Thus, they are unlikely to make bad choices and are much more likely to live balanced lives which include the right foods, the right amount of exercise and the right amount of rest and relaxation. One patient who was an addict explained his experience and felt that his meditation practice helped him to respect his body and mind. He felt that his teacher had taken his mind back to basics and had reconstructed it, because the drug use had literally torn his life apart. Now, forty years later, the calmness that was learned through meditation is the only reminder of the folly of his youth, but it's a valuable reminder that has strengthened him through all kinds of indecision in the day to day running of his life.

One of the things that is highlighted in many illnesses of a psychiatric nature is that subjects find it difficult to sleep. Sleep is a vital factor when it comes to day to day health and wellbeing and without that sleep, the psychiatric problems can be exaggerated and brought to the forefront because people become too tired to deal with their problems.

However, introduce meditation and life becomes easier to manage. People also learn to breathe correctly and that helps the levels of oxygen in the body to normalize. If you have ever seen someone in a panic breathing into a paper bag, it's done for a very good reason. When people panic, they tend to breathe in too much air and the levels of oxygen in the body become too high. When you breathe into a bag, you rebreathe the same air and thus bring those levels down.

Breathing

The fact that meditation circles around breathing means that it's a natural thing, and that people who learn to breathe in the way that meditators do will be able to get more control over themselves and their situations. People who have suffered from bereavement will be able to find a little peace away from depressive thought. Those who suffer from anxiety will also be able to find more control through the breathing methods that are taught.

Coupled with relaxation exercises, therefore, meditation really can be of help to those who are seeking to overcome obstacles placed in their lives by psychiatric conditions. That does not, however, mean that this should replace any pills or medications that are prescribed to a patient. In fact, it would be dangerous to stop treatments without proper supervision and if this is your intention, you need to talk to professionals so that they can work through the process with you, so that you are not making changes to your body that are drastic for your body to take. For example, some serotonin enhancers in the way of medications work long term and cutting them instantly can return the patient to a very low feeling. Thus, if you want to try meditation, then this should be included in your treatment at first, rather than replacing it. Many of the medications today are for long term, build up use, so please do talk to your professional before making changes to prescription medications. All I can do is point out the benefits, but every individual will be different and their needs will be different. All I can say for sure is that meditation will help people whose lives are troubled by anxiety, depression or mood swings. Lack of sleep will also be tackled, as will over-eating and meditation can even help with eating disorders.

# Chapter 6: Meditation for Stress Relief

Before we proceed with this guided meditation, I want you to find the most comfortable place in your house or office. Find a place where you can lie down entirely and feel at ease with your own body. My advice is to use a yoga mat or anything soft, so that you can spend the next several minutes in complete harmony with your body and with who you are, without thinking of pain, stress, what you have to do today at work or what you left undone at work, what college your kids are going to, or even what to eat tomorrow.

Find a place where it's just you and your body, and then lie down. If you need more comfort, bring a pillow or a blanket to prop your legs up or to support your head more. You should not feel distracted by anything, not even a sore inch of your body. The entire duration of this guided meditation is meant to make you feel fresh and anew. It is meant to give you a reboot, both mentally and physically.

Alright now. Are you lying down? Do you feel comfortable? And most importantly, do you feel that you could stay there, like that, for the next fifteen minutes?

If you do, then let's go on.

Lie down and make sure you do not put any kind of stress on your body. This body is here to sustain your life on Earth, so treat it kindly every time you can. It is a sacred mechanism you have been given so that you can fulfill your goals. Your biggest dreams. Your most hidden, secret aspirations.

This body is all yours. Nobody has the right to do anything with it that you don't want them to. Not even yourself.

So lie down, stretch out your legs, and make sure your neck is not stiff. Let your whole body be loose. Let yourself go in the most meaningful way there is. Every muscle in your body deserves to be nothing less than 100% comfortable now. YOU deserve to be comfortable.

You have a whole world of stress and anxiety to deal with outside of this little bubble of comfort you have created for yourself here—but that world is **outside**. And you are here, perfectly in tune with your body, with who you are, with everything the world has given you, perfectly accommodated on this floor or on this bed you have chosen to use while walking the path of meditation with me.

Nothing bad can happen to you here, and the positive feelings you will gain throughout this meditation will overflow into your external life as well. You will smile more. You will be kinder to yourself and those around you. You will emanate nothing but light. Eventually, all stress will disappear as well, and for the first time in what is most likely a long time, you will finally be able to think clearly. You will finally be able to remove the dark clouds of stress and anxiety from your life and see it as it is: a gift, an opportunity, your own game in your own house.

How does your body feel right now? Do you feel the need to adjust a little? If so, do it slowly. You don't have to be anywhere right now, other than here, with your own mind and with your own body. You don't have to do anything else than treat yourself kindly and allow your body to fully relax.

There are hundreds of muscles in your body helping you move every day, helping you feed yourself, helping you talk, helping you smile, and helping you breathe. The muscles in your body are one of the main reasons you can **function** every day at your pace. Treat them kindly, for they are there to stay with you not for today or tomorrow only, but for the rest of your life.

Slowly start to relax as you continue lying down. Breathe in deeply. Breathe out. Inhale. Exhale. Deep and slow. You have all the time in the world right now. No rush, no deadlines, no places to be, no mad bosses to handle. You are everything and you are sufficient. Right here, on your mat, or on your bed, you are you in the fullest and most meaningful sense of the world.

There's nobody who can take you from this state of full and complete relaxation.

Because you are **enough** and you are the only one who can control your life. Not your parents, not your boss, not your family, not your friends, not anyone on TV.

Just you.

You have a purpose here, and you are on your way to making your dreams come true because this wonderful body you have been gifted with, in its own shape, covered in a skin that is its own shade, is more than enough. Your muscles are now soft because you have finally given them time to take a break.

As you relax, you feel like you are sinking into the ground. You feel that everything around you has been liquified, and you feel that every inch of your body becomes the surrounding space. There is no boundary between you and the bubble of relaxation and wellness surrounding you.

You are one.

One with yourself.

One with your past.

One with your present.

One with your future.

You are enough and you have more than enough time on your hands to do everything you want.

What is it that you want to do?

What is your final purpose?

To build something? To raise your children beautifully? To achieve a life of equilibrium and wellbeing that emanates grace, just like the music you are listening to right now does?

Of course, you can do all that—and more! Because nature has engineered you to do it; it has given you a body that can help you do it and a brain that is able to control every single second of your life in a relaxed, gracious, beautiful way.

Your back is fully aligned with the surface you are lying on. There is no strain on it. There is no strain on your life anymore because from here on out you have taken control of every single inch and every single second of who you are and where you are and the time at which you are now.

Your fingers are completely unwound, and your palms are facing the world, ready to absorb all the positive energy in the universe. You are enough. Your body is enough as it is. Nothing can deter you from the path of pure success and happiness that lies ahead of you.

Deadlines do not exist. They are imaginary boundaries the world has placed on you. The only reason you adhere to them is because you feel that you have to.

But in reality, you don't have to do anything at all. Just be yourself. And yourself is enough.

Breathe in deeply and absorb this state of wellbeing into your body and into your mind. This is your moment to recharge yourself before you go out again and handle everything in an efficient way. A way that leaves stress at the door, outside of your space of beauty and grace.

Your legs have sunk into the ground, and they have become one with it. From the tip of your thumbs to the top of your head, everything is fully at ease.

You don't have to run anywhere. You don't have to chase anything or anyone. You just have to be with yourself, because you are the perfect mechanism—one that is fueled with clean air and positive energy only. One that is at ease.

No nerve in your body should feel any tension now.

You are one with everything, and everything is one with you. You are absorbing everything that's good in the universe and leaving behind everything that's bad. Yes, stressful situations happen, but from this moment on, you are handling them with a focused mind and a new, energized, recharged battery.

Everything is mellow and soft around you, and you are sinking into this state of complete balance and love. Everything and everyone around you loves you, and you love them back. And from the infinite love in which you are sinking now, the face of the person you love so much appears.

They are smiling back at you and taking your hand, slowly leading you to the place where you went out on your first date or a place that means something to you. You still cherish that memory so much! With all that's been going on lately, though, you might feel that you have forgotten this memory and shoved it to the back of your mind where no beam of light ever reaches.

But your loved one is there to finally open the door to that place and let that wonderful feeling of excitement and sheer joy beam throughout all the darkness of the room it has been hiding in, exploding into a state that is nothing but pure energy.

You see your loved one smiling so happy that they have brought this memory back to your attention and so happy that they were able to shed the darkness and allow light back into your mind.

You go back to that moment and you can feel everything that is surrounding it: the perfume of the place; the beauty of your loved one; the light in the room or the sunset that was setting down on the two of you; the heat of the moment; the fact that, back then, it was just the two of you and all the dreams you shared with each other, and all the jokes, and all the minutes of bliss that brought you to love them deeply, uncontrollably, madly, and irremediably.

Your loved one is laughing with you, remembering a sweet moment of that first date or that time in space. They are taking your hand and bring the palms of your hands together, to absorb all the good energy of that moment and bring it to the center of your mind.

This is the well from which you will fuel yourself with grace and beauty from here on out. No matter what happens, you will always have this amazing memory that makes you smile every single time. It is right there, at the very core of your mind, radiating happiness and relaxation and goodness all around you.

It is where you will go every time you feel the need to, now that you have finally pulled this memory out of the attic and you are ready to take on the world, knowing that you have an unbreakable shield of strength that can protect you from everything negative and stressful in your life.

Your loved one is slowly fading away now that they have made their purpose clear and now that they have created a moment of sheer joy you can always go back to, knowing that you can hydrate your mind with positivity and grace every time you feel like drowning in deadlines, anxiety, and the overall stress of modern life.

Your loved one's image is fading out, but you hold on to the feeling of miraculous discovery, of sheer passion and calmness. The feeling, the emotion, will never fade completely, not when you are out in the world and not when you are here, with my voice, in this bubble of earnestness and beaming goodness.

Breathe in and out, slowly. Maintain a rhythm of breathing that is in full accord with your life and with everything you have ever done. This is you here, nobody else, and you are not defined by anything other than the good things that have happened to you so far, the beautiful memories, the people who love you most. Deadlines are nothing more than man-made limits. Speed is unnecessary in a world where everyone is heading in the same direction. Stress is futile because you are in full control of your emotions, of your actions, of your thoughts, and of the ways in which you achieve your own dreams.

In, out, in, out.

Right now, the core of your body feels warm and fuzzy, just like that memory you are holding on to. It feels that nothing can break this center of strength and beauty, like nothing can derail you now from your path to happiness.

This core is the essence of everything you are amazing at. It might be that you make the best cookies in the world. It might be that you sing divinely. It might be that nobody can handle a spreadsheet as well as you do. Whatever it is, your core is made of the positive thoughts, the amazing memories, and the things you are absolutely best at.

Let this core of **you** expand slowly, reaching out past its imaginary boundaries and overflowing into your entire abdominal cavity and chest. Take your time; this will overflow in its own rhythm, just like the lava of a volcano reaches every crack of soil without rush, without a deadline, without being anything else than lava.

The warmth in you is not destructive, though. It is only goodness, for the parts of your body this warm feeling reaches are blessed with energy, aptitude, loving grace, and miracle. Every inch of your body that is touched by this river of fuzziness that has sprung from your core is meant to be perfect just the way it is.

You are OK. You are MORE than OK. You are the kind of person that can really move mountains, precisely because your core is made out of the things that truly define you: love, compassion, the power to change, and the power to be kind.

The feeling of warmth has now reached your lower abdominal cavity and you can feel it flowing over the body itself into its extremities. Your shoulders and your hips are the first ones to feel this amazing energy that is filling out your entire being. And from there on, your elbows and your knees will feel it too.

It's a slow process, but there's no need to rush anywhere. In this bubble you have created, time has simply ceased to exist because time is nothing but a relative, man-made concept. This is the absolute zero of time—the moment from which the entire universe has sprung from. And you are there, one with the absence of time, one with the absence of any physical restriction.

By now, the fuzzy feeling has overflown into every inch of your body. Your toes, the tip of your nose, your eyes, your brain, and even your hair—they are all gracefully embraced by this feeling of utter well being and relaxation. And from here, you start to overflow your state of calmness into your bubble and everything surrounding it.

Because you have the power to bring this not only upon you but on everyone that comes into contact with you. In fact, right now, the main source of your stress outside the bubble you have created with yourself is looking at you. And you feel nothing but kindness.

You want to show them that you are enough and that your entire being is capable of creating pure positivity.

You reach out your hand and touch theirs with a firm, but gentle touch. At first, they are skeptical to receive anything from you, even if it's just a simple touch. But the more you reach out to them, the better it is. You are giving them some of your light and watching them being taken over by it.

They slowly start to become much less reticent to everything you are and everything you are sharing with them because there is nothing more and nothing less than beauty between the two of you. This might be your boss, it might be a negative person in your family, or it might be an object in itself. But right now, you can see nothing wrong and nothing dark in them, just the pure light you are sharing with them, watching them melt down their own walls and become one with this bubble of calmness.

The threat of their stress is basically null right now. It simply does not exist, the same way as nothing existed before the world and the universe were created. The negativity they had been bombarding you with is not there anymore, and as you start to fill them with this positive feeling, they start to melt down, and they reach out to you with their other hand.

You are now holding both of their hands, transferring goodness and calmness. Because, no matter who they are and what they do, people deserve to know you are this amazing source of power, efficiency, and courage.

They start to smile back at you, flooded with the positive emotions you have been sharing with them. And, the more they smile, the more they want to hug you, and you want to share this embrace.

You are slowly approaching each other, ready to embrace each other as you are. You are enough. They are enough. And this moment and this feeling of purity and love and commitment to goodness are enough.

Their image slowly starts to fade away, but as this happens, you hold on to this emotion of grandeur and ultimate power. You have beaten your worst enemy, the thing that has been darkening your days and nights, the thing that was the main source of negativity and stress in your life.

From here on out, you not only **manage** each other. You **are** each other, and you are enough in the world and you know that your goodness and your calmness can contain anything negative that may come from them. You know that you can share with them this feeling of utter beauty, and you know that they will never affect you the way they have been doing until now.

Because whatever the reason behind your struggle may have been, it is now over. You have won over it, not by clenching your fists and baring your teeth, but by loving them as they are and by allowing them into your bubble of calm and relaxing vibrations.

As you realize you have the power to change not only yourself and your own mindset, but also show it to the world that you are enough, you slowly start to come back to your room as well. Your core is filled with nothing but greatness now, because you are worthy of it and because you have created this within you, with that one good memory you had.

If one great event from the past can do so much for you, can you imagine how it would feel to open the door to every small joy and big achievement you have ever had? Can you imagine a life where you don't have to roam the halls of your life, hiding in fear of what might happen next, because you KNOW for a fact that you are enough and that you can do anything, beyond time restrictions, beyond physical restrictions, beyond whatever others might say and do to you?

You are everything you have. The body on this floor is everything you need. The mind that controls it and who you are is all that you should ever turn to to make your dreams come true, to achieve a life of perfect balance and harmony.

You cannot change others. You cannot change the past, You cannot change all that is bad in the world. They will always continue to be there. But from here on out, you have a core of strength and light you can easily turn to whenever times get rough. You have a life of happiness and excitement and love and compassion and kindness to share. You can control how others make you feel because you know, deep inside, that you are who you are and they are who they are and embracing them and everything life throws your way means using less of your energy to make this a bad situation for you and more of it to turn it around and transform it into a cascade of more and more happy memories.

Your body is slowly returning to its shape, maintaining the same amount of energy within it as you felt it at the peak of its light overflow. As you come back, you feel your legs have become yours again, and the tips of your toes start to be **there** more than any time before. You can move them slowly, just a little, just to feel what an amazing thing it is that you can control them, that your brain can send an order and your toes can execute without fault.

The same happens with everything in your life. Your brain can send an order and everything else will fall into place to make it come true. The materialization of your love is precisely that: the power your brain has to not only recharge itself and your body but also to show the world that you are powerful and that you can overcome anything you want. Because you are a gift for the world and the world is a gift for you.

Your fingers start to come to their senses too. As you breathe in and out, you slowly start to acknowledge your physical space. You are on your mat or lying down on the bed, and you feel the warmth of your environment and the light, and you slowly start to become conscious of my voice again.

Breathe in and out. Take your time. No rush. It's just you and this voice and the energy you have been building inside of you all this time.

You are here. Now. Breathing air because your body can do this. Holding on to the positivity and calmness you have gained because your mind can do this.

Take a very deep breath and, with your eyes closed, pull your body into a sitting position. Don't rush anywhere, there is no hurry. Inhale and exhale. Sit up in a lotus position or however else you feel comfortable in (maybe you want your legs stretched out or just slightly bent?). Breathe.

The air you breathe in fuels the wonderful feeling of calm, relaxation, and gratitude you have been working toward during this break.

Slowly breathe in and out, deeply. Open your eyes. Start to wiggle your toes and your fingers. Look ahead of you. There's a life of amazing grace waiting for you once you exit your room and start facing your tasks.

They might not always be easy. But what is important is that you now know that you have the power and the energy to handle everything.

# Chapter 7: Tools Needed to Meditate

Lots of people are under the impression that you need to invest money into meditation, but you don't need to at all. The things that you are likely to need are simple. You may need a yoga mat for comfort that is not a costly item and it can be very useful to have one because this means that when you meditate outdoors, you can use this to protect yourself and cushion yourself from the ground. This is something that is useful for other things than meditation, so it isn't a huge investment and can be used on the beach. It may also be a good idea to have a small cushion. This is used to sit on, as many people cannot achieve the lotus position easily since they are not accustomed to sitting in that pose and may have limbs that are not flexible enough to get comfortable in the lotus pose.

I don't want to add a lot of illustrations to the book, but the lotus pose leg position isn't comfortable for people who are starting off with meditation. There's too much bend of the legs and it's not easy for people to tuck their feet in. Thus, if you sit and bend your knees and cross your ankles, you will find it a whole lot more comfortable if you have a cushion to prop up your behind. You can use a meditation stool if you prefer and some people find that this gives their back much better support.

It's a common misconception that you have to sit in any one given position to meditate. You don't. As long as you have a comfortable position, even a chair will be good enough. Those who do yoga and Buddhist meditation tend to choose this position because it's a good position to ground yourself and after achieving the lotus or beginner lotus, they tend to put their hands face upward onto their knees. This helps them to stay focused on what they are doing.

You will need loose clothing, but don't necessarily have to spend money on fancy gear. That's your choice. Avoid clothing that has a tight waistband or anything that is uncomfortable and likely to draw your mind away from the meditation that you are about to do. Thus, even if you choose your most comfortable pajamas, these are very adequate for meditation.

Other things are really up to you. You may want to create a space within your home where you meditate and add things to it that you find to be inspirational. Some people like to have a Buddha statue. Others like candles and scents. However, remember that the main purpose of meditation is concentrating inwardly, so these are not the most important things in the world.

There is something that I found to be very helpful. I bought a set of beads for meditation for a specific purpose. When you are meditating, you are asked to concentrate on something – whether it's the environment around you as in the case of mindfulness meditation – or your breathing in the case of other types of meditation, but you may also be expected to count. I found that by using meditation beads, I could cut out the counting and simply move onto the next bead and that this acted as my counting method thus taking away one more thing to think about. For people who have very active minds, like I had when I started, these can really help because then you can concentrate on the breath rather than the counting.

There are some beautiful beads on Amazon.com for meditating and once you have circled the whole set of beads, you will know that you have reached the number of 108. Instead of going back to one again when you start to think of other things, you merely feel your way back to the beginning of the beads again and this works a treat.

Although none of the extras are essential to your practice, I also found that having an Om singing bowl was useful. With one of these, which you can obtain on markets or on Amazon, you can set the mood for meditation because the sound that you make with the bowl is so mellow. The sound is produced when you move the mallet around the rim of the bowl and as well as being very aesthetically pleasing, I find that slowing down from the busy day is actually enhanced by starting a meditation sessions with a little Om from the bowl.

Of course none of the items that I have suggested are obligatory, but they may just help enhance your meditation and help you to enjoy your retreat into the world of meditation. Anything that positively enhances your experience or that gives you the incentive to ensure that you practice daily is worth it. These could also be little things that you ask friends for, for Christmas, or you can improvise and make things to fit into your meditation space that inspire you. These may be photographs. They may be flowers or plants or anything that makes you feel at peace within your chosen meditation area.

# Chapter 8: Learning All About Relaxation

If you were to start meditating without knowing what relaxation is, then it's likely that you would fail. The reason is that you are going from a very busy life to a time when you are expected to sit and think of nothing. Not only are you making the task hard because of the contrast between your life and meditation, but you haven't yet learned to still your mind. Relaxation helps you to do this and this chapter is all about learning to still the mind and to concentrate on the way that you breathe.

Lie down on a bed or even on a yoga mat and make sure that your head is comfortably propped without too many pillows. One is ideal because this puts your neck in the right position to breathe the best that you can because your windpipe is freed up and air is allowed to pass through your body easily. You need to be dressed in clothing that is not at all restrictive and should ensure that your legs are straight out. When you eventually do the relaxation exercise, your hands will be down by your sides, but for the time being, we need to teach you to breathe correctly.

Place one hand on your upper abdomen. This hand is there for the express purpose of feeling the pivoting motion as you breathe. Many people breathe too lightly or do not allow sufficient air to enter their bodies. Some breathe in too much and over-oxygenate. The way that you breathe is central to meditation.

Breathe in through the nose to the count of 3 and instead of thinking of what's going into your body as being air, think of it as being energy. Hold that energy within you and you should feel your upper abdomen rise to the count of three. Then, exhale through your mouth to the count of 5. The reason that the exhale is longer is because you are trying to get rid of impurities that you may have built up within your breathing system.

Do this several times because you need to get accustomed to the rhythm of your breathing and the counting, so that you do this without really thinking of the timing. It's worthwhile spending a little time on the breathing exercise as once it is automatic, you will be able to do the relaxation exercise that follows in a much more fluent way.

### Relaxation exercise

This exercise is one that can help you to relax and can help you to sleep at night, but it's also a very useful exercise to teach you to put thoughts out of your mind. When you start meditation, you will be expected to empty your mind of thoughts. Since this is something that you are not accustomed to doing, it's hard at first, which is why people concentrate on breathing. It gives the mind something to mull over.

As you continue to breathe in and out as we have shown you, concentrating on that pivot motion and the amount of time you spend on inhaling and exhaling, we are going to turn our attention to each of the parts of the body. First of all, think of your toes. Tighten the muscles around your toes and feel them tensing up. Then relax them totally and feel them getting heavier. You need to do this with each area of the body and it makes sense to start from the toes and to work through all the body parts all the way up the body to the top of the head. I have put down the things that you should be thinking of and should be concentrating on:

- Sole of the foot

- The ankles

- The shins

- The knees

- The thighs

Then move up to the items below:

The hips, the stomach, the waist, the chest or breast area, the wrists, the forearms, the upper arms, the shoulders, the neck, the back of the head, facial features if you want to include these (lips – nose – eyes – cheeks).

By the time that you have worked over the whole body, you should be very relaxed indeed, but while you are doing these, do concentrate on that part of the body that you are relaxing and do not think of other things. If you find that you are thinking of other things, then you need to start back at the toes again.

# Chapter 9: Treatment approaches

Somatization is a complex condition with combined causality of body and mind. Scientists have worked to find out the exact mechanism of development so that they can find the correct and effective treatment. Usually, when a physician confronts with symptoms that can't be explained, he/she becomes frustrated, and the patient becomes confused because he/she doesn't know whether his/her condition is severe. The doctor usually reassures him/her to be patient and does another analysis. As the person complains of symptoms more and more, a physician is forced to begin any treatment that may help in this situation. These treatments are often not helpful, or only partly helpful. Still, the diagnosis stays unknown.

In general, these people that are in the process of searching for the diagnosis should improve their lifestyle, dedicate time to relaxation and doing what they like, and also give up the bad habits and apply some new ones related to physical activity and healthy eating. This doesn't mean that the symptoms aren't being taken as serious, it is a plan for the beginning of the effective treatment on a healthier body.

Treatment includes various methods - pharmacological, that is with medications, psychological, and life coaching. Some are more and some less effective, and it is up to the healthcare provider to refer the patient to the right specialist that may begin the appropriate treatment.

When you have unexplained symptoms that have been present for months or even years, you will seek for a diagnosis. Not everyone around you will share your worries. They can't understand the severity of your symptoms, and when the various diagnostic procedures don't clarify the cause, they are doubtful whether it is even real. Many people experience a lack of support and trust.

Some don't even share the issue with close people, knowing that they would be mocked or not trusted. The symptoms are usually characterized the wrong way because of their unusual characteristics. For example, there's pain that is present in one part of the body then moves to another part without any visible explanation. Therefore, a person may be given advice from family or friends to give up, that it will resolve by itself, that they are imagining or that it is only in their heads. A person is usually confronted with non-acceptance and frustration, which may make the symptoms even worse. Creating a stable and supportive atmosphere is crucial for the treatment.

Some patients, on the other hand, experience rejection from various medical specialists, who tell them that their illness isn't their field of expertise. A person may find himself or herself trapped in their bodies, with no clear help in sight, and the symptoms can continue for a long time. However, with more and more scientific research, general medical practitioners are able to recognise and consider that a person might be having somatization disorder.

The main cause is, in fact, psychological. Some unresolved frustrations, tension at work, or in family, or unexpressed emotions and anxiety are transformed into physical symptoms without visible damage. Thus, the treatment that is helpful is also a psychological approach. These psychological methods require some time and motivation but are actually teaching you new ways to look at your life. A person might feel uncomfortable accepting that something is "mentally wrong" with them and can experience difficulty handle the stigma behind it, which is understandable. A stable psychological structure is actually a part of our normal functions, much like the digestive or respiratory system, and sometimes require some help and treatment. The whole process and treatment needs time for adaptation. You should note that some treatments can't resolve the situation entirely, so you should be ready to try different approaches or combine them with others.

If there are other conditions that have a known cause, your healthcare provider may first concentrate on them and treat that symptomatology. They may be responsible for your other symptoms. If that therapy is of little help, he/she will refer you to a cognitive-behavioral therapist, since a CBT has shown the best results in treatment of somatic symptom disorder.

## Medical (pharmacological) treatment

Medical treatment is often used to cover the symptoms and make a person's life much easier. However, the condition may continue to exist even after treatment. Anxiety and depression may be associated with somatization. So, in these situations, the disorder is known but the physical symptoms still exist with no explanation. Medications that are commonly used are antidepressants. Despite their name, they are not only used for depression and similar mood disorders but also in long-term neuropathic pain, eating disorders, phobias, anxiety, post-traumatic stress disorder, multiple sclerosis, etc. They are also helpful in the treatment of somatic symptom disorder.

Antidepressants may be divided into subcategories:

SSRIs Selective serotonin reuptake inhibitors

SNRIs Serotonin and noradrenaline reuptake inhibitors

TCAs Tricyclic antidepressants

Atypical antipsychotics

Antiepileptic medications

Herbal medication St. John's wort

**1.) Selective serotonin reuptake inhibitors (SSRI) or SSRIs** are most commonly used antidepressant medications. They are efficient in treating depression, phobias, anxiety, eating disorders, obsessive-compulsive disorders, and also fibromyalgia, irritable bowel syndrome, and premenstrual syndrome. They are effective and have minimal side effects. They work by blocking serotonin absorption into the nerve cell, which prolongs its effects. Serotonin is a chemical in our body that is responsible for good mood, reduction of pain, social behaviour, appetite and digestion (serotonin is also located in large amounts in gastrointestinal system), sleep, memory and sexual function. In depression and all of the above mentioned-disorders, serotonin levels are low, and the right way to increase it is with SSRI-s. SSRI-s are tablets that your healthcare provider may begin the treatment with, preferably in small doses. It takes 2-4 weeks for the treatment to take effect.

They are not recommended for pregnant women and those who breastfeed, as well as for persons under the age of 18. Other medications should be considered if a person has some chronic illness like diabetes, kidney, heart, or liver disease. People with glaucoma and epilepsy shouldn't use it either. Some caution is needed when drinking caffeinated drinks. Driving is not advised if a person experiences dizziness and nausea when using SSRIs. They can induce seizures in people with epilepsy.

Side effects are dry mouth, dizziness, nausea, nervousness, insomnia, blurred vision, headache, diarrhoea, and erectile dysfunction. Serotonin syndrome appears when serotonin accumulates in the body, usually when SSRI are mixed with some other drugs that increase serotonin effects, which your healthcare provider will inform you of. The symptoms are confusion, tremors, restlessness, irregular heartbeat rate, dilated pupils, high or low blood pressure, diarrhoea, change in body temperature, nausea, and vomiting. These symptoms require treatment in a hospital.

Most commonly used are:

**2.) Serotonin and noradrenaline reuptake inhibitors (SNRI)or SNRI** are medications that work similarly as SSRI, but instead of only increasing the effect of serotonin, they also increase the effects of norepinephrine (noradrenaline). Norepinephrine is a sympathetic neurotransmitter, similar to adrenaline (epinephrine) and it is important for energy and mood improvement. Serotonin and norepinephrine are low in people who suffer from depression, so that is why these are indicated for this condition. Other indications for their use are in anxiety disorders, chronic pain, fibromyalgia, back pain, osteoarthritis, and somatization.

They are not recommended for pregnant women and those who breastfeed, as well as people under the age of 18. Other medications should be considered if a person has some chronic illness like diabetes, kidney, heart, or liver disease. They can induce seizures in people with epilepsy.

Side effects include dry mouth, dizziness, nausea, nervousness, insomnia, blurred vision, headache, erectile dysfunction, excessive sweating, change in appetite, cough, and weight loss. It is also possible for a person to develop serotonin syndrome.

Most commonly used are:**3.) Tricyclic antidepressants (TCA) or TCAs** are a group of antidepressants that could be helpful even in people with somatic symptoms that are based on the body-mind relationship. Their mechanism of action is to block the serotonin and norepinephrine reuptake, but in a different way than SNRI, and increase the effects of serotonin and norepinephrine. This may be of help in improving mood, decreasing anxious and phobic thoughts, for pain relief, eating disorders, managing premenstrual syndrome, and prevention of migraine and headaches. TCAs can be used for children and adolescents. It takes 2 to 4 weeks for TCAs to take effect.

Persons who are taking this medication should note that they might induce sleepiness and drowsiness, so they affect the ability to drive or operate machinery.

Possible side effects include dry mouth, dizziness, nausea, blurred vision, problems with urination, excessive sweating, weight gain or weight loss, tremors, erectile dysfunction, diarrhoea, and abdominal pain. They can induce seizures in people with epilepsy.

Most commonly used are:

| TCAs |
| --- |
| Amitriptyline (Vanatrip, Elavil) |
| Amoxapine (Asendin) |
| Desipramine (Norpramin) |
| Doxepin (Silenor, Sinequan) |
| Imipramine (Tofranil) |
| Nortriptyline (Pamelor) |
| Protriptyline (Vivactil) |
| Trimipramine (Surmontil) |

**4.) Atypical antipsychotics** can be used for pain relief and also serotonin inhibition in cases where it is very high and inducing the symptoms. Olanzapine (Zyprexa) and Clozapine may be useful for repeated headaches and migraine. (43) Side effects may include low blood pressure, dizziness, drowsiness, blurred vision, confusion, dry mouth, abdominal pain, constipation, problems with urinating, heat intolerance, low white blood cell count, and irregular heart rhythm. There is particularly an increased risk if similar drugs are used. Vehicle driving and machinery operation are forbidden if a person is experiencing dizziness and drowsiness.

Paliperidone is a type of antipsychotic that is usually combined with SSRI (Citalopram mostly) and may be used in somatic symptom disorder.

**5.) Antiepileptics** - Gabapentin and Pregabalin are not only used for epilepsy but for somatic symptoms disorder as well. They improve the general condition and provide relief from pain and can be used in people with fibromyalgia. They are also useful in treating conditions that are linked with anxiety and anxious thoughts. They are used in small doses. Side effects include dizziness, drowsiness, tremor, dry mouth, blurred vision, erectile dysfunction, swelling, and weight gain.

**6.) Herbal medication - St. John's wort (Hypericum perforatum)** many studies suggest this as a good remedy against many illnesses. St John's wort is a flowering plant that is widely known to help in depression, nervousness and anxious thoughts, difficulties sleeping, and even some infections. Active substances in this herb are hypericin and hyperforin, among others (rutin, quercetin, and kaempferol). Hypericin can be helpful in treating conditions that are linked with mild to moderate depression, and hyperforin is also helpful in infection treatment.

St John's wort grows on open space, and has spread from Africa and Europe to Asia and America as well. Its effects are known from ancient history when Greeks used it to improve mood and to heal wounds. They can be used in tablets, capsules, teas, and tinctures (0.3% hypericin derivatives, 300-mg capsules Ze 117- 50% ethanolic extract, and some others). The recommended daily dosage is Ze 117.

Hypericin is found in plant flowers in the black dots. Hypericin and Hyperforin are used to treat somatic symptom disorders. Through the increase of serotonin, dopamine, and norepinephrine, it improves the mood, relieves pain, prevents headaches and migraine, and also treats gastrointestinal symptoms.

Side effects that might occur are gastrointestinal discomfort, allergic reactions, dizziness, confusion, nervousness, and dry mouth. It is possible to develop photodermatitis, which is an abnormal skin reaction to sunlight, while using St. John's wort. A similar reaction could be noticed in the eyes. Normal precaution and protection is advised while spending time on the sunlight. All of the side effects are temporary and mild. Precaution is also needed when using some medications (antihistamines, Digoxin, Amitriptyline, Verapamil, sedatives, oral contraceptives, warfarin, antifungal medications, SSRI-possibility for serotonin syndrome, and some other food supplements and herbs). It is advised to consult your healthcare provider before beginning to use St. John's wort because of possible adverse effects and to evaluate whether it is the appropriate medical agent for you. (44)

Pharmacological treatment is in many cases not advised for their adverse effects that may sometimes bring worse results than the symptoms themselves. That is why medications are not considered to be the main course of action for treating somatoform disorders. They are often used along with other types of treatment (psychological), while carefully choosing the type of medications because of their possible side effects.

Another issue is the treatment of children and adolescents. Many of these medications, antidepressants mostly, are not suggested, because of increased risk for adverse effects. Even though somatoform disorders are much more present in adults, adolescents and children have a higher chance of conversion disorder than adults. The best treatment for them is talk therapy, but it is sometimes not as helpful. However, in this situation, a specialist should evaluate the risks and benefits of using medication therapy. It is usually recommended to children and adolescents to undergo psychosocial therapy, which includes therapy with help of family members and close friends. The psychosocial approach may be effective in the whole society to prevent psychological crises and to prepare for managing emotions and stressful situations.

## Psychological

A psychological approach has shown much more effects, and a wide variety of methods can be deployed depending on what the most comfortable and effective one is. Scientists and psychologists developed various methods in relieving symptoms. Cognitive behavioural therapy showed good results and is usually the first type of psychological therapy. Others are combined with a CBT for better effect. Some of them are a part of cultural tradition with the purpose of clearing the mind.

Work with somatization begins not only when somatic symptoms appear, but rather with education and learning about properly confronting conflicts, frustrations, sudden and shocking situations, expressions of emotions, etc.

These are cognitive behavioural therapy (CBT) with activity monitoring (increasing underactivity/reducing overactivity), overcoming unhelpful behavior, pacing activities, managing sleep problems, managing unhelpful thinking linked to anxiety and depression, assertive and social techniques, relaxation, psychoeducation, and some other non-specific approaches.

### Cognitive behavioural therapy (CBT)

Cognitive behavioural therapy (CBT) is a crucial type of treatment on both psychological and physiological level. CBT focuses on conversation with a psychologist or psychotherapist to create a healthy attitude and ideas for solutions of problems, or importing attitudes into a person's behavior that would later become incorporated with his/her thoughts. These corrected behaviour and thoughts find use in confronting with difficulties in life. Sessions usually don't take long, usually less than an hour of regular visits and talks once a week. The longevity depends on the needs of a person.

Example for cognitive behavioral therapy includes finding an approach for a person to participate in positive activities that would negate fear or stressful situations. In time, it would result in positive thoughts when the negative situations come up. CBT's goal is to achieve specific results toward a subject of psychological imbalance. CBT teaches a person how thoughts and attitudes reflect on behaviour and the other way around. A therapist talks with persons about positive and negative thoughts and behavior. The key is to identify which are which, and to promote what is more healthier and beneficial in managing all of the troubling events/situations. Somatoform disorders have increased risk to occur in people who are just prone to have more negative perspective on things, and this comes from automatically applied thoughts and beliefs that are established in childhood. In time, they triggered a negative reaction in troubling situations. A therapist will help you detect those automatic thoughts and help you change them into useful ones.

You might be seeking reassurance from the doctor that your symptoms indicate a serious illness, even though the diagnostic tests have shown otherwise. You may try a different approach with CBT. A doctor will always have on his/her mind that he/she must take good care of you, and if there is any indication of a serious illness, he/she would determine it in time.

At the beginning of treatment, a therapist will ask directly about the current situation and troubles in your life (using the BATHE technique usually). A person with unexplained symptoms that are likely to be somatization from psychological imbalance will probably have a subject to talk about, and this subject doesn't have to be at first a clear cause for the frustration, but conversation needs to be structured and following certain principles. During the process, a person will learn to cope with some problems, fears, or emotions, and then change the way they react to them.

Particular use of CBT in treating somatoform disorders is characterised by:

introducing relaxation techniques

correcting automatic thoughts and attitudes, and facing fears as well as gradually confronting them

creating new approaches to situations, and illness/symptoms

facilitation of emotional expression and giving value for certain emotions,

elimination of pre occupational thoughts about symptoms,

improving communication with other people regarding the illness or the problem, assertiveness, and social skills,

introducing satisfactory and pacing activities and combining it with necessary and routine activities.

CBT also tends to include a spouse or a family member in the treatment, at least in the beginning. It is important to identify and single out certain thoughts that become blockages and to try to restrict them, which may require support from a significant other.

A person's views on his/her illness should also be modified. No matter how strangely symptoms appear to a physician and a person, there is a background that explains it all without the need to announce the person as mentally ill or sick from an insidious disease. A person will need to change their approach to symptoms. They are present indeed, and troublesome, but the behaviour toward the illness has to change with giving less value and attention to it. With this, a lot of other techniques for positive thinking may be of help.

Some techniques can be attempted as a way of self-help. These include managing the frightening situations that are listed by hierarchy on a paper, and working through them, from the least frightening to the most frightening. Others may be mind experiments, such as thinking about previously experienced situations and thinking of other approaches to that situation, then finding resolutions and seeing them from negative and positive aspects. Some people are given advice to record their feelings or thoughts on something and then carefully and objectively think about them. The key is to learn to see things from another angle and change behaviour accordingly. Very often, CBT is used along with some relaxational methods such as visualisation, breathing exercises, meditation (mindfulness methods), and yoga.

Cognitive behavioural therapy isn't just about talk, but instead it is about acquiring skills and learnings about thoughts and actions and their connection. Usually, the therapist gives a patient assignments that he/she has to achieve, and the effects are later discussed during the session. The treatment usually consists of planning and conceptualising the problem and thoughts about it. Setting the goals isn't about not feeling the pain, nausea or any other symptom, or not feeling anxious, but rather more specific, concrete, and actually achievable. Goals are set using this formula:

Specific
Measurable
Achievable
Realistic
Time bound

Solutions to the problem are discussed. A patient then gets an assignment for coping with the issue. CBT in severe somatization disorder can't be brief, but it should rather last for at least 10 months.

Very often, CBT is combined with antidepressants to treat the associated condition and to increase its effects. Sometimes the treatment can be done individually or in groups, both of which should be offered. CBT alone showed more effects than relaxation methods. While having CBT treatment, patients are advised to also visit the general practitioner for evaluation of physical symptoms once a month. (45)

## Activity monitoring-increasing underactivity/reducing overactivity/boom bust cycle

Activity monitoring is one of the first steps of cognitive behavioural therapy. Having somatic symptom and confronting with the fact that reason for them is unknown and more likely psychological can be difficult to perceive and difficult to handle within interpersonal relationships. It is often that these people are more likely to begin excluding themselves from society and becoming more and more inactive, or begin practising some unbeneficial activities. A person may come to conclusion that is much safer or more comfortable to become passive and do nothing. A person will avoid certain activities with the fear of the pain becoming greater, or that they would be embarrassment by the symptoms and what other people think about them.

Cognitive behavioural therapy revolves around inclusion into activities. Activities are chosen by using the SMART formula. At first, a person needs to create a routine and activities that are repeated each day. These include everyday preparation of meals, buying groceries, reading, etc. Then, he/she needs to determine the necessary activities that occur on a daily basis. These include, going to work, paying the bills, taking the children to and from school, visiting parents, and cleaning. Then a person needs to create a list of everyday pleasurable activities and hobbies that involve different amounts of time. These activities could either be reading, relaxing, watching TV series, listening to music, painting, or dancing and doing sports, etc.

It is preferred for a person to individually organise these activities to fit all three types of activities in a day. Activities should be sorted from the easiest to the hardest. A person should try doing all of them without exception, but evenly organised. It is recommended that a person keep a diary of the activities, at least at the beginning.

Correcting activation and behaviour may work the opposite way, especially to the persons who are overworking themselves to avoid unwanted thoughts. This can't be helpful because the underlying problem is only hidden and covered and not solved through healthy behaviour. There is also another situation when a person forces him/herself to overwork. This happens when symptoms are appearing from time to time and a person tries to deal with the illness itself and the impact that it has on the professional or personal life. This is called Boom and Bust cycle. Boom and Bust cycle activity is a term that comes from business/economy and refers to a person becoming more productive at work when the symptoms aren't present. Boom and Bust cycle is more present in the professional area of activities. This situation pushes a person to achieve as much as possible until the symptoms are back again. This too, arises from fear of the illness, and requires a healthier attitude which is, of course, difficult sometimes to manage. A person feels that work needs to be done and feels incapable or guilty if it's not. It may be that when symptoms are gone, he/she would try to forget about them and ignore their existence and working beyond the limits of physical possibilities. It can also lead a person to feel exhausted and less motivated and induce feelings of unhappiness. It brings more tension because of increased feelings of incapability or failure.

Professional activities are experienced as obligational, and people become more unsatisfied with them and avoid doing them for fear of promoting the symptoms. With time, a person becomes less productive and less active and then needs more time for recovery and rest.

Setting time and effort limits to an activity can prevent this cycle from happening. Also, activities should be equally organised throughout the day. The level of activity should be the same on good days as on bad days to avoid overactivity on good days and underactivity in bad days. Some therapists recommend three Ps :

*Prioritising*
*Planning*
*Pacing*

## Pacing activities

Pacing is a skill that allows you to do activities, but in a reasonable amount and with organisation. Overactivation can make symptoms increase in intensity, and under activating or doing nothing makes you less motivated and depressed. That is why pacing is a good way to do activities. You may think that this way, your productivity becomes lower than if you had worked all day, or you may think of those activities as boring obligations. However, pacing allows you to become constant with work without your symptoms increasing. With time, you shall see that this actually makes you happier and self-satisfied with the amount of work done and time spent for rest or relaxation.

Pacing is particularly suggested to people who are struggling with pain, headaches, and fatigue. They probably need more rest than other people. However, having more rest would solve problems only temporarily. Pacing is all about gradually taking control over your activities and how much you can handle. It may be difficult to cope with, but it would help you to feel better.

The time needs to be divided into activity time and rest time, and they should be equally distributed throughout the day. For people who are becoming more and more tired and have increased their activity with pacing, they need to increase the activity gradually. They should set their own limits and as they feel ready and full of energy, they may proceed and move the limits further.

Some activities need to be divided into the ones that require more energy from those who require less energy. This way, the activities would be properly spread throughout the day. Tough activities can be divided into two parts with a pause. **Planning** in pacing is crucial. You should dedicate a certain amount of time to activity that would require medium energy, and that wouldn't induce symptoms in you. Planning should be taken seriously and with reasonable deadlines to perform the activities that are productive but also not as exhausting.

Some activities need to pass the **priority** test. Not all of the activities are necessary. It isn't a sign of weakness if you ask someone from your family or your friends to help you with some activities. You don't need to do things alone, or don't have to burden yourself because you feel that it is only your duty, because it isn't. You should also include activities that which you enjoy and not just activities that you are obligated to do. Doing fun activities induces pleasure and makes us happier, taking our minds off of the symptoms, pain, or fatigue.

So, with **pacing,** you will avoid overactivity during the days when you feel fine, and also you will escape from pointlessness when you are experiencing symptoms. This requires a plan that you should be motivated to follow. The time that you dedicate to a certain activity needs to be respected. Even though when you are feeling fine you are more productive, focused, and concentrated you shouldn't forget about the burn-out syndrome. It can be difficult to estimate how much time to dedicate to relaxation and how much to continuous working when you don't feel tired or in pain at the moment. Good pacing is all about making sure you know when to quit. It's not when you're already experiencing symptoms, because it will take you longer to rest and recover.

Pacing activities include doing one thing at a time. That way, energy is only used for one activity, and our focus is centred on one thing, which makes us more relaxed and less tense. It may appear difficult as people are getting used to your pacing or they will make their own appointments that would prevent you from following your schedule, or they will assign you with tasks to do. However, it is important that you have control over your energy and time, even if you disappoint others. Your schedule is as important as theirs, and you can't put everyone else first.

There are differences between cognitive behavioural therapy, adaptive pacing therapy, graded exercise therapy, and specialist medical care, and they can benefit persons with somatization individually or combined. Even though they seem to overlap, some of them individually proved to be more useful than the others.

**Adaptive pacing therapy** revolves around letting the body fight with whatever the cause is while providing the best conditions for it to happen. A person organises time and spreads activities in such order that he/she spends energy in an economical way, which would prevent the boom and bust cycles and overusing energy for unnecessary purposes and then not being able to be active at all.

**Graded exercise therapy** refers to approaching previously set activities step-by-step, increasing the effort and energy needed for the activity. Some people become less active due to symptoms and in fear of symptoms intensifying.

**Specialist medical care** includes specific therapy for specific symptoms, even though they have no clear causality. Treatment usually includes medicines and advice on how a person can affect on the symptoms through behaviour.

**Cognitive behavioural therapy** consists of changing the thoughts and behaviour in ways that are more realistic and logical and at the end healthier and more helpful. Certain thought and/or behaviour may be the key for treating some of the symptoms.

A study that compared those four approaches, concluded that graded exercise therapy and CBT had more positive effects than adaptive pacing therapy and specialist medical care alone. (46)

Overcoming avoidance behaviors and other unhelpful behavior. Overcoming fears.

With time, as symptoms seem to last too long and become chronic, a person becomes more distressed. Social, personal, and professional priorities come as second and third now that a person's health is unexplainably disrupted. Avoidance of social and professional activities may develop from fear of the symptoms increasing, or from fear of the rejection from other people due to symptoms. Many people don't show empathy in a way that is encouraging to people. This has to be changed since it creates a stigma against somatization disorder, which hinders with how to cope with it.

Cognitive behavioral therapy tends to focus on activities that are not beneficial for dealing with somatization symptoms. The not beneficial and unhealthy activities are

Avoiding activities or overdoing things

Constantly changing lifestyle and eating habits to try to improve symptoms

Boom and bust cycle

Fears of symptoms getting worse and from illness, and behaving accordingly.

The natural response to any potentially harmful situation is to fight or flight (escape). These actions are both regulated by the sympathetic involuntary system, which starts a reaction for preparing to deal with potentially harmful situations: increased heartbeat rate, breathing, and others. In both, dealing with anxiety towards the symptoms is with creating the fear from the situation, and it prevents consequences from happening in the first place. Avoiding thoughts of a certain problem can make it all worse, but the same way a person may choose certain activities to prevent consequences from happening with excessive and extreme measures (for example, a person cleans the house thoroughly every day to prevent illnesses from germs).

Avoidance and safety behaviour are activities that a person performs due to fear or anxiety of something. Safety behaviour includes taking extreme measures to prevent some events. They may not appear so evidently as avoidance, so a person is usually not aware of all of the activities he/she does in order to escape from the symptoms.

Cognitive behavioural therapy introduces the person to gradual exposure to real situations and helps in overcoming difficulties or fear from difficulties with symptoms in everyday life. A person makes a list of fearful thoughts, specific ones regarding one situation/problem. The list is put in hierarchy from the easiest to achieve and overcome to the hardest. The list is a person's ladder in overcoming unhelpful thoughts and behaviour. During talks with a therapist, a person may discover those activities and focus on dealing with them gradually and switching to more helpful behaviour. By gradually overcoming these situations stage by stage, a person becomes more aware of the benefits of different thinking and how he/she actually is capable of dealing with consequences or problems due to symptoms with the removal of negative thoughts.

You can actually break the fear itself into smaller pieces and try confronting them separately. Thinking of scenarios that could happen is sometimes healthy and sometimes not. However, there is no harm in trying. Sometimes, it is helpful to think of your greatest fear and writing a story about it. You shall notice that, the more you think of it, the less you can do to change any unexpected negative outcome, but you can become aware of healthy ways to become involved in your health. For example, if you are having a very intensive abdominal pain or headache, you may become fearful about a dangerous tumour that might be destructive in your body. However, there isn't much for you to do but to watch from the positive and negative side. After you finish the frightening story, you should read it repeatedly. At first, your emotions would interfere and you would find it hard to continue reading, but as you read it many times, you will experience fewer emotions linked to the fear or event itself, which can lead you to the conclusion of the preciousness of life, and you may feel more motivated to focus your attention not on overthinking about the illness and instead try to live a fulfilling life.

## Managing sleep problems

Disturbing thoughts during the day make the nights even harder. Sometimes when we're distracting ourselves from the core of the problem, we can't fall asleep, because now this subconscious discomfort prevents the brain from shutting down and entering sleep mode.

Some things that you can do to improve sleep is to make your room comfortable with fresh air and with proper ventilation. Loud sound and bright lights should be removed. You shouldn't watch TV or check your smartphone before sleep because it triggers your brain into delaying the process of falling asleep. Also, you should avoid drinking or eating before sleep, especially caffeine. It also depends on how many hours you need to be asleep to recharge. Some people only need 6 hours, while others need 8 or 10.

The real reason behind not being able to fall asleep could be worrying thoughts that appear even in the most comfortable room for sleeping. Think of how many times you would think about your symptoms and the way they interrupt and deconcentrate you during the day. Do they indicate an illness that you are afraid of? Lack of sleep will only make you feel worse. In any case, if you can't sleep, don't obsess over it. Relax and focus on finding different approaches to your worries.

# Chapter 10: Treatments for Anxiety and Depression

Compared to people in a calmer state of mind, the thoughts and feelings of people with chronic anxiety and depression are heavily influenced by information coming in from the limbic system and brain stem. Hence, conscious, logical "top-down" approaches to calming the brain in the anxious and depressed tend to be less effective than "bottom up" approaches which focus on the body, or hybrid "right-brain" approaches which combine talk therapy with body awareness. The goal of somatic therapy is to guide the brain and body back towards **homeostasis** – a balanced state in which there is a moderate level of nervous arousal in most situations and the autonomic nervous system doesn't swing wildly between sympathetic over-arousal and parasympathetic under-arousal. This involves finding ways to release unnecessary muscle tension and desensitize yourself to stressful memories, without triggering the brain's alarm centre in the amygdala. This means it's crucial that you feel relatively safe and comfortable when trying to release chronic tension (the so-called "safe space" referred to in trauma therapy). Otherwise you will subconsciously tense up (both physically and emotionally) to protect yourself from real or perceived threats.

When the inner critic in your mind is loud and persistent, as is often the case when you're anxious or depressed, it can be extremely difficult to calm yourself with rational thinking. Writing down your thoughts can be useful, but this only tends to be of modest benefit, and isn't a very practical solution when you're otherwise engaged in a hands-on task. However, shifting your attention from your negative thoughts and feelings to your physical sensations can be a powerful way of "grounding" yourself and feeling safer and more relaxed. A key aspect of grounding is reducing unnecessary nervous arousal in the upper half of the body. When your nervous system is over-aroused, you can literally feel ungrounded because there is too much muscle tension (and blood flow) in the upper half of your body, and too little in the lower half of the body. So when you're in an over-aroused state it often helps to focus on the lower, or peripheral, parts of the body such as the legs, feet and hands. In turn, this helps to slow down breathing, increase blood flow to hands and feet, and reduce unnecessary muscle tension throughout the body.

The Window of Tolerance

When the brain and body are in homeostasis, your ability to tolerate moderately stressful events is much higher than when your nervous system is dysregulated.* This is why somatic therapists focus on trying to increase their client's "window of tolerance" – how much mental and physical stress they can handle without becoming under or over aroused. Hence, if a client's window of tolerance is increased, they will find it easier to deal with stressful situations.

Limitations of Top-down Talk Therapy

If conventional talk therapy was as good as many of its practitioners claim, then rates of anxiety and depression would be a lot lower than they are.* However, there are a number of drawbacks to conventional talk therapy which limit its usefulness in helping deal with these disorders. One problem I've already mentioned is that **it's very difficult for the logical, verbal neocortex to calm the instinct-driven brain stem and the emotion-driven limbic system.** This makes it's very challenging for us to resolve symptoms of depression or anxiety by just talking about our personal problems. Sometimes we may acquire useful insights into why we are depressed or anxious (for example, we might find that one of the reasons why we have social anxiety is because we were bullied as a child) but simply finding explanations for our emotional problems rarely helps us to feel much better. Think of a common psychological issue such as a phobia of spiders. Just talking about your fear of spiders with someone else isn't going to change your gut reaction when you next have a surprise encounter with a hairy arachnid. You're still going to experience the same feeling of dread that first triggered your phobia. Another weakness of conventional talk therapy is the emotional release that can occur from talking about or expressing powerful feelings rarely brings lasting relief or closure. Hence, you might gain some short-term benefit from punching a pillow or seeing a counsellor and having a frank talk about your personal problems, but this "cathartic" emotional release rarely has long-term benefits.

When talking about emotionally-charged issues, clients can often feel threatened at a subconscious level, and flight, fight, or freeze responses can easily be triggered. Once these instinctive survival responses are triggered, the left-frontal part of the brain (which controls speech and self-talk) will shut down, and it can become very difficult for clients to express their thoughts and feelings in words. Those who instinctively favour the fight response may become verbally aggressive, those who favour the flight response to threats may become fearful and defensive, while those who gravitate towards the freeze response may switch off emotionally and become mentally scattered. Even just getting people to turn up for talk therapy can be a big challenge. Many (if not most) people are instinctively uncomfortable about discussing personal problems with strangers, and regular one-on-one talk therapy with a qualified psychologist can be very expensive. People who are prone to freezing in stressful situations can also be quite shy individuals who don't like confrontation or drawing attention to themselves. Hence they often have an instinctive aversion to therapy and can easily be scared off.

Since the 1980s the most successful form of talk therapy has been cognitive behavioural therapy which, according to some scientific studies, has a 50 percent success rate in helping to reduce anxiety and depression among those who follow through with it. CBT was developed in the 1960s and 70s and is based on the idea that our thoughts determine how we feel. So by recognising your negative thoughts and replacing them with more positive or constructive thoughts, you can eventually think yourself out of anxiety or depression. But despite being a relatively successful form of talk therapy, CBT requires a lot of commitment from the client and relatively few people are willing to commit to an extended course of treatment. In particular, clients with chronic depression find it very difficult to motivate themselves to stick with this form of therapy, and those with major depression often have to take high doses of powerful antidepressants before they feel positive enough to try it.

Brain-body therapists say that while talk therapy techniques like CBT can be useful for some people with mental trauma and mood disorders, they need to be preceded with body work aimed at calming the nervous system. Otherwise the client will either abandon the treatment, emotionally disconnect themselves from the therapy, or become even more nervous by opening themselves up to repressed thoughts and feelings they aren't equipped to deal with. Challenging strongly-fixed beliefs can also lead to an ego-clash between therapist and client, and some clients can become angry, frightened, or resentful if the therapist tries to talk them out of beliefs and coping strategies which are providing some relief from problems they otherwise aren't able to deal with.

### Limitations of Medication

While some people with anxiety and depression experience major benefits from using antidepressant medication, the majority who take them experience either modest improvements, or no benefit at all. Furthermore, many people who do experience some benefit from medications find they are associated with unpleasant side-effects, and for some users these troublesome side-effects (such as nausea, dizziness, insomnia, weight gain, and sexual dysfunction in males) outweigh the modest benefits. Another limitation of antidepressants is they aren't very effective at treating anxiety and depression that is moderate but long term. Hence, someone with low-grade, chronic depression and generalised anxiety is less likely to find an antidepressant helpful than someone with major depression or an extreme case of obsessive compulsive disorder. This suggests that antidepressants work best in people who have chemical (or neurotransmitter) imbalances in their brains, and that most people with mixed anxiety and depression of a moderate but chronic nature do not have neurotransmitter imbalances.* Instead, they have dysregulated nervous systems and or maladaptive approaches to dealing with stress. Antidepressants can also make it harder to sense physical feelings while engaged in body-based therapies, and many brain-body therapists recommend using low doses that still allow patients to stay in touch with their physical sensations (such as half a Prozac tablet per day, instead of the standard adult dose of one to two tablets per day).

## Limitations of Non-Specific Brain-Body Treatments

In addition to pills and talk therapy, many people with symptoms of anxiety and depression use non-specific forms of somatic therapy, such as yoga and aerobic exercise. While these approaches have some benefits, they are probably best regarded as somatic therapy-lite. By that I mean they have some benefits, but aren't focused strongly enough on calming the nervous system and discharging traumatic memories. Arguably the most commonly used form of physical therapy for mood disorders is good old-fashioned physical exercise. Hundreds of scientific studies have shown that aerobic exercise and weight-lifting can have some positive effects on mood and muscle tension, and studies show people who don't exercise are more at risk of developing mood disorders. However, the short-term benefits of exercise only last a few hours, and according to somatic therapist David Berceli, physical exercise only gets rid of surface muscle tension. So you can still experience a lot of deep muscle tension even if you engage in vigorous exercise on a regular basis. Thus physical exercise is a useful complementary therapy for managing nervous arousal on day-to-day basis, but it isn't really powerful enough to have a major, long-term effect on chronic anxiety and depression.

Another popular therapy for anxiety and depression is meditation. Various forms of meditation are all the rage these days, but as with physical exercise, meditation rarely goes deep enough to have long-term effects. Meditation is good for temporarily calming the mind and relaxing the body, but to get major benefits you need to meditate like a Buddhist monk and spends hours meditating every day - ten or fifteen minutes in your lunch time just isn't going to cut it if you are trying to deal with a mood disorder. Sitting for long periods of time while meditating can also be very difficult for some people with high levels of nervous arousal, particularly those with the hyperactive/impulsive form of ADHD or "Type A" personalities. People who are prone to daydreaming and dissociation also tend to space out during meditation, and this makes it difficult for them to get any real benefit from it (if you're trying to use meditation to improve concentration, it's recommended you meditate for very short periods, like a minute or so, and take a break whenever you lose focus)

Among the popular alternative therapies for mood disorders, yoga is arguably the most beneficial since it involves both the mind and body and some of the poses can be very useful for achieving a relaxed yet focused state of mind. However, somatic therapy experts such as Peter Levine and Pat Ogden say that yoga is relatively non-specific and doesn't adequately address core physiological processes. As with meditation, some studies do show that regular yoga practice can help to reduce symptoms of anxiety and depression, but it usually take many years of regular practice for major change to occur. Hence, while the stretching poses in yoga can help to relax the body and mind when done on a regular basis, they aren't particularly effective in helping to release high levels of chronic stress and muscle tension that have built up over many years.

Similarly, if you do have a lot of chronic muscle tension then you are likely to have a poor level of physical flexibility, and you may find it very frustrating and uncomfortable to do some of the yoga poses that are taught in a typical yoga session. For example, as a middle-aged male with chronically tight hamstrings, I found it impossible to do the popular "down dog" position, which is a core exercise in many yoga classes. I eventually did get some benefit and enjoyment from incorporating some yoga poses into my exercise routine, but that was only after I had already made progress in loosening up my body through tension release exercises. Admittedly, a yoga class that is specifically aimed at people with anxiety or depression is likely to be more effective than a more generic yoga class, but it's probably better to use yoga as a complementary therapy rather than a primary tool for tackling chronic symptoms of anxiety or depression.

If you can't find a yoga instructor who specialises in yoga for trauma or stress, you may get some useful benefits from doing "intuitive" stretching exercises at home. Instead of doing a set routine of standard yoga poses, just close your eyes and do whatever form of stretching exercise you feel like doing in the moment. So rather than using your conscious mind to force yourself do a specific set of poses (whether you want to or not) you are allowing your subconscious to decide what type of stretching you do (which could include anything from specific yoga poses, to dance moves, to very simple stretches such as flexing your shoulders or shaking your right hand). Sometimes this type of freestyle stretching can be a very useful tool for reducing physical tension because you are targeting a particular areas of the body where your subconscious is sensing high levels of tension. For example, in a standard set of yoga poses you will probably spend a few minutes on each of the main muscle groups in the body – which could include areas of the body where you aren't very tense. However, when you work intuitively you might spent ten or fifteen minutes on just one area (such as the hips) where you are subconsciously noticing a lot of tension. Music can be very helpful with this form of exercise as it helps you to switch off your logical brain and get your body moving instinctively. When I first start doing this type of stretching exercise I was a bit concerned I might injure myself, particularly when focusing intensely on one particular area of the body. However, not once in doing this form of exercise on a regular basis have I sustained an injury. It seems that your subconscious has a pretty good idea of what your physical limits are, and won't push you do things that are likely to lead to pain or injury.

# Chapter 11: Somatic or "Right-Brain" Psychotherapy

Most forms of talk therapy focus on the left side of the brain that deals with talking and logical thought. For example, in cognitive therapy you discuss your negative thoughts and feelings with your therapist and try to think of more positive or constructive ones. In "person-centred" counselling (the most common form of counselling) you discuss your personal issues with your counsellor and your counsellor provides periodic feedback. In somatic therapy, the client shifts from discussing and analysing their thoughts, behaviours, and personal history to focusing on their internal sensations. For example, the therapist might notice that the client looks uptight and distressed. She then asks where the client is experiencing physical tension. The client mentions tension in their jaw and shoulders, and a feeling of irritation and anger related to a recent argument with a relative. Hence, there is a shift in mental activity from the logical, verbal, left neocortex to the right side of the brain, which is a more intuitive part of the brain that interacts more closely with the body, brain stem, and limbic system.

A big advantage of this type of therapy is that it avoids many of the ego-clashes than often occur in traditional talk therapy. Instead of probing deeply into your personal history or situation, the main focus is on your physical sensations. This means that the therapist isn't challenging the client to radically change their attitude, thinking or behaviour, and the client doesn't have to divulge lots of personal information if they don't want to. The primary requirement is being willing to focus on your **physical sensations** and take note of any related thoughts or feelings – a process that tends to peak most people's curiosity and which can often be quite pleasant (particularly if you unlock an area of physical tension or discomfort). Another benefit of somatic therapy is it tends to be less mentally demanding that cognitive therapy, which can require a lot of mental effort and discipline on the part of the client.

Sometimes the therapist may engage in small experiments with the client, such as asking them to exaggerate a tension pattern in the shoulders, or seeing how the client reacts if they increase or decrease eye contact. As somatic psychotherapy progresses, the therapist works within the client's window of tolerance while slightly pushing their boundaries to help them widen their window of tolerance. For example, if the client is looking relaxed during therapy, the therapist can test their comfort zone by doing role play exercises, and seeing how their body language changes when they are forced to act in a way they aren't used to. The client and therapist may also set specific goals, such as increasing social confidence, or increasing their ability to tolerate feelings of restlessness and boredom without resorting to drugs or alcohol. If the goal is to improve social confidence, the focus might be on sensing their posture and tolerating unpleasant sensations in the chest and belly. If the goal is to explore feelings of sadness, body awareness might be directed towards facial expressions and the downward tilt of the head.

The main drawback of somatic psychotherapy is a lack of trained therapists with the skills to take full advantage of it. It can take a lot of training and experience for the therapist to know what body language cues are meaningful indicators of underlying mental stress, and which are not, and most psychologists and counsellors receive very little training in somatic therapy or body awareness. This is despite an increasing amount of research showing that somatic therapy can be useful for a number of stress-related disorders such as post-traumatic stress disorder. Some somatic therapists say the relative lack of interest in this form of therapy is due to cultural factors.* Over the last few hundred years, western culture has tended to see the mind and body as independent of one another, and some critics, some as medical historian Edward Shorter, say this tendency has been a problem in 20th century psychiatry, with its over emphasis on Freudian psychotherapy in the 50s and 60s and later, by drugs aimed at correcting supposed chemical imbalances in the brain. However, the increasing popularity of eastern mind-body practices like yoga is sparking a greater interest in developing western mind-body practices that incorporate the latest scientific knowledge about the wider nervous system and its effects on the mind and body.

Where somatic psychotherapy is unavailable or unaffordable, body-based somatic therapy can be combined with self-administered cognitive therapy. In self-administered cognitive therapy, as outlined in popular self-help books like David Burns' **Feeling Good: The New Mood Therapy**, you keep a written record of persistent negative thoughts, then critique your thoughts and come up with constructive responses.* This basic DIY cognitive therapy approach can be combined with somatic, brain-body approaches, such as the following exercise suggested by Pat Ogden:

-identify a persistent negative belief (eg, I'm an angry person and can't do anything about it)

-observe how your body reacts to the negative belief (eg, my jaw and shoulders tense up, and I can't think clearly)

-think of a different physical movement you could make (eg, I could clench my left hand, or shake my shoulders)

-make the alternative movement several times

-make a mental or written note of any improvement in your thoughts or feelings (eg, I feel less tension in the upper body, and I don't feel quite so angry).

Self-administered cognitive therapy has been shown to be quite effective for mood disorders, so there's every reason to expect some positive benefits combining self-administered cognitive therapy with body-based therapy.

# Chapter 12: Somatic Release Method

Our life experiences impact our mind-body either consciously or unconsciously. Events such as loss of any kind, for instance a loved one, financial loss, job loss or similar; illness, fearful thoughts, accidents and the like often result in emotional traumas. Emotional traumas create an imprint in the psyche and are reflected in our body language, posture as well as its expressions. In some cases, past traumas may express themselves in the form of physical symptoms such as pain, digestive challenges, hormonal imbalances, sexual or immune system dysfunctions, depression, addiction, etc. Trauma symptoms are the effects of instability of the Autonomic Nervous System. The influence of the traumas on the Autonomic Nervous System as well as the symptoms created as a result of this influence often stay in the mind-body until the experiencer reconnects with that part of their mind-body to resolve the trauma. Mind-body practitioners report that the flow of the breath is often obstructed in the areas where the trauma information is stored within the mind-body.

I am offering the Genco Method Somatic Release in this recording as a meditative somatic release tool, which uses breath awareness as a gentle discovery and resolution technique from the tension one might have experienced. Soma comes from the Greek word for body. The somatic approach to emotional release supports practitioners to holistically observe their mind-body during the practice. The somatic release combines the body's intelligence with the practitioner's sensate experience to formulate a strategy for change.

The Genco Method Somatic Release is a process that facilitates enablement of a new breathing pattern where the disruption is observed, gently releasing the somatic tension, and reestablishing a healthier breathing pattern within the cell tissue. This process is supportive of releasing the trauma or the tension and bringing the cell, hence the mind-body, into a healthier state of being.

In a study reported in the February 26, 1998 issue of Nature (Vol. 391, pp. 871-874), researchers at the Weizmann Institute of Science have conducted a highly controlled experiment demonstrating how a beam of electrons is affected by the act of being observed. The experiment revealed that the greater the amount of "watching," the greater the observer's influence on what takes place. Quantum Physicists Dr. Fred Alan Wolf states that according to quantum mechanics there is no reality until that reality is perceived and we change reality simply by observing it. This means that by observing mind-body's existing response, becomes an acknowledgement of the trauma or tension is experienced, which in turn is a major step towards resolving the issue taking place.

In the beginning of the Genco Method Somatic Release practice, the practitioners are asked to choose something they desire to release. This could be a tension that is being experienced in the mind-body or a certain behavioral pattern. This part of the process is for the practitioners to inform their subconscious mind about their new choice.

# Chapter 13: Genco Method Somatic Release©

**Preparation:** Get ready for the Genco Method Somatic Release. Keep your eyes closed and your body still. If you would like to make any adjustments to your posture, please do so now. (Pause). Once you have adjusted yourself, invite the stillness and keep your body at rest until our practice is over (Pause).

Gradually become quiet within, as quiet as you choose to be at this moment. Take three deep, long breaths and each time you breathe in, sense that your conscious breath is coming to you with the increased levels of peace and harmony. (Pause). And as you breathe out, know that by choice, you are releasing what is already expired and needs to be released from your mind-body. (Pause). Keep observing that with the flow of natural and conscious breath cycles you are inhaling peace and harmony and releasing toxicity and tension. A natural elimination process is taking place by your choice. (Pause) With each breath, you are arriving to a state of enhanced peacefulness; your body is progressively feeling weightless, while you are finding yourself sliding deeper and deeper into your consciousness. (Pause).

Now, see yourself in front of a door that opens into a silent environment that will host only you and your higher consciousness; no external or internal chatter can exist in this Sacred Silent Space. See with your mind's eye that there is your name at the door, and it is reserved only for you. Open the door, go inside and before you close the door, put the do not disturb sign on the door knob. This sign is an instruction to your subconscious mind to not to interrupt the process. Your subconscious acknowledges this command.

During our practice, allow the sound of my voice to guide your journey into the depths of your consciousness. Use my voice as an informing white light that reveals what is on your path, just like a light on a helmet does in the darkness of a cave. Let the sound of my voice assist your journey in and out of the depths of your consciousness.

**Resolution:** Now is the time to intentionally state the resolution you wish to experience through this practice. Take a deep breath, with conscious awareness and clear choice; state your resolution quietly in your heart space three times with full feeling and attentiveness. Your resolution is your conscious choice that is given to your mind-body to undertake through our practice. Notice that your subconscious receives and acknowledges your instructions on what you choose to resolve.

**Restoring the Wellbeing:** Bring your attention to the organic, reverent, capable, quiet breath. Become aware how the breath breathes you. Notice how the breath moves through in and out of the nostrils. *(Pause)* The organic breath flows through both nostrils, meets at the top of the nose to form a triangle. (Pause) The conscious breath enters through the nostril openings moves upwards and draws together to form a triangle with its apex in the eyebrow center. *(Pause)* Observe the breath passing through both nostrils like a gentle dance inside the nostrils... Notice the breath movements in each nostril separately, (Pause) and simultaneously. (Pause) Observe individual movements of the breath in each nostril and their reunion at the eyebrow center. (Pause.)

Continue your awareness of breathing. Imagine you are now breathing through alternate nostrils. In through one nostril, and out through the other; up and down the sides of the triangle and back again. *(Pause)* Start practicing immersing your consciousness with the consciousness of the breath and direct the breath in through one nostril and out through the other. Inhale

580

through the left nostril and exhale through the right. Continue to practice directing the breath towards alternate nostril breathing left in, right out; right in, left out. (Long Pause)

Now, enhance your capacity to interact with the breath. Deepen your connection with the awareness that brings the breath in and out of you. Locate the consciousness of the breath over the crown of your head. Continue engaging with the consciousness of the breath, by breathing through the crown of your head while inviting the conscious awareness into you, into your mind-body. (Pause) Once the breath starts to arrive to you with this directed awareness, then you can guide the consciousness of the breath to arrive at the places that feel uneasy or stuck to offer freedom from it.

Know that the conscious breath is arriving with powerful vibration of the truth. Now see your awareness immersed with this consciousness, observing your body from the level of unattached and highest levels of perception. From these heightened levels of cognizance start observing your body to identify where the information is stored inside your mind-body regarding to the resolution you made. The cells that carry the emotional trauma or tension that is relevant to your resolve make themselves known to you at this time by their dimmed grayish projection of light and denser texture compared to the healthier cells. See their grayish light and locate them inside of you. (Pause). Become fully aware where they are in your body. (Pause) Take a moment to observe them just as if you are observing a piece of art in a gallery, with full awareness, detachment, awe, curiosity, compassion, love and care. (Pause)

Recall your resolve. Let the intention of your resolve charge your breath with the midnight blue light of consciousness. Allow this conscious breath to come in like a laser beam and touch the grayish cells that have made themselves known to you earlier.

Grant permission to the midnight blue light to enable the change towards your resolve with its highly charged levels of truth, consciousness, mercy, peace and harmony. Direct this breath to touch the cells that are ready to release the trauma.

Each time the beam of midnight blue light touches the illumined cell, you see gray matter leaving that cell and the cell starts to shine with the authentic midnight blue, clear divine consciousness of that cell. Know that the original intention of that cell is restored. (Pause) Go through your mind-body cell by cell to clear all the outdated programming and ask the gray matter that has left your body to return to the source that it came from. Take 7 breaths in this level of freedom, release, peacefulness, truth and heightened awareness. (Long Pause)

Confirm the completion of your practice by repeating your resolve quietly in your heart space three times with full feeling and attentiveness. Send your gratitude to your mind-body for its support and cooperation for the resolutions received.

You are now ready to return to the normal state of awareness. In a moment, I will play a chime for you. Once you hear that chime, you will return to normal levels of consciousness, fully restored, rejuvenated, relaxed and feeling much freer than before. As you come out of this wonderful state of peacefulness you will feel fully rested, energetic, healthy and grounded. I will now ring the chime and when you hear the chime, you will come out of the deep relaxation state feeling an increased sense of peacefulness, freedom and wellness, bringing with you all the benefits of this experience. (Chime). It is now time to return to normal levels of awareness.

# Conclusion

Clinical Somatic Education is slowly becoming a mainstream option for treating mobility, flexibility and posture issues. This is, in no small part, thanks to the efforts of Eleanor Hanna who has carried on the work of Thomas. Thomas Hanna was the first person to start using the phrase somatics when he developed the clinical somatic education treatment option. This was a result of his years of research, building upon the work of several other respected scholars. Unfortunately, Thomas died in a car accident just five days into his first training course. The course was never finished, although, thanks to his impressive organisational skills the information had already been shared; the remainder of the course was intended to be reiteration and discussion. This made it possible for both his wife, Eleanor, and two of his students to develop the program further and teach it to the rest of the world. Thomas Hanna and Eleanor Hanna established the Novato Institute for Somatic Research and Training. After Thomas's death in 1980 Eleanor continued to run and build the institute to ensure that as many people as possible could benefit from somatic exercises. As the name suggests the facility continues to research new ways of applying somatics to aid people in leading a fuller, balanced life.

Somatic exercises are designed to reawaken the mind and help everyone discover their own ability to improve their movement and reduce pain which has been impossible to eliminate via more conventional, or traditional means. They are founded on the belief that everyone has the power within them to control their own destiny, eliminate pain, improve mobility, flexibility and, ultimately, become more effective in any activity they choose to undertake. The institute is spreading the word and potential of this treatment method via regular newsletters, magazines, books and training courses. It also offers a three year course to become certified as a teacher of Somatics; the ultimate aim is to have a teacher in every town across the country, ensuring that everyone has the opportunity to benefit from this ability to awaken the mind.

Clinical somatic education gives you the opportunity to release your body from the pain and suffering that you may have come to accept is part of life. The exercises are designed to remind your brain that, despite the sheer number of things that are demanded from it on a daily basis, it is possible and essential to control your own muscles and not to become a victim of habituation. It is only through regaining this level of control over your own body that you will be able to enjoy a pain free life which will provide you with the opportunity to achieve anything.

It is important to mention that although the book has focused on the ability for somatic exercise to relieve pain and aid in movement, flexibility and even posture, there are other a great many other conditions which can be helped by using somatics. Some of the more common ailments which have been shown to benefit are:

• Arthritis

• Balance Problems

• Dizziness

• The need to urinate frequently

• Obesity

• Sciatica

• Tendinitis

• Uneven Leg Length

- Whiplash

In fact there are a host of other disorders which can be aided by the intervention of somatic exercises. The list is likely to grow as research looks into how this technique can be applied to other issues. Somatic exercising may be a relatively recent addition to the list of alternative or complementary therapies but it is proving to have a huge range of potential.

You will have probably started this book with a loose idea regarding what somatics is and how it may benefit you. The book has introduced you to a brief history of the practice and how it came into being. It has also disclosed the main uses for somatic exercises as originally envisioned by Thomas Hanna; in particular how it can aid with movement, flexibility and posture. By now you should also be aware that it can be of great benefit to a wide variety of other disorders or conditions as well. Learning to train your mind is surprisingly easy; the example exercises are simple, yet effective. They release the tight muscles and allow your mind to exercise full control over all the parts of your body; eliminating pain and restoring full function, to parts of you that you may have thought would be limited for the rest of your life.

There is also a range of tips and tricks for how to get started practicing somatics and a list of the many advantages of this technique as well as a few risks; which should be considered before you start practicing.

But perhaps the most important message that you should take away from this book is the power of the human mind. It is possible to heal your own body by applying your brain to the problem and not relying on human prescription medications. Whilst there remains a place in anyone's life for traditional medical responses it is an electrifying feeling to know that you have the power to heal yourself and live a better life. This feeling comes from an awareness of the power which resides within everyone and how it can be reached by focusing the mind.

Somatic exercises are simply one key towards unlocking the full power of the human mind, a mind that is currently only used to less than a tenth of its potential. This book should have opened your eyes to what is possible. Start by using small exercises to alleviate painful muscles and other injuries or illnesses, the logical end of this path is the ability to self heal.

Clinical somatic education also has the potential to help people with mental health disorders and those with low self-esteem. This is because learning to heal yourself will help you understand who you are and what you are capable of. Somatics will open up your options; use this book as a guide to exploring the capabilities of your own mind.

www.ingramcontent.com/pod-product-compliance
Lightning Source LLC
Chambersburg PA
CBHW030232030426
42336CB00009B/75